It has been said that history repeats itself, because we learr don't learn from history! Dr. Mortenson has thoroughly docum Bible-believing geologists in Britain in the 1820–1840 period who resolutely resisted those inside and outside the church who placed human reason above divine revelation, thus undermining the Scriptures and the Christian gospel. These men were the roots of the modern creation movement. Not surprisingly, the arguments from the Scriptures, the geologic evidences debated, and the tactics of the scientific establishment have not changed in almost two centuries. This is a must-read for all Christians, who need to be informed so as not to repeat the mistakes of our forefathers in compromising the clear teaching of Scripture about creation and the Flood as the true history of the earth and thus the only basis for geological inquiry.

Dr. Andrew Snelling
Professor of Geology
Institute for Creation Research

College and seminary students would benefit much from reading the compilation of individual biographies as well as from consideration of the thorough survey of the historical background in which these men lived and studied. Some readers will be challenged and find it a valuable resource tool, others will perhaps pick it up from time to time just to dip into the biographies for a quick reminder of how men of God observed their world with their Bible in hand.

Dr. Trevor P. Craigen
Assoc. Professor of Theology
The Master's Seminary

I read Dr. Mortenson's book and frankly could not put it down because at last I found a scholarly work that I as a minister with no training in geology or science in general could comprehend. This book makes a valuable contribution to an area that has not been explored very much. I can see it being helpfully consulted by seminary professors, college instructors, pastors and interested lay people.

Dr. Jack C. Whytock
Pastor and theologian
Moncton, New Brunswick

The Great Turning Point deals very carefully and comprehensively with the crucial era of historical geology in the light of the Genesis record: the early 19th century. Many evangelical scholars today have ignored the original source materials and have therefore misunderstood the Genesis-geology controversies of that generation, and thus of ours as well. This outstanding volume will go far to set the historical record straight.

Dr. John C. Whitcomb
Theologian, author, and conference speaker

Galileo, Bacon, Newton, Cuvier, and Lyell are all familiar to students of the history of science and geology. However, Penn, Bugg, Ure, Fairholme, Murray, Young, and Rhind (all from the 19th century) have remained virtually unknown until Mortenson's revealing historical analysis. *The Great Turning Point* provides a new look at the Genesis-geology debate that cannot be ignored.

Dr. William Barrick
Prof. of Old Testament, Dir. of Doctoral Studies
The Master's Seminary

If your high school students (or you!) need a break from the relentless secular "wisdom" of every credible scientist in all ages adhering to the idea of an earth millions of years old, Dr. Mortensen's book is a great lesson in the true history of science. It thoroughly explores the origin of replacing God's Word with man's wisdom using geological hypotheses. The lives of seven scientists who did not depart from the clear teaching of Genesis are chronicled. Read this book, written in language understandable to the lay reader, to be able to refute those who would say that creationism teaching is just a side issue.

Monica Cook
Home-schooling mother
General Editor, *The Old Schoolhouse*

In the midst of the current creation-evolution debate, several misconceptions cloud the issue and detract from careful reflection: (1) The theory of evolution was first articulated with the publication of Charles Darwin's *Origin of Species* in 1859. (2) Not until Darwin's "discovery" did some people read the Genesis accounts of divine creation and the Noahic flood in less-than-literal ways. (3) By the first part of the 19th century, no scientifically responsible person held to the historical truth of the biblical accounts of creation and the Flood. (4) Prior to the rise of the young-earth creation movement and the intelligent design movement during the last part of the 20th century, no scientifically and philosophically credible responses to the theory of evolution over millions of years had been offered by Christians. Terry Mortenson thoroughly addresses and definitively dispels these misconceptions by focusing on the British "scriptural geologists" from the first half of the 19th century. For anyone interested in the debate over evolution (and especially over the age of the earth) and the history of Christian responses, *The Great Turning Point* is must reading.

Dr. Gregg Allison
Assoc. Prof. of Christian Theology
Southern Baptist Theological Seminary

Terry Mortenson
Isa 66:1-2

THE GREAT TURNING POINT

The Church's Catastrophic Mistake on Geology — Before Darwin

Terry Mortenson

First printing: August 2004

ISBN: 0-89051-408-9
Library of Congress Number: 2003114508

Printed in the United States of America

In this book frequent reference is made to two very well-known reference works: Leslie Stephen and Sidney Lee, editors, *Dictionary of National Biography* (Oxford: Oxford University Press, 1917), 22 volumes; and Charles C. Gillispie, editor, *Dictionary of Scientific Biography* (New York: Scribner, 1970–90), 16 volumes. These will be abbreviated as *DNB* and *DSB* respectively.

All emphasis in all quoted material is that of the original author, unless indicated otherwise. Any comments in square brackets [. . .] appearing in the quotations are my additions to clarify the quotation, based on the context of the original source.

Further source information on footnote references can be found in the bibliography.

ACKNOWLEDGMENTS

So many people made possible my Ph.D. research (upon which this book is based). Without them I could not have produced this book.

I would like to thank the very helpful library staff at the Bodleian Library (particularly Mr. Richard Lindo, Mrs. C. Mason, Mr. Richard Bell, Mr. W.H. Clennell. and Miss Jackie Dean), the Radcliffe Science Library in Oxford, and at the London British Library. Their assistance was invaluable, not only in making use of the library facilities and resources, but in locating some hard-to-find sources about my subject matter.

I am also indebted to the librarians at several other libraries and museums outside Oxford. Ms. Susan Bennett at the Elgin (Scotland) Museum, Mrs. Jane Pirie of the archives department of Aberdeen University Library and Miss A.M. Stevenson, the archivist at the Museum of the Royal College of Surgeons in Edinburgh, supplied me with biographical information on William Rhind. Mr. Harold Brown at the Whitby Museum and Mr. Paul Ensom at the Yorkshire Museum in York provided a little treasure of biographical information on George Young. The Kettering Library staff sent me a very helpful recent article on George Bugg, and Mrs. Jill Crowther at Hull Central Library supplied some details about his death. Thanks are also due to Mr. Gary Archer at the Leamington Spa Library for tracking down the death notice on George Fairholme and to Mr. Andrew Martin at the Royal Museum of Scotland in Edinburgh for information about Fairholme's home parish. In addition, Mrs. Waveney Jenkins of the Isle of Man and Mr. Gerald Fairholme of London, two living relatives of George Fairholme, were enthusiastic in their help to this foreigner by providing access to private family papers related to their great, great grandfather. Mr. and Mrs. Jane Farr, the present owners of the former Fairholme estate near Gordon, Berwickshire, also contributed useful information.

I appreciate the help of my two oldest daughters (at that time teenagers), Sara and Anna, who worked hard in typing many of the long quotes included in this work. Our financial survival during the Ph.D. research would have been impossible without our many friends in America and England who believed in the importance of my research enough to financially support us so that I could study full-time. Also helpful were the grants from the Sandy Ford Foundation and the Christian Scholarship Foundation, both in America.

Because our house in Guildford, England, was small and our family was large and we were on a tight budget, I would never have completed this research without the gracious and free provision of a place to study and write, first in the home of the late Mrs. Dorothy Jelley and then (when she had to move into a nursing home) in the home of Dick and Helen Battersby. I am indebted to the Steve Daughtery family for letting us live in their beautiful and spacious house at incredibly low rent, when we had to vacate our first home eight months before completing my Ph.D. thesis and to the Adrian Peckham family who took us in for the last few months when the Daughterys found a buyer for their house.

In the process of transforming my thesis into a book, I very much appreciate the work of the editors of the *Technical Journal* (now simply *TJ*, the Australian creationist journal which previously published many chapters of my thesis) and to the staff at Master Books, especially Tim Dudley, Jim Fletcher, and Judy Lewis.

My last expressions of gratitude to fellow humans go to the five people who were most helpful in the research for this book. First, my two Ph.D. supervisors, Prof. Colin Russell and Dr. Gordon McConville, patiently worked with me as initially I produced some abysmally poor writing. In their own unique styles, they wisely guided me when I was a bit perplexed about how to proceed and they provided encouragement and advice, along with strong and specific criticisms, to stimulate me to do my best in research and in writing. I am also grateful for the challenging oral Ph.D. exam administered by Prof. John H. Brooke and Dr. Paul Marsten, and for their insightful criticisms which led to revisions that strengthened the thesis before its final approval. Of course, I take full responsibility for the deficiencies and errors which yet remain and for the conclusions in the finished product.

I also must and gladly want to express my deep, deep gratitude to my dear wife, Margie, who has served, loved, encouraged, and supported me in innumerable ways. She also read every part of my thesis and this book, sometimes more than once, and gave valuable suggestions for improvement. I could not have completed it without her.

Finally, I acknowledge my gratitude to God, who graciously provided for me and my family during the research, and who, I have no doubt, guided me in my study. To Him be all the glory!

TABLE OF CONTENTS

INTRODUCTION

Geologist H.H. Read prefaced his book on the granite controversy a few decades ago with these words, "Geology, as the science of earth history, is prone to controversy. The study of history of any kind depends upon documents and records. For the history of the earth's crust, these documents are the rocks and their reading and interpretation are often difficult operations."[1]

This book analyzes one such controversy, and an extremely important one at that, during the first half of the 19th century in Britain, which has sometimes been called the "Genesis-geology debate." At that time a tenacious and denominationally eclectic band of scientists and clergymen (and some were both) opposed the new geological theories being developed at the time, which said that the earth was millions of years old. These men became known as "scriptural geologists," "Mosaic geologists" or "biblical literalists."

The label "scriptural geologists" is preferred since three of their book titles used these terms and it was the most common label used by their contemporaries and by later historians. However, we need to be aware of the label's liabilities. It has not always been used carefully, resulting in confusion and inaccurate analysis. Calling them scriptural geologists obscures the fact that some of them were competent geologists while others were not (and did not claim to be). Conversely, it sometimes is and was used by opponents to imply, erroneously, that these men all developed their objections to old-earth geological theories solely on the basis of Scripture. Also, at least one of their contemporary critics, an old-earth geologist, also described himself by the same title.[2] Finally, a few of their contemporary critics and several later historians have lumped scriptural geologists together with their opponents under

1 H.H. Read, *The Granite Controversy* (1957), p. xi.

2 For example, see various letters by a Christian geologist, to the editor of the *Christian Observer* in 1839: Jan. (p. 25–31), Mar. (p. 145–148), April (p. 210–216), June (p. 346–348), July (p. 471–474). He obviously wanted to be considered by his fellow Christians as a "scriptural" geologist, even though he advocated an old-earth view.

this label.[3] So it is necessary to have a clear view of what they believed.

The scriptural geologists held to the dominant Christian view within church history up to their own time, namely, that Moses wrote Genesis 1–11 (along with the rest of Genesis) under divine inspiration and that these chapters ought to be interpreted literally as a reliable, fully historical account.[4] This conviction led them to believe, like many contemporary and earlier Christians, that the Noachian flood was a unique global catastrophe, which produced much, or most, of the fossil-bearing sedimentary rock formations, and that the earth was roughly 6,000 years old. From this position they opposed with equal vigor both the "uniformitarian" theory[5] of earth history propounded by James Hutton and Charles Lyell, and the "catastrophist" theory[6] of Georges Cuvier, William Buckland, William Conybeare, Adam Sedgwick, etc.

They also rejected, as compromises of Scripture, the gap theory,[7] the day-age theory,[8] the tranquil flood theory,[9] the local flood theory,[10] and the myth theory.[11] Though all but the myth theory were advocated by Christians who believed in the divine inspiration and historicity of Genesis 1–11, the scriptural geologists believed their opponents' theories were unconvincing interpretations of Scripture based on unproven old-earth theories of geology.

THE NEED FOR A RE-EXAMINATION OF THESE MEN

There are several reasons, besides merely satisfying our historical curiosity, why it is important to gain a better understanding of these scriptural geologists and the Genesis-geology debate.

First, these British writers have received limited scholarly analysis and in what has been done they have been generally misunderstood and often mischaracterized, both by their contemporaries and by later historians. Typical is Charles Lyell, the leading uniformitarian geologist of their day, who described them in 1827 as "wholly destitute of geological knowledge" and unacquainted "with the elements of any one branch of natural history which bears on the science." He said that they were "incapable of appreciating the force of objections, or of discerning the weight of inductions from numerous physical facts." Instead he complained that "they endeavor to point out the accordance of the Mosaic history with phenomena which they have never studied" and "every page of their writings proves their consummate incompetence."[12]

---

3 Lyell's fellow uniformitarian, George P. Scrope, did this, according to a quotation in Martin J.S. Rudwick, "Poulett Scrope on the Volcanoes of Auvergne: Lyellian Time and Political Economy," *British Journal for the History of Science*, vol. VII, no. 27 (1974), p. 226. Also, a scathing anonymous reviewer in the *Christian Remembrancer*, vol. XV (1833), p. 390, lumped together the old-earth geologist, William Higgins, and the scriptural geologist, George Fairholme. Baden Powell did the same in his *Revelation and Science* (1833), p. 44.

Among historians, Marston did this with William M. Higgins, in his "Science and Meta-science in the Work of Adam Sedgwick" (The Open University, Ph.D. thesis, 1984), p. 280. Roy Porter classified William Buckland as a "Mosaic geologist" in "The Industrial Revolution and the Rise of the Science of Geology," *Changing Perspectives in the History of Science* (1973), M. Teich and R.M. Young, editors, p. 341. Frances Haber did the same with several old-earth opponents in his *The Age of the World* (1959). In *Genesis and Geology* (1951), p. 163, Charles Gillispie likewise lumped together Fairholme, Ure, and John Pye Smith, the latter being the old-earth critic of the former two.

4 Some of their evangelical and high church opponents held the same view of Genesis, but they differed with the scriptural geologists over what they believed to be the literal interpretation, as will be seen later.

5 In this theory, geological features of the earth were formed over long ages by slow gradual processes of erosion, sedimentation, and faulting operating at the same rate and intensity as we observe today.

6 This view held that many regional or global floods had been the primary agents during untold ages for the development of the geological record.

7 The vast geological ages occurred before Genesis 1:3 and the rest of Genesis 1 is an account of recreation in six literal days on the geological ruins of the previously destroyed earth.

8 The "days" of Genesis 1 are figurative, representing the vast geological ages.

9 The Noachian flood was a global historical event, but it was such a peaceful event that it left no significant and lasting geological effects.

10 The Flood was catastrophic but affected only the Mesopotamian valley.

11 Genesis 1–11 is myth, which contains theological truths, but has little or no historical accuracy.

12 Charles Lyell, Review of *Memoir on the Geology of Central France* by G.P. Scrope, *Quarterly Review*, vol. XXXVI, no. 72 (1827), p. 482. Lyell likely had in mind, among others, Granville Penn, George Bugg, and George Young, who all wrote substantial works on the subject before 1827 as will be discussed later.

Turning to the historians, we find an equally disdaining view. In 1896, Andrew White, whose views had enormous influence on the next generation of historians, referred only to clerical scriptural geologists, such as James Mellor Brown.[13]

Quoting Brown and others out of context, White said that these scriptural geologists believed that geology was "not a subject of lawful inquiry," "a dark art," "dangerous and disreputable," and "a forbidden province."[14] Also in 1896, William Williamson, professor of botany in Manchester, described the work of George Young, the most geologically competent scriptural geologist, as "prejudiced rubbish."[15]

Moving into the 20th century, the scriptural geologists have been described as "scientifically worthless,"[16] "scientifically illiterate Bibliolaters," and "obscurantists."[17] And they were "vociferous," negative, and defensive in their reaction to geology.[18]

Particularly pertinent to the present analysis of George Fairholme, John Murray, William Rhind, and George Young are comments by the late Harvard University geologist Stephen Gould: "By 1830, no serious scientific catastrophist believed that cataclysms had a supernatural cause or that the earth was 6,000 years old. Yet, these notions were held by many laymen, and they were advocated by some quasi-scientific theologians."[19]

Davis Young, a Christian geologist, progressive creationist, and prominent writer on the creation-evolution debate in America, has implied a similar view — these scriptural geologists had no real geological knowledge.

> A torrent of books and pamphlets were published on "scriptural" geology and Flood geology, all designed to uphold the traditional point of view on the age and history of the world.[20] The "heretical" and "infidel" tendencies of geology were roundly condemned by some churchmen, few of whom had any real knowledge of geology. Those who had geological knowledge were now largely convinced that the earth was very old.[21]

---

13 He is not discussed in this book but see the article on him at<www.answersingenesis.org>.

14 Andrew D. White, *A History of the Warfare of Science with Theology in Christendom* (1896), I: p. 223.

15 William C. Williamson, *Reminiscences of a Yorkshire Naturalist* (1896), p. 56.

16 Martin Rudwick, "Charles Lyell, F.R.S. (1797–1875) and His London Lectures on Geology, 1832–33," *Notes and Records of the Royal Society of London*, vol. XXIX, no. 2 (1975), p. 237. The same remark appears in Rudwick's "Introduction" to the 1990 edition of Charles Lyell's *Principles of Geology*, 1990, p. xi (footnote 3) and p. xvii. In his 1986 essay "The Shape and Meaning of Earth History," in *God and Nature*, David C. Lindberg and Ronald L. Numbers, editors (1986), p. 312, Rudwick makes the passing comment that some of the scriptural geologists supported their ideas "by at least some empirical fieldwork," but he mentions no names.

17 Walter F. Cannon, "The Impact of Uniformitarianism," *Proceedings of the American Philosophical Society*, vol. 105, no. 3 (1961), p. 302; Walter F. Cannon, "The Problem of Miracles in the 1830s," *Victorian Studies*, vol. IV (1961), p. 15, 22–23; Walter F. Cannon, "Scientists and Broad Churchmen: An Early Victorian Intellectual Network," *Journal for British Studies*, vol. IV (1964), p. 82. A similar view is expressed by Owen Chadwick, *The Victorian Church* (1971), p. I:559-561.

18 J. David Yule, "The Impact of Science on British Religious Thought in the Second Quarter of the Nineteenth Century" (1976, Ph.D. thesis, Cambridge University), p. 328 and 331.

19 Stephen J. Gould, "Catastrophes and Steady State Earth," *Natural History*, vol. 84, no.2 (1975), p. 16.

20 Here in an endnote Young cites, without comment, the 1822 work of Granville Penn and the 1837 book by George Fairholme. In 1987, Young said of these two men that "despite some acquaintance with geology, [they] overlooked many important details of geology. The views of literalists no longer carried weight with Christians thoroughly trained in geology." He mentions no other scriptural geologists of the period. See Davis Young, "Scripture in the Hands of Geologists (Part One)," *Westminster Theological Journal*, vol. 49 (1987), p. 25.

21 Davis Young, *Christianity and the Age of the Earth* (1988), p. 54. In his most recent book, *The Biblical Flood* (1995), p. 124–128, he is a little more generous when he states that "a few were competent field observers who had described regional geology." He names George Young, but he briefly discusses only the views of Granville Penn, George Fairholme, and William Kirby. He does not mention John Murray and William Rhind, who along with Young were the most geologically competent scriptural geologists, and are discussed later.

Charles Gillispie, an evolutionist and one of the most influential recent historians of early 19th century geology, was even more stinging in his general evaluation of the scriptural geologists when he stated that they were "men of the lunatic fringe," who published "their own fantastic geologies and natural histories," none of which "marked any advance on Kirwan," who wrote at the turn of the 19th century. In fact, their ideas were all "too absurd to disinter."[22] He later continued:

> The productions of men like George Fairholme, Andrew Ure, and John Pye Smith set forth sillier, less well-informed systems (than Vestiges[23]) reconciling the Mosaic record with empirically misconceived fact. Their errors cannot have seemed sufficiently damaging to science to merit professional refutation because no one bothered to refute them.[24]

In commenting on their significance, Gillispie concluded:

> Although too neat a generalization would be erroneous, the arguments of one generation of purely theological disputants more or less reflected the interpretations of the obstructionist side in the discussions among scientists of the preceding generation. Granville Penn, for example, Dean Cockburn of York, and George Fairholme, to name three of the opponents of geology in Buckland's time, leveled against the whole of the science — catastrophist as well as uniformitarian — arguments very similar to those with which Deluc and Kirwan had attacked the Huttonians 25 years earlier. . . . After Kirwan, no responsible scientist contended for the literal credibility of the Mosaic account of creation.[25]

Millhauser similarly described them as "foes of science" who were woefully ignorant of science and especially geology.[26] Referring to these scriptural geologists, Haber condescendingly asserted that "geological science and the advancement of scientific truth [were] pilloried and stoned by the ignorant literalists" who vainly fought against "the heroic warriors in the army of science."[27] More recently, James Moore has expressed an equally negative view of these scriptural geologists: "Thus their typical ploy of ransacking geological works for contradictory assertions, for passages of which no real understanding is shown but which serve admirably to exercise and display the interpreter's own proficiency in logic and linguistics."[sic][28]

Quite unlike most other contemporary historians, Nicolaas Rupke was somewhat positive in describing some of the scriptural geologists as competent naturalists. In his view, even some of the clergy were quite expert in the local geology around their parishes.[29] Paul Marston acknowledged that they were not anti-geology, but only opposed to the

22 Charles C. Gillispie, *Genesis and Geology* (Cambridge, MA: Harvard University Press, 1951), p. 152.

23 This was a book published anonymously (but written by Robert Chambers) in 1844, which presented a radical evolutionary view of the origin of biological life. It was vehemently opposed by virtually all scientists at the time, though it helped prepare the ground for Darwin's *Origin of Species* 15 years later.

24 Gillispie, *Genesis and Geology*, p. 163. Again there is confusion. Fairholme's work was ignored by contemporary geologists. However, Ure's received a scathing critique by Sedgwick, which will be analyzed, and Pye Smith's views were greatly appreciated by the leading geologists, precisely because he favored the old-earth views, unlike Ure and Fairholme.

25 Gillispie, *Genesis and Geology*, p. 223–224.

26 Milton Millhauser, *Just Before Darwin* (1959), p. 52–56. Tom McIver largely follows Millhauser's interpretations in his remarks on various books by scriptural geologists in his *Anti-Evolution: An Annotated Bibliography* (1988).

27 Francis C. Haber, *The Age of the World* (1959), p. 204. Haber mentioned none of the geologically competent scriptural geologists. He referred to Penn only by name and devoted a page to Bugg, whom he called "a typical example of literalist opposition" to old-earth geological theories (p. 212). He named no scriptural geologists of the 1830s, when their writings were most numerous.

28 James R. Moore, "Geologists and Interpreters of Genesis in the Nineteenth Century," in *God and Nature* (1986), edited by David C. Lindberg and Ronald L. Numbers, p. 337.

29 Nicolaas A. Rupke, *The Great Chain of History: William Buckland and the English School of Geology 1814-1849* (1983), p. 41–47.

old-earth geological theories.[30] Nevertheless, these are very much minority views among historians.

Whenever a group of people is so severely castigated by contemporaries and later historians, the student of history can be excused for being just a little suspicious that maybe there could be another side to the story. So it is important to investigate the evidence more closely and carefully, and as objectively as possible. As we shall see, the above evaluations of the scriptural geologists are wildly inaccurate.

A second reason for studying these men is that their views are very similar to those of modern young-earth creationists (YEC), even though there is no literary dependence of the latter on the former and most YEC have never heard of the scriptural geologists (prior to my research). The historical facts about the scriptural geologists stand as a strong corrective to the misleading argument of respected church historian, Mark Noll, who has castigated young-earth creationists for the scandalous use of their minds and for interpreting Genesis in a way that "no responsible Christian teacher in the history of the church" (before the 20th century) has.[31]

A third reason for studying the scriptural geologists is a fact closely related to the last point, namely, that recent historians of science have written a number of articles and books giving reinterpretations of the historic relation of science to religious belief.[32] In this area the "warfare" thesis of White and Draper dominated scholarly thinking for far too long. According to them, science and Christianity were constantly in conflict and science won every battle.[33] Brooke points out that this warfare thesis was flawed because 1) White and Draper only considered the extreme positions and neglected those who saw religion and science as complementary, and 2) they evaluated past scientific achievements on the basis of later, rather than contemporary, knowledge.[34] Rudwick summarized the need for such fresh reinterpretations of the past when he stated:

> This kind of scientific triumphalism is long overdue for critical reappraisal. Its claims to serious attention have been thoroughly demolished in other areas of the history of science, but it survives as an anomaly in the historical treatment of the relation of science to religious belief. This may be because the historians' own attitudes are conditioned by the immature age at which religious beliefs and practices are abandoned by many, though not all, intellectuals in modern Western societies. This common experience may explain why many historians of science seem incapable of giving the religious beliefs of past cultures the same intelligent and empathic respect that they now routinely accord to even the strangest scientific beliefs of the past.[35]

This difficulty in giving a fair treatment of scientists who held strong religious beliefs, especially

30 V. Paul Marston, "Science and Meta-science in the Work of Adam Sedgwick" (The Open University, Ph.D. thesis, 1984), p. 290–308. However, in his discussion he gave only two sentences to the geologist George Young and makes no mention of John Murray, William Rhind, or George Fairholme.

31 Mark Noll, *Scandal of the Evangelical Mind* (1994), p. 12–14. Noll mistakenly follows the agnostic Ronald Numbers, who in his book *The Creationists* (1992) attempts to root young-earth creationism in the teachings of Seventh Day Adventism.

32 See, for example, David C. Lindberg and Ronald L. Numbers, editors, *God and Nature* (1986); Roy Porter, "Charles Lyell and the Principles of the History of Geology," *British Journal for the History of Science*, vol. IX, no. 32, Part 2 (1976), p. 91–103; Rhoda Rappaport, "Geology and Orthodoxy: The Case of Noah's Flood in Eighteenth Century Thought," *British Journal for the History of Science*, vol. XI (1978), p. 1–18; R. Hooykaas, *Religion and the Rise of Modern Science* (1972); R. Hooykaas, "Genesis and Geology," *New Interactions Between Theology and Natural Science* (1974), p. 55–87; Eugene M. Klaaren, *Religious Origins of Modern Science* (1977), Nicolaas A. Rupke, *The Great Chain of History: William Buckland and the English School of Geology 1814-1849* (1983).

33 A.D. White, *A History of the Warfare of Science with Theology in Christendom* (1896). John W. Draper, in his *A History of the Conflict between Religion and Science* (1875), held the same view but focused his attention on Catholics, rather than Protestants.

34 John H. Brooke, *Science and Religion* (1991), p. 35–37.

35 Martin J.S. Rudwick, "The Shape and Meaning of Earth History," in *God and Nature* (1986), edited by David C. Lindberg and Ronald L. Numbers, p. 296–297.

orthodox Christian beliefs, calls for a more careful assessment of the scriptural geologists, to whom the warfare myth continues to be applied.

Lastly, the battle that the scriptural geologists fought sheds much light on the modern creation-evolution debate in many countries and especially on the controversy within the church over the age of the earth. As will be seen, contrary to popular opinion both inside and outside the church, the controversy is not between science and religion, but between anti-biblical religions/philosophies and biblical Christianity. And those Christians who favor the approach of the "intelligent design" movement will have cause to reconsider the validity of that position on the age of the earth and on its strategy to reform science and culture.

HOW THIS BOOK IS ORGANIZED

After a discussion of the historical context of the Genesis-geology debate, a separate chapter is devoted to each of seven scriptural geologists (presented roughly in chronological order). These seven writers wrote the most on this subject and represent the diversity of the scriptural geologists who were most active in the years 1820–45.[36] In each of these chapters a biographical sketch is followed by a summary of the man's views.

It is essential, as Porter has said, for the historian to allow people from the past to speak for themselves and to endeavor to understand them and their ideas in their own terms.[37] Therefore, in the process of summarizing their arguments, I quote liberally from their writings. To do so is especially important because their works are not easily accessible to most readers, even to scholars.[38]

Having considered them individually, the last part of the book will make overall comparisons and generalizations in analysis and evaluation of the debate. I will suggest reasons for their engagement in the debate and for the response they received from their contemporary opponents.

A remark is in order about how the seven men I have analyzed were selected. The study has been restricted to Great Britain, because this was the heart of the debate.[39] There were many other scriptural geologists who wrote on the subject in pamphlets, a chapter of a book, or book-length treatises during the years 1820–45, the period of their most intense opposition to old-earth theories.

In addition to the ones on which this book concentrates, the works of about 25 other scriptural geologists were also examined, though some in much less detail. These included the writings of Anglican clergymen such as Thomas Gisborne, Henry Cole, Samuel Best, William Cockburn, James Mellor Brown, Frederick Nolan, and Sharon Turner. The Methodist clergyman and geologist Joseph Sutcliffe, and the Anglican clergyman and famous entomologist William Kirby, likewise defended the view.

Others were Thomas Rodd (a bookseller), Fowler de Johnsone (a clergyman in an unknown denomination), William Brande (a prominent chemist and professor at the Royal Institution), William Martin (a natural philosopher), Walter

---

36 Most of the scriptural geologists were in Great Britain where for cultural, religious, and scientific reasons the debate was most intense. I found a few in America and there may have been some on the European continent, but I did not discover any.

37 Roy Porter, *The Making of Geology: Earth Science in Britain, 1660–1815* (Cambridge, England; New York: Cambridge University Press, 1977), p. 7.

38 The writings of some of the scriptural geologists (Brown, Penn, Fairholme, Murray, and Young), along with some of their old-earth opponents (Chalmers, Pye Smith, and Miller) have been republished, though at exorbitant prices that only libraries are likely to pay. See "Creationism and Scriptural Geology, 1817–1857" at <www.thoemmes.com/science/creationism.htm>.

39 As far as I know, the American and continental European scenes in the early 19th century still await a similar detailed study. Byron Nelson, in his *The Deluge Story in Stone* (1931), briefly referred to several American and European scriptural geologists at that time. A recent article on the American scriptural geologists is Rodney L. Stiling, "Scriptural Geology in America," in David N. Livingstone, D.G. Hart, and Mark A. Noll, editors, *Evangelicals and Science in Historical Perspective* (1999), p. 177–192. Regarding Germany, help may be found in Stephan Holthaus, *Fundamentalismus in Deutschland: Der Kampf um die Bibel im Protestantismus des 19. und 20. Jahrhunderts*, Biblia et Symbiotica 1, Bonn: Verlag für Kultur und Wissenschaft, 1993. This is a Ph.D. dissertation from ETF-Leuven.

Forman (a Royal Navy captain with strong interests in physics and astronomy), and Robert FitzRoy (Royal Navy captain of the H.M.S. *Beagle* on which Charles Darwin made his famous voyage).[40] Six of these were discussed at length in my thesis (Gisborne, Cole, Best, Cockburn, Brown, and de Johnsone).[41] All of the works related to the Genesis-geology debate of these 25 men not discussed here are listed in the bibliography, for those who care to pursue the subject further.

As a result of this broader study, I am satisfied that the seven men analyzed in this book accurately represent the whole class of writers. This provides a sound basis for the generalizations and conclusions at the end of the book.

The Reverend Joseph Sutcliffe, an early scriptural geologist and Methodist pastor.

40 Revised chapters of my thesis on Gisborne, Best, Cole, and Brown can be found on the Web at www.answersingenesis.org.

42 It should be noted here that from 1790 to 1820 Richard Kirwan, André Deluc, James Parkinson, and Joseph Townsend were four prominent scientists who wrote in defense of Scripture, especially the Flood account, and therefore have sometimes been grouped with the "scriptural geologists" under study in this book. But like William Buckland in the 1820s, Deluc, Parkinson, and Townsend believed in a very old earth, and held to a day-age theory. Kirwan did not clearly state his view on the age of the earth, though probably he believed in a recent creation. See the bibliography for their works on the subject. Although these men were occasionally classed as "scriptural geologists," the label was most generally applied in the early 19th century to those who rejected all old-earth theories.

THE HISTORICAL CONTEXT

Before considering some of the individual scriptural geologists, we need to consider the intellectual and religious background and the history of geology leading up to the early 19th century, the cultural milieu at that time, what the Bible commentaries on Genesis were saying, and the marks of geological competence in the early 1800s.

INTELLECTUAL AND RELIGIOUS BACKGROUND

The controversies in early 19th century Britain regarding the relationship of the early chapters of Genesis to the geological discoveries and theories did not, of course, take place in a vacuum. They were part of a complex movement of thought with philosophical, theological, social, political, and ecclesiastical dimensions, which pulsed through the educated minds of Europeans in general and of Britons in particular. The following highlights some of the most important people, events, and currents of thought leading up to and contributing to a revolution in world view which profoundly affected the 19th century Genesis-geology debate.

The Galileo Affair

Shortly before his death in 1543 and with some hesitation, Nicholas Copernicus (1473–1543), the Polish mathematician and astronomer, published *On the Revolutions of the Heavenly Spheres*, in which he argued that the earth was not the center of the universe, as generally believed, but rotated on its axis and revolved with the other known planets around the stationary sun. Over the subsequent decades, opposition to his theory (as a description of physical reality, rather than merely as an alternative mathematical description) arose because it seemed contrary to common sense, was opposed to Aristotelian physics, lacked convincing astronomical evidence, and was contrary to a literal interpretation of various Scriptures. Approximately 150 years passed before his theory was generally accepted. But it was soon embraced by Johannes Kepler (1571–1630) and Galileo Galilei (1564–1642), though the latter was at first reluctant to publicize his views.

In 1613, Galileo finally came out in the open in his *Letters on Sunspots*. He argued that his observations of the heavens by means of the recently

invented telescope were consistent with what Copernicus had proposed was the actual relationship and movement of the earth and heavenly bodies. Initially, the Roman Catholic authorities accepted Galileo's assertions as compatible with the teachings of the Church. Eventually, however, Jesuit university professors (who were ultra-orthodox defenders of Catholic dogma and embraced the geocentric theory) were sufficiently provoked by Galileo's further writings so that they pressured the pope in 1633 to force Galileo to recant the heliocentric theory on threat of excommunication. He did recant, but was still under house arrest for the remainder of his life.[1]

This incident gave considerable support to others at the same time and later, who insisted (following Galileo) on a complete bifurcation between the study of the creation and the study of Scripture.[2] The Bible was written to teach people theology and morality, not a system of natural philosophy (i.e., science), it was argued. Or as Galileo said, the intention of Scripture is "to teach us how one goes to heaven, not how heaven goes."[3] Therefore, Galileo concluded that:

GALILEO GALILEI (1564–1642)

> Nothing physical which sense experience sets before our eyes, or which necessary demonstrations prove to us, ought to be called in question (much less condemned) upon the testimony of biblical passages which may have some different meaning beneath their words. . . . On the contrary, having arrived at any certainties in physics, we ought to utilize

1 Much has been written about this complex Galileo affair. See Thomas Schirrmacher, "The Galileo Affair: History or Heroic Hagiography?" *Creation Ex Nihilo Technical Journal,* 14(1), 2000, p. 91–100 (at http://www.answersingenesis.org/Home/Area/Magazines/tj/docs/TJ14_1-Galileo.pdf); Charles E. Hummel, *The Galileo Connection: Resolving Conflicts Between Science & the Bible* (Downers Grove, IL: InterVarsity Press, 1986); Colin A. Russell, *Cross-currents: Interactions Between Science and Faith* (Grand Rapids, MI: W.B. Eerdmans Pub. Co., 1985), p. 37–54; Colin A. Russell, R. Hooykaas, and David C. Goodman, *The "Conflict Thesis" and Cosmology* (Milton Keynes: Open University Press, 1974); William R. Shea, "Galileo and the Church," in *God and Nature*, David C. Lindberg and Ronald L. Numbers, editors (Berkeley, CA: University of California Press, 1986), p. 114–135; John Dillenberger, *Protestant Thought and Natural Science* (Garden City, NY: Doubleday, 1960), p. 22–28; Thomas S. Kuhn, *The Copernican Revolution* (1971), p. 219–228.

2 There had been others before, too, such as the moderate Lutheran, Rheticus, who studied mathematics and astronomy under Copernicus and helped get his book published. Rheticus had virtually the same view of the interpretation of Scripture in relation to the study of nature that Galileo had and he wrote about it in a pamphlet in 1539. See R. Hooykaas, *G.J. Rheticus' Treatise on Holy Scripture and the Motion of the Earth* (1984).

3 Galileo Galilei, Letter to the Grand Duchess Christina (1615), from Stillman Drake, transl., *Discoveries and Opinions of Galileo* (1957), p. 186, reprinted in D.C. Goodman, editor, *Science and Religious Belief 1600-1900: A Selection of Primary Sources* (Bristol: J. Wright [for] the Open University Press, 1973), p. 34.

these as the most appropriate aids in the true exposition of the Bible.[4]

With frequent reference to Galileo, this approach to the relation of science to the interpretation of Scripture was demanded by all the opponents of the British scriptural geologists of the early 19th century. The old-earth proponents believed that, prior to the work of Copernicus, Kepler, and Galileo, it was quite natural for Christians to take various verses in the Bible to imply an immovable earth surrounded by the revolving heavenly bodies because they had no philosophical or observational reasons to think otherwise. But once the new mathematical descriptions and telescopic observations had been made known, they were forced to reinterpret those verses so as to remove the apparent contradiction between the truth revealed by Scripture and that revealed by God's creation. In exactly the same way, the old-earth proponents reasoned, geology has brought forward observational proof that the earth is much older than previously thought and so Christians must interpret Genesis 1 and 6–9 differently, so as to harmonize Scripture with this newly discovered teaching of creation.[5]

It should be noted now that the Galileo affair was focused exclusively on the present structure and operation of the universe, rather than on how it came into being and attained its present arrangement. By way of comparison, Galileo interpreted the account of the miracle of the long day of Joshua 10:12–15 as literal history, though he explained the stationary position of the sun in terms of Copernican theory and the language of appearance. He apparently also took the account of the creation of the sun on the fourth day of Genesis 1 to be literal history.[6] At the end of this book I will return to this distinction between what are sometimes called "operation science" and "historical science."

Baconian Science

The famous English politician and philosopher Francis Bacon (1561–1626) also had an enormous influence on the subsequent development of science and on the views of later Christians regarding the relationship of Scripture to science. He too promoted the separation of Scripture from scientific study of the physical world. Bacon advocated the concept of the two books of God: the book of Scripture and the book of nature. In *Advancement of Learning* (1605) he made his well-known statement of the relationship of Scripture to nature:

> For our Saviour saith, "You err, not knowing the Scriptures, nor the power of God;" laying before us two books or volumes to study, if we will be secured from error; first the Scriptures, revealing the will of God, and then the creatures expressing his power; whereof the latter is a key unto the former: not only opening our understanding to conceive the true sense of the Scriptures, by the general notions of reason and rules of speech; but chiefly opening our belief, in drawing us into a due meditation of the omnipotency [*sic*] of God, which is chiefly signed and engraven upon his works.[7]

Later in the same work he criticized the "school of Paracelsus"[8] and others for pretending "to find the truth of all natural philosophy in the Scriptures; scandalizing and traducing all other philosophy as heathenish and profane." He continued in general terms:

> For to seek heaven and earth in the word of God, whereof it is said, "Heaven and earth shall pass, but my word shall not pass," is to seek temporary things amongst eternal; and as to seek divinity in philosophy is to seek the living amongst the dead,

4 Ibid., in Drake, *Discoveries and Opinions of Galileo* (p. 182–183); and in Goodman, *Science and Religious Belief 1600-1900* (p. 32–33).

5 It will be seen later, however, that this thinking developed in stages in geology generally and in the minds of individual geologists. At first only Genesis 1 was reinterpreted, while the Flood of Genesis 6–9 was seen as a global, geologically significant event. After 1830, Genesis 6–9 was reinterpreted to mean a local and/or geologically insignificant flood.

6 See Galileo Galilei, Letter to the Grand Duchess Christina (1615), from Drake, *Discoveries and Opinions of Galileo*, p. 211–216), reprinted in Goodman, *Science and Religious Belief 1600-1900*, p. 47–49.

7 Francis Bacon, *The Advancement of Learning* (1906 Oxford edition), p. 46 (Book I, part VI.16).

8 Parcelsus (1493?–1541) was a Swiss doctor and chemist.

Sir Francis Bacon (1561–1626)

so to seek philosophy in divinity is to seek the dead amongst the living. . . . And again, the scope or purpose of the spirit of God is not to express matters of nature in the Scriptures, otherwise than in passage, and for application to man's capacity and to matters moral and divine.[9]

Fifteen years later, Bacon developed these ideas further in *Novum Organum* (1620). Here, in condemning the mixture of superstition and theology in the works of Greeks (such as Pythagoras and Plato), he argued that it was foolish to attempt to found "a system of natural philosophy" on the basis of the first chapter of Genesis, Job, or other sections of the Bible, because such an "unsound admixture of things divine and human" would produce not only an erroneous philosophy, but also a heretical religion.[10] In particular, Bacon chastised the scholastic theologians of his day for this unwise mingling of "the disputations and thorny philosophy of Aristotle with the body of Religion in an inordinate degree."[11]

Another key part of Bacon's scientific methodology was that he insisted that accurate knowledge of the physical world could only expand on the basis of inductive reasoning from a wealth of data collected by observation and experimentation. Errors resulted from speculation based on too few facts.

These two ideas (i.e., the separation of the study of Scripture and science and the method of inductive reasoning from much observed data) were fundamental to the objectives of the Geological Society of London, founded in 1807, and many old-Earth geologists repeatedly highlighted their dependence on Bacon.[12]

But for this study, it will also become important to consider a little-noted passage relating to Bacon's influence on geology. Just a few pages before the first quotation above from *The Advancement of Learning*, Bacon noted that the Levitical laws of leprosy teach:

A principle of nature, that putrefaction is more contagious before maturity than after. . . . So in this and very many other places in that law, there is to be found, besides the theological sense, much aspersion of philosophy. So likewise in that excellent Book of Job, if it be revolved with diligence, it will be found pregnant and swelling with natural philosophy; as

9 Bacon, *The Advancement of Learning*, p. 229 (Book II, part XXV.16).

10 Francis Bacon, *Novum Organum* (1859), Andrew Johnson, transl., p. 42 (Book I, Part LXV).

11 Ibid., p. 82 (Book I, Part LXXXIX).

12 Martin J.S. Rudwick, "The Foundation of the Geological Society of London: Its Scheme for Co-operative Research and Its Struggle for Independence," *British Journal for the History of Science*, vol. I, no. 4 (1963), p. 325–355; James R. Moore, "Geologists and Interpreters of Genesis in the Nineteenth Century," in *God and Nature*, David C. Lindberg and Ronald L. Numbers, editors, p. 322–350.

for example cosmography and the roundness of the earth; [here he quoted the Latin of Job 26:7] wherein the pensileness of the earth, the pole of the north, and the finiteness or convexity of heaven are manifestly touched. So again matter of astronomy; [here he quoted the Latin of Job 38:31–32] where the fixing of the stars ever standing at equal distance is with great elegance noted. And in another place, [here he quoted the Latin of Job 9:9] where again he takes knowledge of the depression of the southern pole, calling it the secrets of the south, because the southern stars were in that climate unseen. Matter of generation [here he quoted the Latin of Job 10:10] etc. Matter of minerals [here was another partial quote of Job in Latin] and so forwards in that chapter. So likewise in the person of Salomon [*sic*] the King, we see the gift and endowment of wisdom and learning. . . . Salomon became enabled not only to write those excellent parables or aphorisms concerning divine and moral philosophy, but also to compile a natural history of all verdure, from the cedar upon the mountain to the moss upon the wall (which is but a rudiment between putrefaction and an herb), and also of all things that breathe and move.[13]

Earlier he had briefly expressed his apparent belief in a literal six-day creation, after which the creation was complete. He also believed that the Flood and the confusion of the languages at the Tower of Babel were judgments of God.[14] Some of these beliefs were expressed in more detail in his *Confession of Faith*, first published posthumously in his *Remains* (1648), but written some unknown time before the summer of 1603.[15] This eight-page confession[16] reads like a detailed, orthodox creed.

Of particular relevance to this study is his statement that during the six days of creation God "made all things in their first estate good," each day's work being a "perfection," but that "heaven and earth, which were made for man's use, were subdued to corruption by his fall." He believed that God ceased His creation work on the first sabbath and never resumed it. Since then He has continued His providential work of sustaining His creation and after the Fall He has been doing His redemptive work. According to Bacon, "the laws of nature, which now remain and govern inviolably till the end of the world, began to be in force when God first rested from his works, and ceased to create; but received a revocation, in part, by the curse, since which time they change not."[17] So clearly in Bacon's mind, the laws of nature which scientists should endeavor to discover by observation and experimentation were not the means by which God created the fully functioning universe and earth with its various kinds of plants and animals, and man.

These various remarks by Bacon about creation, the commencement of the laws of nature, Scripture, and the study of nature might seem at

13 Bacon, *The Advancement of Learning*, p. 43–44 (Book I, part VI. 9-11). It might be argued that since Bacon said that Solomon gained his insights on the natural world from learning, he was simply stating that Solomon was a good natural philosopher, anticipating Bacon's methodology. But this interpretation is debatable because Bacon said that Solomon was also endowed with wisdom about divine and moral philosophy and it is doubtful that Bacon thought this wisdom came by Baconian-style scientific methods of analysis. Furthermore, there is no indication that Bacon believed that the use of such scientific methodology was the way Moses discovered the laws of leprosy or the men in Job's day discovered these geographical and astronomical truths.

14 Ibid., p. 40-42 (Book I, points VI.2-8). Bacon's statement on the days of creation reads (p. 40–41), "It is so then, that in the work of the creation we see a double emanation of virtue from God; the one referring more properly to power, the other to wisdom; the one expressed in making the subsistence of the matter, and the other in disposing the beauty of the form. This being supposed, it is to be observed that for anything which appeareth in the history of the creation, the confused mass and matter of heaven and earth was made in a moment; and the order and disposition of that chaos or mass was the work of six days. . . . So in the distribution of days we see the day wherein God did rest and contemplated His own works, was blessed above all the days wherein he did effect and accomplish them."

15 DNB on Bacon, p. 824.

16 Francis Bacon, *The Works of Francis Bacon* (1819), II: p. 480–488.

17 Ibid., p. 482–484.

first sight to be inconsistent or contradictory and we might surmise that his remarks about separation of science from Scripture in *Novum Organum* represent a recantation of earlier statements. But there is no clear evidence that this was so.[18] All his remarks are important for understanding the 19th century Genesis-geology debate, in which old-earth geologists and many scriptural geologists disagreed over what it meant to be "Baconian" in one's reasoning about the created world. It will be shown that one scriptural geologist, Granville Penn, argued (and some other scriptural geologists explicitly agreed with him) that Bacon's beliefs, based on scriptural revelation, about the nature of the original creation and about when the present laws of nature came into operation, were as much a part of Bacon's philosophic principles as his belief that the study of Scripture and the study of the natural world should not be unwisely mixed. In other words, the scriptural geologists believed that the former principles of Bacon qualified the meaning of his latter principle. Therefore, it was unBaconian to reconstruct earth history based solely on the present laws of nature. Scriptural geologists also contended that it was unBaconian to be dogmatic about an old-earth general theory of the earth, when so little of the earth's surface had been geologically studied in the early 19th century. So while the old-earth geologists claimed to be Baconian in a one sense, the scriptural geologists considered that they too were following Bacon in important respects. We will return to this Baconian aspect of the debate at the end of the book, especially under the discussion of the problematic nature of geology.

The Enlightenment

The Enlightenment or "age of reason" in the 17th and 18th centuries was a time when reason was elevated to the place of supreme authority for determining truth. Some, such as René Descartes (1596–1650) and John Locke (1632–1704), sought to use reason to defend the Christian faith, but others used reason to discard all other forms of authority, especially tradition, religious experience, ecclesiastical leadership, and the revelation of Scripture. Ironically, they often relied heavily on the writings of Locke and Descartes to do so. Hazard observed:

> Was there ever a more singular example of the way in which after a while a doctrine may develop ideas completely at variance with those with which it started? . . . To the cause of religion, the Cartesian philosophy came bringing what seemed a most valuable support, to begin with. But that same philosophy bore within it a germ of irreligion which time was to bring to light, and which acts and works and is made deliberate use of to sap and undermine the foundations of belief.[19]

Descartes used the tools of examination, free inquiry, and criticism to attempt to establish with certitude issues such as the existence of God and the immortality of the soul. Skeptics used those same tools to overthrow those beliefs.

One of those Cartesian skeptics was the Dutch apostate Jew, Benedict de Spinoza (1632–77), who in 1670 wrote a most damaging book called *Tractatus Theologico-Politicus*. It was opposed by Jews, Protestants, and Catholics, for it swept away key traditional Judeo-Christian beliefs. Spinoza rejected the Scriptures as the prophetic revelation of God, believing them to be crusted over with errors and ancient culture. Not surprisingly, Spinoza strongly rejected the miracles in the Bible as being contrary to the universal laws of nature. His primary concern in *Tractatus* was to establish a scientific method of hermeneutics. Spinoza attempted unsuccessfully to interpret the Bible impartially without any presuppositions.

Although Spinoza's ideas were strongly opposed at the time, they made their impact on the early 19th century in two ways: through the teaching of the English deists and through the German and French biblical critics, many of whom were also deists.

Deists viewed the Creator as a great watchmaker, who, once He had wound up the world, allowed it to run without interference according to the laws of nature. As a result, miracles were

18 Thomas Fowler, "Introduction," in Francis Bacon, *Novum Organum*, p. 45.
19 Paul Hazard, *The European Mind: 1680–1715* (London: Hollis and Carter, 1953), p. 160.

denied along with fulfilled prophecy and divine revelation. Deism received a firm response from orthodox churchmen so that by the 1750s openly deistic writers had essentially died out in England. Nevertheless, deistic ideas took root and spread into the 19th century, often hidden in works on natural theology which were so prevalent in the early decades. (Natural theology considers the theological/moral truth about God that can be gleaned from the study of His creation, i.e., nature.) Brooke notes:

> Without additional clarification, it is not always clear to the historian (and was not always clear to contemporaries) whether proponents of design were arguing a Christian or deistic thesis. The ambiguity itself could be useful. By cloaking potentially subversive discoveries in the language of natural theology, scientists could appear more orthodox than they were, but without the discomfort of duplicity if their inclinations were more in line with deism.[20]

One Anglican clergyman wrote in 1836 that as a result of the growing influence of natural theology and German neology "a large portion of what passes as Christianity is but deism in disguise!"[21]

In Germany and France deism flourished, especially in biblical scholarship, where the German philosopher Immanuel Kant (1724–1804) and Spinoza had great influence. Reventlow concludes his thorough study by saying:

> We cannot overestimate the influence exercised by Deistic thought, and by the principles of the Humanist world view which the Deists made the criterion of their biblical criticism, on the historical-critical exegesis of the 19th century; the consequences extend right down to the present. At that time a series of almost unshakeable presuppositions were decisively shifted in a different direction.[22]

As critical biblical scholarship gained the upper hand on the continent in the late 18th and early 19th centuries, its penetration into the British (and North American) churches was hindered, no doubt partly because of lasting effects of the evangelical revival led by the Wesleys and Whitefield.

So a revolution in theological and philosophical world view was in full bloom by the early 19th century. Its development can also be traced in the history of geology and cosmogony.

HISTORICAL DEVELOPMENTS IN GEOLOGY, PALAEONTOLOGY, AND COSMOLOGY

The fundamental features of geological study, namely, field work, collection, and theory construction, were not developed until the 16th to 18th centuries. Previously, back to ancient Greek times, many scholars believed that fossils were the remains of former living things and many Christians (including Tertullian, Chrysostom, and Augustine) attributed them to the Noachian flood. But other scholars rejected these ideas and regarded fossils as either jokes of nature, the products of rocks endowed with life in some sense, the creative works of God, or perhaps even the deceptions of Satan. In the 16th and 17th centuries the debate among naturalists intensified. One of the prominent opponents of the organic origin of fossils was Martin Lister (1638–1712). John Ray (1627–1705) favored organic origin although he respected Lister's objections. But from his microscopic analysis of fossil wood, Robert Hooke

20 John H. Brooke, *Science and Religion* (Cambridge ; New York: Cambridge University Press, 1991), p. 194.

21 William J. Irons, *On the Whole Doctrine of Final Causes* (1836), p. 13. Similarly, T.H. Horne, a great Anglican biblical scholar, wrote an 81-page tract for wide distribution called *Deism Refuted* (1819). I consulted the sixth edition of that first year. Another edition appeared in 1826 and an American edition came out in 1819. It was warmly reviewed in the *Edinburgh Monthly Review*, Vol. II (1819), p. 661–670, where the writer complained of deistic belief spreading among the lower classes. Other tracts or books refuting deism included Reverend Thomas Young's *Truth Triumphant* (1820); Francis Wrangham's *The Pleiad; or A Series of Abridgements of Seven Distinguished Writers, in Opposition to the Pernicious Doctrines of Deism* (1820); Robert Hindmarsh's *Christianity Against Deism, Materialism, and Atheism* (1824); and the anonymous translation from French called *Alphonse de Mirecourt; or The Young Infidel Reclaimed from the Errors of Deism* (1835).

22 Henning G. Reventlow, *The Authority of the Bible and the Rise of the Modern World* (Philadelphia, PA: Fortress Press,1984), p. 412.

JOHN WOODWARD
(1665–1722)

(1635–1703) confirmed that fossils had once lived. However, he did not believe they were the result of Noah's flood.

Prior to 1750, one of the most important thinkers was Niels Steensen (1638–86), or Steno, a Dutch anatomist and geologist who established the principle of superposition: sedimentary rock layers are deposited in a successive, essentially horizontal fashion, so that a lower stratum is older than the one above it. In his *Forerunner* (1669) he expressed belief in a 6,000-year-old earth and that organic fossils and the rock strata were laid down by the Flood.[23] Shortly after Steno, Thomas Burnet (1635–1715), a theologian, published his influential *Sacred Theory of the Earth* (1681) in which he argued from Scripture, rather than geology, for a global Flood. He made no mention of fossils and though he believed in a young earth, he took each day in Genesis 1 to be a year or longer. Following him, the physician and geologist John Woodward (1665–1722) invoked the Flood to explain stratification and fossilization, in *An Essay Toward a Natural History of the Earth* (1695). In *A New Theory of the Earth* (1696) William Whiston (1667–1752), Newton's successor at Cambridge in mathematics, shared similar views to the above. But he offered a cometary explanation of the mechanism of the Flood and he added six years to Archbishop Ussher's date of creation by his argument that each day of Genesis 1 was one year in duration. Some of his points were later used by those who favored the day-age theory for Genesis 1. In his *Treatise on the Deluge* (1768) the geologist Alexander Catcott (1725–79) used geological arguments to defend the Genesis account of a recent creation and global Flood which produced the geological record. On the other hand, another geologist, John Whitehurst (1713–88), contended in his *Inquiry into the Original State and Formation of the Earth* (1778) that the earth was much older than man and, although the Noachian flood was a global catastrophe, it was not responsible for most of the geological record. On the continent, Johann Lehmann (d. 1767) studied German mountain strata and believed the primary, non-fossil-bearing rocks were from creation week, whereas the secondary fossiliferous rocks were attributed to the Flood. Other geologists like Jean Elienne Guettard (1715–86), Nicholas Desmarest (1735–1815) and Giovanne Arduino (1714–95) denied the Flood and advocated a much older earth.[24]

In France, three prominent writers developed philosophically naturalistic explanations related to earth history (i.e., explaining the origin of everything by the present laws of nature). In his *Epochs of Nature* (1778), Comte de Buffon (1708–88) espoused the theory that the earth had originated from a collision of a comet and the sun. Extrapolating from experiments involving the cooling of

23 In 1650, Archbishop James Ussher published his now famous calculations that set the date of creation at 4004 B.C. This scholarly work has been masterfully retranslated and edited. See *The Annals of the World* (Green Forest, AR: Master Books, 2003).

24 For further discussion of these 17th and 18th century writers on geology, see Martin J.S. Rudwick, *The Meaning of Fossils* (Chicago, IL: University of Chicago Press, 1985), p. 1–93; Davis Young, *Christianity and the Age of the Earth* (Grand Rapids, MI: Zondervan Publ. House, 1988), p. 27–42.

various hot materials, he postulated that in about 78,000 years the earth had passed through seven epochs to reach its present state. He believed in spontaneous generation, rather than evolution, to explain the origin of living species. In an apparent attempt to avert religious opposition, he interpreted the days of Genesis 1 to be long ages, an idea which became popular among some 19th century British Christians. The astronomer Pierre Laplace (1749–1827) was strongly motivated by his atheism to eliminate the idea of design or purpose from scientific investigations. As a precursor to modern cosmic evolution, he proposed the nebular hypothesis to explain why the planets revolve around the sun in the same direction and in roughly the same plane. According to this theory, published in his *Exposition of the System of the Universe* (1796), prior to the present state there was a solar atmosphere which by purely natural progressive condensation had produced rings, like Saturn's, which eventually coalesced to form planets. This theory made the age of creation even greater than that which Buffon had suggested. Jean Lamarck (1744–1829) was a naturalist specializing in the study of fossil and living shells. Riding the fence between deism and atheism, he had a strong aversion to any notion of global catastrophe. In *Zoological Philosophy* (1809) he attempted to explain the similarities and differences between living and fossil creatures by four laws of gradual evolutionary transformation commonly summarized as the inheritance of acquired characteristics. He believed in spontaneous generation, rejected the notion of extinctions, and became a fierce opponent of the catastrophist Georges Cuvier.[25]

So by the latter part of the 18th century, a number of factors were preparing the ground for the geological revolution of the coming century. Though most Christians believed in a straightforward literal reading of the creation and Flood narratives, some were suggesting that the earth was much older than Ussher had calculated. In addition, the deists and atheists were proposing alternative cosmologies to the one found in Genesis. The idea of an initially fully functioning creation, much like today's, was beginning to be replaced by the notion of created or uncreated, initially simple matter, which gradually, by the laws of nature operating over untold ages, was transformed into the present state of the universe. A major shift in world view, involving the existence and nature of God, the nature of His relationship to the creation and the nature of the relationship of science to biblical interpretation, was underway.

Neptunist-Vulcanist Debate

The years 1790–1820 have been called the "heroic age" of geology. During this time, geology truly became established as a separate field of scientific study. More extensive geological observations began to be made, new methods were developed for systematically arranging the rock formations, and the Geological Society of London, the first society fully devoted to geology, was born. But it was also during this period that geology became embroiled in the so-called Neptunist-Vulcanist debate.[26] Neptunism was named after the Roman god of the sea and viewed water as the most important agent of geological change. Vulcanism takes its name from the Roman god of fire and saw the internal heat of the earth as the dominant factor. The founders of the two positions were, respectively, Abraham Werner (1749–1817) of Germany and James Hutton (1726–97) of Scotland.

Werner was one of the most influential geologists of his time, even though his theory was rather quickly discarded.[27] As a result of intense study of the succession of strata in his home area of Saxony, which were clearly water-deposited, he developed the theory that most of the crust of the earth had been precipitated chemically or mechanically by a slowly-receding primeval global ocean. The strata were then ordered by their mineral content. Werner did acknowledge volcanic activity, but put this as

25 For further discussion of these three writers, see Brooke, *Science and Religion*, p. 234–242, and Roger Hahn, "Laplace and the Mechanistic Universe," in *God and Nature*, p. 256–276.

26 Charles C. Gillispie, *Genesis and Geology* (Cambridge, MA: Harvard University Press, 1951), p. 41–82; A. Hallum, *Great Geological Controversies* (Oxford; New York: Oxford University Press, 1992), p. 1–29.

27 Werner's influence on many of the most influential 19th century geologists in Britain and Europe is discussed in Rachel Laudan, *From Mineralogy to Geology* (Chicago, IL: University of Chicago Press, 1987), p. 93–112, 222–228.

the last stage of his theory, after the primeval ocean had receded to its present level.

Many objections were soon raised against his theory, but it was an attractively simple system. Furthermore, as an excellent mineralogist, Werner was an inspirational teacher for 40 years at the University of Freiberg, where he attracted the great loyalty of his students, many of whom came from foreign countries. He was not a prolific writer but recent studies of private correspondence and lecture notes have shown that he believed and taught his students that earth history lasted at least a million years. He felt that the earth's crust provided more reliable historical information than any written documents. As a deist, he also felt no need to harmonize his theory with the Bible.[28] Nevertheless, some writers, such as Richard Kirwan and André Deluc, used Werner's theory in support of the Genesis flood.

Hutton's geological views, published in his *Theory of the Earth* (1795), were significantly different from Werner's. He did most of his geological work in and around Edinburgh, which is set on volcanic rocks, and he argued that the primary geological agent was fire, not water. Rocks were of two origins, igneous and aqueous. The latter were the result of detrital matter being slowly deposited in the ocean bottoms which was gradually transformed into rock by the earth's internal heat.

Another characteristic of Hutton's view was its uniformitarianism: everything in the rock record must and can be explained by present day processes of erosion, sedimentation, volcanoes, and earthquakes.[29] Earth history was cyclical — a long process of denudation of the continents into the seas and the gradual raising of the sea floors (by the internal heat of the earth) to make new continents, which in turn would be eroded to the sea only to rise again later. This theory was inspired, in part at least, by his deism: God's wise government of the rock cycle was for the benefit of all creatures.[30] It obviously expanded the age of the earth almost limitlessly. In fact, Hutton denied that geology should be concerned with origins. He asserted instead that he saw "no vestige of a beginning or prospect of an end" in the geological record. His view was a clear denial of any global catastrophe, such as Noah's flood, which was for him a geological non-event.

Hutton received harsh criticism from two prominent naturalists. Richard Kirwan was an Irish mineralogist and chemist who viewed Hutton's views as atheistic. In *Geological Essays* (1799), he objected that Hutton's theory was based on false evidence and was contrary to the literal interpretation of Genesis. André Deluc, a geologist and French-born resident of England, gave a gentler, but still negative, critique of Hutton. He took a fairly literal view of Genesis, but he was severely criticized by Kirwan for believing that the days of Genesis 1 were "periods of time" and that the universal Flood left some of the mountaintops unscathed as island refuges for vegetable and animal life.

In his *Illustrations of the Huttonian Theory of the Earth* (1802) John Playfair (1748–1819), mathematician and Scottish clergyman, republished Hutton's ideas in a more comprehensible and less overtly deistic style. He defended Hutton against Kirwan's charge of atheism by arguing that Hutton was just following the path of natural theology by observing the beautiful design in the systems of the earth: Hutton's ceaseless cycles of geological processes were like Newton's laws of regular planetary motion. Although Playfair made no attempt to harmonize Hutton with Scripture he did defend Hutton's notion of the earth's great antiquity by saying that the Bible only addresses the time scale of human history, which Hutton did not deny was relatively short, as a literal interpretation of the Bible indicated. Like Hutton, Playfair also argued that the Flood was tranquil, not a violent catastrophe.

---

28 *DSB* on Werner, p. 259–260.

29 This was not a new idea; Aristotle expressed similar views in his *On Meteorology*. See Martin J.S. Rudwick, *The Meaning of Fossils*, p. 37–38.

30 O'Rourke has argued that it was empirical philosophy (i.e., all knowledge is based on experience) more than deism, that underpinned his theory. But these are closely related, since deism insists on explaining everything from the laws of nature, which are known only through experiential analysis of the world. Whether Hutton was an empirical deist or deistic empiricist, his world view was anti-Christian. See J.E. O'Rourke, "A Comparison of James Hutton's Principles of Knowledge and Theory of the Earth," *ISIS*, vol. 69, no. 246 (1978), p. 5–20.

William Smith
(1769–1839)

Neither the Neptunists nor the Vulcanists paid much attention to the fossils. In contrast, William Smith (1769–1839), a drainage engineer and surveyor, worked on canals for transporting coal all over Britain. After many years of studying strata (revealed in the canal and road cuttings he helped design) and the fossils in those strata, he published three works from 1815 to 1817, containing the first geological map of England and Wales and explaining the order and relative chronology of the stratigraphic formations as defined by certain characteristic fossils rather than the mineralogical character of the rocks.[31] He became known as the "father of English stratigraphy" because he gave geology a descriptive methodology, which became critical for the establishment of the theory of an old earth. Though Smith believed that a global flood was responsible for producing the gravelly deposits scattered over the earth's surface, he never explicitly linked this with the Noachian flood and believed that all of the sedimentary strata were deposited many long ages before this flood by a long series of supernaturally induced catastrophic floods and recreations of new forms of life.[32]

Another important development at this time in Britain was the establishment of the Geological Society of London in 1807. The 13 founding members were wealthy, cultured gentlemen, who lacked much in geological knowledge but made up for it by their enthusiasm to learn. They met monthly at the Freemason's Tavern (until the society outgrew it) and after an expensive dinner they discussed the advancements of geology. The cost of membership and the initial restriction of membership to London residents were two reasons why most practical geologists associated with mining and road and canal building, such as William Smith, John Farey, and Robert Bakewell, did not become members.[33] The stated purpose of the society was to gather and disseminate geological information, help standardize geological nomenclature, and facilitate cooperative geological work, though in fact it also sought, without much success, to be a stabilizing and regenerating socio-economic influence in the face of potential and actual French-style unrest in Britain.[34] From its inception, it

31 William Smith, *A Memoir to the Map and Delineation of the Strata of England and Wales, with Part of Scotland* (1815), *Strata Identified by Organized Fossils* (1816), and *Stratigraphical System of Organized Fossils* (1817).

32 See John Phillips, *Memoirs of William Smith* (1844), p. 25–26, and William Smith, *Deductions from Established Facts in Geology* (1835). The latter work (a large one-page explanatory diagram) was Smith's last and clearest statement on his view of earth history and was obviously intended to be a response to Lyell's uniformitarianism. Though, when he referred to the "Deluge" he possibly meant the Noachian flood, he made no reference to Scripture. However, he was quite emphatic about the supernatural nature of the many revolutions and creations.

33 Horace B. Woodward, *The History of the Geological Society of London* (1907), p. 17–20, 53. For a discussion of possible social and political reasons why these practical geologists were not in the Geological Society see Martin J.S. Rudwick, "The Foundation of the Geological Society of London: Its Scheme for Cooperative Research and its Struggle for Independence," *British Journal for the History of Science*, vol. I, no. 4 (1963), p. 325–355, and George Grinnell, "The Origins of Modern Geological Theory," *Kronos*, vol. I, no. 4 (1976), p. 68–76.

34 Paul J. Weindling, "Geological Controversy and Its Historiography: The Prehistory of the Geological Society of London," in L.J. Jordanova and Roy S. Porter, editors, *Images of the Earth* (Chalfont St. Giles: British Society for the History of Science1979), , p. 248–271.

was dominated by men who held the old-earth view (the relation of Genesis to geology was never discussed in its public communications), though it did not overtly favor either uniformitarianism or catastrophism, as its first president and influential member, George Greenough, believed, on the basis of Bacon's principles, that in the 1810s and 1820s it was too early in the data collection process to formulate theories of the earth.

By the end of the 1820s the major divisions of the geological record were quite well defined. As Table 1 on the following page shows, the *primary* rocks were the lowest and supposedly oldest and were mostly igneous or metamorphic rocks devoid of fossils. The *secondary* rocks were next and were predominantly sedimentary strata that were fossiliferous. The *tertiary* formations were above these, also containing many fossils, but which more closely resembled existing species. Lastly, were the most recent *alluvial* deposits of gravel, sands and boulders topped by the soils.

In the early 1800s Georges Cuvier (1768–1832), the famous French comparative anatomist and vertebrate palaeontologist, developed his theory of catastrophism[35] as expressed in his *Theory of the Earth* (1813). This went through several English editions over the next 20 years, with an appendix (revised in each later edition) written by Robert Jameson, the leading Scottish geologist. The son of a Lutheran soldier, Cuvier sought to show a general concordance between science and religion.[36] In his *Theory,* he seems to have treated post-flood biblical history fairly literally, but did not interact at all with the text of the scriptural accounts of the creation and the Flood. He reacted sharply against Lamarck's evolutionary theory of the inheritance of acquired characteristics and his denial of extinctions. From his study of the fossils of large quadrupeds found in the strata of the Paris basin, Cuvier concluded that there had indeed been many extinctions, but not all at once. Rather, he theorized that in the past there had been many catastrophic floods. Like William Smith, he believed that each of the strata was characterized by wholly unique fauna. The fauna had appeared for a time and then were catastrophically destroyed and new life forms arose. In opposing Lamarckian evolution, Cuvier presumably believed these new species were separate divine acts of special creation, but he did not explicitly explain this. He believed that earth history was very much longer that the traditional 6,000 years, but that the last flood had occurred only about 5,000 years ago. This obviously coincided with the date of Noah's flood, but Cuvier never explicitly equated his last flood with it.[37] These violent catastrophes were vast inundations of the land by the sea. But they were not necessarily global so that therefore whole species were not always eliminated in these catastrophes. According to Cuvier, man had first appeared sometime between the last two catastrophes.

William Buckland (1784–1856) was the leading geologist in England in the 1820s and followed Cuvier in making catastrophism popular. Like many scientists of his day, he was an Anglican clergyman. He obtained readerships at Oxford University in mineralogy (1813) and geology (1818), and was a very popular lecturer. Two of his students, Charles Lyell and Roderick Murchison, went on to become very influential geologists in the 1830s and 1840s. In his efforts to get science, and especially geology, incorporated into university education (which was designed at the time to train ministers) Buckland published *Vindiciae Geologicae* (1820). Here he argued that geology was consistent with Genesis, confirmed natural religion by providing evidence of creation and God's continued providence, and proved virtually beyond refutation the fact of the global, catastrophic Noachian flood. However, the

35 The term "catastrophism," like "uniformitarianism," was coined by the historian and philosopher of science, William Whewell, in his anonymous review of Lyell's *Principles of Geology*, in the *Quarterly Review*, vol. XLVII, no. 93 (1832), p. 126.

36 *DSB* on Cuvier; William Coleman, "Cuvier and Evolution," in *Science and Religious Belief*, p. 229–234, reprinted from William Coleman, *Georges Cuvier, Zoologist* (Cambridge, MA: Harvard University Press, 1964), p. 172–175.

37 It was the editor and publisher of Cuvier's English editions, Robert Jameson, who made the clear connection between Cuvier's last catastrophe and Noah's flood, no doubt to make it more compatible with British thinking at the time. The Oxford geologist, William Buckland, made this idea even more popular. See Martin Rudwick, *The Meaning of Fossils*, p. 133–135.

Formations	Circa 1790	Circa 1840		Modern	
Alluvium	Post-diluvial	Alluvium	CAINOZOIC Tertiary	Holocene	CAINOZOIC Tertiary
Glacial deposits	Diluvial	Newer Pliocene		Pleistocene	
Sicilian strata		Older Pliocene		Pliocene	
Subappenine strata	TERTIARY	Miocene		Miocene Oligocene	
Persian strata		Eocene		Eocene Palaeocene	
Chalk		Cretaceous	MESOZOIC	Cretaceous	MESOZOIC
Oolites Lias		Jurassic		Jurassic	
Muschelkalk New Red Sandstone	SECONDARY	Triassic	Secondary	Triassic	
Kupferschiefe		Permian		Permian	
Coal Measures		Carboniferous		Carboniferous	PALAEOZOIC
Carboniferous (Mountain) Limestone			PALAEOZOIC		
Old Red Sandstone		Devonian		Devonian	
Wenlock Limestone				Silurian	
"Grauwacke"	TRANSITION	Silurian		Ordovician	
		Primordial (Cambrian)	(Protozoic)	Cambrian	
Longmynd strata	PRIMARY	AZOIC (Primary)		PRE-CAMBRIAN	
Scandinavian schists etc.					

TABLE 1 — Chart to illustrate the division of the geological time scale about 1840, with modern equivalents. Some characteristic formations mentioned in the text are shown in the left-hand column. The major divisions recognized about 1790 are given in the second column; but it should be noted (a) that much more detailed divisions were being applied at this date to particular regions, although correlation between them was uncertain, and (b) that the categories "Transition" and "Primary" have no exact equivalents in later schemes, because they included slightly or highly metamorphosed rocks of many ages (though predominantly of the ages shown). From Martin J.S. Rudwick, *The Meaning of Fossils* (Chicago, IL: University of Chicago Press, 1985), p. 213.

geological evidence for the Flood was, in Buckland's view, only in the upper formations and surface features of the continents; the secondary formations of sedimentary rocks were antediluvian by untold thousands of years or longer. To harmonize his theory with Genesis he considered the possibility of the day-age theory but favored the gap theory. Like Cuvier, he held to the theory of multiple supernatural catastrophes and creations and the recency of the appearance of man and the Flood.

As a result of further field research, especially in Kirkdale Cave in Yorkshire, he published in 1823 his widely read *Reliquiae Diluvianae*, providing a further defense of the Flood. However, the uniformitarian criticisms of John Fleming and Charles Lyell eventually led Buckland to abandon this interpretation of the geological evidence. He publicized this change of mind in his famous two-volume *Bridgewater Treatise* on geology in 1836, where in only two brief comments he described the Flood as tranquil and geologically insignificant.[38] Buckland showed in personal correspondence in the 1820s that, for him, geological evidence had a superior quality and reliability over textual evidence (e.g., the Bible) in reconstructing the earth's history.[39] In his view, this was because written records were susceptible to deception or error, whereas the rocks were truthful and cannot be altered by man.

Adam Sedgwick (1785–1873) was Buckland's counterpart at Cambridge, receiving the chair of geology in 1818. Through the influence of these two and others (e.g., George Greenough, William Conybeare, Roderick Murchison, and Henry De la Beche), old-earth catastrophist (or diluvial) geology was widely accepted in the 1820s by most geologists and academic theologians.

For several reasons most geologists at this time believed the earth was much older than 6,000 years and the Noachian flood was not the cause of the secondary and tertiary formations.[40] First, it was believed that the *primitive* rocks were covered by an average of at least two miles of secondary and tertiary strata, in which was seen evidence of slow gradual deposition during successive periods of calm and catastrophe. Second, some strata were clearly formed from the violent destruction of older strata. Third, different strata contained different fossils; it was especially noted that strata with apparently terrestrial and fresh-water shells alternate with those containing marine shells and that strata nearest the surface contained land animals mixed with marine creatures. Fourth, generally speaking, it appeared that the lower the strata were, the greater was the difference between fossil and living species, which to old-earth geologists implied many extinctions as a result of a series of revolutions over a long time. Fifth, the evidence that faults and dislocations occurred after the deposition and induration of many strata implied a lapse of time between the formation of the various strata. Finally, there was the fact that man was apparently only found fossilized in the most recent strata. From this evidence, the earth was believed to be tens of thousands, if not millions, of years old and the relatively recent Noachian flood was considered to be the cause only of the rounded valleys and hills carved into consolidated strata and of the loose gravels and boulders scattered worldwide over the surface of those strata.[41]

A massive blow to catastrophism came during the years 1830 to 1833, when Charles Lyell (1797–1875), a lawyer by training as well as a former student of Buckland, published his masterful three-volume work, *Principles of Geology*. Reviving the ideas of Hutton and stimulated by the writings of John Fleming, the Scottish minister and zoologist, and George Scrope, a member of Parliament and volcano expert, Lyell's *Principles* set forth how he thought geology should be done. His theory was a radical uniformitarianism in which he insisted that only present-day processes

38 William Buckland, *Bridgewater Treatise* (1836), I: p. 16, 94–95. The full title of this two-volume work was *On the Power, Wisdom and Goodness of God as Manifested in the Creation: Geology and Mineralogy Considered with Reference to Natural Theology*, but as one of the eight *Bridgewater Treatises*, it is often referred to with the latter title.

39 Nicolaas A. Rupke, *The Great Chain of History* (Oxford: Clarendon Press; New York: Oxford University Press, 1983), p. 60–61.

40 See William Buckland, *Vindiciae Geologicae* (1820), p. 23 and 29–30; George Cuvier, *Theory of the Earth* (1813), p. 12–18; and John Phillips, *Illustrations of the Geology of Yorkshire* (1829–36), I: p. 13–18.

41 See Buckland, *Vindiciae Geologicae*, p. 37–38.

at present-day rates of intensity and magnitude should be used to interpret the rock record of past geological activity. The uniformity of rates was an addition to Hutton's theory and was the essential, distinctive feature of Lyell's view.

Although the catastrophist theory had greatly reduced the geological significance of the Noachian deluge and expanded earth history well beyond the traditional biblical view, Lyell's work was the *"coup de grace"* for belief in the Flood,[42] in that it explained the whole rock record by slow gradual processes (which included very localized catastrophes like volcanos and earthquakes at their present frequency of occurrence around the world), thereby reducing the Flood to a geological non-event. His theory also expanded the time of earth history even more than Cuvier or Buckland had done. Lyell saw himself as "the spiritual saviour of geology, freeing the science from the old dispensation of Moses."[43]

Catastrophism did not die out immediately, although by the late 1830s few old-earth catastrophists in the United Kingdom, America, or Europe believed in a geologically significant Noachian deluge.

Lyell's uniformitarianism applied not only to geology, but to biology as well. Initially he had held to a sense of direction in the fossil record, but in 1827, after reading Lamarck's work, he had chosen the steady-state theory that species had appeared and disappeared in a piecemeal fashion (though he did not explain how). Lamarck's notion that man was simply a glorified orangutan was an affront to human dignity, thought Lyell. He held man alone to be a recent creation and even after finally accepting Darwinism he believed that the human mind could not be the result of natural selection.

From the mid-1820s, geology was rapidly maturing as a science. Smith's stratigraphic methodology (using fossils to correlate the strata) was applied more widely by a growing body of geologists to produce more detailed descriptions and maps of the geological record. There was still debate over the nature and origin of granite and although Cuvier's interpretation of the Paris basin was widely accepted, it also was being challenged. By the early 1830s all the main elements of stratigraphic geology were established, and maps and journal articles became more technical as geology was making the transition from an amateur avocation to a professional vocation. The 1830s and 1840s saw much debate about the classification of the lowest fossiliferous formations (the Cambrian to Devonian) and the glacial theory began emerging to explain what the earlier catastrophists had attributed to the Flood. By the mid-1850s, all the main strata were identified and the nomenclature was standardized. However, none of these developments added any fundamentally new reasons for believing in a very old earth. So whether the scriptural geologists were arguing against the old-earth theory before or after Lyell's *Principles of Geology*, they were dealing with the same basic arguments that had been dominant since around the turn of the century.

So in the early 19th century there were three competing views of earth history which can be graphically represented as shown on the following page.

In response to these different old-earth theories, Christians were confronted with the choice of various ways of harmonizing them with Genesis. Many of these old-earth proponents believed in the inspiration, infallibility, and historical accuracy of Genesis. But they disagreed with the scriptural geologists about the correct interpretation, in some cases even the correct *literal* interpretation, of the Biblical text.

REINTERPRETATIONS OF GENESIS

In a sermon to his church in 1804, the gap theory began to be propounded by the young pastor, Reverend Thomas Chalmers (1780–1847), who soon became one of the leading Scottish evangelicals. His views reached a wider audience when in 1814 he wrote a review of Cuvier's theory.[44] This became the most popular old-earth view among

42 Gillispie, *Genesis and Geology*, p. 145.

43 Roy S. Porter, "Charles Lyell and the Principles of the History of Geology," *British Journal for the History of Science*, vol. IX, part 2, no. 32 (1976), p. 91.

44 William Hanna, *Memoirs of the Life and Writings of Thomas Chalmers* (1849–52), p. I:80-81; Thomas Chalmers, "Remarks on Curvier's Theory of the Earth," *The Christian Instructor* (1814), reprinted in *The Works of Thomas Chalmers* (1836–42), XII: p. 347–372.

Early 19th Century Theories of Earth History

The Uniformitarian View (e.g., Hutton, Lyell, Fleming)

[B?]——————————————————[P]——————————————[E?]

(B to P: "untold ages")

The geological phenomena provide no trace of a beginning [B?] or an end [E?] to the world. Although Fleming certainly believed in both a supernatural beginning and supernatural ending, Lyell's private writings indicate that he probably did not believe in either. During the untold millions of years since the initial creation and leading up to the present [P], the processes of nature such as volcanoes, earthquakes, local floods, wind erosion, rain erosion, deposition in river deltas, coastal sea erosion, etc., have always operated uniformly with the present degree or range of intensity, rate, and geographical extent of effect. Therefore, large-scale geological change is slow, steady, and gradual. The Noachian deluge was seen as geologically insignificant, whether it was local or global.

The Catastrophist View (e.g., Cuvier, Buckland, Sedgwick)

[SB]——[C/C]——[C/C]——[C/C]——[C/C]——[F]——————————[P]——[C/C?]——[SE]

(SB to P: "untold ages")

The universe had a definite supernatural beginning [SB] untold millions of years ago. Initially, God created matter in some primitive form which over the ages organized itself according to the in-built laws of nature. However, from time to time [C/C] a *natural* regional or global catastrophe (or revolution) has destroyed most or all of life and created huge geological effects, after which God *supernaturally* intervened to create some new forms of life. During these revolutions, some of the processes of nature operated with vastly greater energy, duration, and geographical extent than at present [P], thereby rapidly producing major geological and geographical changes on the earth. Prior to about 1835, most catastrophists believed the Noachian flood [F] was the last such revolution. Though catastrophists did not, to my knowledge, discuss the future, presumably they believed that other natural revolutions followed by divine supernatural creations might occur again before God would supernaturally bring the world to an end.[45]

The Scriptural Geologists' View

[SB]——[F]——————————[P]————[SE]

(SB to P: ca. 6,000 years)

God supernaturally created a mature creation in six days about 4000 B.C. [SB] and then ceased creating.[46] During the next approximately 1,600 years before the Noachian flood [F], the laws of nature operated basically as now, though with some different parameters (or initial conditions), which produced some effects different from the present [P], such as a generally global tropical climate, greater plant and animal growth, etc. The unique, year-long, global Noachian flood [F] was initiated and attended by some supernatural acts of God. In other words, along with the extraordinary effects of this divine interruption of the normal course of nature (e.g., simultaneous global rains and volcanic/earthquake activity), the processes of nature produced the same, though greatly magnified, natural effects of modern localized and brief floods, volcanoes, earthquakes, etc., to produce much of the sedimentary rock record and a greatly changed earth surface. As in the beginning, the world will have (at some unknown time in the future) a *supernatural* ending [SE], when the present laws of nature will be suspended or altered by God as He makes new heavens and a new earth.

Thomas Chalmers (1780–1847)

widely accepted by Christians until Hugh Miller (1802–56), the prominent Scottish geologist and evangelical friend of Chalmers, abandoned the gap theory in favor of the day-age theory, shortly before his death by suicide.[50]

Also in the 1820s, the evangelical Scottish Presbyterian and zoologist, Reverend John Fleming, began arguing for a tranquil Noachian deluge, and in the late 1830s the evangelical Congregationalist theologian, John Pye Smith (1774–1851), advocated a local creation and a local Flood, both of which occurred in Mesopotamia.[51]

Hugh Miller (1802–1856)

Christians for about the next half century. From 1816 onward, Bishop John Bird Sumner, who later became the archbishop of Canterbury, also favored the gap theory.[47] The high church Old Testament professor at Oxford, E.B. Pusey, likewise endorsed this interpretation of Genesis 1 in the 1830s.[48]

The respected Anglican clergyman, George Stanley Faber (1773–1854), began advocating the day-age theory in his *Treatise on the Genius and Object of the Patriarchal, the Levitical, and the Christian Dispensations* (1823).[49] This figurative interpretation of the days of Genesis 1 was not

---

45 The nature of God's activity (providential or miraculous) in these revolutions and creations was problematic and not clearly explained, though the general concensus seems to have been that the revolutions were part of the course of nature (under divine providence, expressed through the laws of nature), whereas the creations of new forms of life were completely supernatural. Presumably, most catastrophists believed that the Noachian flood was supernaturally induced, but, if so, this is generally unclear from their statements. See, for example, Adam Sedgwick, "Annual General Meeting of the Geological Society, Presidential Address," *Philosophical Magazine*, n.s. vol. VII, no. 40 (1830), p. 308; William Smith, *Deductions from Established Facts in Geology*; Buckland, *Vindiciae Geologicae*, p. 5, 18–19, 30, and *Bridgewater Treatise* (1836), I: p. 18–19, 295; Gideon Mantel, *Fossils of the South Downs: Geology of Sussex* (1822), p. 304–305; William Whewell, *The Philosophy of the Inductive Sciences* (1840), II: p. 134.

46 A couple of scriptural geologists believed that maybe God supernaturally created some plants and animals immediately after the Flood receded.

47 John Bird Sumner, *Treatise on the Records of Creation* (1816), II: p. 356.

48 See Pusey's footnotes to William Buckland, *Geological and Mineralogical Considerations with Reference to Natural Theology* (1836), I: p. 22–25.

49 See Volume 1, Chapter 3; also Faber's articles in the *Christian Observer*, Vol. XXIII (1823), p. 420–425, 480–487, 551–556, 693–697.

50 Hugh Miller, *The Two Records: Mosaic and the Geological* (1854) and *Testimony of the Rocks* (1856), p. 107–174.

51 John Fleming, "The Geological Deluge as Interpreted by Baron Cuvier and Buckland Inconsistent with Moses and Nature," *Edinburgh Philosophical Journal*, vol. XIV (1826), p. 205–239; John Pye Smith, *Mosaic Account of Creation and the Deluge Illustrated by Science* (1837) and *Relation Between the Holy Scriptures and Some Parts of Geological Science* (1839).

Another approach was taken by the Anglican clergyman and Oxford geometry professor Baden Powell and other liberal Christians. In company with many contemporary continental biblical scholars, they treated Genesis as a myth which conveyed theological and moral truths and which one should not attempt to harmonize with geology at all.[52]

Nevertheless, many evangelicals and high churchmen still clung to the literal view of Genesis (i.e., a recent creation and global geologically significant Noachian flood) into the early 1840s.

Besides these great changes of thought transpiring in theology and science, there were other upheavals in the 19th century which contributed to a major world view change in society.

THE EARLY 19TH CENTURY SOCIAL AND RELIGIOUS MILIEU

A Time of Revolution

Two revolutions had a significant effect on life in Britain and the wider Western world in the 18th and early 19th centuries: the socially disruptive Industrial Revolution and the physically violent French Revolution.

The Industrial Revolution (roughly 1760–1840) was a time of great transformation from a society based on agriculture and craft industries to one based on industrial factory structure and urban living. The population had begun to grow rapidly as a result of increasing life expectancy due to improvements in diet, medical care, sanitation, and housing. Transportation and communication were greatly improved during the period through the building of canals, better roads, bigger ports, and more railway lines. And, of course, it was a time of exciting invention. The Industrial Revolution expanded the middle class and raised the standard of living for most people.[53] But more importantly the technological and economic advances elevated science to become the queen of knowledge (over theology and philosophy) and scientists became the new priesthood of society.

The French Revolution of 1789–99 was a violent revolt of the peasants, working class, and middle class against the oppressive rule of the king. Though democracy was not achieved, the Revolution spread democratic ideas of liberty and equality all over Europe, which tended to restrict the power of monarchs. While for some it symbolized the destruction of despotism in the church and state, most Britons saw French atheism as the root cause of much-feared political anarchy and public immorality and so wanted England to remain a Christian nation.[54]

The Make-up of the British Church

The established Church of England was also beginning to undergo important changes in the first half of the 19th century. It was roughly divided into three sections: the high (or orthodox), the low (or evangelical), and the broad (or liberal) churchmen, though of course there were people whose beliefs bridged the boundaries of these categories. The 18th century evangelical revival was still having a significant effect and evangelicals, motivated by biblical convictions and led by the Clapham Sect, were largely responsible for many of the social and political reforms as they fought to end slavery; improve the working conditions of children; supported Catholic political

---

52 In the 1820s, Powell expressed his belief that the historical narrative of Genesis (at least the Noachian flood) had some connection with the findings of geology, but he abandoned this view in the 1830s. See Corsi, *Science and Religion*, p. 60 and 138.

53 T.S. Ashton, *The Industrial Revolution 1760–1830* (London; New York: Oxford University Press, 1970); Robin M. Reeve, *The Industrial Revolution 1750–1850* (London: London University Press, 1971).

54 Isser Woloch, "French Revolution," *The World Book Encyclopedia* (1987), VII:450–52; Vernon J. Puryear, "Napoleon I," *The World Book Encyclopedia* (1987), XIV:12–17; J.H. Plumb, *England in the Eighteenth Century* (Harmondsworth, Penguin Books, 1987), p. 155–162.

On the widespread fear of French atheism and its effects, see Owen Chadwick, *The Victorian Church* (1971), p. I:1–2; anonymous review of "The History of Europe During the French Revolution" by Archibald Allison, *Blackwood's Edinburgh Monthly Magazine*, vol. XXXIII (1833), p. 889–890; anonymous, "The Life of a Democrat; A Sketch of Horne Tooke. Part II," *Blackwood's Edinburgh Monthly Magazine*, vol. XXXIV (1833), p. 220–221; Ernest M. Howse, *Saints in Politics: The "Clapham Sect" and the Growth of Freedom* (London: Allen & Unwin, 1976), p. 101 and 127; Paul J. Weindling, "Geological Controversy and Its Historiography: The Prehistory of the Geological Society of London," in *Images of the Earth*, p. 256.

emancipation; started mission and Bible societies; founded schools, libraries, and savings banks; built churches; and improved prison conditions.[55] Up until the mid-1830s at least, the real spiritual force in the church came from the evangelicals and to a lesser extent the high churchmen (strong traditionists in the Anglican Church).[56] Although high churchmen were often critical of "enthusiastic" Methodists and other non-conformists (that is, non-Anglicans), as well as evangelical Anglicans, they all shared much in common in terms of their views of Scripture, the gospel, and the spiritual needs of the church and nation. Two of the most able theologians among the high churchmen were Bishop Samuel Horsley (1733–1806) and Bishop William Van Mildert (1765–1836). Though effective evangelical clergy were spread all over the country, two high concentrations of leaders were found in Cambridge, where Charles Simeon was most well-known, and in London at the Clapham Anglican Church, where the anti-slavery member of Parliament William Wilberforce and several other prominent men had their base.[57]

The Cambridge Network

The broad church or liberal views were also represented and propagated at Cambridge, through (but not exclusively through) what has been called the "Cambridge network." This was a close-knit group of scientists, historians, university dons and other scholars, and church leaders, which originated in the early 1810s and had the greatest influence in university reform and in the development of science, particularly in the British Association for the Advancement of Science, the Astronomical Society, the Geological Society and the science department of the Royal Society.[58] Not all the people in this network of relationships were theological liberals, but many were, and even the orthodox associated with it may have been influenced to some extent by liberal ideas.[59]

Key men in this network included John Herschel, Charles Babbage, and George Peacock, all undergraduates at Cambridge in the years 1811–13. Herschel soon became one of the world's greatest astronomers; Babbage excelled in mathematics; and Peacock re-founded the Cambridge Observatory, tutored at Trinity College for a time, and eventually became dean of Ely Cathedral. These men were joined in 1818–19 by William Whewell (who became master of Trinity College in 1841 and the leading historian and philosopher of science in the early 19th century), George Airy (who was later appointed Astronomer Royal), Adam Sedgwick (who in 1818 became Woodwardian professor of geology at Cambridge),[60] William Hopkins (prominent physics professor), E.D. Clark (a leading mineralogist), and John Henslow (an important botanist and co-founder with Sedgwick of the Cambridge Philosophical Society).

Added to these scientists were several other men in the network who drank deeply from the wells of German philosophy, biblical criticism, and historiography, and passed on their knowledge to others. Julius Hare and Connop Thirlwall were both students at Cambridge in 1812–14 and even then knew more of German scholarship

55 Ernest M. Howse, *Saints in Politics: The "Clapham Sect" and the Growth of Freedom.*
56 Chadwick says this dominant religious influence extended to the middle of the Victorian period. See Owen Chadwick, *The Victorian Church*, p. I:5.
57 John H. Overton, *The English Church in the Nineteenth Century: 1800–33* (1894).
58 Walter F. Cannon, "Scientists and Broad Churchmen: An Early Victorian Intellectual Network," *Journal of British Studies*, vol. IV, no. 1 (1964), p. 65–88; Walter F. Cannon, "The Role of the Cambridge Movement in Early Nineteenth Century Science," *Proceedings of the Tenth International Congress on the History of Science* (1964), p. 317–320; Jack Morrell and Arnold Thackray, editors, *Gentlemen of Science: Early Years of the BAAS* (Oxford: Clarendon Press; New York: Oxford University Press, 1981), p. 17–35.
59 Some evidence of this influence will be presented in the final section of the book.
60 Paul Marston, in his "Science and Meta-Science in the Work of Adam Sedgwick" (The Open University, Ph.D. thesis, 1984), has shown that Sedgwick held many views in common with evangelicals. Nevertheless, it seems undeniable that Sedgwick also was significantly influenced by the Cambridge Network and shared many of their ideas. As noted in the article on Cole (www.answersingenesis.org/home/area/magazines/tj/docs/tjv13nl_cole.asp), the evangelical *Christian Observer,* which favored acceptance of the idea of an old earth, shared some of Cole's concerns about Sedgwick's views as expressed in his *Discourse on the University*. Other insights into Sedgwick's views will be gained from the later discussion on Ure and the analysis of the nature of geology as a historical science at the conclusion of this book.

than their professors. Both tutored for a while at Trinity College. Later, Hare was an ineffective rural rector but was a successful mentor for his nephew, Arthur Stanley, who later became a liberal canon of Canterbury. Thirlwall became a leading liberal and influential bishop of St. Davids. Together, Hare and Thirlwall published in 1827 their translation of B.G. Niebuhr's *History of Rome* (1811–12), which sold more copies than the German original. This, along with Henry Milman's *History of the Jews* (1829), effectively disseminated the ideas of German skeptical scholarship in the United Kingdom.[61] A small discussion group within the network in the 1820s was the "Cambridge apostles." It was led by F.D. Maurice and absorbed and imparted Niebuhr's "anti-mythical methods to the Bible and to Christian tradition generally."[62] Probably more than any other group, the Cambridge network contributed to the 19th century theological revolution in Britian, which saw the traditional orthodox view of Scripture held by evangelicals and high churchmen dwindle into relative insignificance.

The Oxford Movement

A quite different and opposing movement was centered at Oxford University. In the late 1820s and early 1830s dissenting Protestants (i.e., non-Anglicans) were pushing hard for the disestablishment of the Church of England and several acts of Parliament brought changes improving the position of Protestant dissenters and Roman Catholics. A few leading Oxford professors connected with Oriel College, such as John Keble, Henry Newman, Edward Pusey, and Hurrell Froude, saw this governmental infringement as a threat to the apostolic authority of the Anglican Church and to the stability of the nation. So in 1833 they began to express their opposition publicly in the form of sermons and *Tracts for the Times*, from which they gained the label "Tractarians." They spoke out against critical rationalism, skepticism, spiritual lethargy, liberalism, and immorality. They elevated the authority of church tradition over the Scriptures, revived 17th century sacramental attitudes toward nature and the world, and paid careful attention to church furnishings and worship services. Ironically, in spite of the anti-popery of many of these tracts, many in the Oxford movement eventually left the Anglican Church in the mid-1840s and joined the Roman Catholic Church. Those who stayed, such as Pusey, developed the Anglo Catholic party.[63]

Though evangelical Anglicans shared the Tractarians' concern for the continued establishment of the Church of England, they rejected three of their most important beliefs: the supreme authority of tradition (instead of Scripture) for the Church, their Catholic view of justification, and their Catholic views of ministry and the sacraments.[64]

The *Bridgewater Treatises*

Another strand of the theological tapestry of those days was the emphasis on natural theology. With the Baconian notion of the "two books" (Scripture and creation) firmly in mind, natural theology began to develop in Britain in the late 17th century. Throughout the next century, science was seen by leading Christian scientists, philosophers, and theologians as a means of demonstrating the existence and providence of God, and so serving as a support for Christian faith. By the time of William Paley's celebrated *Natural Theology* in 1802, scientific knowledge of creation was being used in a design argument that not only "proved" the existence of God and His providence in creation, but also demonstrated the attributes of God.[65] One of the last expressions

---

61 Nigel M. de S. Cameron, *Biblical Higher Criticism and the Defense of Infallibilism in Nineteenth Century Britain* (Lewiston, NY: E. Mellen Press, 1984), p. 37–38.

62 Walter F. Cannon, "Scientists and Broad Churchmen: An Early Victorian Intellectual Network," *Journal of British Studies*, vol. IV, no. 1 (1964), p. 78.

63 Owen Chadwick, *The Victorian Church*, I: p. 60–75, 167–231; Michael Hennell, "The Oxford Movement," in *Eerdmans' Handbook to the History of Christianity* (Grand Rapids, MI: Eerdmans, 1977), edited by Tim Dowley, p. 524–526; D.A. Rausch, "Oxford Movement," in *Evangelical Dictionary of Theology* (Grand Rapids, MI: Baker Book House, 1984), edited by Walter A. Elwell, p. 811–812.

64 Peter Toon, *Evangelical Theology 1833–1856: A Response to Tractarianism* (Atlanta, GA: John Knox Press, 1979). From Toon's and my own research it appears that no scriptural geologists were significantly involved in writing against tractarianism.

65 John H. Brooke, "Natural Theology in Britain from Boyle to Paley," in *New Interactions Between Theology and Natural Science* (1974), edited by John H. Brooke et al., p. 5–54; John H. Brooke, *Science and Religion*, p. 192–225.

of this kind of writing was the collection of eight *Bridgewater Treatises*, first published in the years 1833 to 1836.[66] Seven prominent scientists and one prominent theologian were commissioned (and paid £1000 each[67]) through the will of the recently deceased Earl of Bridgewater to present from various fields of science the abundant evidence in creation of God's power, wisdom, and goodness.[68] The treatises were full of scientific information which illustrated Paley's thesis, but they did not defend the legitimacy of the inference from design in nature to a designer God. Though they referred to Scripture occasionally, they generally did not comment on the relation between science and the Bible.[69] One of the biggest criticisms of the treatises was their overly optimistic handling of the difficult problem of pain, disease, disaster, and death seen in creation. Generally, they either ignored the problem or dealt with it superficially, attributing the evil in a mysterious way to divine beneficence.[70] For this study, the most important treatise was William Buckland's on geology, for it attracted much criticism from the scriptural geologists.

The BAAS and Other Scientific Organizations

As indicated earlier, great technological advancements and more comfortable living, for the middle and upper classes especially, were elevating the importance and influence of science and scientists in society. The British Association for the Advancement of Science (BAAS) also greatly contributed to this. Founded in 1831 in York, it was modeled after the German association, Deutsche Naturforscher Versammlung. The BAAS sought to stimulate friendships among scientists, increase public knowledge and government support of science, coordinate scientific research (especially by what it hoped would be a growing number of amateur scientists), and facilitate intercourse with foreign scientists. As a means of achieving these aims, it held its annual meeting in a different provincial city each year, opened its meetings to the public, and opened membership with lower dues than those of any other philosophical society. Its constitution embraced two Baconian principles for interpreting nature: 1) to focus on intermediate, rather than final, causes, and 2) to avoid dogmatic systems of philosophy by concentrating on the objective gathering of facts. In light of this, the BAAS insisted on broad religious tolerance in order to transcend doctrinal differences and avoid religious controversy. In the early years it faced strong opposition. Charles Dickens, the *Times* newspaper in London, and others criticized it for the pomp, extravagance, and self-laudation of its annual meetings. More significantly, Tractarians accused it of religious pluralism and deistic science, which they believed was contributing to the de-Christianizing of the universities.[71] One scriptural geologist, Reverend William Cockburn, was critical of the BAAS on similar grounds.[72]

---

66 John M. Robson, "The Fiat and Finger of God: The Bridgewater Treatises," in *Victorian Faith in Crisis* (Stanford, CA: Stanford University Press, 1990), edited by Richard J. Helmstadter and Bernard Lightman, p. 71–125; W.H. Brock, "The Selection of the Bridgewater Treatises," *Notes and Records of the Royal Society of London*, Vol. XXI, No. 2 (1966), p. 162–179; D.W. Gundry, "The Bridgewater Treatises and their Authors," *History*, n.s. Vol. XXXI (1946), p. 140–152.

67 According to Martin J.S. Rudwick, *The Great Devonian Controversy* (Chicago, IL: University of Chicago Press, 1985), p. 461, these amounts were "positively princely," being roughly equivalent in modern terms to £40,000 (or $60,000).

68 The scientists were John Kidd, William Whewell, Charles Bell, Peter Roget, William Buckland, William Kirby, and William Prout. The theologian was Thomas Chalmers. Buckland, Whewell, and Kirby were also Anglican clergymen.

69 Among these eight writers, only William Kirby, a distinguished entomologist and a scriptural geologist, attempted to address this issue. See his *On the History, Habits and Instincts of Animals* (1835), I: p. xvii-lvi.

70 Kirby and Chalmers were more thorough than others on this issue. Kirby was quite explicit in attributing the evil in creation (including pestiferous insects) to the curse at the fall of man. See Kirby, ibid., I: p. 9–17, 42–43, 324–331. Chalmers linked all human suffering to man's moral perversity, but did not comment on the fall of man or on death and suffering in the animal world. See Thomas Chalmers, *The Adaptation of External Nature to the Moral and Intellectual Constitution of Man* (1833), II: p. 97-125.

71 A.D. Orange, "The Idols of the Theatre: The British Association and Its Early Critics," *Annals of Science*, vol. XXXII (1975), p. 277–294; O.J.R. Howarth, *The British Association for the Advancement of Science: A Retrospect 1831–1931* (1931); Jack Morrell and Arnold Thackray, editors, *Gentlemen of Science: Early Years of the BAAS*; Colin Russell, *Science and Social Change 1700–1900* (New York: St. Martin's Press, 1983), p. 186–192.

72 William Cockburn, *A Remonstrance, Address to His Grace the Duke of Northumberland, upon the Dangers of Peripatetic Philosophy* (1838).

The BAAS annual meetings were not the only means of increasing the understanding and influence of scientific knowledge in society. In the 1820s, mechanics institutes began to form in a number of provincial cities. These were intended to teach artisans and mechanics the scientific information that would be practically useful in their trades. For a number of reasons they failed in this objective, though they did help to encourage young people to pursue scientific studies, and some of the institutes went on to become polytechnics or universities. From an examination of the contents of many of their libraries, it would appear that in the early to mid 1800s little attention was paid to geology and it is unlikely that the writings of scriptural geologists were found in those libraries.[73] The Society for the Diffusion of Useful Knowledge began about the same time and sought to produce and distribute cheap and useful books, many of which dealt with science. The middle class also had access to scientific knowledge (along with other subjects) through lectures, libraries, and museums of the many Literary and Philosophical Societies that sprang up in major cities in the 1810s to 1830s. Many of these contributed significantly to the study of local geology and collection of fossils. In the following decades, natural history societies and field clubs also provided amateur science students the opportunity to contribute to the growth of knowledge in botany, zoology, and geology.[74]

BIBLICAL INTERPRETATION

To assess properly the debate that the scriptural geologists were involved in, one needs also to understand the views of Scripture generally and Genesis 1–11 in particular held by evangelicals and high churchmen, especially as revealed in the Bible commentaries. The following summarizes first the views of four of the most influential older commentators (Augustine, Luther, Calvin, and Wesley) and then the commentaries in use in the early 19th century.

Augustine, Luther, Calvin, and Wesley

Augustine of Hippo (354–430) was perhaps the greatest theologian of the early Christian church and through his voluminous writings he had a tremendous influence on the thinking of Christians for nearly 13 centuries.[75] After two previous attempts at commenting on Genesis, both of which took a decidedly allegorical approach, Augustine published in 415 his last commentary on the first three chapters of Genesis, *The Literal Meaning of Genesis*, which was "the most significant attempt made during the patristic period" to clarify the meaning of these chapters.[76] Based on the Latin translation of Genesis,[77] he endeavored to do what his title indicated — give a literal historical interpretation to Genesis rather than looking for allegorical meanings, into which, however, he often slipped. Concerning the meaning of the six days of creation, he openly struggled in uncertainty and leaned toward an allegorical interpretation. This uncertainty of interpretation in Genesis continued apparently throughout his life. Two years after completing his commentary on Genesis he wrote "As for these 'days,' it is difficult, perhaps impossible to think — let alone to explain in words — what they mean."[78] Later, near the end of his life, he remarked about his Genesis commentary: "In this work, many questions have been asked rather than solved, and of those which have been solved,

73 D.A. Hinton, "Popular Science in England, 1830–1870," (University of Bath, Ph.D. thesis, 1979), p. 223, 254–256. Hinton said that even Lyell's *Principles of Geology* was not commonly stocked and suggested that the avoidance of geological works was probably due to the controversial nature of geology.

74 For a more detailed discussion of these different organizations, see Russell, *Science and Social Change 1700–1900*, p. 151–186.

75 N.L. Geisler, "Augustine of Hippo," in Elwell, *Evangelical Dictionary of Theology*, p. 105–107; A.D. White, *History of the Warfare of Science with Theology in Christendom* (1896), I: p. 211.

76 Augustine, *The Retractions* (1968), translated by Mary Inez Bogan, p. 78 (footnote by Bogan), 170–171 (footnote by Bogan).

77 Augustine knew no Hebrew and not until he was an old man did he develop a modest ability in Greek. See J.H. Taylor's "Introduction" to his translation of Augustine's *The Literal Meaning of Genesis* (New York, NY: Newman Press, 1982), p. 5.

78 Augustine, *City of God: Books VIII–XVI* (1952), translated by G.G. Walsh and G. Monahan, p. 196 [Book 11, chapter 6].

few have been answered conclusively. Moreover, others have been proposed in such a way as to require further investigations."[79]

Though insisting that he was interpreting "day" literally, he tended to regard at least the first three days before the creation of the heavenly bodies to be non-literal, unlike modern days, which are measured by the sun, moon, and stars. He never ventured to say how long these non-literal days lasted. He possibly believed that the last three days of creation were literal 24-hour days.[80] If anything, he leaned toward creation being in an instant, rather than over long ages. In any case, he considered that the plants and animals were created miraculously and fully formed in an instant on the various days (rather than gradually by present-day processes of nature) and that creation was complete on the seventh day.[81] In rejecting the uniformitarian and catastrophist views of his day,[82] he argued that 6,000 years had not yet passed since the creation of Adam, the first man, and that the antediluvian patriarchs had literally lived some 900 years.[83] He argued at some length that the Noachian flood was a historical global catastrophe and that all men were descended from Noah, having been dispersed throughout the earth after the confusion of languages at the Tower of Babel.[84]

Martin Luther (1483–1546) started his verse-by-verse commentary on the Book of Genesis in 1535 and completed it ten years later.[85] Criticizing Augustine at several points for his lapse into allegorical interpretations, Luther frequently insisted that the first 11 chapters were literal history.[86] He took the days of creation as literal 24-hour days, with the sun and other heavenly bodies created on day 4 and that he believed all this took place less than 6,000 years before. Referring to Exodus 20:11, he argued that Genesis 1:1 was the beginning of the first day and was not describing a creation before the first day.[87] He stressed that at the end of the week of creation, everything was perfect and God ceased (and never resumed) His creative work; procreation of life continues under His providence.[88] The animals initially were vegetarian and some only became carnivorous as a result of God's curse at the Fall, which Luther believed affected the whole earth, not just man.[89] This curse was made more severe at the Flood, which destroyed the whole surface of the earth, obliterating among other things the Garden of Eden, which, according to Luther, is the reason we cannot find it today. He said the pre-Flood world was like a paradise compared to the earth afterward.[90]

79 Augustine, *The Retractions*, translated by Bogan, p. 169.

80 Augustine, *The Literal Meaning of Genesis*, translated by Taylor, I: p. 103–107, 124–125, 134–136, 141, 149.

81 Ibid., I: p. 125, 141–142.

82 He did not name specific people and theories but only spoke generally of those who believed that earth history was an eternal cycle of destruction and renewal, either in piecemeal fashion or on a global scale from time to time. See Augustine, *City of God: Books VIII–XVI*, translated by Walsh and Monahan, p. 263–267 [Book XII, ch. 10–13].

83 Ibid., p. 436–440 [Book XV, ch. 11–12]; *City of God: Books XVII–XXII* (1954), translated by Walsh and Honan, p. 148–149 [Book XVIII, ch. 40].

84 Augustine, *City of God: Books VIII–XVI*, translated by Walsh and Monahan, p. 480–484 [Book XV, ch. 27], p. 504–507 [Book XVI, ch. 9–10]. He did not believe in a flat earth, as some have suggested, but rather that no men were living on the other side of the world because, it was thought, no one could cross the ocean to the other side. See ibid., 504–505 [Book XVI, ch. 9] and Jeffrey Burton Russell, *Inventing the Flat Earth* (New York: Praeger, 1991), p. 20–23 and 40–45.

85 I referred to the English translation of *Luther's Works*, edited by Jaroslav Pelikan, Vol. I: Genesis 1–5 (1958) and Vol. II: Genesis 6–14 (1960).

86 Ibid., I: p. 5, 19, 89, 122–23; II: p. 150–153.

87 In his lengthy footnote in Buckland's *Bridgewater Treatise*, I: p. 25, Edward Pusey, regius professor of Hebrew at Oxford, said that Luther allowed for the possibility of the gap theory in that the 1557 edition of Luther's German translation of the Bible placed a "1" in the margin at Genesis 1:3. Pusey's interpretation of this marginal notation was in error, however. Luther's commentary makes this clear. But also, Luther's 1523 translation of Genesis has nothing in the margins and the 1545 version has the numbers of the days in the margin at the end of each day's description (so "1" is at verse 5). See *D. Martin Luthers Werke: Die Deutsche Bibel* (Weimar, 1954), p. 8. Band, where the two versions face each other on opposite pages. Also, the 1558 and 1576 versions of *Biblia* (Wittemburg) follow the 1545 edition in this matter.

88 Martin Luther, *Luther's Works*, edited by Jaroslav Pelikan, I: p. 75–76.

89 Ibid., I: p. 36, 77–78, 204.

90 Ibid., I: p. 87–90, 204–208; II: p. 3, 65–66, 74–75, 93–95.

The other great reformer, John Calvin (1509–65), also took the early chapters of Genesis as reliable history handed down faithfully and without corruption from Adam to Moses.[91] Many have remarked on Calvin's notion of accommodation.[92] He said that Moses sometimes "accommodated his discourse to the received custom" of the Jews (as in the reckoning of the days from evening to evening rather than morning to morning)[93] and "does not speak with philosophical acuteness" but "addresses himself to our senses" using a "homely style" (as in the case of the "two great lights," the sun and moon, described in Genesis 1:14–15, in comparison to the more exact way that astronomers speak).[94] However, it has often not been noted that Calvin nevertheless contended for a creation of the world in six literal days less than 6,000 years ago.[95] He emphasized the literal order of the creation events, especially that light was created on day 1 before the sun and other celestial bodies on day 4, and the literal creation of Adam from dust and Eve from the rib of Adam.[96] In his view, the Fall brought a curse on creation, not just on man, and the global Flood, which was "an interruption in the order of nature," destroyed the animals and the surface of the Earth along with man.[97]

John Wesley (1701–91) clearly valued the practical benefits of science and wrote two books to popularize useful knowledge in medicine and electricity. But he was wary of theoretical science because of its potential for leading people toward deism or atheism. In his two-volume *Survey of the Wisdom of God in the Creation* (1763) he relied heavily on the work of others in presenting the traditional arguments from design for God's existence, which were so popular in 18th and early 19th century Britain.[98] He never wrote extensively on creation or the Flood, but in this work he stated his belief that the various rock strata were "doubtless formed by the general Deluge" and that the account of creation, which was about 4,000 years before Christ, was, along with the rest of the Scriptures, "void of any material error."[99] In several published sermons he repeatedly emphasized that the original creation was perfect, without any moral or physical evil (such as earthquakes, volcanoes, weeds, and animal death), which both came into the world after man sinned.[100]

---

91 John Calvin, *Genesis* (1992), translated by John King, p. 58–59; John Calvin, *Institutes of the Christian Religion* (1994), translated by Henry Beveridge, p. 141–142.

92 For example, R. Hooykaas, *Religion and the Rise of Modern Science* (1972), p. 117–124; Russell, Hooykaas, Goodman, *The "Conflict Thesis" and Cosmology*, p. 71–72.

93 See Calvin, *Genesis* (1992), translated by John King, p. 78.

94 Ibid., p. 84–87 and 256–257.

95 On the days of creation he said, "It did not, however, happen from inconsideration or by accident, that the light preceded the sun and the moon. . . . Therefore, the Lord, by the very order of the creation, bears witness that he holds in his hand the light, which he is able to impart to us without the sun and moon. . . . Here the error of those is manifestly refuted, who maintain that the world was made in moment. For it is too violent a cavil to contend that Moses distributes the work which God perfected at once into six days, for the mere purpose of conveying instruction. Let us rather conclude that God himself took the space of six days, for the purpose of accommodating his works to the capacity of men." See Calvin, *Genesis*, p. 76 and 78.

On the age of the earth he wrote that in Genesis, "the period of time is marked so as to enable the faithful to ascend by an unbroken succession of years to the first origin of their race and of all things. This knowledge is of the highest use not only as an antidote to the monstrous fables which anciently prevailed both in Egypt and the other regions of the world, but also as a means of giving a clearer manifestation of the eternity of God as contrasted with the birth of creation, and thereby inspiring us with higher admiration. We must not be moved by the profane jeer, that it is strange how it did not sooner occur to the Deity to create the heavens and the Earth, instead of idly allowing an infinite period to pass away, during which thousands of generations might have existed, while the present world is drawing to a close before it has completed its six thousandth year." John Calvin, *Institutes of the Christian Religion* (1994), translated by Henry Beveridge, p. 141.

96 Calvin, *Institutes of the Christian Religion*, p. 58, 76, 111, 132–133.

97 Ibid., p. 286.

98 John Dillenberger, *Protestant Thought and Natural Science* (Garden City, NY: Doubleday, 1960), p. 156–158.

99 John Wesley, *Survey of the Wisdom of God in the Creation* (1763), II: p. 22, 227. On the Flood see also his sermon on original sin in *The Works of the Rev. John Wesley* (1829–31), IV: p. 54–65.

100 Wesley, *The Works of the Rev. John Wesley*, IV: p. 206–215 ("God's Approbation of His Works"), IV: p. 215–224 ("On the Fall of Man"), VII: p. 386–399 ("The Cause and Cure of Earthquakes"), IX: p. 191–464 ("The Doctrine of Original Sin, According to Scripture, Reason and Experience," especially pages 196–197).

Commentaries in the Early 19th Century

We now turn to the 19th century commentaries. Extremely important in this regard is the work of Thomas Hartwell Horne (1780–1862), who was an Anglican clergyman, although for much of his working life he also served as assistant librarian in the department of printed books at the British Museum. He did not write a commentary on the Bible, but he was one of the great biblical scholars of his time. Among his numerous literary productions, his greatest work was the massive *Introduction to the Critical Study of the Holy Scriptures,*[101] first published in 1818 in three volumes (1,700 pages) after 17 years of research. Not finding an adequate resource for his own study of the Bible, Horne had read, and in many cases bought, the writings of the most eminent biblical critics, both British and foreign.[102] Continually revised and expanded, Horne's work grew to five volumes by the ninth edition in 1846, with two more editions after that in the United Kingdom and also many editions in America during these years. In spite of its size and cost, those editions sold over 15,000 copies in the United Kingdom and many thousands in the United States.[103] From the start, it received high reviews from magazines representing all the denominations (and both high church and evangelical Anglican) and was one of the primary textbooks for the study of the Scriptures in all English-speaking Protestant colleges and universities in the British empire.[104] A one-volume abridged version, designed for the common man, was *A Compendious Introduction to the Study of the Bible,*[105] which was first published in 1827 and eventually reached a tenth edition in 1862.

Given Horne's great influence on the Church, both its clergy and laity, it is noteworthy to know that he thoroughly explained and defended the divine inspiration of Scripture and the Mosaic authorship of the Pentateuch. He maintained that the Bible "is free from error, that is any material error," adding that "this property must be considered as extending to the whole of each" of the books of the Bible and that "it is enough for us to know, that every writer of the Old Testament was inspired, and that the whole of the history it contains, without any exception or reserve, is true."[106] This view of the inerrant inspiration of Scripture was expressed by Horne throughout his life as well as by other biblical scholars at this time.[107]

Referring to the arguments of continental biblical critics such as Astruc, Eichhorn, Rosenmüller, and Bauer (as well as Geddes from Scotland), Horne vigorously contended for the literal historicity of Genesis, especially the first three chapters, stating that Genesis "narrates the true origin and history of all created things, in opposition to the erroneous notions entertained by the heathen nations."[108] Horne also responded to objections against a global Noachian flood, which he believed was confirmed by fossils, the paucity of the human

---

101 Hereafter referred to simply as *Introduction to the Scriptures.*

102 T.H. Horne, *Introduction to the Scriptures* (1818), I: p. 3.

103 S. Austin Allibone, *A Critical Dictionary of English Literature* (1877), p. 890.

104 Ibid., p. 889; *DNB* on Horne. Sample reviews are quoted in the preface to T.H. Horne, *A Compendious Introduction to the Study of the Bible* (1827, second edition) and included *Christian Remembrancer* (high church Anglican), *Evangelical Magazine* (non-conformist), *Congregational Magazine, Home Missionary Magazine, Wesleyan Methodist Magazine* and *Gentlemen's Magazine.*

105 Hereafter referred to as *Compendious Introduction.*

106 Horne, *Introduction to the Scriptures* (1828), I: p. 515–516. The exact same remarks on inspiration appeared in the 1846 edition, I: p. 474–476. For the common man, a similar explanation was given in Horne's *Deism Refuted,* p. 32, and in his *Compendious Introduction to the Study of the Bible* (1827, second edition), p. 29–31, where he responded to (and rejected) the notion that the Bible contains the Word of God but is not in its entirety the Word of God. The tenth edition (p. 33–35) in 1862, the year of his death, said the same.

107 Thomas Scott, *The Holy Bible . . . with Explanatory Notes* (1841), p. 3. Scott wrote this preface in 1812. See also Reverend William Symington's introduction to Scott's work, p. xi–xii; Thomas Stackhouse's *A New History of the Holy Bible* (1737), p. xvii, xxii–xxiv; and Bishop George Gleig's unabridged edition of Stackhouse's work, with his own additional comments (1817), as well as the introductions to the Old Testament and to Genesis (no page numbers given) in George D'Oyly and Richard Mant, *The Holy Bible, with Notes Explanatory and Practical* (1817 and 1823 editions).

108 Horne, *Introduction to the Scriptures* (1818), II: p. 18–38.

population, the late inventions and progress of the arts and science, and the flood traditions of other peoples from around the world.[109] In 1834, he considered Granville Penn's (one of the scriptural geologists) *Comparative Estimate of the Mineral and Mosaical Geologies* to be the best harmonization of geology and Scripture, whereas in 1839 he favored George Fairholme's (another scriptural geologist) *Physical Demonstrations of the Mosaic Deluge*.[110] Not until the 1856 edition of his *Introduction* did he accept the gap theory and local flood theory.[111]

To the proper interpretation of Scripture, Horne devoted about 480 pages. He argued that a word in a given context had only one intended meaning, but that there were two senses: the literal and the spiritual sense. Because of the past abuse of the spiritual sense, he cautioned against too much use of it. Instead he said the "plain, obvious literal meaning" should be sought, and not abandoned for a figurative interpretation unless there is "absolute and evident necessity" in the text or wider Scriptures.[112] Such necessary cases were those in which the literal meaning contradicted doctrinal or moral teachings of other Scriptures or clearer passages on the same subject or in which it resulted in a logical absurdity (though he cautioned against too quickly concluding that there was a real absurdity).[113]

These then were the dominant views of Scripture (and particularly Genesis) at the time of the Genesis-geology debate in the years 1820–45. Table 2, on the pages 46 and 47, shows how many of the commentaries in use in the early 19th century interpreted key verses in Genesis, as well as a few verses elsewhere which refer to the relation of the sun to the earth so as to compare the commentator's view of Copernican astronomy. It should be noted that Alexander Geddes (1737–1802) was a Roman Catholic Bible scholar, whose thoroughly liberal views of the Bible were censored by his bishop. Joseph Priestley (1733–1804) was a unitarian minister (and scientist). The rest were considered to be orthodox Christians. Most of the works were recommended by Horne[114] and all were in use in the early decades of the 19th century, although the most popular were those by the respected scholars Thomas Scott (1747–1821, evangelical Anglican), Matthew Henry (1662–1714, non-conformist), Adam Clarke (1762?–1832, Methodist), George D'Oyly (1778–1846, high church Anglican), Richard Mant (1776–1848, high church Anglican), Andrew Fuller (1754–1815, Baptist), and John Gill (1697–1771, Baptist).

Thomas Scott (1747–1821)

From this analysis it is seen that at the time of the scriptural geologists the dominant view of the

109 Ibid., I: p. 485–490, II: p. 37.

110 Ibid., (1834), I: p. 148–165; T.H. Horne, *Manual of Biblical Bibliography* (1839), p. 283.

111 T.H. Horne, *Introduction to the Scriptures* (1856) I: p. 583–590. He indicated that old-earth proponents William Buckland and John Pye Smith were the two primary influences in his change of thinking.

112 Horne, *Introduction to the Scriptures* (1818), I: p. 207–208.

113 Ibid., I: p. 198–209.

114 Ibid., II: Appendix p. 25–34. Geddes and Priestley were cited for the sake of completeness, but Horne did not approve or recommend them. He also listed the commentary by the German, J.D. Michaelis. All commentaries in the chart are listed in the bibliography.

biblical commentators was that Scripture was infallible and unerring, in matters of history as well as theology and morality. Most of them also believed that Genesis 1–11 was historical narrative describing a creation which was only about 6,000 years old. Though many of them expressed their belief that the earth rotates on its axis and revolves around the sun and that in relation to astronomy the biblical writers used the common language of appearance (which also fit the astronomical understanding at the time they wrote), these commentaries took the account of the long day of Joshua as literal history, just as they did Genesis 1–11.

Although the commentaries in widespread use in the 1820s and 1830s defended the young-earth view, this did not reflect the views of all evangelicals and high churchmen, as noted earlier. In addition to the prominent old-earth proponents previously discussed, the editors of the high church magazines, *British Critic* and *Christian Remembrancer*, and the evangelical magazine, *Christian Observer*, also generally accepted the old-earth view, though they did not firmly commit themselves on how it should be harmonized with Scripture (i.e., day-age or gap theory on Genesis 1, and local or tranquil Noachian flood). All these Christians adopted their old-earth interpretations of Genesis because of the influence of the new geological theories, but they all professed to believe that the Scriptures were divinely inspired, infallible, and historically reliable. So for these evangelical and high church old-earth proponents the issue was not the nature of Scripture, but rather its correct interpretation and the role of science in determining that interpretation.

ASSESSING GEOLOGICAL COMPETENCE

Having considered some of the historical background and social, intellectual, and spiritual context in which the scriptural geologists opposed the old-earth theories, we must look at one more issue to properly understand the debate. Before we can ascertain the level of geological ignorance or acumen of any of the scriptural geologists, we must define, as best we can, what constituted a competent geologist in the early 19th century. How do we distinguish a "real geologist" from a "quasi-geological theologian" at this time? What qualified a person to critically evaluate geological arguments for an old earth? In answering these questions we will see that some of the scriptural geologists were very competent to judge old-earth theories.

In his mapping of the field of geological competence, the respected historian of geology Martin Rudwick broadly defined geological competence as the ability to deliver reliable information or ideas on the subject. But measuring such competence in the 1820s and 1830s was and is difficult, partly because the definition was not static or suprahistorically absolute,[115] but was being progressively refined as geological development approached 1850. Therefore, Rudwick said, "to talk of a geological 'community' at the time of the Devonian controversy [1834–37] is misleading on many counts, not least because it suggests anachronistically a strong-boundaried professional group marked by standardized training and certification, with only the uninitiated lay public outside."[116] He went on to say that therefore "the formal hierarchies of position and influence are by no means coincident" with what he termed "the informal and tacit *gradient of attributed competence*."[117] Rudwick described three zones of this gradient of attributed competence in the mid-1830s (see figure 1 on page 49).

Zone 1 was the small group of "*elite* geologists," who were characterized by a primary commitment to geology (rather than some other science), high activity in the affairs of geological institutions and in practical fieldwork, and significant production in the publication of geological information. Most importantly, they considered themselves, and others considered them, to be the competent arbiters of the most fundamental questions of geological theory and methodology. According to Rudwick, this class included not only the most well-known geologists (Sedgwick, Murchison, De la Beche, Lyell, Greenough, Buckland, Conybeare, Phillips, and

115 Rudwick, *The Great Devonian Controversy*, p. 419.
116 Ibid., p. 418.
117 Ibid., p. 419.

TABLE 2 — COMMENTARY COMPARISONS

Name (year)[b]	Date of creation	Gen. 1:1[c]	"Day"	Gen. 1:14 Sun-Day 4[d]	Flood	Josh. 10:12[e]	Ps. 19:5-6[f]	Ps. 96:10[g]
Ainsworth (1639)	4004 B.C.	Day 1	24 hr	nc	global	nc	nc-a	nc-a
Richardson (1655)	4004 B.C.	Summary	24 hr	nc	global	lm	rh	nc
Stackhouse/Gleig[a] (1817/1737)	ages ago?[h]	nc	24 hr	nc	global	lm-h	nc	nc
Patrick (1809/1738)	4004 B.C.?[i]	nc	24 hr	created	global	lm, nc-a	nc	nc
Gill (1809/1763)	4004 B.C.	Day 1	24 hr	created	global	lm-h	nc-a	nc-a
Purver (1764)	4004 B.C.	Summary	24 hr	nc	global	lm-h	nc-a	nc-a
Dodd (1765)	4004 B.C.	Day 1	24 hr	created	global	lm-h	nc-a	nc-a
Henry/Blomfield (1810/1765)	~4000 B.C.	Day 1	24 hr	created	global	lm, nc-a	nc-a	nc-a
Brown (1816/1777)	4004 B.C.	Day 1	24 hr[k]	created	global	nc	nc-a	nc-a
Geddes (1792)	ages ago	Summary	ages	appeared	myth	myth	nc	nc
Priestley (1803)	ages ago	nc	ages	appeared	global?	lm, nc-a	nc	nc
Fuller (1806)	4004 B.C.?	nc	24 hr[k]	created	global	nc	nc	nc
D'Oyly/Mant[a] (1817)	4004 B.C.	Summary	24 hr	created	global	lm-h	nc-a	nc-a
Horne[a] (1818/1856)[j]	4004 B.C.	nc	24 hr[k]	nc	global	nc	nc	nc
Clarke[a] (1836)	4004 B.C.	nc	24 hr	created?	global	lm-h	la	law-unbroken
Scott[a] (1841/1812)	4004 B.C.	nc	24 hr	created	global	lm-h	nc-a	nc-a, law-unbroken

NOTES:

a. This indicates that the author consciously defended his position in reference to rival cosmologies, whether pagan or geological.

b. The years are first that of the edition I consulted, followed by the original publication, where known, or the date when the author made his last revisions, whichever is latest. D'Oyly, Mant, Scott, Horne, Dodd, Patrick, Richardson, Stackhouse and Gleig, were Anglicans, Gill and Fuller were Baptists, Clarke was a Methodist, Brown was a Presbyterian, Geddes was a Catholic, Henry (edited by Blomfield) was a non-conformist, Priestley was a Unitarian, Purver was a Quaker. According to Horne, Ainsworth was Jewish, but to me he appears Christian in doctrine.

c. "Summary" means that Genesis 1:1 was taken as a summary statement of the whole creation week; "day 1" means this verse was understood to refer to the first act of creation on day 1; "nc" means the author did not make a specific or clear comment.

d. "Created" means that the sun was actually created on day 4; "appeared" means it only appeared on day 4, having been created some time before.

e. "nc" means no comment was made on the passage; "lm" means a literal historical miracle; "lm-h" means a literal miracle described according to appearance, not according to the heliocentric view which the commentator accepted as true; "nc-a" means no comment was made in relation to astronomy; "myth" means the passage was taken as a myth, not as history.

f. "nc" means no comment was made on the passage; "nc-a" means no comment was made in relation to astronomy; "rh" means the commentator rejected the heliocentric view; "la" means the commentator believed that the biblical writer used language of appearance.

g. "nc" means no comment was made on the passage; "nc-a" means no comment was made in relation to astronomy; "law-unbroken" means that the interpretation of the phrase "the earth cannot be moved" was that the earth cannot be moved from its relative place compared to the other heavenly bodies, i.e., the laws governing the earth and universe cannot be broken.

h. Stackhouse believed the earth and solar system were created at Genesis 1:1, but the rest of the universe of celestial bodies may have existed for an immense time before this. Gleig, on the other hand, believed that Genesis 1:1 referred to all the heavenly bodies. Although he believed the text would allow for a gap theory (either of chaotic matter existing for ages or this world being built out of the wreck of another), he was not convinced that this was what actually happened. Both men believed that the events beginning from Genesis 1:3 onward occurred in 4004 BC.

i. Patrick said that the text would not rule out the possibility of a long time period before Genesis 1:3, when the literal six-day creation occurred about 6,000 years ago. But he conceived the earlier formless and void creation to have been a chaotic mass of muddy matter, which was void of any plants or animals.

j. Horne continued to hold these views on creation and the Flood until the 1856 tenth edition of his work, when he embraced the gap theory.

k. Though Brown, Fuller, and Horne made no explicit comment about the length of the creation days, they clearly took them as 24-hour days. This is evident in the fact that Brown and Horne believed the date of creation was 4004 B.C. and although Fuller was not explicit about the date of creation, he believed the creation of the sun was literally on day 4.

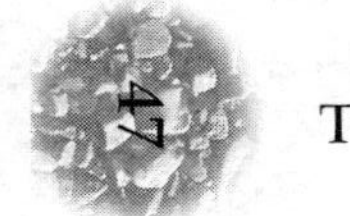

Darwin), but also the non-geologists, Whewell and Humboldt, because of their weighty achievements in other sciences and their appreciable work in geology.

Zone 2 was what Rudwick termed the "*accomplished* geologists." This zone contained two different groups. One comprised those scientists whose primary commitment was to some other science in which they were regarded among the elite, but their scientific judgment impinged in an auxiliary way on geology. They did little or no geological fieldwork and did not publish much, if anything, on the subject. Men in this category of "accomplished geologists" included the botanists Lindley and Brongniart, the fish expert Agassiz, and the conchologist Sowerby. The other group of "accomplished geologists" was comprised of men who were primarily focused on geology and were expert on a particular geographical region, group of strata, or group of fossils. Their geological opinions were highly regarded by the elite geologists, but in matters of theory their judgments were only respected on points where the elite had less expertise.

Zone 3 was the "*amateur* geologists," men and a few women whose geological knowledge was restricted to a very localized area. This group included country gentlemen and ladies, physicians, lawyers, and clergymen with intimate knowledge of the area near their homes, as well as government officials, military officers, and others whose jobs took them to isolated parts of the world. Their knowledge was trusted by the elite only at the strictly "factual" level.

Within these zones of attributed competence, the elite geologists regarded only themselves as competent to propose the most fundamental, theoretical, or global claims to geological knowledge.[118] Beyond these three zones lay the general public. The geological statements of people in this category (which included quarrymen and miners) were never accepted as reliable until checked and corroborated by those with recognized geological competence.

As enlightening as Rudwick's discussion of these three zones is for understanding geological competence in the mid-1830s during the Devonian controversy, there are at least six reasons to conclude that this analysis is not obviously applicable to the assessment of the geological competence of the scriptural geologists to critically evaluate the arguments in favor of an old earth.

First, although Rudwick accurately describes competence relative to the famous "Devonian controversy" of 1834–37,[119] his study does not enable us to adequately place people who were not involved in that debate, such as William Smith, Robert Bakewell, and leading American geologists, who were recognized by many geologists to have broader and deeper knowledge of geology than the "accomplished geologists" (and even the "elite geologist" Whewell), but who were not considered to be in the elite category.

Second, Rudwick pictured diagrammatically (see figure 1) the fact that some of the scriptural geologists were included within the class of "amateur geologists,"[120] whom the leading geologists at the time of the Devonian controversy "regarded as at least modestly active and competent in geology."[121] However, it would be difficult to prove in 1822 (after the scriptural geologist George Young had published four scientific journal articles on geology and his *Geological Survey of the Yorkshire Coast,* in which he objected to old-earth theory) that Young was any less active in geological fieldwork and geological reading or any less capable of geological theorizing than Sedgwick, Buckland, or Lyell (or Smith, Cuvier, Hutton, or Werner), especially given the great amount of exposed strata in Yorkshire which represented a major portion of the secondary formations and were right at Young's doorstep.

Third, to say that experts in other scientific fields (with little or no fieldwork or publications in geology) were more competent than scriptural geologists (who did both activities) is to imply that social standing in the scientific establishment and general scientific reasoning ability were far

118 Ibid., p. 425.
119 This involved the proper placement of the "Devonian formation" in the lower part of the so-called "geological column."
120 Rudwick gave no names of scriptural geologists whom he considered to fit in this category.
121 Rudwick, *The Great Devonian Controversy*, p. 29 (explanatory paragraph for figure 2.3).

more important criteria of geological competence (at least in the minds of the geological elite) than actual first and secondhand knowledge of geological phenomena. But this is a strange definition. On this basis, the scriptural geologist Andrew Ure should be ranked higher in geological competence than George Young, a conclusion most inconsistent with the facts (as will be shown) and the actual opinions of the recognized geologists of the time.

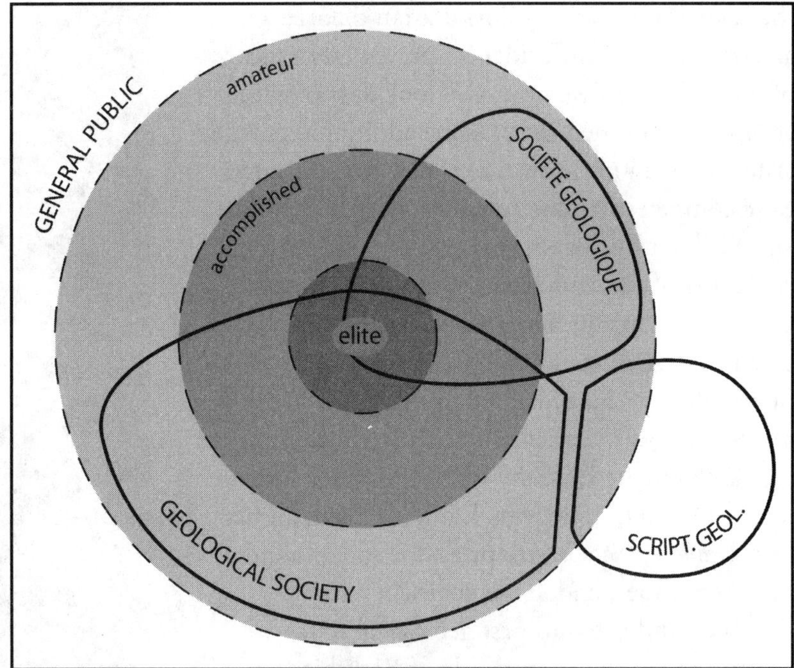

FIGURE 1 — RUDWICK'S DIAGRAM OF THE WORLDWIDE COMMUNITY OF ACTIVE GEOLOGISTS IN THE MID-1830S.

From Martin Rudwick, *The Great Devonian Controversy* (Chicago, IL: University of Chicago Press, 1985), p. 29.

Fourth, this definition of competence was determined by a small group of "elite geologists," some of whom gained their elite status *before* they themselves had achieved a high level of geological competence. Sedgwick, for instance, attained the prestigious position of Woodwardian Professor of Geology at Cambridge in 1818 when, by his own admission, he knew very little about the subject and had done virtually no fieldwork.[122]

Fifth, the definition does not objectively reflect a person's knowledge of geological literature, and his intellectual ability to understand geological arguments and evaluate the logical soundness of induction from agreed-upon geological facts.

Finally, and perhaps most importantly, the authors of the catastrophist and uniformitarian theories of a very old earth constructed those theories and presented their geological evidence in defense of their theories long before the Devonian controversy illuminated and developed a more restrictive definition of geological competence. Hutton, Werner, and Cuvier (along with Buffon and Laplace, both non-geologists) were the chief authors of the old-earth view.[123] But at the time they proposed their theories they were not very geologically competent by the standards of the mid-1830s. Furthermore, while the Devonian controversy involved very technical discussions, it was not introducing or finally establishing the old-earth theory, but only hammering out details within the old-earth interpretive framework, and therefore only one or two scriptural geologists even made mention of the Devonian controversy. In the late 1810s, when the old-earth view was firmly established in the minds of geologists at the universities of Cambridge, Oxford, and Edinburgh, other institutions of higher education, the Geological Society of London, the provincial philosophical societies, and in similar institutions on the European continent, Hutton, Werner, and Cuvier would have only satisfied Rudwick's criteria of "amateur geologists."

So in order to assess the geological competence of the scriptural geologists to critically evaluate

122 *DNB* on Sedgwick, p. 1117; John W. Clark and Thomas M. Hughes, *The Life and Letters of the Reverend Adam Sedgwick* (1890), I: p. 199, 287.

123 Lyell did not really lengthen geological history in any way relevant to the scriptural geologists' contention about the age of the earth. When he devised his modified version of Hutton's uniformitarianism in the late 1820s, the old-earth paradigm was in place and the Noachian deluge had already been judged to be of minimal geological significance compared to the vast drafts of time imagined before the Flood.

the catastrophist and uniformitarian theories of an old-earth and the evidences presented in favor of those theories, we must also look at geological competence in the light of some additional possible criteria as seen in the lives of those who, all agree, were competent geologists, such as Charles Lyell and William Buckland, two of the greatest British geologists of the 19th century, as well as others.

In terms of education, Buckland, son of a clergyman, studied classics at Oxford from 1801–05 in preparation for his ordained ministry. However, his real interest was in science, particularly geology, and he learned much from the writings and lectures on mineralogy and geology by Dr. John Kidd, an Oxford University chemistry professor and a founding member of the London Geological Society.[124]

Buckland took his first geological tour in 1808 alone in the countryside of Berkshire and Wiltshire, and soon after began to give an annual eight-lecture series on mineralogy (from 1813) and on geology (from 1819). Lyell studied at Oxford and later Lincoln's Inn to become a lawyer, which was his vocation until 1828. While at Oxford he attended Buckland's eight geology lectures in the springs of 1817 to 1819. Sometime before 1826 he had read Robert Bakewell's *Introduction to Geology*[125] and John Playfair's *Illustrations of the Huttonian Theory*, the latter of which had a significant influence on the development of his own ideas about the history of the earth.[126]

Some people in Britain had studied mineralogy or chemistry as a background for their geological investigations. This was particularly true of the Scots. They had geological instruction at Edinburgh University much earlier than Oxford and Cambridge, and Robert Jameson, one of their most prominent geologists, was an alumnus of the German institute, Bergakademie Freiberg, where the famous old-earth mineralogist, Abraham Werner, taught from 1775 to 1817.[127] But Buckland and Lyell had a more limited educational background in the subject area. Their expertise came predominantly through self-education. It was the same with other leading British geologists of the 19th century. George Greenough, the first president of the Geological Society of London, trained in law. Roderick Murchison, who was significant in working out the Devonian and Silurian systems of strata in the 1830s and 1840s, had a military education. In fact, it is said that he chose to learn stratigraphical geology because it did not require the academics of mineralogy. Henry De la Beche similarly had a military education. He eventually headed up the

Roderick Murchison (1792–1871)

124 Woodward, *The History of the Geological Society of London*, p. 41; Buckland, *Vindiciae Geologicae*, preface; Rupke, *The Great Chain of History: William Buckland and the English School of Geology, 1814–1849*, p. 7–8; Elizabeth O. Gordon, *The Life and Correspondence of William Buckland, DD, FRS* (1894), p. 1–12.

125 First published in 1813, it went through five revised editions by 1838 and was considered to be "undoubtedly the best of the early textbooks." See Woodward, *The History of the Geological Society of London*, p. 84.

126 Leonard G. Wilson, "The Development of the Concept of Uniformitarianism in the Mind of Charles Lyell," *Proceedings of the Tenth International Congress on the History of Science* (1964), p. 993–996.

127 *DSB* on Werner, p. 257.

geological survey of Britain for the government and led the efforts to found the School of Mines in London.[128] As noted earlier, Adam Sedgwick admitted that he was practically ignorant of geology when in 1818 he was elected to the Geological Society and to be Woodwardian Professor of Geology at Cambridge. What he did know of geology came from reading, not field experience, though this quickly changed after 1818.

William Fitton, who later became president of the London Geological Society, was rather emphatic on this matter of education, when he defended the society in 1817, saying:

> It has been remarked by critics that the want of education is sometimes of advantage to a man of genius, who is thus free to the suggestions of invention, and is neither biassed in favour of erroneous maxims, nor deterred from the trial of his own powers by names of high authority. On this principle it is evident that the members of the Geological Society have derived great benefit from their want of systematic instruction. At the time of its formation there was, in fact, no English school of mineralogy where they could imbibe either information or prejudice. They were neither Vulcanists nor Neptunists nor Wernerians nor Huttonians, but plain men, who felt the importance of a subject about which they knew very little in detail; and, guided only by a sincere desire to learn, they have produced, with a rapidity that is truly surprising, publications of the greatest interest and importance upon the subjects to which they have devoted.[129]

So while university studies in chemistry or mineralogy were seen by some as helpful, they were not necessary to be regarded as a competent geologist in the 1820s and 1830s. In fact, professional training in science generally did not become established until the late 1840s.[130] In any case, it will be seen in subsequent chapters that many of the scriptural geologists had just as great a desire and intelligence to learn as any founding member of the Geological Society or other "elite" geologists.

Certainly we would expect that a non-negotiable characteristic of a good geologist was his personal firsthand observations of the rocks, fossils, and strata of the earth's crust. Buckland and Lyell both had ample experience here. Buckland regularly explored the geological features in the countryside and took students on field trips. He had an extensive collection of fossils and rocks, which he always used in his lectures. His most famous field work was related to the fossils found in the Kirkdale Cave in Yorkshire and incorporated into his early apparent defense of the Noachian flood in *Reliquiae Diluvianae* (1823).[131]

Lyell, though a practicing barrister until 1828, spent some considerable time in the field before writing his *Principles of Geology* (1830–33). In the summer of 1823 he visited Paris and met the catastrophists Humboldt, Cuvier, and Brongniart and made some geological excursions in the area. In 1825 he went on geological field trips in southwest England and later with Buckland in Scotland. And he spent three months in 1828 in the Auvergne region of France with Roderick Murchison studying the river valleys. Many more trips followed as he gave up law and pursued geology on a more full-time basis. However, the original two-volume manuscript of his *Principles* was given to the publisher in late 1827, six months before he made his first major geological tour, which was through France and northern Italy.[132]

In addition to geological reading (or education) and field work, other criteria could be suggested

128 Rudwick, *The Great Devonian Controversy*, p. 54–72, 457–458.

129 William Fitton quoted in Woodward, *History of the Geological Society of London*, p. 52–53. Fitton's original article was in *Edinburgh Review*, Vol. XXIX (1817), p. 70–94.

130 Susan F. Cannon, *Science in Culture: The Early Victorian Period* (1978), p. 142–143.

131 The scriptural geologists recognized it as a subtle attack on the Flood because it attributed to the Flood only the superficial loose sand and gravel deposits and the valley systems, relegating the vast sedimentary rock formations to catastrophes long before the creation of man.

132 Charles Lyell, *Principles of Geology* (1830–33), III: p. vi; Martin J.S. Rudwick, "Lyell on Etna, and the Antiquity of the Earth," in Cecil J. Schneer, editor, *Toward a History of Geology* (Cambridge, MA: M.I.T. Press, 1969), p. 289.

which might be assumed to be necessary marks of a competent geologist, but which in a study of the recognized geologists of the 1820s and 1830s prove not to be essential.

1. A competent geologist need not be a member of the Geological Society of London.

William Smith, the "Father of English Stratigraphy," was considered to be one of the best practical geologists in early 19th century Britain. But he was never a member of the Geological Society. In fact, many of the leading practical geologists (i.e., those involved in mining, building canals, railways and roads, and digging wells, etc.), such as John Farey and Robert Bakewell, were not members of the GSL and many of the early members and officers of the society were not geologists, even well into the late 1820s after its birth in 1807. Furthermore, Rudwick has estimated that at the time of the "Devonian controversy" (1834–37) only two-thirds of the competent geologists in Britain were members of the society.[133]

2. Being well-traveled, especially internationally, or having first-hand knowledge of the geology and geography of an area was not essential to write competently on geology.

John Macculloch was praised by Lyell as an excellent geologist, who had a lasting and powerful influence on geology and even on Lyell's own thinking, even though Macculloch was a catastrophist and his two-volume *System of Geology* (1831) had many imperfections, including outdated information.[134] Yet in defense of the fact that Macculloch based his *System of Geology* mainly on what he observed in Britain, he stated:

> Geologists have been acused [*sic*] of founding theories upon single and favoured districts; yet have I drawn my chief illustrations from Britain? It is true: but there is no resemblance in the applications: as I can also justify this proceeding. Geological facts have no relation to geography: the Earth is everywhere of the same general structure. And I need not hesitate to say, that excepting volcanoes, and little more, this little island contains every fact in the world, with much that is almost peculiar to itself; and that more knowledge can be acquired from a careful examination of it, than from all the writings of all those who have prided themselves on the extent of their travels.[135]

Like the scriptural geologist George Fairholme, Lyell wrote on the causes and age of Niagara Falls in his *Principles of Geology* based on the writings of other reliable observers, long before he himself visited America (including the falls) in 1841–42.[136] Nevertheless, Lyell discredited the great German mineralogist Abraham Werner because Werner made a universal theory of the earth based on very little personal knowledge of the geology of areas outside his native Saxony. Ospovat has pointed out, however, that James Hutton, forefather of Lyell's own uniformitarian ideas, likewise traveled little outside his native Scotland.[137] In fact, Hutton first published his cyclical theory of the earth in 1785 before he had studied any rocks in the field and he traveled very little outside Scotland to look for confirmation of his theory.[138]

Similarly, Georges Cuvier, who did not explore much geology outside the environs of Paris, based his *Theory of the Earth* (1813) exclusively on a study of the Paris Basin, or rather a study of the fossils found there by others, for he himself relied on others, primarily Alexandre Brongniart, for the geological information.[139]

---

133 Rudwick, *The Great Devonian Controversy*, p. 419.

134 Charles Lyell, presidential address (Feb. 19, 1836), *Proceedings of the Geological Society of London*, Vol. II (1836), p. 359; Woodward, *The History of the Geological Society of London*, p. 36, 87, 286.

135 John Macculloch, *System of Geology* (1831), I: p. vi-vii.

136 Lyell, *Principles of Geology*, I: p. 89, 179–181.

137 Alexander M. Ospovat, "The Distortion of Werner in Lyell's *Principles of Geology*," *British Journal of the History of Science*, vol. IX: 32 (1976), p. 190–198. William Whewell was also critical of Werner and Hutton for prematurely developing theories of earth history based on very limited knowledge of the earth. See Whewell's *History of the Inductive Sciences* (1837), III: p. 604–605.

138 Stephen J. Gould, *Time's Arrow — Time's Cycle* (Cambridge, MA: Harvard University Press, 1987), p. 70–72, 76.

139 *DSB* on Cuvier, p. 525; Cuvier, *Theory of the Earth*, p. 111–114.

3. A person did not need to be gainfully employed as a geologist in order to be considered a competent geologist in the 1820s and 1830s.

Murchison was an independently wealthy, retired military man, who did not take a job as a geologist until he replaced De la Beche in the 1840s in the governmental Department of Geological Survey. De la Beche himself initially did his geological work living off funds from his father, a plantation owner in the West Indies, before becoming a government geologist in the mid-1830s. Lyell was initially a lawyer by profession. Then for a short time he earned a little from geological lectures presented to a paying public. But for most of his life he lived off the royalties of his successful geological writings. George P. Scrope married into wealth, which funded his early geological research on volcanos and valleys in France and he spent most of his professional life as a member of Parliament from Stroud (for 35 years) before resuming geological work in his retirement. George Greenough, the first president of the Geological Society and active in geology for many years after that, was likewise independently wealthy.[140] In fact, it was not until the late 1840s, in large measure because of the Devonian controversy, that we see the rise of the professional specialist (as opposed to the independently wealthy gentleman) in geology.[141]

4. A competent geologist in the early 19th century did not necessarily have a good knowledge of conchology.

One might think that this would be absolutely essential, since shells were by far the most common fossils found in the geological record and the most important fossils used to identify, correlate, and relatively date the strata in various locations. However, William Smith, who was recognized for having developed this technique for classifying the strata, said the following in 1817 about his *Stratigraphical System of Organized Fossils*:

> Errors in [my] stratified arrangement can be corrected by those only who are locally acquainted with the strata, and the numerous organized Fossils they contain. On this principle I have ventured, without much knowledge of Conchology, and with weak aids in that science to give the outlines of a systematic arrangement [of the geological record].[142]

Similarly, Lyell based his uniformitarian theory largely on the fossil shells of the tertiary, but he did not start studying conchology until 1830, the year Volume 1 of his *Principles of Geology* was published and two years after the theory was firmly fixed in his mind.[143]

5. Finally, and perhaps most important to note, for a person to be considered competent in geology it did not mean that he was unbiased and unaffected in his geological theorizing by non-scientific considerations.

Nicholaas Rupke has argued persuasively that Buckland's catastrophist geology was significantly influenced by his involvement in university and social reform. Speaking of the reform going on in Britain at the time, Rupke wrote:

> The geological notion of progressive earth history cannot be separated from this historical milieu. The progressivism of the English school [of geology, of which Buckland was a leader] was formulated at a time when the idea of progress was becoming a major determinant of cultural expectation in English society.[144]

In other words, the perceived progressive nature of the geological record was used as a basis for, and to some extent shaped by, the idea that man and society were improving.

Lyell likewise was not a purely objective observer of the geological facts. A number of recent

140 Rudwick, *The Great Devonian Controversy*, p. 53–72, 457–458; Woodward, *The History of the Geological Society of London*, p. 12, 73; *DNB* on Greenough.

141 Rudwick, *The Great Devonian Controversy*, p. 449. See also Roy Porter, "Gentlemen and Geology: The Emergence of a Scientific Career, 1660–1920," *The Historical Journal*, vol. XXI, no. 4 (1978), p. 809–836.

142 Smith, *Stratigraphical System of Organized Fossils*, p. vi.

143 Katharine M. Lyell, editor, *Life, Letters and Journals of Sir Charles Lyell, Bart.* (1881), I: p. 304, 397.

144 Rupke, *The Great Chain of History: William Buckland and the English School of Geology 1814–1849*, p. 255.

historians of science and geologists have shown that politics, economics, and deistic (or unitarian) theology had a significant bearing on the interpretation of geological formations given by Lyell (and Scrope, upon whom Lyell heavily relied).[145] In his discussion of Lyell and the uniformitarian catastrophist debate in the 1820s and 1830s, geologist Derek Ager, a leader in the 20th century renaissance of geological catastrophism, remarked:

> My excuse for this lengthy and amateur digression into history is that I have been trying to show how I think geology got into the hands of the theoreticians [uniformitarians] who were conditioned by the social and political history of their day more than by observations in the field.[146]

American old-earth geologist, Edward Hitchcock, argued that both the French geologists and Lyell had a hostility against the Bible, which very much affected their interpretation of the Noachian flood and the geological evidence.[147]

So, the definition of geological competence was not fixed in the 1820s and 1830s as geology matured as a science and certainly, as Rudwick has shown, there was a gradient of competence. But the level of competence necessary for proposing or debating a detailed stratigraphy of a particular region within the old-earth framework (such as in the Devonian controversy of the mid-1830s) was much higher than that needed to propose the old-earth framework and state its supporting evidences (in the years 1790–1815) or to criticize those theories and arguments, as the scriptural geologists did. Upon consideration of further criteria than those proposed by Rudwick, it may be argued that a competent geologist in the 1820s and 1830s was one who devoted a significant portion of his time to firsthand observation of the geological formations in the field and was knowledgeably conversant with current geological literature, facts, and theories. If, added to these, his field observations were not just regional, but national or international in extent, if he published his research in reputable scientific journals and/or books, if he was a member of one or more scientific societies, if he had personal contact with recognized geologists, if he added new facts to the pool of geological knowledge, if he earned his living from his geological work, etc., then so much the better. But these latter attributes were not *necessary* in the 1820s and 1830s to qualify as a competent geologist who was able to critically evaluate the theories of an old earth and the geological evidences adduced as proof of those theories.

These considerations assist in the evaluation of the Genesis-geology debate and the part which the scriptural geologists played in it. As we will see, George Young, John Murray, William Rhind, and George Fairholme were quite competent in geology (possessing even some of the extra characteristics mentioned above) and had as much or more first and secondhand geological knowledge than some of those categorized by Rudwick as *accomplished*, or even *elite*, geologists. It will also be shown that some of the other scriptural geologists were better informed geologically than was (or is) generally acknowledged by their critics.

---

145 Martin J.S. Rudwick, "Poulett Scrope on the Volcanoes of Auvergne: Lyellian Time and Political Economy," *British Journal for the History of Science*, vol. VII, no. 27 (1974), p. 205–242 (especially, p. 227); Martin J.S. Rudwick, "Transposed Concepts from the Human Sciences in the Early Work of Charles Lyell," in Jordanova and Porter, editors, *Images of the Earth* (1979), p. 67–83; Salim Rashid, "Political Economy and Geology in the Nineteenth Century: Similarities and Contrasts," *History of Political Economy*, vol. XIII, no. 4 (1981), p. 726–744; Rupke, *The Great Chain of History*; George Grinnell, "The Origins of Modern Geological Theory," *Kronos*, vol. I, no. 4 (1976), p. 68–76; Walter F. Cannon, "Scientists and Broad Churchmen: An Early Victorian Intellectual Network," *Journal of British Studies*, vol. IV, no. 1 (1964), p. 65–88; James R. Moore, "Geologists and Interpreters of Genesis in the Nineteenth Century," in Lindberg and Numbers, editors, *God and Nature*, p. 322–350; Corsi, *Science and Religion*, p. 106–123.

146 Derek Ager, *The Nature of the Stratigraphical Record* (New York, Wiley, 1981), p. 46.

147 Edward Hitchcock, "The Historical and Geological Deluges Compared," *The American Biblical Repository*, vol. IX, no. 25 (1837), p. 131–137. At this time (1837) Hitchcock, along with Benjamin Silliman (another prominent American old-earth geologist), still believed the geological evidence indicated that a geologically significant global catastrophe had occurred at the time of Noah.

SEVEN INDIVIDUAL PORTRAITS

We have considered the historical context of the British scriptural geologists. They wrote at a time of incredible change. Politically, monarchial government was moving in the direction of representative democracy. The Industrial Revolution was bringing an explosion of new technology, thereby helping to elevate the social status of science. Reason was being raised to the place of supreme authority in determining truth, and deists and atheists were openly or subtly challenging the Christian world view. This had an effect not only on scientific assumptions and methodology, but also on biblical scholarship and faith in the Scriptures.

In the early 19th century, science and scientists were just beginning to become specialized in the way that we know them to be today, and the study of geology was still very much in its infancy, more as a "gentlemen's avocation" than as a profession. Though in Britain there were strong defenders of Christian orthodoxy among both high churchmen and evangelicals, liberal theology was slowly penetrating and transforming the churches. And after several centuries of close ties between geology and Scripture, the study of the rocks and fossils was being divorced from the study of the Bible, resulting in a departure from the dominant, traditional interpretation of the early chapters of Genesis.

We are now prepared to consider individually seven of the scriptural geologists. They are presented roughly in the chronological order of their writings on geology. After we have looked at each of these men and his arguments, we will then be in a position to make overall comparisons, summarize their common objections to the old-earth theories, and draw general conclusions about the nature of the debate in which they were engaged.

GRANVILLE PENN (1761–1844)

Granville Penn was born in Spring Gardens, a hamlet in the parish of Wooburn, Buckinghamshire,[1] on December 9, 1761, the fifth but second surviving and youngest son of Thomas Penn, and the grandson of William Penn, who founded the colony of Pennsylvania in America.[2]

He matriculated, without taking a degree, from Magdalen College, Oxford, in November 1780, and then became an assistant chief clerk in the War Department, from which he received a £550[3] pension.

He married Isabella, daughter of General Gordon Forbes, on June 24, 1791, and they settled in London for many years. Together they had four sons and five daughters, with one of each dying in infancy.[4] Of the three sons who reached manhood, all received an M.A. from Christ Church, Oxford. One became a barrister and another became an Anglican clergyman.[5] This family information, in the absence of other contrary data, suggests that Penn himself was an Anglican.

In 1834 when Penn's brother John died, he took over the family estates of Stoke Park, Buckinghamshire, and of Pennsylvania Castle, Portland. When he died at Stoke Park on September 28, 1844, he willed to his son and his heirs £3000/year[6] for 500 years out of an perpetual annuity of the £4000[7] granted to the Penn family by an act of Parliament to compensate for losses sustained in America.[8]

Unless otherwise noted, this biographical section is based on the *DNB* article on Penn.

1 William Page, editor, *The Victoria History of the Counties of England* (1925), III: p. 105–106.

2 *Imperial Dictionary of Universal Biography* (1865), III: p. 526.

3 According to Martin J.S. Rudwick, *The Great Devonian Controversy* (Chicago, IL: University of Chicago Press, 1985), p. 461, this princely sum was equivalent in modern terms to about £22,000 (or $33,000).

4 *Gentlemen's Magazine* (1844), II: p. 545–546.

5 John Burke, *History of the Commoners of Great Britain and Ireland* (1836), III: p. 491.

6 Rudwick, *The Great Devonian Controversy*, p. 461, about £120,000 (or $180,000) in modern currency.

7 Ibid., about £160,000 (or $240,000) by today's value.

8 See footnote 2.

William Penn (1644–1718), founder of the colony of Pennsylvania and grandfather of Granville.

Penn loved the study of languages (being fluent in French, Greek, Latin, and possibly Hebrew) and ancient literature. He was a Fellow of the Society of Antiquaries,[9] wrote several books dealing with biblical criticism and published a number of competent translations of ancient Greek works, including a critical revision of the English version of the New Testament. He also wrote some theological works particularly related to biblical chronology (past and future) and the early history of post-Flood mankind. Many of these works went through more than one edition.

His major work on geology[10] was *A Comparative Estimate of the Mineral and Mosaical Geologies.* ("Mineral geology" is how Penn referred to the old-earth theories. "Mosaical geology" refers to the young-earth view he was defending.) It was first published in 1822, received a supplement in 1823 in response to Buckland's theory on Kirkdale Cave, and was revised in light of criticism and greatly enlarged to two volumes for a second edition in 1825.[11] The later edition will be the focus of this study.[12]

Geological Competence

Penn made no claim to be a geologist, but he was well read in the geological literature of his day. His book contains many quotations, most of them long and all well documented, from the most recent books (or most recent editions of books) by leading British and French geologists, as well as geological articles in prominent British and French science periodicals. In addition, he carefully read and responded to the journal reviews of his first edition of *Comparative Estimate.*[13]

Throughout *Comparative Estimate* Penn gave little indication of firsthand observation of geological phenomena. Nevertheless, he was not insensitive to the charge from the geologists, to whose theories he was offering critique, that he was not qualified to comment on the subject. In his long appendix on Buckland's Kirkdale Cave theory he seems to intimate the extent of his own observations of geological phenomena, when he wrote:

> I am well aware, that it has long been a common resource of many who, after laborious and hazardous enterprises to collect facts in geology, find the conclusions which they have drawn from those facts questioned by others who have not engaged in the same particular enterprises, to exclaim, that the objections are those of *"mere cabinet naturalists,"* who have not inspected the objects on which they pretend to deliver an opinion. But, this *"argumentum ad silentium"* has no

9 Joseph Foster, *Alumni Oxonienses* (1887), p. 1093.

10 The *DNB* article on Penn and the leading library catalogs attribute to Penn (apparently erroneously) the book *Conversations on Geology*, published in 1828 (second edition in 1840). But according to the *Magazine of Natural History*, vol. I (1829), p. 280 and 463–466, which reviewed this anonymous book, it was supposedly written by J. Rennie, a respected scientist and former editor of the *Foreign Medical Journal.*

11 Volume I contains 353 pages, plus an 80-page introduction, and volume II has 426 pages.

12 Hereafter it will be cited as *Comparative Estimate.*

13 Penn's responses are scattered throughout the second edition but most of them are concentrated in the introduction to Volume I.

> title to *produce it*; for, *the facts reported, are certainly of no value whatever to science, if they do not enable all reflecting and philosophical minds to reason effectually and conclusively upon them*; and, no one can at the same time, both impart his knowledge to others, and keep it all back to himself. And, that the sobriety of *"the cabinet"* is materially needed to revise and regulate the often hasty and impassioned combinations of *actual inspection*, is virtually admitted in the concession of Cuvier; "that many who have made excellent collections of observations, though they may have *laid the foundations* of true geological science, have not therefore been able to *raise and complete the edifice*." Besides, it does not follow, because a writer *meditates in his cabinet*, or, because he has not visited the limestone caves of England and Franconia, that he has not *made researches out of it*: or, because he abstains from a recital of his travels, that he has not explored the *mountainous chains of the Alps*, or the *Pyrennees*, or sought the interior of the earth in various places, as, at *Hallein* in Salzburg, *Bex* in Switzerland, *Mont St. Pierre* near Maestricht, and elsewhere; which are no negative instructors in preparing the mind for geological investigation.[14]

Furthermore, Penn argued, it is sound logical induction, more than the quantity of geological observations, that is critical to the erecting of a reliable geological history of the earth.

> The mineral geology [i.e., old-earth theories] confidently reposes on its delusive error, that he who *sees most, judges best*; and it expects, by that rule, to secure the palm in every geological contest. As if *judgment* were the necessary product of *vision*. But, as the two faculties have no such necessary ordination and dependence; he who sees *enough*, with a *more instructed* judgment, will better apprehend the fundamental truths of *geology*, than he who sees *more than enough*, with a judgment *less instructed*. It is one thing to *accumulate data*, and another thing to *reason soundly* upon them when accumulated: as will be frequently exemplified in the progress of this work. . . . Certainly, he who has read numerically *most books* [*sic*], is not necessarily the *best critic*; and, by the same principle, he who has seen numerically *most rocks* [*sic*], is not necessarily the *best geologist*. . . . Although, then, it is undeniably true, "that those who have contributed most to the advancement of Natural Philosophy, have had, at the same time, a *tendency to generalize*, and an accurate knowledge of *a great many particular facts*;" yet, it was not the *tendency*, but the *sound ability*, that enabled them to contribute to that advancement.[15]

In response to Buckland's assertion in *Vindiciae Geologiae* that a qualified natural philosopher cannot be content with mastering one branch of science but must have a breadth of knowledge over the whole range of science, Penn added that in the area of historical geology other branches of learning were also essential.

> But, it is also no less certainly true; that all the *physical* sciences combined cannot serve the *philosopher* to apprehend the *historical basis* on which alone the complex Science of *Geology* can securely stand, unless he is further succoured by the concurring auxiliaries of *Sacred and*

14 Granville Penn, *Comparative Estimate* (1825), II: p. 285–286.

15 Ibid., I: p. 50–51. At the end, he was quoting from Humboldt's *Superposition of Rocks* (1823), p. 32. He continued on page 52, "In Newton, intuitive *logic* was dominant; and *mathematics*, were only the steps by which his *logic* ascended to the elevation to which it attained. In the mineral geology, *physical impressions* are dominant; and its *logic*, is only an artificial instrument which it seeks to employ for arranging those impressions. *How many eminent mathematicians had seen apples fall to the ground, before the intuitive LOGIC of Newton's mind apprehended the phenomenon!* How different that *logic* was from the logic of the mineral geology, we have seen by the difference of their respective conclusions."

Ancient Learning. If he would attain to that apprehension, he "can no longer be allowed to remain satisfied" with the exclusive illumination of the *Physical Sciences*.[16]

Some indication that Penn's work did not reflect complete geological ignorance, or misunderstanding of the geological works he read, may be gained from two reviews of his book. One review was in the form of a book published anonymously in 1828, called *Conversations on Geology*, which primarily compared Penn's geological theory of earth history with those of Werner and Hutton and generally considered Penn's the best, though the author did not agree with Penn on every point.[17] The geologically informed author of *Conversations on Geology* remarked, possibly on the basis of personal acquaintance, that Penn was an "excellent geologist," "who is extensively acquainted with the facts and theories of modern *Mineral Geologists*," and who "is a pupil of the celebrated Saussure," and had been "long among the Alps and Pyrennees."[18]

A two-part review of Penn's first edition and the subsequent supplement on Kirkdale Cave appeared in the *Quarterly Journal of Science, Literature and Arts*.[19] The reviewer hailed Penn's "valuable" book "with unfeigned satisfaction."[20] He said that Penn "invariably supports his assertion by reference to some writer of established authority" and his argument was "remarkable for the closeness of its reasoning" and "for the spirit of upright honesty and manly candour which animates every page."[21] As for Penn's discussion on the formation of coal, the reviewer felt that Penn handled the subject "with the judicial caution which the obscurity of the subject demands."[22] The reviewer highly recommended the book because:

> . . . its philosophy is founded on that of Bacon and Newton; its reasonings on the mode of first formations and secondary causes, are in strict harmony with that philosophy, and at least as plausible as any that have been advanced by the Huttonian and Wernerian schools . . . and its excellent moral and religious tendency.[23]

---

16 Ibid., I: p. lvi, footnote.

17 This work received a very positive review in the *Magazine of Natural History*, vol. I (1829), p. 463–466, and, as noted earlier, was attributed to J. Rennie, a respected scientist. Of this book the reviewer wrote, "It may be objected to these *Conversations on Geology*, that they contain too many objections, and leave many parts of the subject in utter uncertainty: but we may be permitted to reply to this, that all the systems of geology are precisely in the state in which they are here represented, uncertain and imperfect in their theories and speculations; though these are generally illustrated by interesting and well-ascertained facts, and sufficiently plausible arguments. The author of the *Conversations*, therefore, it would appear to us, has acted judiciously in representing the actual imperfections of geology, rather than concealing them, and in expressing doubts upon points imperfectly ascertained, rather than dogmatizing" (p. 466). Another positive review of *Conversations on Geology* appeared in *Athenaeum*, 47 (Sept. 17, 1828), p. 737–738.

18 [J. Rennie], *Conversations on Geology* (1828), p. 293, 44, 306.

19 *Quarterly Journal of Science, Literature and Arts*, vol. XV (1823), p. 108–127; vol. XVI (1823), p. 309–321. The reviews are not signed, but probably were done, or at least approved, by the editor, William Brande (1788–1866), by whose name the journal was commonly known.

Brande was professor of chemistry at the Royal Institution and close associate of Michael Faraday and Sir Humphry Davy. He also had a keen interest in and knowledge of geology. In 1817 he published his *Outlines of Geology*, which consisted of his lectures on geology at the Royal Institution in 1816. The book was revised and nearly doubled in length before coming out in a second edition in 1829, in which Brande described Penn's second edition of *Comparative Estimate* as a "masterly work" (p. 3). Brande's book was a purely descriptive geology which avoided theoretical speculations. Apart from attributing the diluvial deposits (loose gravels and sands above the consolidated strata) and valleys of denudation to the global Noachian flood, Brande did not commit himself on the age of the earth.

Brande was also a leading fellow of the Royal Society, serving as a secretary from 1816–26, and an original fellow of the University of London, as well as a member of several foreign scientific societies. According to the *DNB* article on Brande, "During forty-six years Brande laboured most industriously in the front ranks of science."

20 Ibid., vol. XV (1823), p. 108.

21 Ibid., p. 110.

22 Ibid., p. 125.

23 Ibid., p. 127.

The *Supplement* only strengthened this reviewer's convictions about the "talents and right-mindedness" of Penn and the "logical precision and force" of his objections against Buckland's theory that Kirkdale Cave was an antediluvian hyena's den, though the reviewer objected to some points in Penn's argument.[24] Finally, he praised Penn for the "gentlemanly tone" and "respectful terms" he used in reference to Buckland.[25]

Geology and Geologists

Penn never expressed any opposition to the study of geology or any other science. On the contrary, he affirmed that geology is a "delightful study," and mineralogy is a "sound and valuable science."[26] Furthermore:

> The science of GEOLOGY, the last of those *reserved measures of light* which have been opened upon us, has this remarkable character above all the preceding physical sciences; that, it not only conducts the intelligence, like them, to the discernment of the *God of Nature*, but advances it further, to a distinct recognition of that *God of Nature* in the *God of Scripture*.[27]

Throughout his work he showed great respect for the "eminent and distinguished" geologists with whom he disagreed.[28] Wherever he could, he frequently expressed respect and appreciation for the research and philosophical inductions they had made.

When Penn disagreed with these respected geologists it was over the *interpretation* of the facts, not the facts themselves, except when so-called "facts" were, in his opinion, really just disguised theoretical inferences from the facts. He contended that the old-earth geologists erroneously relied on a "seductive principle" that the "facts in geology are *self-evident*, and need only to be *seen* to be *believed*."[29] He was convinced and attempted to show that the geologists themselves were not aware that many of their "facts" were theory-laden. After quoting Humboldt's expressed desire to avoid hypothesis in his factual description of the crust of the earth, Penn wrote:

> Yet, notwithstanding this emphatic disclaimer of all *hypothesis*, notwithstanding this determined advocacy of *facts*, and *facts only*, the *"Geognostical Essay"* is governed throughout by a *masked theory*; of which its eminent author appears to be hardly conscious, but of which the attentive reader will have caught some surmise from the *reservation* claimed by the author; "of *adding* what is *only probable*, (that is, in his own opinion) to what appears *completely verified*," and thus, of *incorporating theory with the facts of his observation and experience*. This *theory of probabilities*, I shall now proceed to unmask; in order that we may be able to distinguish and ascertain exactly, how far his *geognosy of fact* is also a *geognosy of hypothesis*, and thus reveals itself to be only another variety of that *Alchymical Geology*, which has already been examined and exposed.[30]

For these reasons, Penn distinguished between what he considered to be the legitimate science of mineralogy, which like botany and zoology explores the present *nature* of the relevant objects of study, and the "spurious and baseless science" of "mineral geology" or "geognosy."[31] Penn used the term "mineral geology" to collectively describe all the old-earth theories which tried to explain, solely by observation of the geological phenomena and reference to secondary physical and chemical causes, "the two *historical facts*; viz. *the* MODE *of first formation* of the primitive mineral substances

24 Ibid., vol. XVI (1823), p. 310, 319.
25 Ibid., p. 321.
26 Penn, *Comparative Estimate*, I: p. xxvi, 51, 140.
27 Ibid., I: p. xiv.
28 Ibid., I: p. lvii.
29 Ibid., I: p. 89.
30 Ibid., I: p. 329–330.
31 "Mineral Geology" was a term taken from Cuvier's *Ossemens Fossiles*. D'Aubuisson, following his teacher, Abraham Werner, called this part of mineralogy, "geognosy."

composing this Earth, and *the* MODE *of the changes* which those substances had subsequently undergone," i.e., the original creation and history of the earth.[32]

Penn argued that explaining the original creation (or first formation) of the earth (as a fully functioning habitat for biological life) by the existing laws of nature was a case of anti-Newtonian and anti-Baconian philosophizing. Because the old-earth geologists were wrong on this fundamental point, their old-earth interpretations of the changes of the earth since its first formation were suspect. He did not disallow all reasoning about the past secondary (physical) causes and time sequence of geological effects based on the observed processes of nature, for he himself did such reasoning in his objections to old-earth interpretations. Rather, he argued that mineral geology was as theory-laden (or presuppositionally loaded) as his Mosaic geology and that because the mineral geologists rejected the infallible historical framework of Genesis (what he saw as the true presuppositions for geology) their general interpretation of the geological record in terms of a great amount of time was fatally flawed, in spite of many accurate observations and interpretations of particular geological phenomena. Penn was convinced that this error was because mineral geology contained many notions from the ancient Greek atomic philosophy of chaos. As a view of earth history, Penn's "Mosaic geology" was an alternative to "mineral geology," not to the science of mineralogy. We will come back to this distinction shortly, for it is at the heart of Penn's argument.

The Relationship Between Scripture and Geology

The *DNB* article on Penn, probably following several of Penn's critics, says that he made "an unscientific attempt to treat the Book of Genesis as a manual of geology." But this is precisely what Penn disclaimed and his argument seems consistent with his stated intentions.

First, Penn argued that Genesis and geology ought to be connected because it was philosophically permissible, even necessary, to attempt to identify the God of Scripture with the God of nature, i.e., to show that they are one and the same God, as Scripture itself teaches. And since God had communicated certain historical facts about the original creation of the earth and the Flood, it would certainly not be prudent to disconnect them from the geological study of the surface of the earth. Rather, to trace the connection of Genesis to geology would be "of the first importance, in man's relation to God under *Divine Revelation*," as it would contribute to our confidence that Scripture is of divine origin, as we are sure that nature is.[33]

Conybeare and others contended that physical science only had a connection to natural religion, not revealed religion, i.e., science could help only to prove the existence and attributes of the author of nature from His works.[34]

Penn countered that the Christian already knew this from abundant and obvious physical evidence and that in light of Romans 1:18–20 the unbeliever had no excuse for not acknowledging this fact. The real problem, said Penn, was to show that the God of Scripture is the God of nature.[35] Penn objected to the assertion of Conybeare and other geologists that the study of Scripture and of geology should be dissociated because (as the old-earth geologists asserted) the professed object of revelation was to treat only the history of man.[36] Penn argued that Exodus 20:11 shows that God intended to impart to man special and particular historical knowledge about the origin of the celestial bodies and the plants and animals of land and sea, *before* He imparted a history of man's own origin. "The history of the origin and relations of all and each of these, is therefore as much *a professed object of Revelation*, as the history of the origin and relations of *Man himself.*"[37] Also, if, as Conybeare

32 Penn, *Comparative Estimate*, I: p. 17.
33 Ibid., I: p. xvi–xx.
34 See William D. Conybeare and William Phillips, *Outlines of the Geology of England and Wales* (1822), p. li.
35 Penn, *Comparative Estimate*, I: p. xxxi.
36 Conybeare and Phillips, *Outlines of the Geology of England and Wales*, p. l–li.
37 Penn, *Comparative Estimate*, I: p. xxiii.

admitted,[38] the dealings of divine providence in regard to man were a professed object of scriptural revelation, then a knowledge of the divine judgments at the Fall and the Flood would necessarily be encompassed in that object. But according to the Bible, these judgments had universal physical, as well as spiritual, effects on the earth. Therefore, what the Bible said about the origin, formation, and universal changes to the earth was a professed object of divine revelation.[39]

Penn insisted that the Bible did *not* include a *system* of physical truth, as Conybeare (and others) claimed that people such as Penn did believe.[40] To this accusation, Penn responded that these old-earth geologists argued:

> . . . as if no *physical* FACTS could be imparted to man by revelation without being accompanied, at the same time, with *a* SYSTEM *of physics*. No *system of physics*, is imparted to us; but, *fundamental physical facts* are most certainly imparted to us, in order that we may have a *secure and certain basis* on which to found the *system* which, by the due exercise of our intelligence, we may construct, and which could, otherwise, never have acquired any secure and certain basis at all. Our *reason* is, indeed, to work; but, it is set *right* in the first instance, that it might not necessarily work *wrong*. We have, therefore, *no physical system*, but, we have *grounding physical facts*. . . . those simple *grounding principles* which the Mosaical revelation alone either does or can supply . . . opening to us . . . the *true foundation* on which the *historical science of Geology* must ultimately rest.[41]

Penn repeatedly stressed that geology was different from other sciences in that it dealt with past history, rather than merely presently observable processes. Therefore, expertise in the study of the latter, was no guarantee of accuracy in the reconstruction of the former.

> What true comparison can be made, between the *measurement of present objects of sense* and the *recovery of past facts of history*? Because we can apply rules of arithmetic or mathematics to *present objects*, we are not *therefore* capacitated to recall *past events*. In the former case, we have the evidence of the truth *always with us*; in the latter, we must seek it *elsewhere*, for we can never find it in the *subject matter of our study*.[42]

He quoted with approval the opening remarks of the review of Buckland's *Reliquiae Diluvianae* in the *Quarterly Review:*

> The science, as it is perhaps improperly called, of *geology* (observes a recent learned Journalist) differs from all other sciences in one material respect. It contemplates, not only *what is*, but *what has been*. It embraces the *history* of our globe, as well as its *actual composition*; it endeavours to trace the succession of events which have preceded its present state; to ascertain, not only the changes which have taken place, but the *causes*, or, in other words, the *physical connexion* of those changes; and to determine the *order*, the *time*, and the *circumstances*, under which they were effected. The province of the *Geologist* resembles therefore in some respects that of the *Historian*: he must diligently *examine ancient documents*.[43]

The mineral geologists considered only the geological phenomena as the "documents" of

38 Conybeare and Phillips, *Outlines of the Geology of England and Wales*, p. l–li.

39 Penn, *Comparative Estimate*, I: p. xxiv-xxvi.

40 Conybeare and Phillips, *Outlines of the Geology of England and Wales*, p. l-li did not mention Penn by name but was clearly referring to scriptural geologists.

41 Penn, *Comparative Estimate*, I: p. xxvi–xxvii. In defining the Mosaical Geology on the basis of his detailed consideration of what Genesis teaches about the original creation, Penn re-emphasized this distinction in I: p. 160.

42 Ibid., I: p. 139–140.

43 Ibid., I: p. 7. The quote is from *Quarterly Review*, vol. XXIX (1823), p. 138.

history (from the "book of nature"), which were to be studied and interpreted to reconstruct the past. But Penn argued that these geologists developed faulty theories because they rejected or ignored the written historical documents, i.e., Genesis. The "documents" of the mineral geologist were really only the "monuments and medals" of the past.

> But, what could we make of *monuments* and *medals*, if it were not for the *auxiliary references of history?* The mineral geology has indeed a strong *tendency* to explore, inquire, and collect these relics of the globe's antiquity, in rich abundance; but, to *decipher them when collected*, far exceeds the bounds of its capacity, unless it associates to itself *another and a more authoritative geology*. It was wisely observed by Mr. Kirwan; that *"past geological facts* being of an *historical nature*, all attempts to deduce a complete knowledge of them *merely from their still subsisting consequences*, to the exclusion of unexceptionable *testimonies*, must be deemed as absurd, as that of deducing the history of Ancient Rome solely from the *medals* or other *monuments of antiquity* it still exhibits, or the scattered ruins of its empire, to the *exclusion of a Livy, a Sallust, or a Tacitus*." . . . It is evident to reason, that *certainty concerning a past fact* — such as is, the *mode* by which all material existences were *really first formed, or were really afterwards altered* — must be *historical certainty*: the subject, therefore, is no longer a subject for *philosophical* or *scientific induction*, but for *historical evidence*, it demands *a voucher competent to establish its truth*. Now, the *voucher* that could establish the *fact* respecting the *true mode of first formations*, must have been a *witness of that mode*; but, the *only witness* of the *mode of first formations or creations*, was the *Creator himself*.[44]

Genesis then gives us the Mosaical geology, the historical framework for understanding the monuments of the past. Within this framework, or "general elementary scheme," geologists have plenty of room to investigate and speculate. He wrote:

> Within the limits of this *General Elementary Scheme*, all *speculation* must be confined which would aspire to the quality of *sound Geology*; yet, vast is the field which it lays open, to exercise the intelligence and research of sober and philosophical *mineralogy* and *chemistry*. Upon this *legitimate ground*, those many valuable writers, who have either *incautiously lent their science* to uphold and propagate the vicious doctrine of a *chaotic geogony*,[45] or who have *too cautiously withheld their science* from exposing and refuting it, may geologise with full security; and, transferring their mineralogical superstructures from a *quick-sand* to a *rock*, may concur to promote that true advancement of *natural philosophy*, which Newton held, and demonstrated, to be inseparable from a proportionate advancement of the *moral*. They may thus, at length, succeed in perfecting a TRUE PHILOSOPHICAL GEOLOGY; which never can exist, *unless the* PRINCIPLE OF NEWTON *form the* FOUNDATION, *and the* RELATION OF MOSES, *the* WORKING-PLAN.[46]

Now the reason, said Penn, that many past attempts to interpret the fossils and rocks in the light of Scripture had failed, was not because theology had wrongly meddled in a foreign domain of study, but because either the theologians did not know physical science well enough or the physical philosophers had possessed an inadequate knowledge of the details recorded in the sacred history of the Bible, particularly Genesis. But these errors on both sides were fundamental to the question of the origin and subsequent changes of

44 Penn, *Comparative Estimate*, I: p. 150–152. He quoted from Richard Kirwan, *Geological Essays* (1799), p. 5.
45 This is the theory that the primitive earth was a chaotic mass of matter. We will consider Penn's objections to this later.
46 Penn, *Comparative Estimate*, II: p. 250.

the earth, because "the question at issue is a *compound question*; it is both *physical* and *historical*; for it seeks the *historical truth* of a *physical fact*."[47]

The Philosophical Foundation of *Comparative Estimate*

Volume I deals exclusively with the original creation, or "the mode of first formation," as Penn termed it. Volume II treats the changes to the earth since the first formation, focusing primarily on the Noachian deluge.

After an 80-page introduction in Volume I, in which Penn clarified the arguments in the book by responding to critics of his first edition, he then endeavored methodically to show that mineral geology was contradictory to the Newtonian and Baconian principles of philosophizing. This is the part which, Penn rightly said in his introduction, was ignored by his negative critics, but which was fundamental to his whole argument. So it is important to consider it carefully.

First, he argued that there are only two guides to interpreting the history of the earth reflected in the four geological divisions of the earth's surface (primary, transition, secondary, and tertiary): the Mosaic and mineral geologies. (See Table 1 on page 31.) These, he said, are mutually exclusive, even contradictory guides, for Mosaical geology rested on divine testimony about historical facts whereas mineral geology ignored this inspired scriptural account and constructed its history solely from geological phenomena and chemical and mechanical principles, as then understood. To determine which was true, Penn proposed the application of the test to which mineral geology always appealed, namely, the "reformed philosophy of Bacon and Newton."[48]

On the basis of quotes from D'Aubuisson, Penn carefully defined mineral geology in contradistinction to mineralogy (as noted above) and showed that it claimed to follow the inductive scientific method of Bacon and Newton in explaining how the earth was formed.[49] He reasoned that if mineral geology did not do well by the standard of Newton and Bacon in explaining the first formation of the earth, we would have justification for distrusting its history of the changes and revolutions that had occurred since that first formation.

Using seven pages of quotes from D'Aubuisson, Jameson, Cuvier, Kirwan, and Deluc he showed what the old-earth geologists (whether Huttonian or Wernerian) believed about the first formation of the earth: a once fluid chaotic mass (whether igneous or aqueous) was gradually formed into the present spherical earth with a crust of primitive crystalline rocks, solely by the laws of matter operating over long ages of time. This they claimed was a conclusion resulting from the methodical combination of observation, experimentation, and inductive logic based on proven principles of physics, as advocated by Newton and Bacon. But, quoting from Newton's *Opticks*,[50] Penn contended that this view of first formation was directly opposed to Newton. Newton believed that, by His great intelligence,

47 Ibid., II: p. 273–274.

48 Ibid., I: p. 16.

49 Unfortunately, for later students of this debate, Penn never dealt with the Baconian principle of the necessity of not unwisely confounding the two divine books (the book of creation and the book of Scripture), even though the passages from Bacon's writings, on which Penn concluded that Bacon believed in a literal six-day creation, were just a few pages before the passage about the two books. But likewise I have seen no evidence that the old-earth geologists ever dealt with the passages in Bacon, that Penn did. Compare points VI: p. 2, 5, 6, 8, and 16 in Bacon's *The Advancement of Learning* (1906), p. 40–47.

50 Penn, *Comparative Estimate*, I: p. 33. Adding emphasis, Penn accurately quoted Newton (*Opticks* [1704, 1931 reprint], p. 400, 402) as saying, "It seems probable to ME, that God *in the beginning* formed *matter* in solid, massy, hard, impenetrable, moveable particles, of *such sizes and figures, and with such other properties, and in such proportion to space, as most conduced to the end for which he formed them. All material things* seem to have been composed of the hard and solid particles above mentioned, *variously associated in the* FIRST CREATION *by the counsels of an* INTELLIGENT AGENT. For, it *became* HIM *who created them to set them in order*; and, if HE did so, it is *unphilosophical* to seek for any other origin of this world, *or to pretend that it might rise out of a* CHAOS *by the mere laws of Nature*; though, being *once formed*, it may *continue* by those laws for many ages." In this Newton appears to have changed in his thinking, a fact of which Penn was apparently and understandably unaware. In 1680, 24 years before Newton published *Opticks*, he did entertain the idea that the earth had formed from a chaos by gravity. See his letter to Thomas Burnet in H.W. Turnbull, editor, *The Correspondence of Isaac Newton*, Vol. II (1960), p. 332.

God initially formed the earth, immediately (i.e., miraculously) and perfectly, in a solid ellipsoidal condition suitable to the end for which it was formed (i.e., a habitation for life), and not as a chaotic mass which would evolve by the mere laws of nature to the intended end.

Penn illustrated this perceived contradiction between Newton and mineral geology by considering the spherical shape of the earth. Relying on both Newton's writings and Newton's expounder, Colin MacLaurin (1698–1746),[51] he argued that the old-earth geologists had actually misused Newton's *Principia Mathematica* to defend their notion of a once liquid globe. He contended that Newton merely *supposed* the once liquid state of the earth as a philosophical hypothesis in order to demonstrate something mathematically, but that Newton gave no evidence of believing that this supposition actually was a *geological fact*.[52]

The reason, Penn said, that mineral geology was in opposition to Newton was because these geologists did not carry their analysis and induction back as far as Newton had — to the investigation of the first formation (or creation, as Newton called it) of all matter in general in order to ascertain the most general cause. Quoting from Newton's *Opticks*, Penn contended that Newton attributed the existence and perfection of such things as the planetary systems and the bodies of animals to the wisdom and skill of an eternal Creator.[53] In other words, the three kingdoms of minerals, plants, and animals were originally formed by the same cause — the immediate or instantaneous acts of the supernatural Creator. In light of this Penn remarked:

> Newton's *rules of philosophizing* require that we should refer to the same common cause, all existences which share the same common properties; and, the *three kingdoms of matter*, share equally the same common properties of matter. But, besides sharing the same common properties of matter, they demonstrate a *community of system*; each existing with relation to the others, and having the *reason* of its own existence in *that relation*. . . . The *first formations* of each of which, must of necessity, that is, in philosophical consistency, be referred to the *same operating cause*, and to the *same mode of operation*. If *any one* of the three was originally formed *perfect for its end*, so also were they *all*.[54]

Penn proceeded to build up to the geological implications of this by considering the first formed, or created, animal matter (particularly focusing on the bones of the first man), and the first plants (focusing on the trunk of the first tree). From this discussion he proposed two principles of first formations of plant and animal matter. First, "those first formations of the Creating Agent *anticipated* by an *immediate* act, effects which were thenceforward to be produced only by a *gradual process*, of which He *then* established the laws."[55] In other words, the laws of nature did not begin to operate until after the initial creation; they were not the means of creation.

So if a bone of the first created man persisted and was found mingled with the bones of that man's descendants, the anatomist could not distinguish the

51 Colin MacLaurin, *Account of Sir Isaac Newton's Philosophical Discoveries* (1748).

52 Penn, *Comparative Estimate*, I: p. 40–49. Penn argued, "That he did not *suppose* that the earth had ever *really been fluid*, and that it had *settled itself by laws of matter* into its present figure; is proved, both by the *object* and *hypothetical form* of his proposition, and by his express ascription of its '*figure and properties*,' as of those of *all first formations*, to the intelligent counsels and creative act of God, *immediately*. His own words, were sufficient to have preserved his proposition from the perversion which it has experienced; for, he states it in different modes, by which his intention is cleared from all ambiguity. He does not only argue, '*if the Earth were fluid*,' etc.; but he also argues, '*if all circular diurnal motion were taken from the planets*,' etc.; '*if all matter were fluid*,' etc. That these were only different *hypothetical propositions*, employed to illustrate the same principle, is thus manifest to every capacity" (I: p. 44). Newton's statements are from his *Principia Mathematica*, Book III, Prop. 18, Theorem 16.

53 Ibid., I: p. 57–59; Isaac Newton, *Opticks* (1931), p. 402–403. Adding emphasis, Penn correctly quoted Newton as saying, "Such a wonderful uniformity in the *planetary system* must be the effect of *choice*; and *so must* the uniformity in the bodies of *animals* . . . these, and their instincts, can be the effect of nothing else than the *wisdom and skill of a powerful ever-living agent*."

54 Penn, *Comparative Estimate*, I: p. 64–65.

55 Ibid., I: p. 73.

created bone from the generated one, by the study of physical phenomena alone. Similarly, the botanist would be incapable of discriminating between a part of the trunk of the first tree and that of one of its generated offspring. This naturally led to Penn's second principle of first formations in the case of two of the three kingdoms of terrestrial matter (the plants and animals): "*sensible phenomena alone* cannot determine the mode of their formation, since the real mode was in direct contradiction to the apparent indications of the phenomena."[56]

Having established these points in relation to the plant and animal kingdom, Penn next made the connection to the mineral kingdom. As the first tree was not the result of a gradual process of lignification and the first bone was not the consequence of the presently observed process of ossification, so the first primitive rocks of the earth were not the product of precipitation (or fusion) and crystallization, as the physical phenomena alone would suggest to the observer. This reasoning applied equally to the two varieties of mineral geology: Neptunist (Wernerian) or Vulcanist (Huttonian).

> The *correspondence* and *correlation* of the *three subjects*, are pointed out by physical science itself in the passages which have just been quoted; for, *natural history* there points out the analogy of the *wood* in the vegetable structure, and *mineralogy* points out that of *primordial rock* in the mineral structure, with the *bone* in the animal structure. *Solidity* and *consistency*, therefore, are the *common properties* of all the *three*. To *produce that solidity and consistency*, which were as necessary for the surface which was *to sustain*, as for the bodies which were to *be sustained* by it, was equally the *end* of the formation of *each*; and, therefore, according to Newton's *second* rule, we are bound by reason to assign the *same identical cause* for the solidity and consistency of *each*. And it will then necessarily follow; that *primitive immediate crystallization*, can furnish no *data* for computing *time*, more than *primitive immediate ossification*, or *primitive immediate lignification*.[57]

So all of God's first creations in the mineral, plant, and animal kingdoms were made in *correspondence* with the laws of nature, which He inaugurated *immediately after* the original creation, in *anticipation* of the phenomena which would thereafter be produced only by those laws. Put more simply, the original plants, animals, and minerals were created supernaturally with characteristics like those things that were produced later by natural process, which God instituted at the end of the creation week.

But to the anticipated objection of the old-earth geologists that this would implicate God in the wilful deception of human students of His creation, Penn replied:

> Those *phenomena* cannot mislead, deceive, or seduce any òne, who faithfully and diligently exercises his moral and intellectual faculties by the rule which God has supplied for their governance; but, only those who neglect to exercise them by that rule. For, those very faculties, while they direct us to infer *universal first formation by the immediate act of God*, caution us, at the same time, *not to be misled by the phenomena which that act must necessarily have occasioned*. They warn us, that all *first formations* of the *material works* of God, must have received a *specific form* of their substance, and therefore, must have exhibited to the *visual* sense *specific characters*, even at the moment when they were first called from non-existence into being. Whether it were the first formed *bird*, or

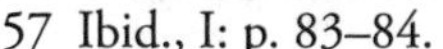

56 Ibid., I: p. 74. This was similar to how Philip Gosse, a biologist, would argue later in his *Omphalos* (1857), except that Gosse used such reasoning to suggest that, in addition to the first plants and animals, the fossils (along with the strata that enveloped them) were also supernaturally created by God (rather than being a result of post-creation processes and the Flood, as Penn argued, or a result of long ages of time before Adam, as old-earth geologists argued). This last suggestion of Gosse was fatal to his otherwise compelling argument about the original, created plants and animals.

57 Ibid., I: p. 83–84.

the first formed *shrub* on which that bird rested, or the first formed *rock* on which that shrub grew, each must have instantly exhibited *sensible phenomena*; the first, of *ossification*, the second, of *lignification*, and the third, of *crystallization*. Yet, the *phenomena* would not have been truly indicative of *actual* ossification and *actual* lignification in the two first cases; and therefore, they would not have been truly indicative of *actual* crystallization in the last; that is to say, of those subjects having actually passed through any of these *gradual processes*. There is no possibility of escaping from the demonstrative power of this *great principle*, which extends itself, equally, to *first formations* in all the *three* kingdoms of terrestrial matter.[58]

Penn insisted that those who rightly used their reasoning faculties would never be in danger of being deceived by primitive phenomena, (i.e., the initial creation) because by rational induction, following the example of Newton and Bacon, they would ascribe them to the supernatural plan and action of God.

In the last two chapters of Part I, on the philosophical problems with mineral geology, Penn raised his objections to the idea that the omniscient and omnipotent God created an initially imperfect chaos, which with time and only by the laws of nature operating as they do now became ordered and perfectly suited to life, especially man. In other words, he rejected the old-earth geologists' notion of the progressive evolution of the earth (an idea which he considered an ancient pagan view) and he objected for three reasons.

First, such reasoning could not be applied to the first creations in the other two kingdoms of matter, plant and animal. God would have created instantaneously perfect bone, perfect wood, so also a perfect rock. Not even the tender condition of nascent plants or animals under the present laws of generation is imperfect, but is a part of the sequence begun at the first perfect creation. At a time when most old-earth geologists firmly rejected the notion of biological evolution, Penn wrote:

> If the mineral geology could shew it to be *probable*, that the *first man* and the *first tree* subsisted at first an *"imperfect substance, which day by day was fashioned when as yet there was none of them,"* then indeed it might infer, with some consistency, "the comparatively *slow progression* of our planet, from a state of *chaos* to a state of *maturity*"; but, that it never can shew; and therefore, it can never draw the latter inference from the laws *now in operation in generated beings*, without renouncing all pretensions to the faculty of grounding or conducting a logical argument.[59]

Second, it was philosophically faulty to say that because every effect must have a cause, every sensible physical effect must have a physical secondary cause. Since the primitive granite rocks had never been observed in the process of forming, mineral geology was involved in very unsound philosophical reasoning to assume either an aqueous or volcanic cause.[60]

Third, in contrast to Bacon and Newton, mineral geology was tending toward atheism or the deification of nature, in its attempts to attribute the first formation of the earth to secondary physical causes. Although most mineral geologists at the time would have assumed that the intelligent First Cause immediately (ie., without the use of secondary causes) created the initial unordered matter, they attributed the present ordered state of

58 Ibid., I: p. 95–96.
59 Ibid., I: p. 107.
60 The origin of granite was at this time by no means certain among the old-earth geologists. The same year of Penn's second edition, 1825, the leading Scottish geologist, Robert Jameson, was still arguing in print for an aqueous origin of granite. See A. Hallam, *Great Geological Controversies* (1992), p. 22. Eight years later, and after much study of volcanoes, Lyell remarked in his *Principles of Geology* (1830-33), III: p. 11: "*Origin of primary rocks.* Nothing strictly analogous to these ancient formations can now be seen in the progress of formation on the habitable surface of the earth, nothing, at least, within the range of human observation."

matter to the laws of nature acting on that initially unordered chaos of matter over a very long time period before man. But God did not need vast ages to create the world suitable for life and man. So for the mineral geologists to say that He molded the earth into a mature habitation ready for man over the course of eons of time impugned the character of God.

> To assume arbitrarily, *a priori*, that God created the matter of this globe *in the most imperfect state to which the gross imagination of man can contrive to reduce it*, which it effectually does, by reducing the creative *Fiat* to the mere production of an *amorphous elementary mass*; and then to pretend, that His intelligence and wisdom are to be collected from certain hypothetical occult laws, by which *that mass worked itself into perfection of figure and arrangement after innumerable ages*; would tend to lessen our sense either of the divine *wisdom* or *power*, did not the supposition recoil with tremendous reaction upon the *supposers*, and convict them of the clumsiest irrationality. The supposition, is totally *arbitrary*; and not only arbitrary, *viciously* arbitrary; because, it is totally *unnecessary*, and therefore betrays a *vice of choice*. For, the laws of matter could not have *worked perfection* in the mass which the Creator is thus supposed to have formed *imperfect*, unless by a power imparted by *himself* who established the laws. And, if He could thus produce perfection *mediately*, through their operation, He could produce it *immediately*, without their operation. Why, then, wantonly and viciously, without a pretense of authority, *choose* the supposition of their mediation? It is entirely a decision of *choice and preference*, that is, of *the will*; for, *the reason* is no party in it, neither urging, suggesting, encouraging, or in any way aiding or abetting the decision, but, on the contrary, positively denying and condemning it. The *vast length of time*, which this sinistrous *choice* is necessarily obliged to call in for its own defense, could only be requisite to the Creator *for overcoming difficulties obstructing the perfecting process;* it therefore *chooses to suppose*, that He *created obstructions* in matter, to resist and retard the perfecting of the work which He designed; whilst at the same time he might have perfected it without any resistance at all, by *His own Creative act*. . . . To suppose then, *a priori*, and without the slightest motive prompted by *reason*, that His wisdom willed, at the same time, both the *formation* of a perfect work, and a series of resistances to *obstruct* and *delay* that perfect work, argues a gross defect of intelligence *somewhere*; either in the *Creator* or in the *supposer*; and I leave it to this science, to determine the *alternative*.[61]

Finally, in the summary to Volume I, Penn quoted Bacon's statement that the present laws of nature only commenced on the seventh day, after God had ceased from creating a perfect, fully functioning cosmos.[62] Convinced that these views of Bacon were just as much a part of Baconian natural philosophy as his beliefs about experimental and observational learning, Penn reasoned from his quotation of Bacon that:

> Bacon's philosophy, no less peremtorily denies all *chaotic formation*, together with all the undeterminable *periods of time* which it is obligated to postulate. He acknowledges no other agency, either in the act of *power* which *"created,"* or in the act of *wisdom* which *"disposed and adjusted"* this globe, than the hand of God himself: the former, in *"one moment of time,"* the latter, in *"six* natural and consecutive *days"*; and he could discern no sound, philosophical objection, to the admission of those facts.[63]

61 Penn, *Comparative Estimate*, I: p. 124–127
62 Ibid., I: p. 280–282. See my earlier discussion of Bacon's views which begins on page 21.
63 Ibid., I: p. 280–281.

So Penn argued (even as an old-earth proponent later did[64]) that the sensible phenomena of the earth, by themselves, with an understanding of the present laws of nature, could never lead us to the right conclusion about the mode of first formation of the earth, any more than they could with relation to the creation of the first animals or plants. In all three kingdoms of matter, the original creation was a perfect, immediate, and humanly incomprehensible work of God. This conclusion about the initial creation, Penn contended, was philosophically consistent with the principles of both Newton and Bacon, and was based on the divine revelation about the history of the early earth, which was relevant to the discussion because geology is a historical science.

Creation According to Scripture

In the second half of Volume 1, Penn proceeded to expound the mode of first formations of the earth according to the Mosaical geology, as laid out in Genesis. In a lengthy and detailed discussion of the six days of creation in Genesis 1, Penn began by reaffirming the fundamental principle, which he argued was consistent with Bacon and Newton, that the mode of the first formations in the three kingdoms of plants, animals, and minerals was by intelligent immediate acts of the Creator. These creative supernatural acts were antecedent to the laws of nature, which God set in operation for the perpetuation of the creation. And he reaffirmed the Genesis record as a reliable divine testimony of those historic events.

He also laid down two rules of proper interpretation of Genesis: 1) all of Genesis, including Genesis 1, is strictly historical, with no vestige of allegorical or figurative description, and 2) this history was adapted to the comprehension of the common man by the use of phenomenological language, so that Moses described "the *effects* of creation *optically*, or, *as they would have appeared to the eye*; and without any assignment of the *physical causes*." By describing effects accurately, "according to their sensible appearances," Moses enabled the reader "to receive *a clear and distinct impression of those appearances*, and thus to *reduce them to their proper causes*, and to draw from them *such conclusions as they are qualified to yield*."[65]

Penn took the "days" of Genesis 1 as literal 24-hour periods. Though expressing great respect for Faber's piety and giving general praise for Faber's *Treatise on the Patriarchal, Levitical and Christian Dispensations* (1823), Penn devoted a 24-page endnote in Volume I to a biblical refutation of Faber's day-age theory. To show that in the Bible *yom*, the Hebrew word translated "day," *only* meant an ordinary day, Penn carefully examined (apparently all) the Scriptures which Faber used to argue that *yom* could denote either one rotation of the earth on its axis, or one revolution of the earth around the sun, or 1,000 years, or an indefinite time period, or even the whole creation week. Penn concluded that the only reason Faber adopted his day-age interpretation was because of the pressure of old-earth geological theories.

To reject the gap theory, Penn argued, using support from ancient Jewish and Christian commentators, that the way the Hebrew conjunction is used at the beginning of Genesis 1:2 would not allow the insertion of long ages of time between verse 1 and verse 2. He also examined the key words *TOHU* and *BOHU* in Genesis 1:2 and showed from the Bible and ancient commentaries that these words meant "invisible" and "unfurnished" and therefore conveyed no sense of chaos or of time. Finally, he spent nearly 30 pages exposing the problems he saw with the interpretations of biblical scholars such as Horsley, Rosenmüller, and Patrick, who had tried to accommodate the theories about pre-Adamite creations or chaos.[66]

64 About 15 years later, the famous historian and philosopher of science, William Whewell, ironically came to the very same conclusions about the original creation compared to present-day physical processes, saying that "geology and astronomy are, of themselves, incapable of giving us any distinct and satisfactory account of the origin of the universe, or of its parts." See Whewell's *History of the Inductive Sciences* (1837), III: p. 687–688, as well as III: p. 580–587 and 620, and his *Philosophy of the Inductive Sciences* (1840), II: p. 134–135, 137, 145, and 157. More about this vitally important point at the end of the book.

65 Penn, *Comparative Estimate*, I: p. 162–163.

66 Ibid., I: p. 169–177, 189–205.

On a close examination of other particulars in Genesis 1:1–5, Penn argued that the earth was created instantly in its present spherical shape with a compact granite surface covered with and yet distinctly separated from a universal ocean of water, rather than of a muddy liquid. Penn believed that the sun, moon, planets, and stars were also created on day 1. The sun's heat immediately caused a universal vapor or fog, which blocked the sun, but not its light, from view on earth.[67]

On day 2, God created the atmosphere lifting the water vapor above it like a canopy, which yet obscured the sun's shape. On day 3, God caused by volcanic force, it seemed reasonable to Penn to assume, the sudden depression of part of the earth's underwater surface to instantly form the seabed and make dry land appear. This deepening of part of the earth's crust was a violent disruption, the first "revolution" of the earth, initiating the new laws and agencies of geological change and causing the surface of the newly formed seabed to be covered with fractured and comminuted materials and soils. This, in Penn's Mosaical geology, was the fragmentary, *transitional* formation (which later became known as the Cambrian-Silurian formations). Thus, the newly created earth was radically modified before the first plants were instantly and perfectly made in a mature condition later on day 3.[68]

On day 4, the canopy of vapor was dispelled so that the celestial bodies became visible on earth. Penn devoted a number of pages to explaining, on the basis of our knowledge of the solar and lunar movements, that the moon was created on the first day in the position of the new moon so that on the fourth day of creation it would be in the right place in the sky to rule the night as it was ordained. He also argued that it was unphilosophical to assign a different cause to the light of the first three days, than that source which caused light on the earth from day 4 onward. This then was another reason for saying the sun was created on day 1. Curiously, in his detailed analysis he did not discuss Genesis 1:16 at all, which other scriptural geologists and most commentators at the time took to mean that God had actually made the sun, moon, and stars on the fourth day. So in this case he was rather arbitrary in his literal interpretation.

The chapters on day 5 and day 6 were brief. Penn emphasized that the various marine, winged, and land creatures were made in fully mature form, just as the first formations of the vegetable and mineral kingdoms had been. He also devoted several pages to countering Saussure's notion of the insignificance of man. In his analysis of day 7, Penn reasoned that when God's creative activity ceased, the laws of nature commenced, by which God now providentially sustains His creation. He also remarked on the issue of time and calendars, with a rejection of the Julian day count developed in the 16th century by Scaligier.[69]

The Flood and Geological Changes Since the Creation

Volume II is devoted to a comparison of the views of the mineral and Mosaical geologies regarding the mode of the changes or revolutions of the earth since the initial creation. Penn argued that since he had established in Volume I the validity of the Mosaical geology and invalidity of the mineral geology with respect to first formations, it was also philosophically sound to compare these two geologies to the rest of the geological features of the earth to determine which theoretical framework best fits the actual observations of the earth. A comparison of Genesis to old-earth geological theory regarding the changes, or revolutions, on the earth since creation was all the more appropriate, in Penn's view, since in the previous few years D'Aubuisson, Cuvier, Dolomieu, Saussure, Pallas, and Deluc had all affirmed that geological evidence clearly proved that the last universal aqueous revolution had occurred at about the time set for the Flood by Scripture and pagan traditions.

Penn first began with a biblical argument that the Flood was universal, violently destroying the surface of the whole earth, not just mankind living on it. This was defended by a technical

67 Ibid., I: p. 182–185.

68 This revolution was viewed by Penn as an act of divine foreknowledge for this disrupted bed would become the base of the future lands of the post-Flood world. See ibid., II: p. 38–39, 172–173.

69 Scaligier set day 1 at Jan. 1, 4713 B.C. See Alexander Hellemans and Bryan Bunch, *Timetables of Science* (1988), p. 199.

discussion (of the Hebrew compared with ancient translations and commentaries) on the explicit statements to this effect in Genesis 3:14–17 and 6:13, coupled with 2 Peter 3:6–7 and Job 22:16. Though at the Fall the Curse in Genesis 3:17 affected the earth to such a degree that people at the time of Noah's birth recalled it (Gen. 5:29), the full consequences of that Curse were not felt until the Flood.

Just as the first revolution on day 3 of creation week suddenly produced the first habitation for man, so the second revolution suddenly resulted in a new earth. The main difference was that in the latter case the revolutionary alteration of the earth's surface transpired over the course of 12 months. To accomplish this destruction and renovation, God resumed immediate creation-type operations in the world, i.e., some of the laws of nature that commenced operation on day 7 were to some extent suspended or altered temporarily during the year of the Flood. As in the first revolution on day 3, God used global volcanic and earthquake activity (which in the Flood was also abetted by winds and 40 days of rains) to cause the eruption of violent inundations.

So, in Penn's view, the Flood was a preternatural event, not a part of the normal course of nature, as many old-earth geologists viewed it, though God used the forces of nature to accomplish His judgment. The ocean transgressed the land by the gradual sinking (over the course of five months) of the pre-Flood continent. During this process the sea was violently agitated until no land remained to cause the flux and reflux of the waters. Similarly, as the continent progressively subsided, the pre-Flood seabed was raised to become the new land.[70]

In light of all this, Penn argued, we ought to expect that the geological phenomena would show evidence of two distantly separated periods of global volcanic activity; that is, two, and only two, revolutions in earth history. Generally, the present continents should indicate that they had been under the ocean for a long time (roughly 1,600 years) and that those waters were removed from the earth at the time assigned by Moses for the Flood. Relying on the descriptions of geological phenomena given by the leading authorities, he sought to demonstrate how the four divisions of the geological record (see table 3 on following page) corresponded to the biblical history. The *primary* geological formations were created instantly on the first day of creation. The *transitional* formations were primarily the product of the first revolution, which occurred rapidly on day 3. The lower portion of the *secondary* formations with their marine plant and animal fossils (including the coal measures[71]) accumulated during the 1,600 years between creation and the Flood and remained largely in a soft state. The upper *secondary* with terrestrial plant and animal fossils and the *tertiary* were attributable to the year-long flood, which also carved the valleys systems.[72]

Having laid out his general theory about the Flood and earth history, Penn then proceeded to deal with the arguments that the old-earth geologists used to defend their notion of many revolutions before the creation of man.

To account for the order and complexity of the fossil record and the presence of tropical plants and animals buried in northern latitudes,

70 Penn clarified his meaning of "sudden" and "gradual" with these remarks on II: p. 36: "Mineral geologists, who acknowledge that the sea once covered our present continents, dispute whether its retreat was *sudden* or *gradual*. Sudden, and gradual, are relative terms; that which is sudden by one comparison, may be gradual by another. A retreat of the entire ocean, effected in the space of *twelve months*, will be a *sudden* operation, compared with that imperceptible mutation of its bed, proceeding through an unassignable number of *ages*, which has been engendered in the imagination of some visionary geologists; but, it will be *gradual*, compared with that immediate and instantaneous operation, by which the universal abyssal waters were originally reduced within the bed of the *primitive sea*."

71 Coal, he argued (II: p. 185–199), was produced from the deposition of marine vegetation, rather than transported land plants. He suggested that lignites, on the other hand, might be the result of terrestrial vegetation floated and eventually deposited during the Flood.

72 Penn was not completely clear on these divisions. He preferred the terms primitive (or creative), fragmentary, sedimentary and diluvial (or tertiary or upper secondary). See *Comparative Estimate*, I: p. 4 and II: p. 69–71, 150, 197, 287, 363. These terms for the various formations of the geological record were still in use in 1825 but were in the process of being replaced by different, soon-to-be standardized nomenclature.

Formations	Circa 1790
Alluvium	Post-diluvial
Glacial deposits	Diluvial
Sicilian strata	
Subappenine strata	TERTIARY
Persian strata	
Chalk	
Oolites	
Lias	
Muschelkalk New Red Sandstone	SECONDARY
Kupferschiefe	
Coal Measures	
Carboniferous (Mountain) Limestone	
Old Red Sandstone	
Wenlock Limestone	
"Grauwacke"	TRANSITION
Longmynd strata	
	PRIMARY
Scandinavian schists etc.	

TABLE 3 — This chart partially illustrates the division of the geological time scale. We have included the full chart on page 31. Based on Martin J.S. Rudwick, *The Meaning of Fossils* (Chicago, IL: University of Chicago Press, 1985), p. 213.

the mineral geologists postulated many revolutions and creations separated by long periods of time, a major climatic change in the past, and that fossil animals generally lived and died where they are buried. Penn rejected these ideas and instead attributed the strata containing the fossil remains of land animals to the Flood. He did this on the basis of a lengthy consideration[73] of "agents now acting generally on the surface of the globe:"[74] the movements of the waters in the present oceans.

Penn reasoned that since the Flood was relatively gradual and successive in covering the land over the course of several months, winds and currents would have produced advances and recessions of the sea relative to land. As we see in the present ocean, the retiring currents would retrograde as the next wave advanced against the land. Also, on a more global scale, there would have been massive and simultaneous fluxes and refluxes of the sea, such as the present equatorial current from Africa to America and the gulf stream from America to Europe. These currents during the Flood would have had the ability to carry debris long distances in a few days. Penn cited several recent examples of this kind of oceanic transport, such as plant debris from Mexico ending up on the shores of Norway, and a ship's mast being conveyed from Jamaica to Scotland. Postulating a different land-sea configuration before the Flood, he figured that whereas today the fluxes and refluxes of the sea predominate in easterly and westerly directions, during the Flood there would have been more of a north-south pattern, therefore bringing tropical creatures to the upper latitudes.

Penn reasoned that during the 40 days of rain at the beginning of the Flood the soils would have been supersaturated and easily eroded away with much plant and animal debris. Because the sea was agitated, the debris would not have been immediately buried but rather transported in masses in different directions and for various periods, depending on the durability of the creature and the power of the currents, before eventually being deposited.

He thought that the pre-Flood seabed was a "yielding paste of differing qualities, arenaceous,

73 Ibid., II: p. 81–123.
74 Ibid., II: p. 86.

argillaceous, or calcareous" into which the plants and animals were imbedded, and cited a modern example of the burial power of the sea in the mouth of the Amazon River at high tide. Cuvier objected that the bones did not show evidence of transport, such as being rolled and triturated or generally buried as whole skeletons. Penn responded that the animals would have entered the water whole and floated on the surface, only gradually becoming dismembered before deposition.

In Penn's view, successive tides would deposit new accumulations of the remains of both marine and land creatures. In the later stages of the Flood the violent retiring transient currents would have also cut the valleys of denudation while the sedimentary strata were still relatively soft.[75] Induration of the sediments was affected by the gravity of the mass and the rate of desiccation.

After this discussion of ocean currents during the Flood, Penn turned his attention to some other reasons that old-earth geologists believed there had been many revolutions before man. One was the lack of fossil humans in the sedimentary strata. Penn responded to this objection in two ways. First, as would be expected in Mosaical geology, this was because man, as the most intelligent creature, would have escaped the rising Flood longer than all the other creatures, and secondly, because the pre-Flood land on which man lived was now at the bottom of the oceans. Still, he conceded, some vestiges of pre-Flood man should be found in the fossil record. Though acknowledging that the famous human fossil found in Guadaloupe in 1812 was no longer convincing evidence, he argued in an eight-page endnote that the discovery of fossil remains in the Cave of Durfort, in France, reported in 1823 by Marcel de Serres, and the human fossils mixed with extinct creatures in the limestone of Köstritz, Germany, both of which formations appeared to be contemporary with the Kirkdale Cave deposits analyzed by Buckland, were strong fossil evidence of pre-Flood man.

Another problem was the extinction of so many creatures. Penn said that the mineral geologists were perplexed by this because they failed to combine morals with physics: the most probable physical cause of extinctions was the Flood, whereas the most probable moral cause was the will of the Creator. For some unknown purpose, Penn reasoned, God planned that only some of the pre-Flood animals should continue in the renovated world. Related to this was the mineral geologists' claim that existing species were never found buried with extinct ones, which therefore implied that they had not coexisted but that there had been many revolutions and creations. Penn challenged the universality of the claim that existing and extinct creatures were never mixed. But he also said that the order and complexity of the fossil record would be what he would expect from an agitated sea (during the Flood) gradually encroaching, with flux and reflux, over the various habitats of land and sea creatures.

To Penn's mind, this conception of the Flood would also explain the mixture and alternation of terrestrial and marine fossils. He argued that fresh-water and marine formations could not be determined by shells, as some old-earth opponents asserted, because the Flood would have easily mixed together freshwater and marine shells and because both Greenough and Humboldt had raised objections about the possibility of successfully distinguishing freshwater and marine shells.[76]

Penn believed that after the Flood, God supernaturally created new vegetation for the earth, since the seeds of pre-Flood terrestrial

75 Penn devoted a whole chapter (II: p. 159–184) to the formation of valleys, arguing that the present rivers running in them could not possibly have cut the valleys.

76 Ibid., II: p. 152. In an endnote (II: p. 371–393) Penn rejected Cuvier's interpretation of the Paris Basin as representing numerous revolutions. His reasons included 1) the difficulty of distinguishing freshwater and marine shells, 2) the fact that gypsum is generally a saltwater formation and Cuvier considered it to be a freshwater deposit on the basis of only a few shells, 3) Cuvier offered no cause for the repeated inundations of the sea and his notion of freshwater inundations seemed impossible, 4) Cuvier offered no explanation for the supposed multiple creations, 5) the insensible transitions (or conformity) between strata that have vastly different fossils, 6) some strata have commingled freshwater and marine shells, and finally, 7) the fact that Cuvier ignored the biblical record.

vegetation would most likely not have survived the nearly year-long Flood. And since fossil animal remains were so different from existing species and many animals were particularly suited to different continents, it was probable that new animals had been created. Furthermore, because "all" does not always have a universal meaning in the Bible, Noah only took some of the pre-Flood species on the ark. Those animals were to be for man's post-Flood food and to be a reminder of the Flood to man.[77]

Before drawing his discussion to a close, Penn remarked on the apparent contradiction of the idea of a global Flood with the description of paradise in Genesis 2:10–14, which mentions two post-Flood rivers — the Tigris and Euphrates. Without stating any justifications, he summarily rejected Deluc's way to resolve the problem, which Penn called a "gratuitous invention." Deluc reasoned that the rivers of paradise were erased from the earth by the Flood and the names were carried over by post-Flood man to attach to new rivers, just as immigrants to new lands often name new places with names of the homeland.[78] Instead, Penn gave a detailed textual argument for why these four verses should be treated as a scribal gloss added to Moses' original text.[79] While his argument was not convincing to some of his sympathetic readers,[80] it was based on sound principles of textual criticism and, in methodology, did not represent a cavalier approach to Scripture (which he considered to be the sacred Word of God), as was charged by some of his critics. He was simply trying to solve the apparent contradiction in Scripture.

Conclusion

Though not a geologist himself, Penn was not completely incompetent to propose his theory of Mosaical geology. He apparently made some geological field observations on the continent, and through careful reading he was well informed about old-earth geological theories and the geological and palaeontological evidence used to support them. He respectfully challenged the logic of the inferences and theoretical interpretations drawn from the geological observations, and legitimately, even if not always convincingly, used facts and arguments of some of his opponents against the reasoning of other old-earth geologists. However, he never argued that because there was disagreement between mineral geologists this proved they were all wrong.

While the mineral geologists were claiming to follow in the philosophical tradition of Bacon and Newton, Penn contended that in the matter of the initial creation and the history of the earth, they were actually contradicting these great philosophers. He argued that it was both Baconian and Newtonian to rely on the divine testimony about the original creation of the earth and the two revolutions since then (day 3 of creation week and the Flood). This, said Penn, was because of the uniquely historical nature of geology compared with other sciences at the time.

In his interpretation of Scripture he used his skills in biblical and literary criticism to build his case for a literal six-day creation about 6,000 years ago with two, and only two, global revolutions, on day 3 of creation week and at the Flood. These two revolutions, along with the work of the sea and its creatures over the approximately 1,600 intervening years, were sufficient to account for the geological record accumulated on the original supernaturally created primitive crust of the earth. However, he displayed some inconsistency in arguing for the literal interpretation of Genesis, while at the same time arguing that the sun was created on day 1, not day 4, and that only two of some, not all, of the kinds of pre-Flood animals were taken onto the ark. Also his treatment of

77 Ibid., II: p. 209–229. Though Penn argued for a global Flood (II: p. 7–19), he did not rely on the use of universal terms in Genesis 6–9 in support of this conclusion. So technically he was not inconsistent in arguing here that not all kinds of antediluvian animals were preserved in the ark. However, he also did not address the obvious exegetical difficulty this creates, and again he was being inconsistent with his general insistence that the text of Genesis should be carefully followed.

78 Ibid., II: p. 231.

79 Ibid., II: p. 231–243.

80 The otherwise positive review in *Eclectic Review*, n.s. vol. XIX (1823), p. 53, called it "ingenious and plausible," but proceeding "wholly upon the dangerous ground of conjecture."

Genesis 2:10–14 as a textual gloss was (and no doubt still is) unacceptable to many sympathetic readers.

Penn was apparently quite secure financially. Clearly, it was his convictions about the truth and authority of Scripture and his genuine interest in philosophically sound argumentation that compelled him to pick up his pen against the theories of the mineral geologists.

GEORGE BUGG (1769–1851)

George Bugg was probably born in 1769, the year he was baptized at the Anglican church in Stathern, Leicestershire. At the age of nine, his mother passed away, which was the first of several mournful experiences for Bugg. Beginning in 1786, he received a few years of private tutoring from Reverend Thomas Baxter, curate of Ufford, Northamptonshire. He was admitted to St. John's College, Cambridge, in May 1791 and received the B.A. degree four years later.

In July 1795 he was ordained deacon in York and became curate of Dewsbury, near Leeds, where he was made priest the same year and served until 1801. Subsequent curacies included Welby with Stoke in Leicestershire (1802), Kettering in Northamptonshire (1803–15), Lutterworth in Leicestershire (1817–18), and Desborough near Kettering (1831–45).[1] By March 1846 he had moved to Hull where he lived with his unmarried daughter Elizabeth and two teenage house servants until his death at home on August 15, 1851, at the age of 82.[2] Shortly before his death, and after a lifetime of ecclesiastic setbacks, he was finally made rector of Wilsford, Lincolnshire, in 1849, though he apparently never lived there.[3]

In 1804 he was married to Mary Ann Adams, daughter of a local prominent draper in Kettering. They had four daughters and one son

Unless otherwise indicated, this biographical section is based on the most extensive biographical material I could find: Rosemary Dunhill, "The Rev. George Bugg: The Fortunes of a 19th Century Curate," *Northamptonshire Past and Present*, vol. VIII, no. 1 (1983–84), p. 41–50.

1 During the years 1818 to 1831 he apparently lived in Lutterworth, though what he did with his time and how he maintained himself is unclear. He made some attempts to appeal his dismissal from his curacy in Lutterworth, but his Christian principles prevented him from going so far as to bring a case to court. See ibid., p. 46. During the first half of these years he clearly spent time reading, thinking, and writing about geology in preparation for the publication of his two-volume work in 1826–27.

2 Both servants were girls and were 18 and 19 years old respectively at the time of Bugg's death, according to the 1851 census return for Hull.

3 In addition to Dunhill, see also J.A. Venn, *Alumni Cantabrigensis* (1940), I: p. 437.

(who died at ten months old), and before Mary's premature death in 1815 she served with George in expanding Sunday school ministry and the work of the Church Missionary Society and the British and Foreign Bible Society. When she died, Bugg was left with the care of his daughters, who were all under the age of seven at the time.

He was brought to personal faith in Christ in his late teens or early twenties,[4] at which time he also apparently became convinced that "the Scriptures are strictly and literally true."[5] Every indication is that Bugg was a fervent evangelical Anglican all his life. His lifelong friend, Reverend Thomas Jones of Creaton, was a leading evangelical Anglican. Bugg was noted for his effective preaching and had good relations with and the respect of many non-conformist (i.e., non-Anglican) ministers. His two books on baptism and regeneration, written in 1816 and 1843, were refutations of the views of Dr. Richard Mant and Dr. Edward Pusey, respectively.[6] He considered the views on baptism of both Mant and Pusey to be virtually identical to the teaching of the Roman Catholic Church (that infant baptism is the means of salvation), and therefore a serious threat to the doctrine of justification by faith, a concern expressed by many evangelicals in the 1830s and 1840s as the Anglo-Catholic "Tractarian" movement spread within the Anglican Church.[7] In both treatises he was respectful toward his opponents, while strongly disagreeing with their views.[8]

Bugg's life was checkered with difficulties and controversies. Besides the death of loved ones and frequent struggles with illness, he was dismissed by two bishops from three of his curacies. In each case the dismissal appears to have been the result of a few prominent non-evangelical parishioners complaining to a liberal Bishop and involved vague charges with no opportunity for redress.[9] Never was he accused of any particular doctrinal error, moral misconduct, or ecclesiastical irresponsibility.

The anti-creationist Michael Roberts asserted, without documentation, that some time after Bugg's last dismissal (1812) he became a unitarian.[10] This was most definitely not the case, however, as noted by his close lifelong friendship with a leading evangelical Anglican, Reverend Thomas Jones. Certainly at the time Bugg wrote his massive two-volume *Scriptural Geology* (1826–27) he was a thoroughgoing Trinitarian, evidenced by two statements he made against Socinians, a unitarian sect.[11] Also, he was equally Trinitarian in his two books on baptism and regeneration, in 1816 and 1843 respectively.

4 George Bugg, *The Key to Modern Controversy* (1843), p. x. Here in 1843, as he refuted Pusey's tractarian views of baptismal regeneration, he said that he had more than 50 years of experiencing the life-changing effects of spiritual regeneration through repentance and faith in Christ.

5 George Bugg, *Scriptural Geology*, II: p. 351. Here, in 1827, he wrote (in probable reference to his conversion), "[I have] lived nearly 40 years under the full and firm belief that the Scriptures are strictly and literally true."

6 George Bugg, *Spiritual Regeneration, Not Necessarily Connected with Baptism* (1816) and *The Key to Modern Controversy, or the Baptismal Regeneration of the Established Church Explained and Justified.* Bugg's doctrine seems to be the same in both books. He had a very polemical style, though in the first he explicitly said that he was not attacking Mant personally, but only his erroneous doctrine (p. vi-vii, 171). On the other hand, in the second, Bugg considered Pusey to be a Romanist in disguise and a false prophet in the Anglican Church (p. vii-xi).

7 Peter Toon, *Evangelical Theology 1833–1856: A Response to Tractarianism* (Atlanta, GA: John Knox Press, 1979).

8 Bugg was also respectful in his response to a fellow Anglican, Reverend J. Cunningham, who in Bugg's view misrepresented both the debate and the debators (Bugg and Mant) on baptism. See George Bugg, *Friendly Remarks on the Rev. J. W. Cunninngham's Conciliatory Suggestions on the Subject of Regeneration* (1816).

9 Bugg's assessment of his dismissals received confirmation from the anonymous *The Curate's Appeal* (1819). This 177-page book went through a second edition the same year and a third appeared in 1820. It was penned "under the direction of a committee of clergymen, and is approved and sanctioned by an increasingly numerous body of divines, both incumbents and curates, but especially the former" (from the preface, p. iii). Although most library catalogs list this book as Bugg's work, Bugg clearly indicated in *Hard Measures* (1820), page 42, that it was written by others who were fully acquainted with and referred to his cases of dismissal.

10 Michael B. Roberts, "The Roots of Creationism," *Faith and Thought*, vol. 112, no. 1 (1986), p. 28. From personal conversation with Roberts on December 15, 1995, it is clear that he was led astray by the fact that a pamphlet entitled *Four Letters from a Unity Man* (1847) is listed in leading library catalogs with the other works by Reverend George Bugg. However, Roberts overlooked the fact that the anti-trinitarian author of these letters (also named George Bugg) was a farmer from Horbling, a town in which Reverend George Bugg never lived.

11 Bugg, *Scriptural Geology*, I: p. 78–79 and II: p. 333.

His other writings included a book of sermons (1817),[12] an account of a legal squabble Bugg had with the husband of a woman who before her death had willed that Bugg distribute some of her money to certain charities (1835),[13] and a pamphlet on the Anglican Prayer Book (1843).[14] By far, Bugg's most significant work was *Scriptural Geology*. Although the work appeared anonymously, a number of his readers knew he had written it and Bugg identified himself as the author in his correspondence with the *Christian Observer*, the leading evangelical magazine of the day.[15] Volume I (361 pages) appeared in 1826, but due to Bugg's poor health, Volume II (356 pages) was delayed until the following year. The work had 200 pre-publication subscribers, who included 85 clergymen, 15 members of the nobility, and 7 students at Cambridge University. Five of the clergymen were leading evangelical Anglicans: Charles Simeon (in Cambridge), Josiah Pratt (in London), William Marsh (in Colchester), Legh Richmond (in Turvey, and whose varied accomplishments included the study of mineralogy)[16] and Thomas Jones (in Creaton).[17]

The Relationship Between Scripture and Geology

Bugg held to the dominant view of evangelicals and high churchmen regarding the infallibility of the Scriptures, not just in matters of religion and morality, but also of history. He also believed that, at least with respect to Genesis, the "plain" and "obvious" literal meaning is the correct one.[18] He reasoned:

> I allow, as I before allowed, that sacred writers may be silent about science or even ignorant of it, without impeaching their infallibility as recorders of divine revelation. But whatever they do declare, and on whatever subject (as we before observed from Bishop Horsley) is certainly true. They were under divine and supernatural guidance, and therefore personal *ignorance* in the *writer* is no *defect;* and *error* is *impossible.*[19]

Therefore, when Bugg chose the title for his book, he was not asserting that the Bible teaches us the details of geology. Rather, on the basis of Genesis, Bugg was cautious not to give "any thing more than bare suggestions" about the geological effects of creation and the Flood, for "the scriptural data certainly afford a mere outline" of the events of the past.[20] It gives clues or the foundational principles for interpreting the geological phenomena.[21]

> Now, though we expect from the Bible, no *detail* of circumstances respecting what are the state and situation of the fossil strata, we have seen enough respecting the *cause* and OPERATIONS of the DELUGE to prove the real *ground* and *principle* upon which we account for the actually existing state of those strata.[22]

Bugg was quite emphatic that the Scriptures do not "establish any peculiar system of

12 George Bugg, *The Country Pastor* (1817).

13 George Bugg, *Plain Statement of an Unusual Case of Prosecution, Biggs v. Bugg* (1835). The problems with Mr. Biggs were solved out of court and Bugg does not appear to have been guilty of any wrongdoing in the handling of the money for Mrs. Biggs. See Rosemary Dunhill, "The Rev. George Bugg: The Fortunes of a 19th Century Curate," *Northamptonshire Past and Present*, Vol. VIII, No. 1 (1983–84), p. 47–48.

14 *The Book of Common Prayer: Its Baptismal Offices, Catechism, and Other Services Explained and Justified, in an Address to the Churchmen of Kettering and Its Neighbourhood* (1840). The work does not bear his name, but it is attributed to Bugg by the Northampton Central Library.

15 *Christian Observer*, vol. XXVIII (1828), p. 235–244. I could discover no reason why his book itself did not identify him as the author.

16 John H. Overton, *The English Church in the Nineteenth Century: 1800–1833* (1894), p. 52, 81, 86–87.

17 Rosemary Dunhill, "The Rev. George Bugg: The Fortunes of a 19th Century Curate," *Northamptonshire Past and Present*, vol. VIII, no. 1 (1983–84), p. 42.

18 Bugg, *Scriptural Geology*, I: p. 126, 173, and many other places.

19 Ibid., II: p. 352–353. He remarked on the infallibility of Scripture several other times (II: p. 20, 272, 351).

20 Ibid., II: p. 99.

21 Ibid., II: p. 348; *Christian Observer*, vol. XXVIII (1828), p. 430–431.

22 Bugg, *Scriptural Geology*, II: p. 349.

philosophy."[23] To the objection that "the Bible is not given to us to teach us geology," Bugg agreed, partially at least, depending on the meaning of the phrase. He contended that geology and the Bible both had legitimate and illegitimate provinces.

> THE BIBLE is certainly *not* given to teach us geology, as a SCIENCE. But it is given to teach us what nothing else can teach us — the *time* and *manner* of the world's creation. It is, moreover, given to inform us that the world has since been destroyed, and *why* it was destroyed. These "*two* events or epochs" are, when received in the light of Revelation of IMMENSE IMPORTANCE. The *one*, displays the *Being* and *natural* perfections of the Deity, or as the Psalmist and St. Paul have recorded it: "The glory of God," and "His eternal power and Godhead." The *other* exhibits him in his moral character, as the just and righteous Governor of the world.
>
> GEOLOGY, in its *modern* character, does not only fall short of both these grand objects, but in its obvious consequences, thwarts, if not destroys them *both*. For, as we have seen, it would merge OUR CREATION among the *geological* REVOLUTIONS, even among the *least* of them, and thus annihilate its CHARACTER. And as to the *time and manner* of the creation, it would make the *"Word of God"* to speak what is *unintelligible* or *erroneous*. With respect to the *other*, its obvious tendency is to diminish, if not subvert the MORAL causes which operated at the DELUGE. For it bewilders and leads away the mind of the beholder from the awful import of *that* catastrophe, by presenting to him indefinite numbers of such events. And it blunts the edge of his *moral feeling* by familiarizing him with the misery and destruction of the earth's inhabitants, so many times repeated, without any connexion of *offence*, with the *suffering beings*.
>
> It is the *province*, then, of *geology*, and not of the *Bible*, to afford us "any curious information as to the structure of the earth." But it is *not* the province of geology, as Mr. Sumner seems to think it is, to "speculate on the formation of the globe." The Bible does *not* "interfere with philosophical inquiry," or repress the researches of mankind." But it *does* forbid us to interfere with "the literal interpretations of terms in Scripture," when such interference would change the *character* of the *thing revealed*, and fritter down *the creation of the Bible* into "THAT *creation* which Moses records, and of which Adam and Eve were the first inhabitants"; and so make "the *Mosaic* account of creation" a mere *epoch* in the progress of *geology* from the *"primitive formations"* to the present times.[24]

Buckland, Sumner, and other old-earth proponents argued that the geological structure of the earth displayed God's wisdom and benevolence in preparing the earth for man. Again Bugg agreed. But it was not the *structure* (i.e., the geological facts) of the earth that was his concern. He objected that the old-earth geological *theory* about the *time and processes of the formation* of that structure was inconsistent with the nature of God. He asked, where is the wisdom, kindness, and justice of many revolutions on the earth before man sinned, which destroyed myriads of creatures? The Bible, on the other hand, taught that God had originally made a perfect, mature, productive, and fertile creation and that there was a holy and wise reason for the one destructive catastrophe, the Flood.

> Thus we see that, when compared with the *Scriptures*, the *modern geological theory* makes every thing unwise, unkind, and perhaps, unjust. It finds no original creation: and it cannot prove a first creation, from *"wise design."* For "primitive" rocks remaining thousands of years *alone* is unwise, because useless. And, dashing these to pieces, in order to mend them and make fresh ones, designates

23 Bugg, *Scriptural Geology*, I: p. 129.
24 Ibid., II: p. 39–41.

> either a want of wisdom in the primitive "design," or a failure in the attempt, and a want of experience and power to *execute* a wise one. But whoever predicates either of these on the Most High, "charges God foolishly." . . . That the location and *adaptation* of the strata to the use of man are wise and good, is fully admitted. But these are *facts*. That the *time and manner* of these formations, however, which the modern geological *theory* professes to develop, shew "wise foresight and benevolent intention," and exhibit "proofs of the most exalted attributes of the Creator," is, I believe, what few will have boldness enough to assert. Yet, if geologists would recommend their *science* (which involves their "theory" of formations), they must not only shew that there is wisdom and goodness manifested in the *formation* of the strata, but in their *theory* of that formation.[25]

On the basis of the scriptural account of creation and the Flood then, Bugg explicitly disavowed "all pretensions to a system of *operations and causes*, as well as classification and arrangement in the stratification."[26] He did believe, however, that the character of the Flood as described by the Bible would correspond with the leading features of the geological phenomena of the earth.[27] This correspondence he attempted to demonstrate, and we will consider it later.

Bugg was mindful that his critics would object that the insistence of binding geology to the Scriptures was a repetition of the mistakes of the Church at the time of Galileo. He replied that there was a significant difference: whereas Copernicus found no difficulty reconciling his theory with Scripture, modern geologists could not harmonize the Bible with their theories, without taking away from the Scriptures all legitimate meaning.[28] However, Bugg did not explain how he came to this conclusion about Copernicus.[29] To the charge that he was attempting, like the Catholic authorities of Galileo's day, to prevent all inquiry, Bugg countered that his two volume work was a "most minute inquiry into every part of the subject in dispute."[30]

Respecting the accommodation of the language of Scripture, Bugg contended that "the history of creation has one plain, obvious, and consistent meaning, throughout all the Word of God." The rest of Scripture offers no hint or key to any other meaning so that if the obvious meaning is not the true one, then the biblical authors have misled their readers and the creation narrative has no meaning, or a false one. Furthermore, argued Bugg, the phenomenological language that the Bible uses to describe the movement of the heavenly bodies is the common language used then as now. Otherwise, it would be intelligible to no one but astronomers. Also, it was foreign to the "office of the sacred writers" to teach the science of astronomy. However, although the Bible also was not intended to teach the science of geology, it did give detailed narratives of the creation and the Flood, which were critically relevant to the discussion of geological theories about earth history.[31]

The historicity of the Genesis account and the historical nature of geological theories were what Bugg repeatedly emphasized. He quoted with approval the words of the *Quarterly Review* of Buckland's *Reliquiae Diluvianae* (1823):

> That in an inquiry into the history of the world to reject the evidence of written records as wholly irrelevant and undeserving of attention, is in itself, *illogical* and *unphilosophical*. It is true that to assume these records to be infallible and above all criticism is to prejudge the question and to supersede all inquiry: but when the case is one of remote concern and full of difficulty, when we are compelled to compass

25 Ibid., II: p. 47–48.
26 Ibid., II: p. 57.
27 Ibid., II: p. 82–83.
28 Ibid., I: p. xii.
29 He cited no writings by Copernicus or others to support this view.
30 *Christian Observer*, vol. XXVIII (1828), p. 237.
31 Bugg, *Scriptural Geology*, I: p. xii–xiv.

sea and land for presumptive and circumstantial evidence, to turn a deaf ear to that Volume which professes to give a direct and detailed account of the whole transaction "is a great" violation of the laws of sound reasoning.[32]

He considered it to be most unphilosophical for the old-earth geologists and divines "to reason from the *operations* of nature to the *origin* of nature, for which they have no data."[33] At best, he argued in chapter 1 of Volume II, they theorized that the primitive mountains were formed out of a fluid. But they never explained the creation of the fluid. In fact, he contended, as they attempted to explain first formations solely by natural causes they were implying, sometimes no doubt unconsciously, an infinite series, which amounted to atheism.

> Thus then, we see with perfect certainty, that the OPERATIONS of nature afford us no data for a theory on first formations; and that it is not the *province* of philosophy, which is concerned only with the *operations of nature*, to speculate about the *time* or *manner* of the WORLD'S FIRST EXISTENCE.[34]

The questions of origins (how? and when?) could only be answered by revelation, said Bugg. "Its Divine Author alone, knows how He made the world; and His WORD therefore in this matter, is our only guide."[35]

Geological Competence

Bugg did not have (or claim) geological competence, but neither was he totally ignorant of geological facts and theories. At the end of his book, Bugg declared that he "sought no instruction (in theory or argument), but that of his Bible."[36] But this did not mean that he had read only the Bible. He admitted that he had little firsthand knowledge of geological phenomena and no skill as a practical geologist, but that he accepted the facts as described by the leading geologists, many of whose writings he had read.[37] His work, representing three to four years of study,[38] contains many lengthy, documented quotations from the current relevant books of such old-earth proponents as Buckland, Cuvier, Faber, Sumner, and Phillips and from relevant recent scientific journal articles. He also indicated that he had read at least some of the writings of prominent old-earth geologists on the European continent.

Geologists and Geology

One of Bugg's critics, "Oxoniensis Alter," complained that Bugg's whole book was an *ad hominem* argument.[39] The editor of the *Christian Observer* said that Bugg "had deviated from simple argument into criminations" and that he had accused Faber, Buckland, Sumner, and others of being perverters of Scripture and abettors of infidelity.[40] As Bugg focused his criticisms on the theories of Cuvier and Buckland, it is true that, because he concluded that their theories were unphilosophical, illogical, and contradicted by their own description of the facts, this reflected quite negatively on these two men and the divines and other geologists who followed their catastrophist theory. However, Bugg repeatedly and explicitly stated[41] that he was not accusing Cuvier, Buckland, Sumner, Faber, Conybeare, Phillips, etc., of evil motives (i.e., of intentionally trying to undermine Scripture by their theories).[42] He did, however, believe that many of the continental geologists did consciously intend to attack Scripture. He said that he had "the highest opinion of Mr. Buckland's

---

32 Ibid., I: p. 10. *Quarterly Review*, vol. XXIX (April 1823), p. 142–143.
33 Bugg, *Scriptural Geology*, I: p. 132.
34 Ibid., II: p. 12.
35 Ibid., II: p. 18.
36 Ibid., II: p. 351.
37 Ibid.; *Christian Observer*, vol. XXVIII (1828), p. 237.
38 Bugg, *Scriptural Geology*, II: p. 118.
39 *Christian Observer*, vol. XXVIII (1828), p. 312.
40 Ibid., p. 647.
41 Ibid., p. 433; Bugg, *Scriptural Geology*, I: p. xii, 17, 204; II: p. 307, 322, 330, 352.
42 Bugg, *Scriptural Geology*, II: p. 321.

integrity, and of Mr. Faber's and the *Christian Observer*'s sincerity."[43] But while their motives may have been commendable (i.e., to vindicate Scripture), Bugg was certain that the actual effect of the old-earth theory was nevertheless very detrimental to the Christian faith.

> I have been particularly cautious not to charge individuals (not even Baron Cuvier) with hostile designs against the Scriptures; but that he has propagated, and others have adopted, a system which is hostile to the Scriptures is the subject for discussion, and is not to be silenced by rebuke or censure.[44]

Several statements that Bugg made, if lifted out of the context of his whole argument, might lead us to think that he was opposed to the study of geology or denied the geological facts. For example, he said that the "modern inquiries into geology may justly lie under the imputation of being dangerous to religion" and he called geology an "insidious science."[45] But generally Bugg was most explicit in saying that what he opposed was the old-earth "theory" or "scheme" or "system" of geology, because he believed it was contrary to reason, the geological facts described by the geologists, and the plain meaning of Scripture. Contrary to the charge of his critics,[46] he emphatically stated that he did not deny the "physical facts" of geology, but opposed the old-earth theoretical interpretations of those facts.

> From an attentive consideration of their writings, it will be seen that Dr. Buckland and Mr. Faber, do much more than admit that the "physical facts" are true which geologists allege. They embrace the theories by which geologists account for the formation of those "physical phenomena," and from which they endeavor to prove, that numerous races of animals lived and died "on our globe during myriads of years before the formation of man." These theories are "inferences," or deductions, which geologists have drawn from their "physical facts." But these theories, inferences, or deductions, are not facts. They are conclusions which geologists assert to arise out of those facts. It is a fact that the "strata" are deposited in a certain form; it is a fact that "animal remains" are found embedded in the strata. These are facts, and, generally speaking, we may say these facts are true.[47]

Like Penn, Bugg went on to say that facts do not speak for themselves,[48] but must be interpreted, and that often the old-earth geologists were guilty of using language which ignored this distinction and therefore clouded the philosophical debate. He remarked:

> The subject now before us is, whether the Scriptures and the modern theory of geology agree. Not "geological PHENOMENA," as your correspondent has put it; but the geological theory. . . . It is an artifice unworthy of philosophy, to say nothing of divinity, to make, as writers on geology very often make, and as Oxoniensis Alter has made, geological *theories* synonymous with geological phenomena; thus bewildering the reader, and involving in the premises what remains to be proved in the process.[49]

43 Ibid., I: p. 56. The *Christian Observer*, though at this time not absolutely convinced of the day-age or gap theory, was clearly leaning toward the latter and did not like Bugg's strong criticisms of Buckland and Cuvier. From 1827 to 1829 it published a number of letters to the editor by Bugg and his anonymous opponents, none of whom gave any indication of being geologists.

44 *Christian Observer*, vol. XXVIII (1828), p. 242; Bugg, *Scriptural Geology*, II: p. 330. Regarding Bugg not questioning Buckland's motives, see also *Christian Observer*, vol. XXVIII (1828), p. 433.

45 Bugg, *Scriptural Geology*, I: p. 78, 83.

46 For example, see *Christian Observer*, vol. XXVII (1827), p. 738–740.

47 *Christian Observer*, vol. XXVIII (1828), p. 237–238. Similar remarks appear in his *Scriptural Geology*, I: p. 6–7; II: p. 304–305.

48 *Christian Observer*, vol. XXVIII (1828), p. 308–309.

49 Ibid., p. 242. Several times Bugg complained that the geologists merely assumed their theory was correct in spite of contrary geological evidence: *Scriptural Geology*, I: p. 259, 272; II: p. 311.

Bugg wrote with strong conviction about many things: for example, the historicity of Genesis, the infallible authority of Scripture, the global and violent nature of the Flood, and the literal meaning of the days of creation. But in his own theoretical attempts to harmonize the geological phenomena with the literal interpretation of the scriptural accounts of creation and the Flood, he explicitly expressed great caution. Examples included such matters as how the breaking of the fountains of the deep during the initial phase of the Flood would have caused faults, dips, and inclinations, how whirlpools in the tumultuous Flood collecting floating animal debris could have formed highly concentrated fossil graveyards, why tropical creatures are found buried in the strata of the northern latitudes, and how the vast pebble and gravel beds were formed.[50] In ending one such discussion he stated the following about the explanation he offered:

> . . . [this] is only suggested as a *probable* circumstance from the analogy of cases. On subjects where data are so imperfect, it were arrogant, not to say impious, to assume airs of importance and confident dictation. The whole of these suggestions may one day prove to be nothing more that mere speculations. However, as the whole seems natural, and, from present data, not improbable, I have thought I might be allowed to throw out the foregoing hints on points on which geologists speak with the fullest confidence.[51]

Creation and the Age of the Earth

Bugg believed in a literal six-day creation and a global Noachian flood that produced most of the fossiliferous strata. He clearly believed the earth was only about 6,000 years old, but he did not discuss the genealogies or the exact age of the earth.[52]

Though he was absolutely convinced of a recent creation and global Flood, he was not dogmatic about every point within this view. Besides the cautious geological speculations mentioned above, he was not dogmatic on each of his interpretations of Scripture. For example, he was undecided whether all the matter of the universe was created at once on the first day of creation and then was formed and organized during the six days, or was successively created over the course of those days.[53]

In defense of this view, he gave refutations of the day-age theory of Faber and the gap theory favored by Buckland and Sumner. Bugg argued that the day-age theory is proven false on several counts. First, in the period prior to the Flood, Cuvier's theory postulated many physical revolutions of the earth after the creation of plants and animals, whereas the Bible declares only one physical pre-Flood revolution,[54] on day 3 before the creation of plants. Second, the number and arrangement of the fossil remains of the supposed geological revolutions is inconsistent with the order of creation in Genesis. Bugg quoted Faber correctly as saying that the succession of organized fossils in the strata agree with "the precise order of the Mosaic narrative." But Bugg replied that a careful inquirer would see that this was obviously false.[55] That the order of Genesis 1 did not fit the order of the fossil record was a conclusion also embraced by most old-earth geologists at the time.

Bugg believed that the matter of the sun, moon, and stars was created at the beginning of the first day, but that they only became endowed with luminosity on day 4. "Day" is clearly literal in Genesis 1:14, where the heavenly bodies are said to be for the purpose of telling time. But there is no reason to think that "day" has any other meaning in the rest of the chapter, so all the days of creation must be literal.[56] To the objection that light from distant stars could not have

50 Bugg, *Scriptural Geology*, II: p. 99, 107, 128, 247, 287.
51 Ibid., II: p. 291
52 Ibid., II: p. 308–315, 332.
53 Ibid., I: p. 117–118.
54 He is speaking of revolution in terms of geological catastrophe of regional or global extent, not in terms of its movement around the sun.
55 Ibid., I: p. 48–59.
56 Ibid., I: p. 134–137.

reached the earth in only a few thousand years, Bugg replied that the distance to stars and the nature of the transmission of light were too imperfectly known to overthrow the clear statements of Scripture.[57] The day-age theory must also be rejected because it makes an absurdity of the biblical statements about the origin of the Sabbath (Gen. 2:1–3 and Exod. 20:8–11).[58] To the objection that too much happened on day 6 for it to be a literal day, Bugg replied that we are too ignorant of how many animals Adam named to say that he could not have done it in a few hours, which, if he did, would have left sufficient time for the other events assigned to that day.[59]

Bugg rejected the gap theory because, first, its notion of a long series of creation-revolution-creation-revolution reduced the biblical account of creation to virtually nothing. His opponents considered the biblical creation account to be a description only of the preparation of the earth's surface for the creation of man[60] and as such only related to a thin section of the total geological record, which itself was only a tiny fraction of the whole globe. Furthermore, the sedimentary rock formation which Cuvier attributed to the creation (which was just below the loam, clay, sand, and gravel attributed to the Flood) was not in any way a suitable preparation for man. In fact, contended Bugg, on the old-earth interpretation of the strata, the Flood would have a greater claim to being called a creation than the creation itself, because the geological results of the Flood were more suitable to plants, animals, and man than the geological effects which the old-earth proponents attributed to creation week.[61]

More general objections to old-earth interpretations of Genesis included the following. Bugg frequently referred to Exodus 20:11.[62] He argued that since this verse says that "In six days the Lord made the heavens, and the earth, and the sea and all that is in them," it must, especially when taken in conjunction with the second commandment and Moses' commentary on this passage in Deuteronomy 4:15–19, refer to the creation of the whole universe and all it contained (including man) at the end of the sixth day, and could not refer only to the refurbishing of the surface of the earth after thousands of ages before man. Also, since in the commandment the six days of God's creation week are linked to a week of literal days, the days of Genesis 1 must be literal. And since they were written directly by the hand of God they come with an added stamp of truth.

Furthermore, several verses expressly connect man with the beginning of creation, not long ages after the beginning (2 Pet. 3:4; Matt. 24:11; Mark 13:19; Isa. 45:6, 12, 18).[63] Buckland said that "the declaration of Scripture is positive and decisive in asserting the low antiquity of the human race" in comparison to the rest of the creation.[64] To this Bugg replied:

> There is not a word or an intimation given which implies that *man* is more modern than the *animals*. If therefore *this narrative* does not deny a *previous* state of

57 Ibid., I:p. 115–116.

58 Ibid., I: p. 150–151.

59 Ibid., I: p. 151–152. He also objected to what he considered to be the atheistic notion that Adam was a barbarian and that man has since advanced in perfection. Instead, Adam was created perfect with extensive wisdom, by which he named the animals, and man and the rest of nature with him have degenerated since the Fall. See also ibid., II: p. 315–316.

60 Buckland's words, correctly quoted by Bugg, were that "Moses confines the detail of his history to the preparation of this globe for the reception of the human race." See William Buckland, *Vindiciae Geologicae* (1820), p. 24.

A few years later, John Phillips remarked similarly, "The historic records of man's residence on the earth are, for most parts of the globe, utterly incomplete; so that, but for the Jewish Scriptures and other documents of eastern nations, we should be in danger of attributing to the human race an origin too recent by thousands of years. Now, as all historic records end, for each country, with the surface, terminate at some point of man's history posterior to the preparation of that tract for his residence, we see how far more ancient than the historic date of the human race is the series of productions which lie below the surface." See John Phillips, *Treatise on Geology* (1837), I: p. 10.

61 Bugg, *Scriptural Geology*, I: p. 26–29, 60–68.

62 Ibid., I: p. 29, 62, 103–107; II: p. 307; *Christian Observer*, vol. XXVIII (1828), p. 239–240.

63 Bugg, *Scriptural Geology*, I: p. 108–109.

64 Buckland, *Vindiciae Geologicae*, p. 23.

the earth, and previous races of *animals*, it does not *deny* the *previous existence* of *other* races of *human beings*. . . . If then the Scriptures are *positive* and *decisive*, and therefore *correct* in what they assert respecting the "low antiquity of the human race," they are equally decisive and correct in asserting the *low antiquity* of animals and fishes of "every race." And, therefore, the vast *antiquity* of the objects of *Geology* are fabulous and visionary.[65]

Furthermore, observed Bugg, in Scripture the heavens and the earth are always presented as being created (or destroyed) synchronously (Ps. 102:25–26; Isa. 51:6; Rev. 20:11 and 21:1; Matt. 24:31; Heb. 1:10–11; and 2 Pet. 3:5–7). Hebrews 11:3 clearly states that the earth was created out of nothing, not out of the wreck and ruins of a more ancient world (as Buckland asserted).[66] Bugg argued that the whole notion of a long series of revolutions causing animal extinctions before the creation and fall of man was contrary to the original perfection of creation as described in Genesis 1:31. He believed, on the basis of Genesis 1:29–30, that all the animals and man were originally herbivorous. Some animals became solely carnivores after the Fall and man was permitted to eat meat only after the Flood (Gen. 9:3). Whether the degeneration of animals into carnivorous habits was the result of a physical change or simply a change in dietary tastes, he was unsure.[67]

Bugg expressed his conviction many times that the old-earth theories denigrated the character of God, especially his wisdom, kindness, and justice.[68] To the idea of many creations and revolutions before the creation of man, who was to be the lord of creation under God, Bugg objected, "Where is the philosophy, the wisdom, yea the common sense in building, destroying, and rebuilding the *mansion* many times over, before its *Lord* is made to occupy it?"[69] To Bugg, such an idea was consistent with a Hindu, rather than Christian, concept of God:

Hence then, we have arrived at the wanton and wicked notion of the Hindoos, viz. that God has *"created and destroyed worlds as if in sport, again and again"!!* But will any Christian divine who regards his Bible, or will any philosopher who believes that the Almighty works no "superfluous miracles," and does nothing in vain, advocate the absurdity that a wise, just, and benevolent Deity has, "numerous" times, wrought miracles, and gone out of his usual way for the sole purpose of destroying whole generations of animals, that he might *create others* very like them, but yet differing a little from their predecessors!![70]

Bugg also complained that professing Christian old-earth geologists exhibited a very careless or superficial handling of Scripture, especially Genesis.[71]

Finally, Bugg objected to the old-earth theories (day-age and gap) because they involved creation by secondary causes, which was really no creation at all. This was because at this time Buckland believed that the successive formations of geological record on the surface of the earth (i.e., from the *primary* to *tertiary*) were the result of many violent convulsions subsequent to the original creation and that these convulsions were produced by secondary causes, superintended by God.[72] Bugg responded that since in this old-earth theory the six-day creation only related to the penultimate revolution, our creation was only part of a series resulting from secondary causes, which philosophers and theologians had always agreed were created causes. "But to speak of 'created

65 Bugg, *Scriptural Geology*, I: p. 142, 157.
66 Ibid., I: p. 109–112.
67 Ibid., I: p. 143–149.
68 Ibid., I: p. 109, 139; II: p. 43–48, 278–279.
69 Ibid., I: p. 142.
70 Ibid., I: p. 318–319.
71 Ibid., I: p. 40, 47, 71, 88; II: p. 322.
72 Buckland, *Vindiciae Geologicae*, p. 18–21.

causes' producing 'creation,' is a solecism in language, [which] reduces that creation to the class of second cause productions, and destroys the nature of creation." Such a view of creation was a revisitation of heathen atheistic notions of an infinite series.[73] Bugg wrote elsewhere about the initial creation of the earth:

> If our geologists therefore will reason from all we see and know to what is gone before, they must not and cannot stop at their "first mixture," for in truth there can be no first. Every stratum will come from a fluid mixture, and every fluid mixture from prior strata. So that in spite of all Mr. Buckland has said, in his Inaugural Lecture, to rescue *modern geologists* from the imputation of holding an *"infinite series"* of formations, the imputation can never be separated from the inevitable consequences of their doctrine.
>
> This theory, and the reasoning of its authors upon it, imply that every thing we see is the effect of some *natural* cause, and is also itself the effect of something else which is also natural. Thus the *origin* of matter is indirectly denied. For if we allow that matter did ever *begin* to exist, we have no data to assert in WHAT STATE it commenced its existence.
>
> If a man therefore asserts that he knows from the strata of a primitive rock *how* that rock was *originally formed*, that man, if he knows what his assertion implies, means to say that that rock arose from a *natural* or *material cause*. For with any other cause or its mode of operation, he has no acquaintance. Then he certainly means that its cause or the mode of its operation is familiar to him. This implies an infinite series, and that there is *no* cause of formations but this.
>
> Such an author ought to know, however he may slight the information, that he is treading upon ground which leads, and not very indirectly, to a denial of the God that made him![74]

If the biblical account of creation is rejected, then we have no account of creation of first formations, Bugg reasoned, for geologists have given nothing in its place.[75]

Bugg was insistent on arguing from analogy to present-day processes, when discussing post-creation history. In other words, apart from the divine miraculous interventions recorded in the Bible (of which one was the Flood), we should assume the uniformity of secondary causes.[76] But to make creation the result of secondary causes was to confuse creation and providence.

> Here then we find the *earth* and the *sea* created immediately by God. We find the earth and sea bringing forth and swarming with life. But the *immediate* and *sole parent* of *all* is *God*. The fishes are generated without spawn — the fowls without eggs — the vegetables without seed, or "a man to till the ground" — and animals, without progenitors. There is no "second cause." God MADE them. He made them out of the waters and earth it is true; but who will call these "second CAUSES." They are not causes at all. They are passive materials at most, and themselves just created by Jehovah.
>
> "And God blessed them, saying, be fruitful and multiply." Out of *this benediction* the earth is replenished.[77] "Second causes" are *henceforth* employed by the Almighty. He has formed a creation *"whose seed is in itself."* And we now know of neither fish, fowl, vegetable, or animal but what springs out of "their kind." Thus

73 Bugg, *Scriptural Geology*, I: p. 79–80, 113.

74 Bugg, *Scriptural Geology*, II: p. 10–11.

75 Ibid., I: p. 69–88, II: p. 1–18. The quote is on I: p. 79.

76 Ibid., II: p. 69–71; *Christian Observer*, vol. XXVIII (1828), p. 368, 429–431.

77 Bugg was using "replenish" as is found in the King James version of Genesis 1:28. Contrary to its use in modern English, "replenish" previously meant simply "fill," rather than "refill," and therefore it was an accurate translation of the Hebrew verb.

animals are generated; and their lives are sustained by food. God also made the "*sun* to rule the day," at the *same time.* It so continues. But *prior* to that arrangement, "second causes" cannot be found in *earth* or *heaven.*[78]

Related to this idea of uniformity of nature and miracles we should note that one of Bugg's frequent objections to Cuvier's and Buckland's theory was that to explain the fossil record they postulated a new creation of plants and animals after each revolution. Bugg found it extremely contradictory and unphilosophical that, in rejecting the biblical account of a miraculous creation and miracle-attending Flood, these old-earth geologists continually, though vaguely, invoked unknown and unspecified miracles to explain their revolutions and creations, while all the time insisting on explaining everything by natural causes.

Cuvier's whole argument about revolutions and different epochs was based on a view of species that allowed for very little biological variation, so that most fossil creatures must be extinct species unrelated to existing ones. In contrast, Bugg believed, as indicated in the above quotation, in the fixity of the original "kinds," but that great variation in size, shape, color, habits, diet, hairiness, etc. could be produced within those original kinds by natural causes such as climate change, population isolation, and different food supplies.[79] Such variation would be adequate to explain the relatively slight differences between existing species and their fossil counterparts. He succinctly summarized his view to the *Christian Observer* this way:

> The only difficulty which needs to be admitted is, the comparatively slight variations in the animal creation, between the fossil remains and the existing species; variations which surely it is no way unnatural to believe divine providence may have effected, by natural causes, in several thousand years. This, however, modern geologists deny; and have therefore invented their present theory. But the theory almost instantly runs into the very difficulty it is constructed to escape; namely, a deviation from the ordinary course of nature.[80]

Bugg did not believe there had been any extinction of the original kinds before or as a result of the Flood. And he doubted whether there had been any since the Flood, because to conclude this man must with certainty know about all the plants and animals now on the earth and must with certainty know that existing races did not arise from the fossil ones. But Bugg contended, man did not have such knowledge.[81] Furthermore, the notions of "genus" and "species" were human categories, and man had as yet insufficient knowledge to say whether his boundaries of classification were the same as the boundaries of nature. Certainly, the diversity of human races descended from Noah demonstrated how much variety there could be in a species.[82] Bugg also cited Cuvier's own statements about the variety of foxes in polar and tropical climates, all belonging to the same species.[83]

The Flood

Bugg argued from Scripture that the Flood waters advanced to their full height above the mountains in 40 days and then receded over the next 273 days, thereby rising seven times faster than they abated. Therefore, the initial stages of the Flood would have been very violent. The waters came from the torrential rains and the "fountains of the great deep," which he took to mean underground water, just as exists today.[84] He did not believe that the Flood significantly rearranged

78 Bugg, *Scriptural Geology*, I: p. 158.
79 Ibid., I: p. 219–227, 315–319; II: p. 24–25, 32–37, 275–302.
80 *Christian Observer*, vol. XXVIII (1828), p. 370.
81 Bugg, *Scriptural Geology*, II: p. 38, 71–72.
82 Ibid., II: p. 284–285.
83 Ibid., II: p. 299–301.
84 Ibid., I: p. 160–172.

the continents or mountain ranges,[85] though it did damage the mountains and deposit the *secondary* formations, by which he meant everything above the *primitive*, except for post-diluvial formations of recent occurrence.[86]

Bugg contended that the geologists dismissed the Flood as the cause of the geological record, because they failed to seriously take into account the violent nature of the Flood, especially the breaking up of the fountains of the deep, a worldwide aqueous and volcanic process, accompanied by earthquakes which elevated and shattered the crust over the subterranean waters (he never explained how such violent action could leave the continents and mountains basically in their antediluvian arrangement).

> From these irruptive fountains and descending cataracts of water we may, without fancy or theoretical pretensions, contemplate a scene most awful and tremendous. The waters would instantly, and from all quarters, descend to the low grounds. For we have no reason to suppose that *gravity* was suspended. These, meeting with waters boiling up from beneath the earth, would disturb each other, and form commotions. The *diluvium*, of whatever it might consist, whether of fragments of rocks, of soil and vegetables from the hills, and the loose or solid earth which the bursting forth of the waters would urge from beneath, would mingle and form unknown compounds. Stones and detritus, and whatever else might come in the way, would be dashed about, and rolled backwards and forwards in proportion to the impetuosity of the commotions occasioned by the issuing and falling waters.
>
> The amount of the wreck, or the extent to which the hilly contents would be mixed with those in the valleys, or from beneath, cannot be calculated. Nor can we say to what distances either laterally, longitudinally, or perpendicularly, any *current* formed by the *issuing* waters, under particular circumstances, might advance. Nor can we conjecture how great a quantity of rocks, stones, mud, detritus, small pebbles, or shells, such a mass of spouting waters, rushing with irresistible impetuosity, might force upon contiguous eminences, or deposit in the neighboring hollows.[87]

As the waters rose and conquered the land, they would have become less violent. The retiring waters, abating at one-seventh the speed back into underground cavities, would have been less violent than the rising waters. Such a year-long catastrophe would have produced far more than just the diluvial detritus assigned to it by Cuvier and Buckland.[88]

Bugg said that although the laws of nature (e.g., gravity, aqueous erosion and transport, sedimentation, and behavior of volcanoes) continued during the Flood, it was not a strictly natural event in the normal course of nature, as the old-earth geologists conceived it. The biblical text indicated that it was attended by some miracles, such as the collection of wild and tame animals for Noah, the breaking open of the fountains of the deep, the preservation and landing of the ark on a mountain instead of in a valley, and possibly the creation of new vegetation to recover the earth after the Flood.[89]

While he often expressed his caution in his geological speculations, he was convinced that, and attempted to explain generally how, the character of the Flood, which he inferred from the biblical account, would have produced most of the present physical features of the earth's surface, namely, both its regularity and irregularity of rock

85 He rejected Penn's notion that the sea and land had changed places during the Flood (ibid., II: p. 61, 68, 85–88). Because the Bible says the Flood covered all the mountains, he concluded that the Flood covered the 28,000-foot-high Himalayas.
86 Ibid., II: p. 84.
87 Ibid., II: p. 61–62.
88 Ibid., II: p. 63–66, 77–81.
89 Ibid., II: p. 69–71.

formations; the mixtures of mineral types; the distinct stratification; the denudation of valleys; the formation of lakes, gorges, basins and barriers; the faults, dips, and inclinations of the strata; the diluvial islands and trap rocks; and the fissures and fractures of the strata. Furthermore, he contended that Cuvier's and Buckland's theory of a number of revolutions during untold ages could not explain these features.[90]

Likewise, Bugg believed that the nature of the Flood explained the fossil record, whereas Cuvier's theory did not. For example, the Flood would be expected to have buried plants at all levels and to mix together land and marine animals and he cited evidence that this was the case.[91] He also quoted evidence from Jameson's appended notes to Cuvier's *Theory of the Earth* and Buckland's report of a recent discovery (in 1826) of an opossum found in the lower Oolite, well below the level it should have appeared according to Cuvier's theory. Added to this was evidence from Conybeare, Phillips, and Jameson showing that supposedly extinct shellfish and land animals were mixed in recent deposits with the remains of existing species, in contradiction to Cuvier's theory, but just exactly as the Flood would be expected to produce.[92]

On Human Fossils

At this time, all the old-earth geologists agreed that human fossils had never been found except in what they considered to be post-Flood deposits. This was stated to be positive proof that there had been many ages of creations and revolutions before man's creation. Bugg contested, however, that the absence of fossils in a formation did not prove the non-existence of man at the time of the creatures found in the formation. This was because the bones of *all* creatures that the old-earth theory said were contemporary were never found all buried together and the bones of modern animals contemporary with man were not only found in the alluvial formations where man was said to be found, but elsewhere also.

Bugg also asserted there was fossil evidence of man in the lower strata, but that Cuvier and other geologists had unjustifiably dismissed the evidence (of which he cited a few examples) because it militated against their theory.[93] In Bugg's mind, the best example of this rejection of evidence was the human fossil of Guadaloupe, found in 1805.[94] He concluded that this fossil did not support the old-earth catastrophist theory, but corresponded with the expected results of the Flood.

His Argument against Cuvier

Since, at the time Bugg wrote, Cuvier's catastrophist theory of the earth was dominant in geology, this is what he primarily criticized. Bugg argued that there were two propositions that needed to be proved in order for that theory of long ages of multiple revolutions to stand. First, "the physical operations in the strata which the assumed revolutions involve, must be consistent with 'physical and chemical science.' " Second, "the evidence of these revolutions arising from the strata and fossil remains, must be so regular, consistent, and uniform, as to admit of no reasonable objection."[95]

Before proceeding to analyze these propositions, Bugg insisted that we need to follow three rules in judging the evidence brought forward in favor of Cuvier's theory. First, to make generalizations from the strata about certain epochs of earth history, the strata must be distinct in character, be regularly and uniformly ordered with respect to the accompanying strata, and be general in extent, in order to prove general (i.e., global) revolutions. Second, if certain fossil species or genera are to prove the theory of the succession of different life forms in different epochs, then they must be universally distributed,[96] exclusive to the strata where

---

90 Bugg, *Scriptural Geology*, II: p. 88–108.

91 However, he did not attempt to explain the vast remains of plants in the form of the coal measures, concentrated in the lower part of the geological column.

92 Bugg, *Scriptural Geology*, II: p. 109–133.

93 Ibid., I: p. 265–270; II: p. 290.

94 Ibid., I: p. 282–312. Charles König, "On a Fossil Human Skeleton from Guadaloupe," *Philosophical Transactions*, vol. CIV, Part 1 (1814), p. 107–120.

95 Ibid., I: p. 181.

96 In other words, they should exist in every part of the world where animals exist and the strata to which they are peculiar are found.

they are found,[97] successive in the order of appearance,[98] and non-recurrent.[99]

Bugg's final axiom for evaluating the favorability of the evidence to Cuvier's theory pertained to the mode of ascertaining the arrangement of the rocks and fossils. Was it based on actual inspection and examination? Since no strata could be exhaustively examined in minute detail to determine what fossils it did and did not contain, probability was the best that the theory could hope to attain. But to attain a sufficiently high probability to vindicate the truthfulness of the theory, the area examined must have three characteristics.

> It must appear 1) that a space sufficiently large has been examined, to warrant a probable opinion respecting the rest, 2) that the parts examined correspond with the rest of the strata, so as to make them a fair specimen of the whole, and 3) that those parts accurately exhibit such phenomena, and such only as the theory requires. . . . For if the specimen by which we determine the rest, be itself refractory, how absurd to suppose that a general correct theory can be proved by an erroneous specimen![100]

Georges Cuvier (1768–1832)

Bugg devoted nearly one hundred pages of Volume I[101] to attempting to show, from the geologists' (mainly Cuvier's and Jameson's) own description of the geological facts, that Cuvier's *Theory of the Earth* failed the above tests fatally.

Regarding the space examined, Cuvier based his theory almost completely on his and Brongniart's investigations of the fossils and strata of the Paris basin.[102] By comparing the surface area of the Paris basin to that of the whole earth, Bugg calculated that Cuvier had only examined one twenty-thousandth of the earth — hardly sufficient to erect a theory of the whole earth. But then by comparing the depth of the Paris formation in comparison to the total stratigraphic record, Bugg concluded that Cuvier could have been familiar with only one twenty-millionth of the fossiliferous strata of the globe — again, objected Bugg, woefully inadequate as a basis for a global theory. Additionally, the Paris formation contained strata only above the chalk (i.e., in the *tertiary* formation) and so was not a fair representative specimen of the strata in general. Finally, as Bugg noted from the writings of geologists, in comparison to other studied basins above the chalk (i.e., under London and on the Isle of Wight off the south coast of England), the strata of the Paris basin did not agree in the number of strata, or their mineralogical content (e.g., Paris didn't have the London clay, London lacked the Paris coarse limestone, and both London and

97 In other words, they should not be intermixed with the remains of other animals which supposedly lived in another epoch.

98 In other words, the same sort of fossils should not be found in successive strata, but rather different species and genera should appear in different strata.

99 In other words, as we move up through the strata, lower fossils should not reappear in the upper strata, but rather new species and genera should appear after the extinction of the lower ones.

100 Bugg, *Scriptural Geology*, I: p. 187.

101 Ibid., I: p. 189–281.

102 Georges Cuvier, *Theory of the Earth* (1822, fourth edition), p. 177–178.

the Isle of Wight were void of the Paris gypsum). Therefore, Bugg concluded, the Paris basin absolutely fails as a specimen on which to build a general theory of the earth.[103]

Next, Bugg turned his attention to the fossil shells in the strata. He reminded his readers that Cuvier's essential principle in his theory was that the species and genera change with the strata (i.e., the animal nature changed with the chemical nature of the depositing fluid), so that species and genera gradually disappeared or became increasingly similar to living species, as one moves up through the strata from the most ancient to the most recent. Accurately quoting Jameson from the appendix to Cuvier's *Theory*, Bugg then argued that this was contrary to the geological facts. For example, two different mineralogical formations, the London clay and the Paris limestone, contained the same fossils. The four different fossiliferous strata of the *transition* formation, the lowest such strata in the geological record, in general all contained (in intermixed fashion) the same fossil species, which were very similar to living tropical species. He also quoted the article on "Organic Remains" from the *Edinburgh Encyclopaedia*[104] to the effect that many fossils appeared throughout many of the strata and that formations of the same mineralogical content in different places had different fossils. Finally, he quoted from Cuvier himself that the same species occurred in different strata, that many strata contained a mixture of land and sea creatures, and that shellfish species could not indicate more than one revolution because the slightest change in the chemistry or temperature of the water could change the species and there was at the time still a great ignorance of testaceous animals and fishes. These facts, Bugg charged, were fatal to Cuvier's theory. He believed this was precisely the reason that Cuvier abandoned shellfish as indicators of earth history and instead focused on fossil quadrupeds as the basis of his theory.[105]

Cuvier said that his whole theory depended on his ability to accurately identify and reconstruct a species of quadruped on the basis of a single fragment of bone.[106] But Bugg contested that even in Cuvier's own field of expertise he displayed the most fallacious reasoning. For example, Cuvier believed that carnivores would have the limbs for pursuing their prey, the jaws to devour it, the claws to seize and rip it, the teeth to cut and divide the flesh, the intestines to digest the flesh, etc.[107] "But," said Bugg, æeven a child knows that carnivorous dogs, wolves, and hyaenas have no such claws." Cuvier said that a cloven hoof footprint would be proof positive that the animal to which it belonged was a ruminant.[108] But Bugg cited Moses (Lev. 11:7) to remind his readers that pigs divide the hoof but do not chew the cud. He seriously questioned therefore why anyone should reject the biblical history to accept Cuvier's theory of revolutions in earth history, based on extinctions which he had inferred from his fossil reconstructions.[109] Very similar criticisms of Cuvier on this matter of his species reconstructions (even of a ruminant) from a single bone were made by John Fleming, an old-earth and tranquil Flood proponent and prominent Scottish zoologist. Like Bugg, Fleming cited the example of a pig to contest Cuvier's "silly gasconading."[110]

Bugg rejected Cuvier's argument for extinctions because of the imprecise definition of a species, the lack of knowledge of the whole world to declare positively an extinction, and Cuvier's too

103 Bugg, *Scriptural Geology*, I: p. 191–199.

104 I attempted to confirm the accuracy of this quote, but did not find the encyclopaedia to which Bugg referred. I presume it was the 1813 edition of the named text, as listed in the *National Union Catalogue*.

105 Bugg, *Scriptural Geology*, I: p. 200–211. Regarding the differences of the rock formations and the similarities of fossils seen in the London, Isle of Wight, and Paris formations, Lyell agreed with Jameson. See Charles Lyell, *Principles of Geology* (1830–33), III: p. 18–19.

106 Cuvier, *Theory of the Earth* (1822, fourth edition), p. 5.

107 Ibid., p. 90–91.

108 Ibid., p. 89–90.

109 Bugg, *Scriptural Geology*, I: p. 212–218.

110 John Fleming, "On the Value of the Evidence from the Animal Kingdom, Tending to Prove That the Arctic Regions Formerly Enjoyed a Milder Climate Than at Present," *Edinburgh New Philosophical Journal*, vol. VI (1829), p. 279–280, and "Additional Remarks on the Climate of the Arctic Regions, in Answer to Mr. Conybeare," *Edinburgh New Philosophical Journal*, vol. VIII (1830), p. 69–70.

limited view of variation within the created kinds. He concluded his discussion as follows:

> From all we have seen of the change in animals since the Deluge, it seems impossible that M. Cuvier can *prove* that a great portion of the fossil bones of animals which he has examined and pronounced extinct, might not vary so much as those vary from the bones of existing animals, by climate, food, and change of place, in the course of four or five thousand years. But upon the *proof* of this point the whole system hangs.
>
> Again. Analogy even from M. Cuvier's own pen is against himself. We remember with respect to *fishes*, how he stated that the species might easily be driven away, or even *changed*, only by the "temperature" of the water. What then should hinder the extreme variation of heat and cold on *land* from producing the same effect?
>
> But even were the globe to be drowned now, not the least evidence from analogy could be derived to M. Cuvier's system. For we find *different* animals in almost every country. Were *these* then to be imbedded where they are, it would be the highest possible absurdity for any naturalist who should examine a small space, like the Paris stone quarries, for instance, to pronounce upon the state of the *globe* from such a *specimen*.[111]

Continuing on, Bugg presented evidence, again largely from Cuvier's and Jameson's own statements, that the fossil quadrupeds in fact were not situated in the strata in a way that supported the notion of successive revolutions. First, he argued that the strata of the Paris basin were not distinct and well defined by Cuvier; that he often spoke in ambiguous terms about where the extinct genera, extinct species, and existing species were found. Nor were the strata regular in their situation relative to other strata and uniform or homogeneous in their composition. Neither were they all extensive enough to warrant the generalizations made. Finally, species were not always confined to one particular formation. Bugg argued that the evidence proved that all the strata of the Paris basin were of contemporaneous formation.[112]

Regarding the fossils, Cuvier's theory required that extinct genera were lower in the strata than extinct species, which were in turn lower than existing species and that these three kinds of fossils (extinct genera, extinct species, and existing species) were never intermixed.[113] Bugg argued that even one example would be fatal to this theory.[114] He cited Jameson's comments about an existing species of roe which had been found with an ancient genera (the palaeotheria) in limestone near Orleans, France.[115] Jameson said that Cuvier explained this anomaly by suggesting that the exact species of roe maybe is only discernable from parts that had not been discovered. Bugg replied:

> It is quite clear that this explanation is equally ruinous to modern geology, with the fact itself. For if this roe cannot be distinguished by the parts which have been discovered, the very pretense of all M. Cuvier's *science* — to discover a genus or distinguish a species by half a bone — is absurd; and he had no more claim to regard on the assumption of anatomical knowledge, than other men.[116]

Bugg then spent the next 15 pages documenting, often from Cuvier's and Jameson's writings, other examples of extinct species or genera intermixed with the fossil remains of existing species, all quite contrary to Cuvier's theory.[117]

111 Bugg, *Scriptural Geology*, I: p. 228–229.
112 Ibid., I: p. 232–253.
113 Cuvier, *Theory of the Earth* (1813), p. 109–111.
114 Bugg, *Scriptural Geology*, I: p. 255.
115 Cuvier, *Theory of the Earth* (1822, fourth edition), p. 374.
116 Bugg, *Scriptural Geology*, I: p. 257.
117 Similarly, in discussing the discovery of recent animal remains with ancient ones, the old-earth geologist Robert Bakewell said, "Such instances should lead us to receive the evidence from animal remains alone, with much caution." See Bakewell's, *Introduction to Geology* (1838), p. 406–407.

Finally, in his attempt to expose the contradictions and fatal weaknesses of Cuvier's theory, Bugg recorded Cuvier's own revealing admissions of his ignorance[118] (see this footnote) about the stratigraphic locations where his Paris fossils had been found and even the correct species identification of the fossils, the two critical factors on which his theory of successive epochs was built. After several long quotations from Cuvier, Bugg vehemently objected, using some of Cuvier's own words:

> This *"theory"* then, which is to establish a new philosophy and change the faith of Christians, is built upon *"vague and ambiguous accounts,"* not on knowledge *"personally"* acquired, respecting the situation of "fossil remains," but on the information of persons ignorant of the subject, and *"still more frequently"* upon no *"information whatever"*!!![119]

So, in summary of Bugg's argument against Cuvier, he contended that the area and depth of geological phenomena upon which Cuvier based his theory was too incredibly tiny to justify the grand generalizations about earth history which completely subverted the "plain teaching of Scripture." Furthermore, Cuvier's own admissions of ignorance about critical details related to the strata and fossils, which he did investigate, made his theoretical inferences exceedingly suspect, in Bugg's mind. Also, even in Cuvier's own book with Jameson's lengthy endnotes, Bugg saw abundant evidence of the complete fallacy of the theory: geological facts that refuted the theory, contradictions, and extremely faulty logic.[120] Finally, Cuvier invoked many miracles to explain revolutions and creations of the past, without any basis in scriptural revelation, while at the same time insisting on referring everything to the laws of nature.

118 Cuvier's words from his *Theory of the Earth* (1822, fourth edition), p. 111–113, which triggered Bugg's response, were as follows. "It must not, however, be thought that this classification of the various mineral repositories is as certain as that of the species, and that it has nearly the same character of demonstration. Many reasons might be assigned to shew that this could not be the case. All the determinations of the species have been made, either by means of the bones themselves, or from good figures; whereas it has been impossible for me personally to examine the places in which these bones were found. Indeed I have often been reduced to the necessity of satisfying myself with vague and ambiguous accounts, given by persons who did not know well what was necessary to be noticed; and I have still more frequently been unable to procure any information whatever on the subject.

"Secondly, these mineral repositories are subject to infinitely greater doubts in regard to their successive formations, than are the fossil bones respecting their arrangement and determination. The same formation may seem recent in those places where it happens to be superficial, and ancient where it has been covered over by succeeding formations. Ancient formations may have been transported into new situations by means of partial inundations, and may thus have covered over recent formations containing bones; they may have been carried over them by debris, so as to surround these recent bones, and may have mixed with them the productions of the ancient sea, which they previously contained. Anciently deposited bones may have been washed out from their original situations by the waters, and been afterwards enveloped in recent alluvial formations. And, lastly, recent bones may have fallen into the crevices and caverns of ancient rocks, where they may have been covered up by stalactites or other incrustations [*sic*]. In every individual instance, therefore, it becomes necessary to examine and appreciate all these circumstances, which might otherwise conceal the real origin of extraneous fossils; and it rarely happens that the people who found these fossil bones were aware of this necessity, and consequently the true characters of their repositories have almost always been overlooked or misunderstood.

"Thirdly, there are still some doubtful species of these fossil bones, which must occasion more or less uncertainty in the results of our researches, until they have been clearly ascertained. Thus the fossil bones of horses and buffaloes, which have been found along with those of elephants, have not hitherto presented sufficiently distinct specific characters; and such geologists as are disinclined to adopt the successive epochs which I have endeavored to establish in regard to fossil bones, may for many years draw from thence an argument against my system, so much the more convenient as it is contained in my own work."

Slightly reworded, these same admissions were made in 1831 in Cuvier's revised edition of his theory, which appeared as the introductory "Discourse" of the 4-volume *Researches on Fossil Bones* (1834, fourth edition), I: p. 68–69.

119 Bugg, *Scriptural Geology*, I: p. 276.

120 The justness of Bugg's criticisms may be indicated by Cuvier's opening remarks in the preface to his 1831 revision of his theory: "The first edition of this work, published in 1812, is nothing more than a collection of Memoirs published successively by the Author. . . . From this mode of publication, many of the chapters remained incomplete, others had been composed of various fragments written at different times and in contradiction with each other. It was not possible to arrange them all in a order sufficiently methodical." See Cuvier's *Researches on Fossil Bones* (1834, identical in this statement to the 1831 edition), I: p. 16.

An analysis of several chapters in Volume II would reveal that Bugg had very similar arguments against Buckland's interpretations of the fossils found in limestone caves, such as the famous one at Kirkdale.[121] In both cases, Bugg concluded that although Cuvier and Buckland attempted, with apparent sincerity, to defend the Flood, they in actuality did the opposite: by limiting its effects to a relatively insignificant part of the geological record, they denied it.

Bugg's book was totally ignored by the geologists at the time, particularly the clerical geologists, such as Buckland, Sedgwick, and Conybeare. His critics in the non-scientific journals were apparently all non-geologists.[122] The only "review" I could find in the scientific journals was a brief statement by "R.C.T."[123] to a reader, who, as "an Admirer of Buckland," was concerned about the impact of Bugg's book and wanted a geologist's response. This author declined to present any refutation of Bugg because "it is wasting words and time to combat with ignorance and prejudice."[124]

A number of facts raise doubts, however, whether this was the real reason for R.C.T.'s lack of critique. First, Bugg was making a biblical response to Buckland's and Cuvier's theories which openly purported to defend the biblical flood and recent creation of man. Therefore. Christian old-earth geologists should have been able and willing to bring biblical and geological arguments against Bugg's criticisms of the catastrophist theory that so many in the church were embracing.

Secondly, several prominent old-earth proponents were criticizing Cuvier's theory, sometimes with very similar arguments to Bugg's. For example, Constant Prevost, a leading French geologist, had opposed Cuvier's interpretation of the Paris basin since as early as 1809. Prevost argued that the marine and freshwater fossils did not depict a succession of alternating environments, but rather contemporaneous lateral deposits in a river-fed saltwater gulf.[125] Geologist John Phillips argued that Cuvier's theoretical conclusions only applied to limited districts, not to the whole earth.[126]

Uniformitarian Charles Lyell favored many of Prevost's interpretations of the Paris basin, and assigned the whole basin to one great epoch. He used some of the same objections to Cuvier's theory that Bugg raised.[127] William Whewell, a very prominent old-earth scientist and historian/philosopher of science, agreed with Bugg (probably unknowingly) when he wrote in 1837:

> We know that serious errors were incurred by the attempts made to identify the tertiary strata of other countries with those first studied in the Paris basin. Fancied points of resemblance, Mr. Lyell observes, were magnified into undue importance, and essential differences in mineral character and organic contacts were slurred over.[128]

And the old-earth zoologist John Fleming wrote a critical review of Cuvier's *Theory*.[129] He argued that Cuvier revealed a great ignorance of geological facts. Like Bugg, Fleming pointed out that Cuvier's and Jameson's stated facts about the location of fossil shells in the Paris basin contradicted Cuvier's

121 Bugg made no reference to the analyses of Buckland's interpretation of Kirkdale Cave done by Granville Penn or George Young.

122 For example, *Christian Remembrancer*, vol. VIII (1826), p. 530–532; *Christian Observer*, vol. XXVII (1827), p. 738–740; vol. XXVIII (1828), p. 98, 311–312, 628–631, 750–755; vol. XXIX (1829), p. 647–648.

123 This was probably the geologist Richard Cowling Taylor (a fellow of the London Geological Society, or FGS).

124 *Magazine of Natural History*, vol. II, no. 6 (1829), p. 108–109.

125 *DSB* on Prevost.

126 John Phillips, *Illustrations of the Geology of Yorkshire* (1829–36), I: p. 23.

127 Lyell, *Principles of Geology*, III: p. 240–256. Like Bugg, Lyell argued that 1) the lowest formation of strata attributed by Cuvier to be a freshwater deposit "is not only of very partial extent, but is by no means restricted to a fixed place in the series"; 2) in the great coarse limestone formation, marine, terrestrial, and freshwater shellfish species were mingled together; 3) in the gypsum and marl formations, the strata repeatedly alternated with a limestone, which in Cuvier's reckoning was placed below them, and 4) shells of the various freshwater formations from the lowest to the uppermost strata were virtually all the same species.

128 William Whewell, *History of the Inductive Sciences* (1837), Vol. III: p. 538.

129 *New Edinburgh Review*, vol. IV (April 1823), p. 381–398.

theory about the fossils changing with the strata. He also considered Cuvier's conclusions to be far too general given the skimpiness of the quadruped fossil evidence. Finally, like Bugg, Fleming felt that the area of the Paris basin was far too small to justly and safely erect a theory of the whole earth.

So then Bugg did make some very substantive criticisms of Cuvier's theory, contrary to the conclusion drawn by the *Christian Observer* that "all the scientific journals hold the same language, plainly stating, that the reason they do not answer Mr. Bugg's book, is, that there is nothing in it to answer; nothing really tangible and solid."[130] Clearly, something else was the cause of the silence.

Conclusion

Bugg was not opposed to the study of geology. For the most part, he accepted the geological facts as he argued against old-earth interpretations of those facts. Though he agreed with his opponents that the Bible was not a science textbook, Bugg was convinced that, since it was the infallible Word of God, it provided a general framework for interpreting geological phenomena and reconstructing earth history, and that within this outline of a recent creation and global flood (which he believed had produced most of the geological record) there was plenty of latitude for speculation about the details. By focusing on accepted geological facts and what appeared to him to be the old-earth geologists' logical contradictions, unproven assumptions (e.g., about the extent of variation within species), and invocation of unwarranted miracles (i.e., multiple creations), Bugg attempted to show that the old-earth catastrophist theory was fatally flawed. He engaged in this controversy, because he firmly believed that the authority and sound interpretation of the whole Bible, the gospel, and the spiritual and moral future of the nation would be undermined and the character of God slandered by the old-earth theory, regardless of the sincere intentions of its authors and defenders to the contrary.

Bugg clearly stated that he engaged in this debate because of his love for the truth.[131] He perceived there was a battle going on. But it was not science against religion. He had no antipathy to the pursuit of knowledge about the physical creation by the method of experimentation and observation. Rather, he saw it as a battle between the Christian faith and ancient heathen, atheistic ideas, which were being revived primarily by continental philosophers and were penetrating the Church.[132] This battle was really only a part of a long-standing strategy of Satan to undermine faith in the inspiration and infallible truth of Scripture, a battle especially intense in the minds of the young men training for ministry at British universities.[133]

Bugg further argued that the old-earth theory reduced the creation and Flood to very insignificant events (contrary to the biblical description), making them part of an indefinite series.[134] By ignoring and in effect rejecting the Fourth Commandment in Exodus 20:8–11 in order to introduce immense time into Genesis 1, old-earth proponents were also introducing a dangerous mysticism into Bible interpretation. The Mosaic narrative professed to be history, said Bugg, and to take it figuratively opens the rest of Scripture to such non-literal interpretation. Out the window then would go the doctrines of the temptation, the Fall, and the redemption of man, thereby destroying the gospel. Gone too would be the basis for keeping the Sabbath and worshiping the Creator, as well as obeying the rest of the Ten Commandments. Missions to the Hindus would also be undermined since their own view of earth history meshed well with the old-earth geological view of many revolutions over millions of years; so

130 *Christian Observer*, Vol. XXIX (1829): p. 648.

131 At the beginning of the work, he wrote that his "sole aim has been to elicit truth, and confront error" (Bugg, *Scriptural Geology*, I: p. xv). He concluded with these words about himself: "Truth he values above all things. But the truths of the Bible alone, have the keys of 'eternal life.' He will, therefore, esteem it his greatest honour and happiness, if, before he go to be judged by *that word*, he shall have done any thing which may tend to illustrate its truth, to unfold its correctness, or to shew its importance" (*Scriptural Geology*, II: p. 355).

132 Ibid., I: p. 113, 277; II: p. 310.

133 Ibid., I: p. 11; II: p. 344.

134 Ibid., I: p. 89–98.

they would not want to convert to belief in a book which they deemed less reliable than their own.[135]

Bugg was a bold preacher and contended firmly for what he believed all his life. His attempted defense of the gospel in his works on baptism and regeneration in opposition to the views of some leading clergymen, his efforts with other ministers to influence a change in the laws regarding the arbitrary dismissal of curates, his battle with an unspecified, but very debilitating illness,[136] the fact that he wrote the book in the face of expected opposition, and his own statement about being tolerant of other's views on "non-essential" but uncompromising on "fundamental doctrines"[137] (which he considered Genesis to involve), all would seem to indicate that this passion for truth, especially the truth of Scripture, was indeed his primary motivation for writing on geology.

135 Ibid., II: p. 328–329, 332–344; *Christian Observer*, vol. XXVIII (1828), p. 239–241.
136 Ibid., II: p. 353–354. Bugg said this illness increased during the writing of the book and at times brought the work to a complete halt with no hope of it resuming.
137 Bugg, *Friendly Remarks on the Rev. J.W. Cunningham's Conciliatory Suggestions on the Subject of Regeneration*, p. 46.

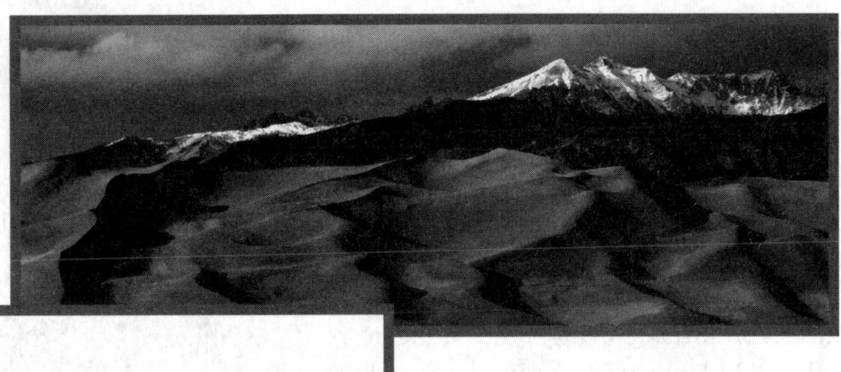

ANDREW URE (1778–1857)

Andrew Ure was born in Glasgow on May 18, 1778,[1] to Anne and Alexander Ure, a cheesemonger. He studied first at the University of Glasgow and later of Edinburgh, obtaining his M.A. in 1798–99 and his M.D. in Glasgow in 1801. After graduation, he served briefly as an army surgeon in the north of Scotland before settling in Glasgow, where he became a member of the Faculty of Physicians and Surgeons in 1803. The following year he replaced Dr. George Birkbeck as professor of natural philosophy (specializing in chemistry and physics) at the recently formed Andersonian Institution (now the University of Strathclyde) in Glasgow.

As well as successful teaching there, for about 20 years he also gave extremely popular evening lectures in chemistry and mechanics for artisans in the city. Attended by as many as 500 people, including up to 50 women, these courses were influential in the development of similar institutes in Edinburgh, Paris, London, and other cities.[2] Of this work, one contemporary wrote, "To Dr. Ure belongs the honor of having taken the lead in a movement which has had incalculable influence in developing national wealth, and promoting the interests both of science and art."[3] In these lectures he covered such topics as electricity, magnetism, heat, light, mechanics, hydrostatics and hydraulics, pneumatics, and astronomy. The lectures all

Unless otherwise noted, this biographical section is based on Copeman W.S.C., 1951. Andrew Ure, M.D., F.R.S. (1778–1857), *Proceedings of the Royal Society of Medicine*, Vol. 44 (1951), p. 655–662, and on W.V. Farrar, Andrew Ure, F.R.S., and the Philosophy of Manufactures, *Notes and Records of the Royal Society of London*, vol. 27, no. 2 (Feb. 1973), p. 199–324.

1 Anon., 1857, Ure's obituary, *Gentlemen's Magazine*, N.S. vol. II (1857), p. 243.

2 W.V. Farrar, "Andrew Ure, F.R.S., and the Philosophy of Manufactures," *Notes and Records of the Royal Society of London*, vol. 27, no. 2 (Feb. 1973), p. 300. Ure attributed this in some measure to the favorable report of his teaching the artisans which was given by Charles Dupin in his *Tour through Great Britain* (1817). The schools following Ure's model included the Edinburgh School of Arts, the Conservatory of Arts in Paris, and the Mechanics' Institutions in London and other cities. See Andrew Ure, *New System of Geology* (1829), p. xxxviii.

3 Ure's obituary, *Gentlemen's Magazine*, N.S. vol. II (1857), p. 242.

included physical experimental demonstrations, and so the course times were split between evening and morning lectures, since some experiments were best done by candlelight and others by daylight.[4]

Additionally, in 1814 he began lecturing during the summers at the Royal Belfast Academical Institution. Eventually, strained relationships with the management of the Andersonian Institution led to his resignation in 1830. He moved to London and became probably the first consulting chemist in Britain, which provided him with a comfortable living, but not great wealth. In 1834 he began to be used regularly as an analytical chemist by the Board of Customs, which did not pay him a salary, but only on a per-analysis basis.[5] In this capacity he demonstrated that he was willing to make financial sacrifices and to risk personal friendships and professional reputation for the sake of scientific truth and the exposure of large-scale criminal activity.[6] As a chemist, he was highly esteemed by contemporary scientists, and Michael Faraday said that not one of Ure's chemical analyses was ever impugned.[7]

ANDREW URE (1778–1857)

In 1809, after a trip to London to meet some of the appropriate leading scientists, he helped establish the Glasgow Observatory and was appointed its astronomer.[8] For several years he resided there, and during this time the famous astronomer William Herschel assisted him to install a 14-foot reflecting telescope, which Ure had designed and manufactured.[9] He was one of the original honorary fellows of the Geological Society of London shortly after it was founded in 1807, was an original member of the Astronomical Society, and became a fellow of the Royal Society in 1822.[10] He was also accepted into the membership of several foreign scientific bodies, such as the Philadelphia Academy of Natural Science and the Pharmacological Society

4 Andrew Ure, *Outlines of Natural or Experimental Philosophy* (1809). This short booklet described his lectures for those who would take the course. The topics covered reflect Ure's great breadth and depth of scientific knowledge gained by both reading and experimentation.

5 *Imperial Dictionary of Universal Biography* (1865), III: p. 857.

6 See Andrew Ure, *The Revenue in Jeopardy from Spurious Chemistry* (1843), especially p. iii, v, and 33. In order to serve the national interest, Ure consumed much time and money on these analyses. Such time and money could have generated more income if invested in non-government work.

7 For Michael Faraday's remarks, and a similar view expressed by E.D. Clark, see W.S.C. Copeman, "Andrew Ure, M.D., F.R.S. (1778–1857)," *Proceedings of the Royal Society of Medicine*, Vol. 44 (1951), p. 659–660. A review of Ure's *New System of Geology* in *Quarterly Journal of Science, Literature and Art*, N.S. vol. V (Jan.–Mar. 1829), p. 113, stated that Ure "has been long esteemed among men of science for his able and intrepid refutation of numerous errors current in some of our chemical systems." The review was possibly by the editor, William Brande, himself a chemistry professor at the Royal Institution, as well as a friend of Ure's. An obituary, in *Gentlemen's Magazine*, N.S. vol. II (1857), p. 243, likewise noted that Ure's "skill and accuracy as an analytical chemist were well-known."

8 Thomas H. Ward, *Men of the Reign* (1885), p. 904.

9 W.S.C. Copeman, "Andrew Ure, M.D., F.R.S. (1778–1857)," *Proceedings of the Royal Society of Medicine*, vol. 44 (1951), p. 658.

10 *DSB* and *DNB* articles on Ure.

of Northern Germany.[11] He wrote extensively throughout his life: seven books and more than 53 scientific journal articles.[12] The books included *A New Systematic Table of the Materia Medica* (1813),[13] *A Dictionary of Chemistry* (1821),[14] *Elements of the Art of Dyeing* (1824),[15] *A New System of Geology* (1829, 621 pages),[16] *The Philosophy of Manufactures* (1835, 480 pages),[17] *A Dictionary of Arts, Manufactures and Mines* (1839, 1,334 pages),[18] and *The Cotton Manufacture of Great Britain* (1836, 2 volumes).[19]

His journal articles primarily dealt with various chemical problems. But other topics included gravity, telescopes, a thermostat, methods of apartment heating and ventilation, gunpowder and detonating matches, thunder-rods, experiments on a human cadaver,[20] and four articles on light. A paper on the latent heat of vapors, published in 1817, was influential in the development of many modern meteorological theories. Many of these articles were republished by foreign scientific journals. He was also a linguist and a fair classical scholar, was well acquainted with English and foreign literature, and had read deeply in theology and biblical criticism. All in all he was "one of those brilliantly versatile men of science" in the early 19th century, who had an "encyclopaedic understanding" covering many subjects.[21]

His marriage to Catherine Monteath in 1807 lasted only 12 years until Andrew divorced her due to her adulterous relationship with Granville Pattison, the professor of anatomy at the Andersonian Institution. During those 12 years, however, the Ures had two sons and one daughter. His daughter married but also remained devoted to him, traveling with him to the continent several times later in life as he sought treatment at spas for what was then diagnosed as gout, which for

---

11 Andrew Ure, *Dictionary of Arts, Manufacturers and Mines* (1839), title page; Anonymous, *Dr. Andrew Ure: A Slight Sketch* (1874), p. 17–18. This anonymous work may have been by William Beattie, according to William A.S. Sarjeant, *Geologists and the History of Geology* (1980), III: p. 2310. Beattie was a Scottish medical doctor and possibly knew Ure from their early years at Edinburgh University.

12 *Catalogue of the Royal Society*. Farrar says there were many more journal articles than listed here. See W.V. Farrar, "Andrew Ure, F.R.S., and the Philosophy of Manufactures," *Notes and Records of the Royal Society of London*, vol. 27, no. 2 (Feb. 1973), p. 304.

13 Ure claimed that this was the first scientific book on pharmacology. See W.S.C. Copeman, "Andrew Ure, M.D., F.R.S. (1778–1857)," *Proceedings of the Royal Society of Medicine*, vol. 44 (1951), p. 658.

14 This was a virtual rewrite of William Nicholson's outdated work by the same title. Ure's version reached a fourth edition in 1835. French, German, Spanish, and Russian translations were also published. The 1841 American edition became and remained the standard chemistry textbook in the USA for many years. See ibid., p. 659.

15 This was a two-volume translation of the French work of Claude Louis and A.B. Berthollet.

16 As the focus of this study, hereafter it will be referred to simply as *Geology*.

17 This work was based on a tour Ure made of the manufacturing districts of Lancashire, Derbyshire, and Cheshire, and it embodied one of the first clear recognitions of the cultural impact of the "industrial revolution" (*DSB* on Ure). In it, Ure displayed a concern that factories be places where workers were well-paid, healthy, educated (in secular and Christian knowledge), and godly in character. He was especially concerned about good education for poor children. He was convinced, and presented some of the evidence that led him to that conviction, that British factories were generally doing well in these areas, though there was room for improvement. Most historians would say that he was overly optimistic about factory conditions. See, for example, Robin M. Reeve, *The Industrial Revolution 1750–1850* (London: University of London Press, 1971), especially pages 65–66 and 76.

A third edition of the book appeared in 1847, a posthumous edition came out in 1861, and a reprint was done in 1967. It was also translated into French and German. See W.S.C. Copeman, "Andrew Ure, M.D., F.R.S. (1778–1857)," *Proceedings of the Royal Society of Medicine*, vol. 44 (1951), p. 661.

18 This was a greatly broadened version of his *Dictionary of Chemistry*. See *DSB* on Ure. It went through several revisions and enlargements before the seventh four-volume edition appeared in 1875. It was translated into almost every European language, including Russian and Spanish. The vastness of research Ure put into it is reflected in the fact that the French translation involved 19 collaborators, all expert in their own specialized subjects. See W.S.C. Copeman, "Andrew Ure, M.D., F.R.S. (1778–1857)," *Proceedings of the Royal Society of Medicine*, vol. 44 (1951), p. 661.

19 This was the first and only work published in an intended series. A posthumous edition appeared in 1861 and a German translation came out in 1834.

20 This reported the results of his sensational public experiment on the electrically induced activation of the muscles of an executed murderer. The article was republished by three French journals, according to the *Royal Society Catalogue*.

21 W.S.C. Copeman, "Andrew Ure, M.D., F.R.S. (1778–1857)," *Proceedings of the Royal Society of Medicine*, vol. 44 (1951), p. 655–656.

many years affected the right side of his body after any physical exertion. On January 2, 1857, at the age of 78 and still maintaining mental sharpness, Ure died after a few days of illness.

Geological Competence

Although in 1805 Ure had visited all the principal mines in the United Kingdom,[22] he acknowledged that he did not write his book on the basis of original geological investigations. Rather, he endeavored to draw "freely from every authentic source of geological knowledge within his reach"[23] and his writings show wide reading in geology books and pertinent articles in leading British and foreign scientific journals. Though his intention was "careful merely to quote his authorities, and to acknowledge his obligations" and generally he did mention a person's name when using their material (which was usually set in a different print type), he could have avoided one criticism of his work by footnoting the actual sources far more often than he did. He specifically expressed his considerable debt to Conybeare and Phillips' *Outlines of the Geology of England and Wales*, though he also "diligently availed himself" of the valuable information in Cuvier's *Ossemens Fossiles*.[24]

Apart from reading, he collected some fossils and did a number of chemical analyses of the composition of various kinds of rocks.[25] Also, with relevance to a theory of earth history, he had very good meteorological knowledge, which he brought to bear on his discussions of the initial creation, the Flood, and the distribution of plants and animals.[26]

As far as his reading of other scriptural geologists is concerned, he made a negative comment about the cosmology of Kirwan and referred positively to Hutchinson's and Catcott's views on valleys of denudation. In defense of a global Noachian flood he said that Penn's *Mineral and Mosaic Geologies* merited "the deepest reverence," though he disagreed with Penn's estimate of the ratio of antediluvian land and sea.[27] He did not give any evidence of having read the works of George Young or George Bugg.[28]

Geology and Geologists

Ure wrote his book for the expressed purpose of promoting the study of geology, that "magnificent field of knowledge."[29] He was very charitable and respectful in his comments about geologists. Conybeare's and Phillips' work was "excellent" and of "inestimable" value, William Smith's work on using fossils to identify strata was "admirable," Von Buch was "second to none in mountain geology," and Scrope and Daubeny had done "ingenious" work on volcanoes.[30] Similar remarks were made of the sagacious work of Buckland, Lyell, Murchison, and other geologists in the United Kingdom and in Europe. There is absolutely no basis in Ure's book for Lyell's charge that Ure wanted all the old-earth geologists "to be burnt [at the stake] at Smithfield."[31]

As far as geological theory was concerned Ure made a strong effort to avoid dogmatism.

---

22 W.V. Farrar, "Andrew Ure, F.R.S., and the Philosophy of Manufactures," *Notes and Records of the Royal Society of London*, vol. 27, no. 2 (Feb. 1973), p. 303.

23 Andrew Ure, *Geology* (1829), p. vii.

24 Ibid., p. vii–viii.

25 Ibid., p. 618, 89–90 (here he gives a quantitative description of the make-up of the major kinds of rock found in the primitive crustal rocks), and 165 (where he said that "I have examined with great care many specimens of coals of the purest quality").

26 Ibid., p. 55–71, 481–499. In this he relied heavily on the *Meteorological Essays* (1823) of John Daniell, the leading scientist in this field at the time. Daniell was one of those influenced by Ure's 1817 journal article on the latent heat of vapor, mentioned above. See Anonymous, *Dr. Andrew Ure: A Slight Sketch*, p. 8.

27 Ure, *Geology*, p. xiv, 366–367, 470, 481.

28 The lack of reference to Young is noteworthy in light of the facts that both were Scottish, both attended Edinburgh University, and Ure, like Young, gave considerable space to a discussion of the Kirkdale Cave (ibid., p. 567–580). However, contrary to Young, Ure favored Buckland's interpretation that it had been an antediluvian hyena den.

29 Ibid., p. 616.

30 Ibid., p. 290, vii, 153, 480, 377.

31 Lyell wrote this comment about Ure in a letter to his sister just prior to the publication of Ure's book. See K.M. Lyell, *Life, Letters and Journals of Sir Charles Lyell, Bart.* (1881), I: p. 238.

> However momentous the interests involved in this inquiry may be, it demands, however, the utmost delicacy and circumspection. Every approach to controversial acrimony should be deprecated. The advocates of religion do not always bear in mind that compassion is the only feeling which they are allowed to entertain towards those who unhappily want the faith essential to salvation. The more violent their rejection of the Christian doctrine, the more gentle should its teachers be in addressing unbelievers. Dogmatic virulence never made a convert.[32]

At several points in his argument Ure displayed caution in his theoretical speculations and calmly presented his reasons for favoring one interpretation of the scientific observations over another.[33] He closed his book by saying:

> In concluding my survey of the primeval world, while I readily acknowledge that many of my views are but partially developed, or faintly shadowed forth, and that some of them may want confirmation, yet I trust that the accordances brought out between scientific induction, and sacred history, are neither fanciful, nor over-strained.[34]

E.L. Scott accuses Ure of an "air of conscious superiority" and "intemperate scorn for his contemporaries and the self-aggrandizement that characterized much of his writing."[35] Farrar repeatedly criticizes Ure, saying that he "seldom expressed himself in calm and moderate terms" but rather used "intemperate polemics" against others.[36] But these portrayals seem to be very exaggerated generalizations in light of Ure's above remarks and the fact that his surviving correspondence shows that he enjoyed good relations with

---

32 Ure, *Geology*, p. xiii.

33 In discussing the primitive atmosphere he stated, "On a subject so transcendent and mysterious as the state of the new born atmosphere, it becomes not man to dogmatize. It is, therefore in perfect humility, that I offer the following suggestions" (ibid., p. 69). Of the primeval ocean and its relation to land he wrote, "In attempting to search into the secondary causes which may have been called into action, when the channel of the sea was hollowed out, and the mountains were upheaved from the abyss, it behooves us to walk with the most humble circumspection. . . . The reproach of presumption will indeed be incurred, if we do not travel closely to the inductive path. We must, above all, beware lest we be misled by vague analogy" (ibid., p. 73). He was also restrained in his remarks about the origin and nature of coal (ibid., p. 163–174), the origin of valleys (ibid., p. 355–357), and the restructuring of the earth during the Flood (ibid., p. 437–348).

34 Ibid., p. 615.

35 *DSB* on Ure, p. 547. Scott wrote the *DSB* article on Ure. Scott also said that Ure wrote "a series of tendentious pamphlets, in which his fellow scientists were frequently castigated." But Scott cited no sources to support this assertion and I could find no such pamphlets in any library catalog or reference made to them by any other primary or secondary sources which Scott did provide.

36 W.V. Farrar, "Andrew Ure, F.R.S., and the Philosophy of Manufactures," *Notes and Records of the Royal Society of London*, vol. 27, no. 2 (Feb. 1973), p. 301 and 306. Farrar made many critical remarks about Ure's character, but more often than not they were assertions without documentation. Several of Farrar's negative assertions, that I was able to check for accuracy, proved to be inaccurate.

For example, in discussing Ure's *Philosophy of Manufactures* (1835) Farrar (p. 318) accused Ure of asserting that working at 150°F was not unhealthy. In fact, Ure never made such a general statement but instead described (on pages 392–393) one particular case of women, called "stove girls," whose job was to supervise the drying of wet dyed cloth in very hot rooms, which they were in for only a few minutes at a time. This was an enviable job among women in the factory and all such stove girls in the factories observed appeared to be in perfect health. On page 316, Farrar said that Ure's last chapter on the commercial economy of the factory system was "a diatribe" in favor of free trade. However, although Ure clearly favored free trade, the tone of the chapter is calm and respectful, not bitterly critical of all other views of commerce.

On the same page, Farrar also said that in that chapter Ure gave a "curious defense of smuggling." But he did no such thing. He merely described the fact that smugglers will always find ways to circumvent bad government trade laws and that ultimately their activities become the stimulus to change faulty legislation. But Ure was not advocating smuggling. Further proof of this was his chemical analyses in 1842–43, which helped the commissioners of Customs to discover a smuggling operation. In the process, Ure regrettably had to expose the errors in chemical analysis done by two prominent chemists, Professors Thomas Graham and William Brande, Ure's friend. See Andrew Ure, *The Revenue in Jeopardy from Spurious Chemistry* (1843).

Finally, on page 320, Farrar erroneously stated that, in relation to this 1843 smuggling investigation, Ure was "an official of the Customs." Ure was most explicit in his *Revenue in Jeopardy* (p. iii) that he was not and received no salary from

many prominent scientists for most of his life and that he had a wide circle of friends, many of them leading scientists in the United Kingdom and abroad, who lamented his death.[37] In any case, such a negative picture would not be a just reflection of the tone of Ure's *New System of Geology*.[38]

Nevertheless, Ure considered Werner's Neptunist theory of earth history to be "a world-building hypothesis, so extravagant, so visionary, and so inconsistent with every principle of mechanical and chemical science."[39] Hutton's uniformitarian theory fared no better in Ure's estimation. Rather, to build a sound geological theory, the example of Bacon and Newton needed to be followed.

> Our age and nation never cease to extol Bacon's inductive logic, and the rigid demonstrations of Newton. One is naturally led to suppose, that those who so loudly profess to be their disciples, should imitate, in some degree at least, the methods of research prescribed and practiced by these great masters of reason and science. We should expect to find the facts subservient to any doctrine, collected with labor and skill, examined with scrupulous caution, and lucidly arranged without deceptive art. It is only facts, thus carefully chosen and candidly compared, which can be generalized into a just theory. If we examine the ablest expositions of the Wernerian and Huttonian geologies by that philosophic standard, we shall find them to fall egregiously short.[40]

The Relationship Between Scripture and Geology

Ure believed that when both the geological phenomena and the Scriptures were rightly interpreted they would agree, since both were the work of God.[41] Like most of his old-earth contemporaries, Ure also believed that the ultimate fruit of scientific and philosophical study was to draw man's attention to the Creator. Of the creation he said, "All its parts display so clearly the work of an Almighty hand, as to impress moral and religious sentiments, on every unperverted naturalist."[42]

In seeking to follow Bacon, he insisted that geology, like any science, must be based on experimentation, careful observation, and sound inductive logic.[43] But he made qualifications to a quoted statement from Bacon's *Novum Organum*[44] to the effect that we should not try to "establish a body of natural philosophy" from Genesis 1 and other portions of Scripture about creation. Ure wrote:

> The censure [of Bacon] here bestowed on those who construct schemes of philosophy on scripture texts, is perfectly just, but it does not apply to those who endeavor to prove, by inductive evidence, that the conclusions of philosophy are not discordant with the order of physical events, recorded by Moses. The object of Bacon's reprobation is not the besetting sin of the present age. Science must now be built up on its own foundations, by its own rules, and with its own materials. The individual who would attempt to deduce

---

Customs. Instead, he was paid two guineas for each individual chemical analysis, regardless of how much time and money each analysis required. Farrar continued by saying that in this pamphlet Ure had attacked his former friend and fellow chemist, Brande, with "unnecessary bitterness." But the *Revenue in Jeopardy*, which is largely comprised of letters and other documents (by Ure, Brande, Graham, and others), did not constitute a bitter attack by Ure against these professors. Nor was his exposure of their mistaken chemical analyses unnecessary since they had erroneously advised the Customs.

37 W.S.C. Copeman, "Andrew Ure, M.D., F.R.S. (1778–1857)," *Proceedings of the Royal Society of Medicine*, vol. 44 (1951), p. 657–658 and 661–662. Another of Ure's biographer said that "his conversation was always most interesting and instructive." See Anonymous, *Dr. Andrew Ure: A Slight Sketch*, p. 17.

38 As further support for this conclusion, it should be born in mind that although Hitchcock, a prominent American old-earth geologist, largely rejected Ure's views, he did commend Ure's temperate expression of them. See Edward Hitchcock, "The Historical and Geological Deluges Compared," *The American Biblical Repository*, vol. IX, no. 25 (1837), p. 113.

39 Andrew Ure, *Geology*, p. xxxiii–xxxiv.

40 Ibid., p. xxi–xxii.

41 Ibid., p. xiii.

42 Ibid., p. 86, also xxxix–xliii and 183–184. This was, in fact, one of the stated purposes of Ure's book (p. xxxviii).

43 Ibid., p. x–xi, 16.

44 Francis Bacon, *Novum Organum* (1859), p. 43 [Book I, pt. lxv]. This was quoted earlier in the section on Bacon.

a single principle in science from any phenomenon described in the Bible, would be regarded as no friend either to philosophy or religion. But when the principles of physics are fairly established on their own bases, it becomes a subject of interest, to examine how far certain natural phenomena related by the inspired historian, are conformable to our digest of the laws of nature. If an accordance can be clearly made out between things so distinct and independent, as ancient testimony, and the results of modern research, faith and reason will enjoy a just triumph, propitious to their mutual influence on mankind. This procedure is just the inverse of what Bacon reprobates. We do not seek the living among the dead; we do not determine the existing or actual properties of matter, from a few brief notices of mighty revolutions which it anciently suffered.[45]

Ure agreed that the Bible was not given to man as a scientific textbook: "Revelation was certainly not imparted to mankind, for the purpose of instructing them in any principles of philosophy, which reason can explore. When the phenomena of nature are described [in Scripture], it is always in popular language, corresponding to the information of sense."[46] So, he argued, the Bible does not teach us "the actual motion or repose of" the heavenly bodies; that is something for astronomers to investigate.[47] Likewise, it does not describe the ratios of land and sea before and after the Flood; that should be considered on the basis of sound principles of meteorology, physics, geology, etc.[48]

But this did not mean for Ure that the Bible was irrelevant to the question of the history of the earth. He made a sharp distinction between the present operation of the universe (and all it contains) and its past origin and history. In his mind, the proper domain of science is in the repeatable and experimental study of the way in which things in creation function in the observable present. But when we turn to the unobservable past we are entering into a great deal of speculation.

> Astronomy never reverts to a state of repose, antecedent to their actual condition. It contemplates the velocities and mutual equilibrium of moving bodies, but does not venture to speculate on a former or a future state, an origin or an end of the actual appearances of the heavens. In this respect, astronomers differ widely from our two famous geologists, Werner and Hutton, who do not confine their inquiries to the existing cycle of phenomena, but boldly remount to a hypothetical order very different from the present, which no human eye ever witnessed.[49]

Because of our "absolute ignorance concerning the origin of our terrestrial system" and because of the great moral implications of the question of origins, he continued, "it would therefore seem not unreasonable to consider such facts as the Deity has thought fit to reveal concerning the formation and garnishing of this globe as an abode of vegetable and animal beings."[50] The Scriptures, "the unerring oracles of God," were seen by Ure to set the boundaries for speculative theories about the early history of the earth.

> That divine revelation was not imparted to man, for the purpose of instructing him in the recondite principles of physics, is a proposition fully laid down in the Introduction. Yet there may be certain primary facts, beyond the horizon of science, shadowed out by prophecy, as limits to speculative temerity and resting points to the pious spirit. Without such supplemental illumination, man can

45 Ure, *Geology*, p. xiv–xv.
46 Ibid., p. xviii.
47 Ibid.
48 Ibid., p. 471.
49 Ibid., p. xviii. In this statement, he forgot Laplace's nebular hypothesis, which he mentioned elsewhere in the book and which was an evolutionary view of the origin of the solar system.
50 Ibid., p. xix–xx.

know nothing of the cause, and manner, of himself, and his companion beings, coming into existence.[51]

His Book on Geology

The full title of Ure's book reads, *A New System of Geology, in Which the Great Revolutions of the Earth and Animated Nature Are Reconciled at Once to Modern Science and Sacred History.* Ure did not write his book to add to the storehouse of geological observations, but to serve as an "introduction and incentive to the study" of other geological works. Of himself he said:

> His leading object has been to distribute the most interesting and best established truths, illustrative of the structure and revolutions of the earth, in the order of their physical connexions and causes; whence certain general inductions might be legitimately seen to flow.[52]

In so doing he sought to present on the basis of physical and geological science "a view of certain intrinsic sources of change" in the earth's constitution, which he believed other natural philosophers had not considered.

He also wanted "to lead popular students of philosophy, to the moral and religious uses of their knowledge."[53] He sensed that a growing number of anti-Christian natural philosophers were using science to undermine morality and faith in the Scriptures. In an allusion to the French Revolution, he said that as these skeptics gained university posts they would contribute to the "loosening [of] the frame work of society [and] bring down a second fearful crash of atheism and crime."[54] He believed that sound natural philosophy would point toward the true and living God of Scripture and so he sought to show the concordances of science and Scripture, thereby "strengthening the faith of the pious."[55]

Ure's book, most of which is descriptive geology, is organized in a reasonably systematic way, with an introduction and then three major sections: 1) the primordial world, which covered creation (pages 1–129), 2) the antediluvian period, which in Ure's view formed the secondary and tertiary strata (pages 129–349), and 3) the Deluge (pages 350–614). It includes 50 wood engravings of fossils and geological phenomena and six plates of fossils representative of some of the geological formations.

Creation and Pre-Flood History

Ure believed in a literal six-day creation of the universe, which was finished in a perfect form about 6,000 years ago.[56] In opposition to both the day-age theory and gap theory, he argued that both the contextual use of "day" in Genesis 1 and God's commentary in Exodus 20:8–11 prove that the creation days were 24 hours long, the length of one rotation of the earth, and that the first day was the beginning of the whole creation.[57]

He contended that the notion that the earth was formed from a chaotic mass by the laws of nature over vast indefinite ages of time was contrary to reason and made God appear as an imbecile. Rather, the primitive earth (with its primitive rocks) was an instantaneous, fiat creation of God.[58] On the appointed day, God also supernaturally and instantly created mature plants and

---

51 Andrew Ure, *Geology*, p. 15–16.
52 Ibid., p. vii–viii.
53 Ibid., p. xxxvii.
54 Ibid., p. xxxix.
55 Ibid., p. xl–xli and lv.
56 Ibid., p. 13–15, 86. He accepted Ussher's date of creation (4004 B.C.), knowing that people would scoff at him. But he asked, if the earth was made for man, why we need to imagine a more distant beginning for earth or the universe of stars, planets, etc., which were the result of one and the same creative mandate. At the end of the book (p. 608–615) he discussed his reasons for rejecting the Hindu chronology (of a vastly older earth) as fabulous myth.
57 Ibid., p. 11, 82.
58 Ibid., p. 7–10. In support of his notion of the primitive earth, he quoted Isaac Newton's *Opticks* (I found Ure's undocumented quotation of Newton in the 1931 edition of *Opticks*, p. 400 and 402). Later, Ure continued, "Had we been told that Deity, in the beginning, created a chaos out of which symmetry was to be educed through a long series of material transmutations, then philosophy might have proffered her conjectures concerning the order of evolution; but ancient chaos is merely a mythological fiction, disavowed alike by the word and wisdom of God. . . . Chaos is, in fact, a dogma borrowed by Pythagoras from the Persian Magi" (ibid., p. 12).

animals (i.e., with the appearance of age).[59] The sun, along with the other stars, was created on day 1 with the earth, when the universal law of gravitation was instituted. But not until day 4 were they invested with rays of light as they "acquired their lucid exterior."[60]

Ure reasoned that the original earth was created instantaneously as a spheroid perfectly suited for life. It had a molten interior with a crust of concentric horizontal strata of gneiss, mica-slate, and clay-slate, with partial layers of semi-crystalline limestone, all of which were initially enveloped by a universal ocean.[61] These were the primitive rocks of day 1 of creation, which explains why they contain no fossil remains. When God made the dry land to appear on day 3, the transition strata began to be formed in the ocean bottom, being increasingly mingled over time with marine exuviae after they were created on day 5.[62] Ure believed that the ocean at this time and prior to the Flood was smaller in surface area (equal in size to the land mass) but deeper, which contributed to warmer and drier antediluvian climate.[63]

When Adam and Eve sinned, God cursed the earth,[64] one effect of which, in Ure's view, was a long series of localized convulsive events all over the more thinly crusted ocean bottom, which culminated finally in God's judgment of a global Flood.[65] During this antediluvian period of 1,600 years, the regular pattern of fossiliferous secondary and tertiary strata was formed on the ocean bottom, as basaltic eruptions agitated the seas causing partial destructions of the land and its inhabitants and local elevations of parts of the seabed.[66]
In this regard, Ure basically accepted the old-earth theory for the deposition of these sedimentary formations over a long period of time and by many catastrophes, though in contrast to old-earth geologists he believed the biblical chronology provided sufficient time for these events. As we have seen, Ure gave only a brief biblical argument against the gap and day-age theories. Apart from short comments showing why he rejected the nebular hypothesis (with its gradually cooling earth) and a limited discussion of how the advancing desert sands of Egypt could serve as a chronometer for measuring the date of the Flood (consistent with Genesis), he did not make much effort to explicitly refute, with geological reasons, the old-earth time scale.[67] He did, however, add a theological argument against

59 In reference to this miraculous creation of plants on day 3, he wrote (ibid., p. 81–82) that such an idea "does not seem to have been made a stumbling block by the botanical student, as the first arrangement of the mineral strata, has been by the geologist. . . . No botanist or zoologist, of sane reputation, inculcates that plants and animals acquired their perfect and unvarying forms, through successive organic depositions and catastrophes, as geognostic theorists have taught with regard to the primitive structure of the earth." In a further rejection of evolution (biological, geological, or astronomical) he added, "The achievement of creation, by distinct and independent acts, was performed on each of six successive days; demonstrating that it was not the result of a blind necessity, or a spontaneous, and therefore continuous, though irregular aggregation of chaotic atoms" (ibid., p. 86–87). Whether Ure denied any variation of the species is not clear. He did believe that after the Flood, God created new forms of life supernaturally, the creatures on the ark only serving as food for Noah and his family until the earth was replenished with other sources of food. On the other hand, we cannot legitimately make too much of this with reference to biological variation, since Ure's view of post-Flood creation was an attempt to explain the difference between the extinct fossilized creatures and existing forms.

60 Ure, *Geology*, p. 17–51, 82. In a lengthy discussion of the undulation (wave) theory of light (with reference to M. Arago's experiments), Ure argued that light had existence before the sun became the primary light-bearer for earth on day 4. He added that had Moses written Genesis 1 on the basis of sense perception and Egyptian education he would not have put the creation of light before the sun. Obviously, it would appear that Ure had not adequately pondered the fact that he was being a bit loose and inconsistent in his interpretation by putting the creation of the sun on day 1 and of its luminosity on day 4. Using interpretation of sun spots given by Herschel, a leading astronomer of the day, Ure rejected Buffon's theory that the sun was the molten parent of the other planets (ibid., p. xxxv–xxxvii).

61 Ibid., p. 89–92.

62 Ibid., p. 129–130.

63 Ibid., p. 495, 599–602, 51–70.

64 In support of this Ure cited Genesis 3:17–19 and 5:29 (ibid., p. 274).

65 Ure, *Geology*, p. 436–439, 470–474, 505–506.

66 Ibid., p. 130, 169, 594–595.

67 Ibid., p. 498, 602–604. Concerning the Egyptian desert, he argued that according to historical records, the fertility of Egypt was much greater at the times of Cleopatra and Caesar Augustus. If the Flood had been more ancient than the date set by Moses, then Egypt should have long before their times become an uninhabitable desert.

the old-earth view: the fossil-bearing strata and diluvium speak of the wrath of God against sin and do not reflect the creative work of God.

> Such a dismal ruin of all organic beings, such a derangement of the fair frame of nature seem to be irreconcilable difficulties in *natural* theism. For is not the wisdom of God impeached in constructing a world on foundations so infirm; his prescience in peopling so precarious an abode, with countless myriads of exquisite mechanisms; and his goodness in plunging indiscriminately every tribe and family of his sentient offspring in mortal agony and death? A creation replete with beauty and enjoyment, suddenly transformed by its Creator's mandate or permission into a waste of waters, is a moral phenomenon which certes no system of ethics can explain. Here, metaphysics, the boasted mistress of mind, with all her train of categories, stands at fault. But here, if reason will deign to forego its pride, and implore the aid of a superior light, the Hebrew prophet will lift up the dark veil from the primeval scene. In revealing the disobedience of Adam, the atrocious guilt of Cain, and the pestilence of sin, almost universally spread among the progeny, he shows, alas! too clearly, how justice outraged, and mercy spurned, inevitably called forth the final lustration of the Deluge. This conclusion, no philosopher can reasonably gainsay, who considers man as a responsible agent, and this earth with all its apparatus of organic life, as mainly subservient to his moral and intellectual education.[68]

The Flood

Ure devoted 240 pages to a discussion of the Flood, which included no detailed analysis of the biblical account of the event. He believed that it was a global, year-long, penal judgment of God, the last in a series of previous smaller catastrophes, which themselves were the secondary cause of the Flood.[69] These pre-Flood catastrophes, though far from universal, were considered significant enough to extend the area of the ocean step by step by permanently submerging some of the land. This process also had a cooling effect on the earth's climate (which is a subject we will return to shortly). So, in a way that he did not fully explain, the Flood was both a divine interruption and a result of the normal laws of nature. Regarding this uniformity of nature he wrote:

> In the Newtonian philosophy, no other causes of natural events can be admitted than what are known to be really operative, and adequate to account for the phenomena. This inductive law prohibits the employment of hypothetical assumptions, whose existence we cannot prove, such as the attraction of a comet in deranging the axis of the earth, or deluging it, by lifting the waters from their ocean bed. Nor will modern discovery suffer the theorist to summon from the bowels of the earth an ideal abyss to serve his purposes; far less allow him to get rid of a meteoric deluge imported by an aqueous *coma* for the occasion. Thus wisely circumscribed, but by no means fettered, we shall have no difficulty in finding actual and potential forces, capable of explaining the principal appearances, incident to the great diluvial catastrophe, and its precursor inundations.[70]

The uniquely global Flood raised many of the secondary and tertiary strata out of the ocean

68 Ure, *Geology*, p. 505–506.

69 Ibid., p. liii, 130, 349, 439.

70 Ibid., p. 373–374. In contrast, he said this about the theory of the earth evolving from a nebulous cloud: "I am not conscious of having employed in the preceding investigation, any causes whose operation is not both actual and sufficient to explain the appearances. I leave others to speculate about the igneous origin of the globe, and its having spontaneously evolved during an indefinite period of refrigeration, successive orders of organic forms. This hypothesis is founded neither on natural or revealed knowledge; nor will it accord with those great and sudden crises of temperature, which innumerable monuments attest" (ibid., p. 498).

as the antediluvian land sank.[71] The evidences of this event were the diluvial deposits of gravel, erratic boulders, and fossils of extinct creatures, the scratches and furrows on the surface of many strata, the trap rocks witnessing to the intensified volcanic activity, and the pagan traditions of such a Flood. In this view he was in considerable harmony with the old-earth catastrophists of his day, such as Cuvier, Buckland, Brongniart, Conybeare, and Phillips.[72] Ure's answer for why no fossil humans had been found was simple: the lands inhabited by antediluvian man were permanently submerged by the Deluge.[73]

Ure devoted a considerable amount of discussion to the climatic impact of the Flood, giving us one of the earliest conceptions of an ice age.[74] He reasoned that at the beginning of the Flood the ratio of land to sea was probably about 1:1. This arrangement, along with a cloud canopy high in the upper atmosphere ("the waters above" of Gen. 1:7)[75] and an initially warmer ocean, had produced a very warm and uniform temperature on the earth.[76] As a result, he conceived that in the pre-Flood world there were no winds to speak of, nor virtually any rain (nor rainbows, which Ure thought was implied by Gen. 9:11–17). Rather, a heavy dew, resulting from the vertical movements of air causing evaporation and condensation, watered the earth (which Ure based on Gen. 2:5–6).[77]

However, the Flood reordered the surface features of the earth, leaving the present ratio of land to sea. This caused a "sudden and vast refrigeration"[78] of the earth accompanied by much precipitation. The result was a rapid build-up of glaciers in the higher latitudes.[79] Ure argued that these glaciers would have transported much diluvial gravel and would account for the woolly mammoths of Siberia and the fossilized tropical plants found in the Arctic by the explorations of Sir William Edward Parry (1790–1855)[80] in 1819–20. For a long time after the Flood the earth would have remained, at least in the extra-tropical zones, relatively damp and cold, gradually passing to a considerably drier and warmer climate and in places producing deserts, such as in northern Africa.

Ure said that another result of the Flood, along with the sedimentation process of the previous 1,600 years, would have been a much thicker crust over the molten interior of the earth, which in turn would produce a more stable post-diluvian terraqueous system (in terms of volcanic and earthquake activity).

---

71 Ibid., p. 350, 471, 475.

72 John Phillips, *Illustrations of the Geology of Yorkshire* (1829). Pages 16–30 present his view of a global flood. William Smith, Phillips' uncle, held a similar view of the geological effects of a global flood, apparently till the end of his life, though he never equated it with the Noachian flood. See John Phillips, *Memoirs of William Smith* (1844), p. 25–26, and T. Sheppard, "William Smith: His maps and Memoirs," *Proceedings of the Yorkshire Geological and Polytechnic Society*, N.S. vol. XIX (1914–22), p. 175 and facing chart.

73 Ure, *Geology*, p. 472.

74 Ibid., p. 483–494, 599–603. Not surprisingly, Hallum makes no mention of Ure in his history of the ice-age theory in the 19th century. See A. Hallum, *Great Geological Controversies* (1992), p. 87–104.

75 Earlier, Ure had given a rather technical discussion of this canopy, based on Daniell's *Meteorological Essays*. See Ure, *Geology*, p. 51–70. In Ure's view, these clouds were not the only or even the major source of water for the Flood. Ure rejected the notion of any "super-aerial ocean" as being contrary to the principles of meteorology. For Ure, the Flood was largely the result of the sinking of the land mass and raising of the ocean bottom by volcanic and sedimentary processes (ibid., p. 475–476).

76 He estimated temperatures of about 120 degrees in the daytime and 110 at night (ibid., p. 599).

77 He said the phenomenon of heavy dew would have been similar to those experienced at the time in Lima, Peru, and other regions of the world (ibid., p. 601).

78 This was far greater than the cooling effect envisaged as a result of the pre-Flood catastrophes.

79 He cited the work of Jens Esmark (1763–1839), a leading Norwegian old-earth geology professor, who, on the basis of his studies in Norway, had concluded that in the past, and on more than one occasion, the whole earth had been covered with ice and snow (and all the water on earth had been frozen), only to completely thaw later. Some of his research and his own peculiar theory of the earth appeared in Jens Esmark, "Remarks Tending to Explain the Geological History of the Earth," *Edinburgh New Philosophical Journal*, vol. II (Oct. 1826–Apr. 1827), p. 107–121. Esmark likewise got no mention by Hallum (footnote 74 above).

80 *DNB* says that Parry was a famous naval explorer who searched for the northwest passage from the Atlantic to Pacific.

One other aspect of Ure's theory about the Flood was that he, like Penn, believed that God supernaturally created new animals to suit the transformed earth.[81] The animals on the ark with Noah would have provided food for the human survivors of the Flood. Their stock probably died out in the course of a few generations. His reasons for postulating this were that 1) extinct fossil animals were so different from existing forms, 2) this seemed to be the only way to explain why some animals are found only in one location on earth, such as Australia, 3) the types of most existing races of animals are not found in the diluvial deposits, 4) the lack of any ape fossils at the time, and 5) Psalm 104, which Ure believed seems to describe the Flood and to speak of God creating animals (v. 30) as He renewed the earth.

Reviews of His *Geology*

Having examined Ure's book, we now have a context for considering several reviews it received, which shed light on the nature of the Genesis-geology debate.

The *British Critic*,[82] while commending Ure's moral and religious objective for writing, considered the book to be no friend of science or Scripture. Among other things, it criticized Ure for not taking a very literal interpretation of Scripture (as he said we should). For example, Ure postulated many land-submerging catastrophes before the Flood, about which the Bible made no mention and he proposed new creations of animals after the Flood whereas the Bible said that the animals on the ark replenished the earth.

The *Quarterly Journal of Science, Literature and Art* gave a very positive review[83] calling it an "interesting, and in many respects original, work," though it could have been better titled as "Geological Physics" or "Philosophy of Geology." To the reviewer, the book displayed Ure's proven "vigilance of observation and logical acumen" and it "has not in the least a controversial texture."[84] Ure's discussion of the primitive formation was praised for its reference to Macculloch's "excellent" papers on granite (published in the same journal) and Von Buch's latest observations on volcanic rocks in the Alps. The reviewer believed that Ure's overview of the secondary and tertiary formations "will contribute essentially to promote the popular diffusion of geological science."[85] One of the vexing problems for geologists at the time was to explain the fossil evidence of tropical plants and animals buried in northern latitudes, which suggested to many that there had been in the past a global tropical climate. The reviewer regarded Ure's proposed explanation "to be equally new and striking."[86] He concluded by saying, "On the whole, we regard this new system of geology, as one of the most valuable accessions lately made to the scientific literature of our country."[87]

The most influential and scathing review was written by the Cambridge geologist, Reverend Adam Sedgwick, in his annual presidential address to the Geological Society.[88] He said Ure's book contained "the worst violations of philosophic rule, by the daring union of things incongruous," and "the bold and unauthorized hypothesis" that

---

81 Ure, *Geology*, p. 500–504.

82 Anonymous review of Ure's *Geology*, *British Critic*, vol. VI, no. 12 (1829), p. 387–412.

83 *Quarterly Journal of Science, Literature and Art*, N.S. vol. V (Jan.-Mar. 1829), p. 113–132. The review is not signed, but like the previously noted reviews of Granville Penn's work, I think (for the same reasons as in Penn's case) that it was probably done by William Brande, the long-time editor of the journal. Farrar suggested, solely on the basis of the style of language used in the review, that Ure wrote the review himself. See W.V. Farrar, "Andrew Ure, F.R.S., and the Philosophy of Manufactures," *Notes and Records of the Royal Society of London*, vol. 27, no. 2 (Feb. 1973), p. 312. Assessing style, however, is a very subjective task. Though Ure contributed a number of articles to the journal and was a personal friend of Brande's, such a serious allegation seems a fanciful speculation, and quite out of keeping with the tenor of Ure's life, as remarked by other biographers, and reflected by his Christian convictions, as expressed in his *Geology*. Farrar's idea would also implicate Brande, who as editor would have approved the review. But he offered no evidence that Brande would be an accomplice to such a deception.

84 Ibid., p. 113–115.

85 Ibid., p. 123–124.

86 Ibid., p. 126.

87 Ibid., p. 132.

88 Reprinted in *Philosophical Magazine*, N.S. vol. VII, no. 40 (1830), p. 289–315. Sedgwick's criticisms of Ure's *Geology* is found on pages 310–313.

REVEREND ADAM SEDGWICK (1785–1873)

the primitive rocks were instantly created by divine fiat.[89] Sedgwick did not have one good thing to say about the book; he did not even acknowledge how much Ure agreed with contemporary catastrophists, as we have noted. While many of his criticisms were valid, a general overview of them suggests that Sedgwick may have been diligently looking for nothing but errors of detail, for he made no comment on any of Ure's theoretical discussions as the review in *Journal of Science* had done.

Sedgwick was very irritated by what he called "a complication of errors as nearly baffles all attempts at description."[90] However, upon careful inspection, some of Sedgwick's examples of error do not appear to be errors at all, or at least Sedgwick's obvious anger about them seems out of proportion to the insignificant nature of the error.[91] Since Sedgwick's review was so hostile and influential, it will be enlightening to consider two of these cases.

Sedgwick charged that "In one place we are told,[92] that the lower secondary rocks are characterized by the simplest forms of the animal kingdom. In another,[93] we find fish enumerated among the fossils of the transition (or submedial) strata."[94] In the first place, we might say that the average reader in Ure's target audience would never have made such a connection of minute detail between such vastly separated pages (about 150). But actually, when the statements are taken in context they are both seen to be true. In the first statement, Ure was describing, in two pages of the "Introduction," a general view of the whole geological record, with relatively simple marine creatures at the bottom, and reptiles, amphibians, and mammals more common at the top. This, in fact, is precisely how Sedgwick himself described the geological record when writing in 1845 to Agassiz about his disdain for the theory of evolution.[95] The second statement Ure made was in the context of a lengthy and detailed discussion of the transition strata and it was also true.[96]

In another example, the details are only those which an expert geologist like Sedgwick (for whom Ure expressly did not write the book) would have known and noticed and, even if the example constituted an error, it was petty. Sedgwick said that Ure had figured the "Steeple Ashton caryophyllia (the characteristic fossil of the middle oolite)" as "a fossil of the inferior system" (i.e., the

89 Ibid., p. 310–311.

90 *Philosophical Magazine*, N.S. vol. VII, no. 40 (1830), p. 312.

91 Sedgwick's censure was especially harsh in light of his own recantation of what he called "geological heresy" (belief that the Flood was the cause of the diluvium), which he made just one year later from the same chair of the Geological Society.

92 Ure, *Geology*, p. xlix.

93 Ibid., p. 143.

94 Adam Sedgwick, "Presidential Address to the Geological Society," *Philosophical Magazine*, N.S. vol. VII, no. 40 (1830), p. 312.

95 "Now I allow (as all geologists must do) a kind of progressive development. For example, the first fish are below the reptiles; and the first reptiles older than man." See John W. Clark and Thomas M. Hughes, *The Life and Letters of Rev. Adam Sedgwick* (1890), II: p. 86. It is also how Buckland presented the geological record pictorially in his *Bridgewater Treatise* (1836), II: Plate 1.

96 In his *Bridgewater Treatise* (1836), I: p. 294, Buckland said fish were found in the transition strata.

lower oolite). In fact, on Ure's cited page (251), the figure is subtitled (in agreement with the wording in the paragraph next to it) less precisely as simply a "Caryophyllia," which Conybeare and Phillips listed as one of the fossils found in the inferior oolite.[97] The majority of Ure's readers would likely not have even noticed, much less remembered and been terribly misguided, by such a slightly erroneous detail. Further, it seems reasonable to assume that Ure was using an available picture of a caryophyllia to illustrate for his non-specialist reader, rather than to precisely distinguish species of caryophyllia, as Sedgwick was doing.

Many of the other specific errors Sedgwick mentioned were completely valid and did reflect that Ure's knowledge of some of the geological details was a little out of date or confused, or that he had not done an adequate job in editing before the book went to press.[98] But Sedgwick's severe reaction seems to warrant the same geologically informed response that "T.E." gave to a similarly negative review. T.E. wrote:

> In general, indeed, I think we should be careful how we magnify molehills into mountains, and, for a few inaccuracies and marks of inattention, throw discredit on a book which, like Dr. Ure's, contains so many pages of sound induction and philosophic reasoning; and although most people will be inclined to differ, more or less, from his theory, or the arguments adduced in its support, yet, as geologists still seem inclined to adhere to one of the three hypotheses mentioned by Mr. Conybeare in his *Introduction*,[99] a book written in support of one of them, by such a man as Ure may not be without its use; perhaps, indeed, we might all be much benefited, and our ideas enlarged, if men qualified for such speculation were to illustrate the other two, in connection with a good practical account of the present state of the science.[100]

The harshness of Sedgwick's criticism also seems inconsistent with his own statement in the paragraph immediately following his critique of Ure, where he said, "It is indeed true that in the very classification of our facts and of our phaenomena, there are difficulties connected with all parts of natural history, which for ages yet to come, may continue to require for their solution a combination of the greatest industry with the greatest skill."[101] It is hard to avoid the conclusion that something other than minor errors was driving Sedgwick's hostility toward Ure's book.

Conclusion

Though a fellow of the Geological Society, Ure was not, and did not present himself as, an original investigator of geological phenomena. Rather, he quoted, too often without adequate citation, from the works of others. In much of his thinking he was in total agreement with the leading old-earth catastrophists of the day: he accepted the

97 William D. Conybeare and William Phillips, *Outlines of the Geology of England and Wales* (1822), p. 245. Conybeare and Phillips did not name the species of caryophyllia. The fossil also was found in lower Mountain Limestone, far below the oolite (ibid., p. 359).

98 In spite of his reputation for meticulous accuracy in his science, evidently he frequently sent his manuscripts off to the printer in haste, without adequate proof reading. See W.S.C. Copeman, "Andrew Ure, M.D., F.R.S. (1778–1857)," *Proceedings of the Royal Society of Medicine*, Vol. 44 (1951), p. 660.

99 Conybeare and Phillips, *Outlines of the Geology of England and Wales*, p. lix–lx. The three views Conybeare discussed were 1) the theory, like Ure's, that the primary rocks were formed in the initial creation of the earth on day 1; the transition, secondary, and tertiary strata were formed during the 1,600 years between day 2 and the Flood; and the diluvium were laid down and the general appearance of the present continents were formed by the Flood; 2) the gap theory in which the primary to tertiary were formed in the supposed millions of years between Genesis 1:1 and 1:2 and the rest was attributed to the Flood; and 3) the day-age theory in which the primary to tertiary were formed during indefinitely long creation days of Genesis 1 and the rest by the Flood. Of course, as we will see in the case of George Young, there was also a fourth view held by some geologists at this time, namely, that the Flood produced the secondary, tertiary, and diluvial deposits.

100 T.E., Anonymous letter to the editor, *Magazine of Natural History*, vol. III (1830), p. 91.

101 Adam Sedgwick, presidential address to the Geological Society, *Philosophical Magazine*, N.S. vol. VII, no. 40 (1830), p. 313.

distinctions and temporal separation of the different strata (though spanning only about 1,600 years), as interpreted by the use of characteristic fossils, and his view of the geological effects of Noah's flood was virtually identical to that of old-earth geologist John Phillips, who published the same year. But what he sought to do was to offer some new perspectives on the facts and incorporate into a theory of creation and earth history information which had not been previously known or applied to this question. For example, the undulation theory of light with reference to the creation of light and the celestial bodies, and meteorological knowledge in relation to the early earth, the Flood and the Flood-induced "ice age" (as it would later be called). He believed that the unerring Scriptures do not teach a system of science, but that they are relevant to the question of origins. That question is outside the realm of experimental science, which studies present-day processes. Though not working out a detailed connection between Genesis and geology, he endeavored to speculate on the basis of current knowledge and within what for him were the limiting boundaries set by Scripture, namely, a six-day creation about 6,000 years ago and a global catastrophic Flood.

Ure's long teaching career up to this point reflects his desire to advance general scientific knowledge among the common people and to show how geology related to Scripture. His commitment to biblical truth and true scientific knowledge and his concern that atheistic science (toward which, he felt, geology was tending) would be detrimental to society and to the Christian faith, motivated him to write on geology.

GEORGE FAIRHOLME (1789–1846)

George Fairholme was born to the wealthy Scottish family of William and Elizabeth Fairholme of Lugate, Midlothian, on January 15, 1789.[1] Coming from a long-established, upper-class family, William made his living from banking and also was a serious art collector.[2]

Nothing is known of George's childhood years except that in 1800, at the age of 11, his uncle bequeathed to him the Greenknowe estate (comprising 5,000–6,000 acres) near Gordon, Berwickshire, which he retained until his death.[3] Given his family's financial situation and the fact that his parents and other relatives were very well read, he was probably tutored at home and self-taught.[4]

According to official university records, he was not a graduate of Oxford, Cambridge, Aberdeen, Edinburgh, Glasgow, St. Andrews, or Dublin. He was affiliated with the Church of Scotland, but he evidently was not too bothered about denomination, since his third son, George, attended the well-known Anglican school in Rugby[5] and his

1 George Fairholme, *Notes on the Family of Greenknowe and on the History of the Estate from 1470 to the Present Time* (1838), unnumbered page of the preface to this unpublished manuscript. This manuscript, of which I have a copy, is in the possession of one of Fairholme's living relatives, Mrs. Waveney Jenkins of the Isle of Man. See also John Burke, *Burke's Landed Gentry* (1965–72), III: p. 315–316.

2 Based on personal conversation on December 14, 1995, with Mrs. Jenkins (see footnote 1), who has a strong interest in and knowledge of the family history.

3 Fairholme, *Notes on the Family of Greenknowe and on the History of the Estate from 1470 to the Present Time*, p. 31. On an unnumbered additional page at the beginning of the manuscript, Fairholme stated that his uncle willed through his father the estate or a sum of money between £6000 and £10,000 (approximately £240,000 to £400,000 or $360,000 to $600,000 in today's value), but his father willed the estate, which proved to be of greater value. This unpublished manuscript is in the possession of Mrs. Jenkins (see footnote 2). Mrs. Jane Farr, wife of the present owner of Greenknowe estate, informed me that the present estate of 1,000 acres is about one-fifth the size that it was when Fairholme owned it.

4 Jenkins (see footnote 2).

5 According to the Mormon *International Genealogical Index*, Fairholme's second son, James, was christened on March 3, 1821 or 1822, in the small village of Kinnoul, Perth. At that time Kinnoul had only a Church of Scotland, according to

fourth son, Charles, was baptized in an Anglican Church in Brussels.[6]

He was married in Dunkeld, Perth, on November 15, 1818, to Caroline, eldest daughter of the 18th Lord Forbes and granddaughter of the 6th Duke of Atholl, and together they had four sons and one daughter.[7] They resided in Perth and Greenknowe for a time, and for part of 1829 they lived near Berne, Switzerland.[8] Apparently, from the late 1820s until about 1832, they resided in Brussels, where George was involved in banking. From there they returned to England[9] to reside in rented accommodation in Ramsgate, Kent, until at least 1843.[10] Throughout his life, however, he traveled extensively, as will be shown later, and seemed to have a favorite spot in Mühlbad near Boppard on the Rhine, just south of Koblenz, Germany.[11]

Fairholme died in Leamington Spa on November 19, 1846, leaving his wife (d. 1865), three sons, and one daughter.[12] Besides his financial assets (e.g., he willed £3000–3500 to each child),[13] land, and four homes in Scotland, Fairholme bequeathed to his wife and each of his children a painting (two of which were by Van Dyke and Correggio), each depicting some scene from the life of Christ. To his daughter he also gave a small cabinet of his collection of fossils shells and rocks.[14] Clearly, Fairholme's Christian faith and the study of natural philosophy, especially geology, were important to him and like many in his day he had the financial resources to pursue his study of geology both in Britain and on the European continent.

Scientific Work and Geological Competence

Fairholme published two lengthy books on the subject of geology: *General View of the Geology of Scripture* (493 pages) appeared in 1833[15] and *New and Conclusive Physical Demonstrations Both of the Fact and Period of the Mosaic Deluge, and of Its Having Been the Only Event of the Kind That Has Ever Occurred upon the Earth* (443 pages) was published in 1837.[16] His *Positions géologiques en vérifications directe de la chronologie de la Bible* (1834), a 32-page booklet critically evaluating Lyell's theory, was published in Munich, but apparently never appeared in English. Also in the area of geology, he wrote three journal articles on

---

the Perth Local Studies Library (phone conversation, October 28, 1995). The information about the schooling is from the Fairholme family history in John Burke, *Burke's Landed Gentry* (1965–72), III: p. 315–316, and confirmed by a phone conversation on December 8, 1994, with Mr. McClain, the librarian of Rugby School.

6 Jenkins (see footnote 2).

7 George and Elizabeth Fairholme's contract of marriage, a copy of which I obtained from Mr. Gerald Fairholme, another relative living in London; Susanna Evans, *Historic Brisbane and Its Early Artists* (Brisbane: Boolarong Publications, 1982), p. 24.

8 George Fairholme, *Geology of Scripture* (1833), p. 125.

9 Jenkins (see footnote 2).

10 He signed all of his published works in Ramsgate, declared himself a resident of Ramsgate in his 1837 will and signed two codicils to his will in Ramsgate in 1842 and 1843. The later two are included in his *Codicils to Trust Disposition and Deed of Settlement* (1847), of which, along with his will, *Trust Disposition and Deed of Settlement* (1837), I have a copy from Mr. Gerald Fairholme (see footnote 7). Ramsgate was a favorite resort town for the wealthy gentry of the day. Margate Library Archives has no record of his residence so he likely only rented property, as many others did at the time, according to personal correspondence on January 4, 1994, from Mrs. Penny Ward, Heritage Officer in Thanet, Kent.

11 His *Codicils to Trust Disposition and Deed of Settlement* referred to this place several times.

12 Death Notices, *Leamington Spa Courier*, vol. XIX, no. 963 (Nov. 21, 1846), p. 3; *Gentlemen's Magazine*, N.S. vol. XXVII (1847), p. 108. According to Fairholme's *Notes on the Family of Greenknowe and on the History of the Estate from 1470 to the Present Time* (1838, unnumbered page of an additional 1846 preface to this manuscript), his second son, James, entered the Royal Navy in 1834 at the age of 13 and soon became a lieutenant. He perished in about 1845, at the age of 24, in the disastrous Franklin expedition to find the Northwest Passage from the Atlantic to the Pacific.

13 Fairholme, *Trust Disposition and Deed of Settlement.* According to Martin J.S. Rudwick, *The Great Devonian Controversy* (Chicago, IL: University of Chicago Press, 1985), p. 461, these amounts were "positively princely," being roughly equivalent in modern terms to £120,000–140,000 (approximately $180,000–210,000).

14 Fairholme, *Codicils to Trust Disposition and Deed of Settlement*, p. 2–4.

15 A second edition followed in 1838. Two American editions were published in Philadelphia in 1833 and 1844.

16 A second edition was released in 1840. Hereafter, these two books will be referred to as *Geology of Scripture* and *Mosaic Deluge* respectively.

GEORGE'S FATHER, WILLIAM FAIRHOLME (1736–1805)
Courtesty of Gerald Fairholme, London

coal, Niagara Falls, and human fossils.[17] He wrote four other journal articles (two of which were translated into German) on the topics of spiders, elephants, microscopic creatures, and woodcocks.[18] These articles reflect his scientific skills in recording careful observations of nature, wide research in relevant scientific literature, personal correspondence or conversation with other naturalists, the use of museum and zoo collections, the application of appropriate experimentation, and a caution so as not to over-generalize from the stated observations. His writing style, vocabulary, and evident literary research skills reflect a high level of education. His English quotations from French and German literature indicate that he was quite fluent in both languages.[19]

Fairholme was not a member of the Geological Society or any other such society, as far as I could determine.[20] He apparently attended the BAAS (British Association for the Advancement of Science) annual meeting in Bristol in 1836 and he read a paper on the nature of valleys to the 1834 meeting of the Deutscher Naturforscher Versammlung (DNV), the BAAS equivalent, in Stuttgart, Germany.[21] The fact that he was invited to make field trips with several German scientists after that 1834 meeting is an indication of the level of respect they had for his geological knowledge. There is also ample evidence that he conducted his own personal geological investigations. In his *Mosaic Geology* (1837), he asserted that he was presenting new scientific facts and inferences from those investigations and made this general statement about his fieldwork (which he said had improved greatly since the writing of his first book in 1833):[22]

17 "Some Observations on the Nature of Coal, and on the Manner in Which Strata of the Coal Measures Must Probably Have Been Deposited," *Philosophical Magazine*, 3rd Ser. vol. III, no. 16 (1833), p. 245–252; "On the Niagara Falls," *Philosophical Magazine*, 3rd Ser. vol. V, no. 25 (1834), p. 11–25; "Mr. Fairholme on Geological Phenomena," *Christian Observer*, vol XXXV (1835), p. 346–350. Hereafter, these articles will be referred to as "Coal," "Niagara Falls," and "Geological Phenomena," respectively.

18 The journal articles were "On the Power Possessed by Spiders to Escape from an Isolated Situation," *Philosophical Magazine*, 3rd Ser. vol. I, no. 6 (1832), p. 424–427 [German translation: "Über die Fahigkeit der Spinne, sich von einem isolirten Orte aus zu entfernen," *Notizen aus dem Gebiete der Natur und Heilkunde*, vol. XXXV (1833), p. 278–281]; "Description of a Species of Natural Micrometer; with Observations on the Minuteness of Animalcula," *Philosophical Magazine*, 3rd Ser. vol. II, no. 7 (1833), p. 64–67; "Natural History of the Elephant," *The Asiatic Journal*, N.S. vol. XIV, Pt. 1 (1834), p. 182–186, [German translation: "Zur Naturgeschichte der Elephanten," *Notizen aus dem Gebiete der Natur und Heilkunde*, vol. XLI (1834), p. 193–198. Note that the *Royal Society Catalogue* is incomplete, listing only the German version]; "Observations on Woodcocks and Fieldfares Breeding in Scotland," *Magazine of Natural History*, N.S. vol. I, no. 7 (1837), p. 337–340.
Hereafter these articles will be referred to as "Spiders," "Animalcula," "Elephants," and "Woodcocks," respectively.

19 George Fairholme, "Coal" (1834), p. 23; George Fairholme, *Mosaic Deluge* (1837), p. 20, 38, 41, 88, 108, 130.

20 The beginning of his 1833 article on natural micrometers and animalcula has "F.G.S." (Fellow of the Geological Society) after his name. But the Geological Society has no record of his membership (personal correspondence from Mrs. W. Cawthorne at the Geological Society, March 2, 1994). It is a mystery how these letters got placed there. His 1833 article on coal has no such initials after his name.

21 Fairholme, *Mosaic Deluge*, p. 94, 108, 130.

22 Ibid., p. 62.

That the line of proof which I now adduce is *new* as bearing on this particular question, will not, I believe, be denied. It has been the subject of patient and attentive study during the last four years, previous to which period, the evidences in question were as completely veiled from my perception, as if they had no existence in nature, although many of them had for years been daily displayed *before my eyes*. I have spared no pains in personally tracing out these proofs, from point to point, not only in our own island, but also over various parts of the continent of Europe: and the simple and obvious nature of many of the facts, in those districts within my reach, has enabled me to extend with confidence the same line of reasoning to every part of the earth, where phenomena precisely similar, are clearly described by travelers.[23]

But his geological research before his 1833 book was not insignificant. He wrote:

In the course of repeated travels over a great part of Europe, I have also had many opportunities of practically forming a judgment of the more visible and tangible evidences adduced in support of those theories.[24]

These field studies involved a longitudinal journey across the United Kingdom, which included descent into several mines.[25] He gave his readers detailed descriptions and many drawings (which often included careful measurements), which he made of the geological features of the English Isles of Sheppey, Thanet, and Wight and of many places along the coasts of England, Scotland,[26] Wales, Ireland, and northern France. Of particular note are his careful observations and measurements of six years' worth of erosion of the sea cliffs near Ramsgate during his residence there,[27] of the peculiar features of the famous western promontory of the Isle of Wight (known as the Needles),[28] and of the French coast near Boulogne.[29]

Other evidence of his geological field research is reflected in the fact that he spent several months exploring the valley system of the French table-lands.[30] During his extended residence on the shores of Thoun Lake in Switzerland in 1829 he engaged in much geological and geographical fieldwork.[31] He described his observations of the winding Neckar river valley in Germany in 1834 this way: "But having, myself, just completed an examination of *the whole course* of the Neckar, from its very source, down to Heidelberg, and having seen *many hundreds* of such windings, both above and below Canstatt. . . ."[32] Such observations led him to reject the burst-lake theory for the formation of the valley explained by the geology professor at the DNV meeting, who had taken him and others on a field trip to the valley. During this time in Germany he also visited a cave to study the stalagmites and some bones found there. He described the careful observations which led him to conclude that the stalactites and stalagmites were for the most part formed rapidly a few thousand years ago, rather than slowly over millions of years by the present rate of dripping water.[33]

One of the reasons that Fairholme believed that most of the sedimentary rock record was

23 Ibid., p. xiv.
24 Fairholme, *Geology of Scripture*, p. 1–2.
25 Ibid., p. 327, 330–332, 381–382.
26 On page 284 of *Mosaic Deluge* he again stressed his own field research: "I cannot expect the reader to follow me through all the details of the Scottish coasts, which I have, myself, studied. . . ."
27 Ibid., p. 208–212, 233–234.
28 Ibid., p. 255–259.
29 Ibid., p. 299–302. This little study also included some historical research regarding a lighthouse built by the Romans near the sea cliffs, from which Fairholme reasoned about the rate of erosion of the sea cliffs.
30 Ibid., p. 117; and also his careful description of the Seine River accompanied by his own illustrative drawing on pages 293–297.
31 Ibid., p. 277–278, 282, 316, 125.
32 Ibid., p. 130.
33 Ibid., footnote on p. 337–339.

produced during the year-long Noachian flood was the gradual, "insensible transitions" (or conformity) between the strata. After first having been alerted to this fact by a French professor of geology in Paris, who because of this fact had rejected Cuvier's theory of multiple catastrophes each separated by long stretches of time, Fairholme said:

> I had ample opportunities, both in Britain and on the continent of France and Germany, of inspecting the junctions of almost all the formations; and I feel persuaded that there is no fact more clear in geology that this, *viz. that the upper surface of almost every formation, was yet soft and moist, when the superincumbent sediments were deposited upon it.*[34]

Although Fairholme wrote about geological formations which he had not personally observed (e.g., Niagara Falls), he was careful to inform his reader of that fact and to cite his sources.[35] In addition to his field research, he studied fossils in the possession of others, such as at the Dublin Museum, in Buckland's Oxford collection, and in the private collections of several German geologists, as well as fossils and rock specimens which he had collected from various places in England, Wales, Ireland, Germany, and even Australia. He understood the way in which fossils were used to identify rock formations:

> I have now before me some fossils and hand-specimens, which were lately sent from New South Wales [Australia]. The first glance at these specimens is sufficient for an experienced geologist to be assured that they belong to the formation termed *mountain limestone*, which lies low in the carboniferous group of strata; and he thus becomes certain that the mountain limestone is found in New South Wales.[36]

Besides the time he had spent with German and French geologists and his attendance at scientific meetings, mentioned above, he also had personal contact with naturalists in India and Africa, from whom he gleaned information about the behavior of elephants, bears, and other creatures, whose bones often were found in the caves and diluvium of England and Europe. By this information he contested Buckland's interpretation of these fossil bones, such as those found in Kirkdale Cave in Yorkshire.[37]

As his writings show, Fairholme was well read in the current books and journal articles (both English and foreign) of the leading geologists, scientists, and experienced explorers, contrary to the charge of some critics.[38] In most cases he quoted liberally from his sources (often a page or more), especially of those with whom he disagreed, which reflects his desire to properly represent their views before he contested their conclusions.

34 Ibid., p. 396–397.

35 In his writing on Niagara Falls, for example, Fairholme relied primarily on the work of Captain Basil Hall and Robert Bakewell, who were also sources for Fairholme's American critic, Henry D. Rogers (later a famous structural geologist and professor of geology in Glasgow), and for Lyell. In confirmation of Hall's conclusions about the falls, Fairholme received information from his personal friend, Sir Howard Douglass, who as a result of many years experience as governor of New Brunswick had become recognized as a well-informed observer of the falls. See George Fairholme, "Niagara Falls" (1834), p. 11, 13, 20, and *Mosaic Deluge*, p. 158–159; also *DNB* on Douglass.

Rogers's critique of Fairholme's 1834 article appeared in *American Journal of Science and Arts*, vol. XXVII, no. 2 (1835), p. 326–335. Lyell's memoir on the falls from his trip to America appeared in *Proceedings of the Geological Society*, vol. III, pt. 2 (1838–42), p. 595–602. See also Lyell's *Principles of Geology* (1830–33), I: p. 179–181.

36 George Fairholme, "Coal" (1833), p. 247; *Mosaic Deluge*, p. 89, 139, 374 (quote). As is clear from his comments, the fossils found in Australia were sent to him by someone; the others appear to be specimens that he himself had discovered. The quote also suggests that Fairholme perceived himself to be an experienced geologist.

Even after his last writings on geology, he evidently continued to collect fossils, as reflected in a passing comment in a report of the meeting of the Geological Society. See *Philosophical Magazine*, 3rd ser. vol. XV, no. 99 (1839, supplement), p. 539.

37 Fairholme, *Mosaic Deluge*, p. 26–32; "Elephants" (1834).

38 For example, Anonymous, Review of Fairholme's *General View of the Geology of Scripture*, *Magazine of Natural History*, vol. VI, no. 33 (1833), p. 256.

In spite of his obvious geological competence, three scathing reviews of his writings stated that Fairholme, like the other scriptural geologists, knew nothing about geology. One said that he knew "scarcely an atom of geology as now taught" or knew "that atom imperfectly," that he was "actually (or wilfully) ignorant of the simplest data of the science [geology]" and that he had a brain with an opening like "a diluvial chaotic pit."[39] Another said he had "little real knowledge of geology"[40] and a third spoke of Fairholme's "want of practical acquaintance" with geology.[41] Yet neither of these latter two critics cited a single example of such ignorance, and of the two errors cited by the first critic at least one is questionable, and neither is significant.

In dealing with the arguments of his opponents, Fairholme displayed a very respectful attitude. One could accuse him of being boring in the use of adjectives, because his most frequent descriptions were "able" or "learned," which he used equally with regard to deistic uniformitarians, such as Lyell, Playfair, and Hutton, and to Christian catastrophists, such as Buckland and Sedgwick. For example, after quoting James Hutton's famous statement that he found "no traces of a beginning, no prospect of an end," which had provoked the charge of atheism from many others, Fairholme refrained from character assassination and simply, but firmly, criticized his conclusions by saying:

> But Hutton, intent only on proving the vast antiquity of the earth, carried his sweeping conclusions far beyond the limits prescribed by his premises; and was thus amongst the first to mislead the scientific world into that tangled labyrinth, which most men now perceive, and which some regard without much hope of ultimate extrication.[42]

Fairholme also critically evaluated the views of those more sympathetic to his own with regard to geology and the Flood, such as André Deluc.[43] Scriptural geologists, to whom he made passing positive reference, were Thomas Gisborne, Sharon Turner, and George Young.[44] In *Geology of Scripture* (p. 431–438), he favored Granville Penn's argument that Genesis 2:10–14 was a textual gloss.

So Fairholme dealt respectfully with his opponents, commending them as persons and acknowledging their contributions to scientific knowledge, while at the same time disagreeing with them where he thought their arguments were weak or fallacious. He also expected and invited response to his ideas from geologists. In his journal article on Niagara Falls he wrote:

> It will give me the greatest pleasure to be set right in the arguments which I have ventured to draw from various distinct, *and otherwise unaccountable,* sources in support of the Scripture statement [regarding the Mosaic Deluge]; and *last,* though not *least,* from the above phenomena of the greatest of known cataracts; and I shall look with some anxiety for a simple and consistent refutation of the subject of this paper.[45]

He was willing to admit his errors, when so proven by the evidence, and to modify his views accordingly, as shown in the appendix to his 1834 article on Niagara Falls and in his introductory chapter to the 1837 book with reference to his 1833 book.[46] In commenting on Buckland's recantation of his belief in the Flood, which Buckland felt obliged to make because of new geological evidence brought to his attention, Fairholme described himself in comparison, saying:

---

39 Anonymous review in *Christian Remembrancer*, vol. XV (1833), p. 391–392.

40 Anonymous review in *Magazine of Natural History*, vol. VI, no. 33 (1833), p. 256.

41 John Pye Smith, *On the Relation between the Holy Scriptures and Geological Science* (1839), p. 220. In his discussion of Fairholme, Smith gave no evidence of having read Fairholme's *Mosaic Geology* (1837), and he was not a geologist either.

42 Fairholme, *Mosaic Deluge*, p. 309.

43 Ibid., p. 320–322.

44 Ibid., p. xi, 2, 274.

45 George Fairholme, "Niagara Falls" (1834), p. 18–19.

46 Fairholme, "Niagara Falls" (1834), p. 23–25; Fairholme, *Mosaic Deluge*, p. 62–63.

So far from condemning these candid admissions of supposed error, I look upon them as in the highest degree praiseworthy; nor can there be the slightest doubt of their disinterested and honorable nature, when we consider that they voluntarily level with the ground, some theoretical structures which were once regarded with general delight and admiration. Nor could I, indeed, be justified in any such censure, as I shall, myself, have occasion, like so many other geological students, to recant, in the following Treatise, some opinions which I had adopted on the same independent grounds, but which a more mature study of facts had subsequently led me to abandon.[47]

In addition to analyzing existing geological theories, Fairholme also attempted to add to the storehouse of geological facts by presenting new knowledge on the basis of his own fieldwork. From his reading of many contemporary and leading geologists, he felt confident in saying that no one had ever made these observations before. The new facts he claimed to present related to the formation of valley systems, sea cliffs, and waterfalls. His work on valleys was especially significant in his mind, because it was the arguments of Lyell, Scrope, and Murchison, in the late 1820s (that valleys had been cut by the rivers now flowing in their bottoms), which had substantially increased doubts about the violent nature of the Noachian flood and led to the recantations of Sedgwick, Buckland, and Greenough. Fairholme wrote:

"To elicit new and prominent facts," says a recent and highly talented writer, "is the lot of few; but all may investigate *truth*, and thus contribute more or less, towards the advancement of knowledge. Moreover, even the humblest contributors may rest assured, that they are imperceptibly raising a structure, which will, sooner or later, include the conspicuous labors of their more fortunate coadjutors; in which structure, their labors will, indeed, still appear conspicuous, though their importance will be diminished as the fabric is extended around them."[48] Under this impression, and in the hope of thus conducing to ultimate good, I am induced to offer this contribution to the general stock of *facts*, on which alone, scientific knowledge can be solidly based. From the critic, I feel that I can look for but little indulgence, while deliberately entering on the field of controversy, in opposition to so numerous a host of powerful combatants. But humbly invoking the divine blessing, without which all scientific efforts, however brilliant, are to man but *"a stumbling block,"* to God *"foolishness;"* and confidently trusting in the simplicity and clearness of the facts which have at length been disclosed, I submit both these facts and the inferences which seem naturally to flow from them, to the candid and unbiassed [*sic*] judgment of the world.[49]

After the presentation of his "new and conclusive" evidences regarding the time of the formation of the present land masses and the changes that have taken place on them since then to the present, Fairholme went to some length to establish that they were, in fact, a totally new contribution to the advancement of geological knowledge. So he quoted extensively from *Discourse on the Study of Natural Philosophy* (1831) by the astronomer Sir John Herschel,[50] who was

47 Fairholme, *Mosaic Deluge*, p. ix–x.

48 He was quoting from William Prout's *Bridgewater Treatise* (1834), p. 548.

49 Fairholme, *Mosaic Deluge*, p. xiv–xv.

50 John Herschel, *Preliminary Discourse on the Study of Natural Philosophy* (1840, identical to 1833 edition), p. 283–286. Herschel was discussing the obscurity of geological knowledge about the commencement of and subsequent changes to the present superficial rock strata of the dry lands and the fact that, at the time, it was difficult to properly evaluate the effects of present causes in geology, such as the annual erosion rates of the continents or coastal erosion caused by the sea. Herschel concluded that "much then, at present, must be left to opinion" and "every possible effort" should be made "to obtain accurate information on such points" in order for geology to move forward as a true science.

a man of encyclopedic knowledge, including of geology, and was almost deified by his contemporaries.[51] Fairholme then remarked of his own present work:

> Such were the judicious observations of this able astronomer, a very few years ago; and such as he describes it, was then the very limited state of our knowledge, with regard to the progress of meteoric and marine agencies, in constant action upon our dry lands. I may, perhaps, be permitted, without presumption, to hope, that the evidences just produced, from sea-cliffs and water-falls, have now become of a sufficiently distinct and definite nature to entitle them to a place amongst such inductive reasoning, as are so beautifully applied to the more experimental sciences. . . . Having thus justified the character of *novelty*, as applied to the facts of *sea cliffs* and *water-falls*, which have now been, for the first time, brought forward in a new light, let us proceed in our proposed summary of the evidences which have now been adduced.[52]

The Relationship Between Scripture and Geology

Fairholme did not discuss at length his view of the Bible. But clearly he held to the traditional Christian view of the inspiration, infallibility, and inerrancy of Scripture.[53] In this belief he was not ignorant of critical biblical scholarship. In the preface to his 1837 book he decried the fact that the "all too common view at present" is that the early chapters of Genesis were mythical or allegorical, the result of successive traditions of ignorant and superstitious people.[54] He believed, like many educated and uneducated Englishmen in his day, including some Christians who opposed his view of Genesis and geology, that the "Sacred Word of God can neither err, nor stand opposed to His works, however blindly or imperfectly man may interpret them."[55] So he made a distinction between the unerring Scriptures and a person's interpretation of them, which could be in error. But, he said, when rightly understood, God's truth in creation would be harmonious with the truth of divine revelation.

It was his conviction that the Genesis-geology debate was foundational to faith in the rest of Scripture. In response to Lyell's insistence on explaining every geological phenomenon by the current laws of nature Fairholme said:

> Such is the line of reasoning by which the distinct testimony of Inspiration is to be set aside, on the subject of the deluge; and such the steps, whether intentional or casual, by which, if acceded to, all confidence in Scripture must eventually be shaken, on subjects of infinitely greater importance than that which we are now examining.[56]

Some of those more important subjects to which he alluded included the historicity of the accounts of the miracles of Jesus as well as the truthfulness of the prophetic statements in the Bible about the future.

But it was as a result of his geological investigations up to 1833 that his "confidence in the unerring accuracy of these Records [Genesis 1–11]

51 Walter F. Cannon, "The Impact of Uniformitarianism," *Proceedings of the American Philosophical Society*, vol. 105, no. 3 (1961), p. 301–314.

52 Fairholme, *Mosaic Deluge*, p. 327, 329.

53 Fairholme, *Geology of Scripture*, title page, x, 24, 135, 493. On these pages, Fairholme used both the words "infallible" and "unerring," though he favored the latter by referring to the unerring character, dictates, truths, and source of Scripture. His comments suggest that he had essentially the same view as modern Christians who hold to the complete "inerrancy" of Scripture.

54 Fairholme, *Mosaic Deluge*, p. x–xi.

55 Ibid., p. xvi.

56 Ibid., p. 59. His response was after a lengthy quote from Lyell's *Principles of Geology* (1830–33), III: p. 271. Later, on page 390, Fairholme similarly stated, regarding the new theories of geology, that bending "His Sacred Revelation to our own fanciful theories, thus rudely shatters the very foundation of our belief on other points, of incomparably greater importance than geology, to the present as well as future well-being of the human race."

[was] firmly established."[57] After another four years of more firsthand study of geological evidence, as well as analysis of the current theories of Buckland and Lyell, he concluded in 1837 that "we find that the combined efforts, even of the ablest men, have proved totally incompetent successfully to contend against the simple yet unbending Words of Eternal Truth."[58]

Though he had this view of Scripture, he decided in his 1837 book to restrict himself to scientific arguments. But in so doing he did not want his readers to think that he was belittling the Word of God. Thus, before proceeding into the last stages of his argument, he made this digression (which reveals not only his view of the Bible, but also his perspective on purely scientific arguments):

> My design is rather to follow the course already pursued in the foregoing chapters, and to draw my inferences from *natural phenomena*, as far as their evidences are exposed to our view. But though this may be the most proper, and the most philosophic mode of dealing with the subject, I would by no means have it inferred that I undervalue, or set aside, the conclusive testimony of Revelation, on this point. On the contrary, I should myself be content to rest, with the fullest confidence, on the unerring truth of revealed testimony, on this as on all other points, especially if they are beyond my own ready comprehension; but as this may not be the feeling of numbers who take an interest in geology, and who conceive that its facts ought to corroborate and explain the more obscure notices of physical events relating to the earth, which are incidentally afforded by Scripture, in recording God's dealings with man, it may be more satisfactory to such persons to exclude, for the moment, what the Scriptures have taught us, with regard to this particular subject, with the distinct reservation, however, that they are in no wise freed from their allegiance to the Word of God, by any imperfection which they may conceive to exist, in the evidences which I may now adduce, in support of that Word.[59]

So in Fairholme's view, all of the Scriptures were produced by divine supernatural inspiration. They are God's unerring revelation, and as such they are completely trustworthy in all that they affirm.

On the Laws of Nature

I have briefly alluded to Fairholme's view of the so-called "laws of nature" when describing his view of Scripture. But since he had more to say about this topic than any other scriptural geologist and since Buckland, Lyell, and his other opponents insisted on explaining the geological phenomena on the basis of such laws, it would be well to note carefully how Fairholme used analogy with the existing laws of nature and how eager or reluctant he was to invoke the First Cause to explain what then-known secondary causes could not. I will quote extensively to let him speak for himself and then will summarize.

First, with regard to the relationship of Scripture to geological reasoning he wrote:

> "A natural deluge, arising from physical causes, within our view," says geology, "may be readily understood and assented to; and of such local convulsions we have numerous proofs, in the strata of the earth; but to a *universal flood*, such as Moses describes, we cannot subscribe, because we can conceive no law in nature, by which it could possibly be effected." It may readily be admitted, that, as a general rule, this determination of adhering closely by the established laws of nature, is most necessary and wise; for, without such rule, human ardor, combined with human blindness would recur, in every difficulty, to a *final* cause. But "although

57 Fairholme, *Geology of Scripture*, p. 493.
58 Fairholme, *Mosaic Deluge*, p. 423.
59 Ibid., p. 356.

> it be *dangerous* hastily to have recourse to final causes,"[60] yet there are some subjects, and those too, not unworthy of philosophic attention, which cannot possibly be credited, without drawing a certain line of exception to this rule. Is the chemist in his laboratory, for example, to refuse his assent to the statement of history, with regard to the physical fact, that, on one occasion, *water* was converted to *wine*, merely because he is certain that the laws of chemistry would not enable *him* to succeed in any similar trial? Is the physician or surgeon to put in the plea of the laws of nature, in objecting to the no less physical facts, respecting the *blind* being made *to see*, the *deaf to hear*, the *dumb to speak*, and even *the dead body*, on which corruption had begun its work, *to rise again into life*, and once more to resume its former station in human society? On similar grounds might the soldier refuse his assent to the statement of Joshua respecting the destruction of the walls of Jericho, on the strength of his never having either seen or heard, in modern warfare, of walls being destroyed by the mere shout of a besieging army. We can, in short, see no bounds to scepticism on such subjects, from the moment that we subscribe to any such objections, however talented they may be, who set us the example. If these, and such like statements of physical facts are to be erased from the Word of God, as being altogether inconsistent with the common laws of nature, then, indeed, *but not till then*, will the Christian geologist be justified in entertaining doubts with respect to the fact of a general Deluge, on the pleas of his inability to account for it, by the fixed laws of nature. . . . We must act with due consistency with regard to such decisions as are here demanded from us. We cannot *believe* one of the above preternatural, yet physical, facts, and *deny* another, simply because we have not discovered the means by which that other was effected. If it can be clearly shown, from natural facts, as I hope to make it appear, that a great change occurred, over all the present dry lands of the earth, at the very period assigned by history to the Mosaic deluge; and if the known laws of nature will not, or cannot, furnish us with any means of explaining how this change was effected; we must, *perforce*, admit into our scientific reasoning, a *preter*-natural power and agency; and thus attribute to the power and will of nature's God, what nature itself can by no means account for.[61]

When Fairholme discussed the erosion of the sea cliffs along the coast of England we see something of his idea of the uniformity of processes and rates of nature and how he argued from analogy.

> We have, in such instances, only to reason with regard to what has been, by a study of what is, and what we see will be, in order to discover the real path of truth. We plainly see in examining all these coasts, that in a thousand, or in ten thousand years, the edge of the cliffs on which we now walk will not exist, and that instead of being elevated, as we are, far above the waves, the geologists of that day, must walk upon what is now the foundation of the rock on which we stand, left dry by the ebbing tide, and covered, like those below us, with a protecting coat of sea-weed. What must thus happen to future philosophers, now happens to ourselves with reference to bygone times, and to masses of solid rock already washed away. Unless we forcibly reject all analogy, our forefathers might have foretold what we now see has taken place; and in the same manner, we can now with certainty foretell what our descendants must witness in succeeding ages; for as an action which

60 He quoted from Buckland's *Bridgewater Treatise* (1836), I: p. 547.
61 Fairholme, *Mosaic Deluge*, p. 59–62.

is ceaseless, is now slowly destroying the lands at D in the plates [see replica below], so has it progressively advanced from A to B and C;

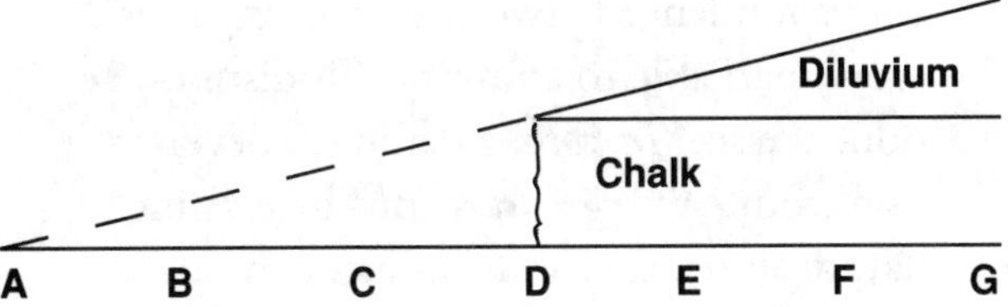

and so must it continue to advance from its present place D to E, F, and G; but beyond the point at A we can by no means advance, under the guidance of the existing laws of nature. We then reach the commencement of a new state of things; and it is as clear as any mathematical demonstration, that as, on a certain day, this action, which is now ceaseless, must have begun, by the breaking of the first powerful surf on a fixed shore, so, before that day, there was there no such action, simply because there was no fixed land for such surf to beat upon. Beyond this point, and beyond the date (whatever it may be, of 5, 10, or 100 thousand years) to which it points, we cannot advance; we must there embark on the obscure sea of theory, without chart or compass.[62]

Concerning the difference between the sedimentary rocks and the sediments being deposited by the present rivers and oceans he stated:

The existing lands consist of all the strata already described. The rivers, by means of which much of the detritus of these lands is carried into the sea, flow over *the whole of them;* and, consequently, the sediments now lodged in the waters, must be a mixture from the destruction of all sorts of rocks. In like manner, the sea coasts are composed of every variety of mineral formation; consequently the destruction by the waves, there so constant, must occasion deposits of moved matter, of a like mixed character, partaking of the composition of the whole, and not confined to that of any one species of rock. One river is perhaps charged more especially with the detritus of *argillaceous* formations; another with *arenaceous* sediments,[63] each according to the prevalence of the rocks, over which it flows. If we view this process on the great scale, we cannot fail to perceive that though the movements of the waters may sift and arrange the whole into distinct strata, such strata cannot have the universality of *character*, which the older formations exhibit. Far less can their fossil contents, consisting of fish, shells, or vegetables, be the same *in all latitudes*, as appears formerly to have been the case. The analogy, then, on which geologists reason, between the *mode* of former depositions, and the result of existing action, can, in no point, hold good, except that water still possesses, as it always has done, the power of arranging its sediments in *strata*.[64]

A few pages later in a discussion of the origin of soils he compared the action of contemporary flooded rivers with that of the Deluge.

I am aware that on the subject of the origin of soils, there are various contending opinions; and a very common idea is, that they have almost entirely arisen from the long-continued action of the sun and air, upon that portion of the surface, and to that particular depth only, which is exposed to this action. But though we cannot doubt that this action of the atmosphere is another proof of design, and that it greatly ameliorates all soils, which, indeed, without it, would soon become barren, it is evident to any one who will examine the sections of that general diluvial covering *which exists only on the surface*

62 Ibid., p. 236–237.
63 Argillaceous rocks are composed of very fine-grained material, such as clay, while arenaceous rocks are composed of sand.
64 Ibid., p. 377–378.

of the earth, that those rich soils, generally termed *vegetable loams*, are quite distinct from any thing found amongst the regular strata beneath. This diluvium, being the result of the action of waters, may perhaps be said to be a *mere natural consequence* of such action, and therefore that we cannot justly attribute to express *design*, what any, and every, flooded river produces, on a smaller scale. But inasmuch as a *general Deluge* covering *the whole earth*, exceeds the flooded brook or river, by so much do the *universal* and *preternatural* effects of the former, exceed the local and merely *natural* effects of the latter.[65]

The catastrophists believed that the geological record revealed that throughout the millions of years of quiet periods interspersed with catastrophes God had periodically, after each catastrophe, interrupted the normal course of nature to create new forms of plants and animals. To this view Fairholme responded:

> We are told by geologists, that with the commencement of certain *mineral* strata, certain *animal and vegetable* forms also *commenced*. Have we any such *commencements* in the present state of nature? And if we find ourselves entirely deprived of all such points of comparison, by which alone we are capable of judging, are we not naturally led, by the *creative* Power which these animal forms so obviously bespeak, to attribute to the same Power and Will, such changes and arrangements *in the mineral strata*, as appear to have accompanied those changes *in organic beings*? If this inference be just and natural, we cannot, without force, separate, as geologists do, the two facts, and suppose that in the one case, a creative Power was exercised, and that in the other, corresponding as it seems to have done in point of time, the mineral formations were the mere casual effects of the same common laws of nature which are still in force around us. The mutual and oft-repeated correspondence between such changes, is too remarkable to admit of this distinction. We see, *in both*, a complete deviation from *existing nature*. But by existing nature alone, can we form just conceptions of things. In the absence, then, of this sole criterion, we are forced to quit the laws of nature, by which philosophy so tenaciously holds; and we are handed over to a different and superior power, of which we can have no knowledge except that it exists.[66]

In 1833 Fairholme had also expressed his rejection of evolution on the grounds that it was contrary to the laws of nature, though he did believe in limited biological variation to produce different races (e.g., of men).[67]

In his final conclusions of *Mosaic Geology*, Fairholme returned to the relation of secondary causes and the First Cause.

> This fact being proved, and the truth of the so long *doubted*, and now *rejected* Mosaic flood, being thus attested, we look around us, into the beautiful volume of the laws of nature, as far as that volume has been graciously unsealed for our perusal, to discover some *law* by which this great event could have been brought about, that we may not unnecessarily have recourse to a *Final Cause*, where *second causes* might be found capable of accounting for the phenomena. But although we find a variety of destructive causes, such as volcanoes, and local floods occasioned by earthquakes, exercising considerable violence in different parts of the earth, throwing up islands from the bottom of the sea,

65 Ibid., p. 381.
66 Ibid., p. 384–385. Clearly, from his writings, Fairholme believed we could have other knowledge of God, but only by divine revelation.
67 airholme, *Geology of Scripture*, p. 7–14, 457–458.

and perhaps even slightly influencing the relative level of sea and land over a limited extent; although we may admit, to the very utmost, the extent of these results (which are, however, often still but problematical), we look in vain for any *law of nature*, by the action of which even a small district like the Isle of Wight *could be at once elevated to the height of several hundred feet*, above the level of its native deep. How much more hopeless, then, the discovery of *a law* which could cause the seas and continents of our planet *to change places*, and this not by a very slow and *gradual*, but by a *paroxysmal* movement! And yet so different has this movement been from any thing that we know *of volcanic effects*, or of terrific and instantaneous earthquakes, that instead of such confusion as these latter almost always occasion, we find an order, a beauty, and a general smoothness pervading the new dry lands,[68] which all bear testimony to the fact that the Final Cause to which we are thus at length driven, could produce, and had produced, the most admirable *good* out of *evil* and the utmost possible *order*, out of the most awful and destructive judgment. . . . The proofs of the *rapidity*, and of the *uninterrupted* deposition of sedimentary matter, so totally different from any existing action on which we can form our judgment, seem to remove the *mode* of these strata entirely beyond the sphere of man's distinct comprehension; and lead us to attribute them *to the action of second causes indeed, but under the special and direct guidance of* THE GREAT FIRST CAUSE, in the same manner as the Deluge, and the present beautiful order of things resulting from it, seem to have been brought about.[69]

Fairholme's ideas can be summarized as follows. He firmly believed in the general uniformity of the processes of nature, such as gravity, the flow of water downhill, the erosive and sorting powers of moving water, the ameliorating effect of the atmospheric forces on the surface of the earth, that earthquakes cause faults, etc. He was therefore strongly committed to the sound and necessary scientific principle of analogy. He assumed, because of the physical evidence he observed, that the present gradual processes, such as wind, rain, river and sea erosion, and river, lake and ocean sedimentation, have continued ceaselessly, since the land masses were elevated. But he did not believe that the rates of these processes had been constant, for in the case of sea cliffs and waterfalls he observed evidence that in the past the present force of water was working against a much smaller rock resistance (i.e., softer rocks), resulting in more rapid erosion.[70]

But by the same process of analogical reasoning, Fairholme concluded that the contemporaneous elevation of the continents was an almost unimaginably great paroxysmal and temporally brief event. He argued that the present-day processes and rates of erosion, sedimentation, volcanos, and earthquakes (which were generally described as the "present processes of nature," the "laws of nature," or the secondary causes of effects) completely failed to explain the major features of the land masses. The present paroxysmal events (e.g., floods, volcanos, and earthquakes) are only miniature analogies of the past singular paroxysm which laid down the geological record of fossiliferous sedimentary strata and diluvial surface rubble all over the earth, raised the continents, and scooped out the valley systems. In this regard he was reasoning very much like the catastrophists of his day, though he believed he had uncovered geological evidence, which corroborated the testimony of Scripture, that there had only been one catastrophe in the past and

68 Here he was referring to the drainage system of valleys on all the continents and the relative rarity of inhabitable (for man) mountain ranges in comparison to the habitable plains and rolling hills. He spent considerable time developing these topics earlier in the book.

69 Fairholme, *Mosaic Deluge*, p. 417–418, 421–422.

70 This was particularly the form of his argument for calculating the time (about 5,000 years ago) of the initial recession of Niagara Falls. See George Fairholme, "Niagara Falls" (1834) and Fairholme, *Mosaic Deluge*, p. 157–203.

that it had not been a *natural* event of nature, which we should expect again in the future, but a unique never-to-be-repeated *preternatural* event associated with the judgment of God on a sinful world.

So Fairholme did not freely invoke miracles to explain what he saw. He sought to find secondary causes for the observed effects, as much as he could. Rather, from his own geological observations he argued against those who said that the present processes (and rates) of nature did explain everything. When he felt that the natural secondary causes demonstrably failed to explain the effects, he concluded that the First Cause had preternaturally acted. As the catastrophists applied this line of reasoning to the biological realm to explain the origin of life forms, Fairholme insisted it could and should be applied to the geological realm as well to explain the features of the earth. In reality he argued that such preternatural divine activity only occurred, with reference to geological history, at the time of the Flood and original creation, as the biblical record testified.

Furthermore, he argued that to insist on explaining everything by present-day processes or "laws of nature" would necessarily involve the denial of all the miraculous elements of the Bible, which in his view was impossible for a Christian.[71]

Summary of His Two Books

The argument of his *Geology of Scripture* (1833), which mainly attempted to refute Lyell's uniformitarian theory, can be summarized as follows.

1. It is unreasonable and unphilosophical to attribute all things to the mere laws of nature. Even if secondary causes can explain the transformation of the original chaotic mass into the present globe, they cannot explain the origin of the chaotic mass, and therefore we are forced to acknowledge a creative power. This logic applies even more forcefully to the origin of animals and plants, which display such evident design. God must have made originally a mature, perfect man, oak tree, bear, etc. When we compare such reasoning to Scripture we realize that God did such creating in six days, which arguably were literal 24-hour days. So the original creation was perfect; it did not improve gradually from an imperfect state over eons of time.

2. The first great geological change on earth took place on the third day, when God made the dry land by divine decree. He did this not by the normal laws of gravity, fluid flow, and slow accumulation, but by the depression of the earth's thin crust in places. From that moment, the ocean, operating in a manner similar to its present action, produced the earliest, non-fossiliferous, secondary formations on the base of the primary primitive rocks created in the initial act of creation.

3. A great portion of the secondary formations (those containing marine fossils, e.g., the chalk) was formed by the current laws of nature operating during the 1,656-year period from the creation to the Noachian flood. The Flood, for which there is evidence all over the dry lands, produced all strata containing the fossil remains of land animals as there was a gradual interchange of the former sea and land. The Flood waters, moving in currents similar to the movements of the present oceans, distributed the floating plants and animals to where they are now buried. The pre-Flood climate was not significantly different than presently, and plants and animals similarly lived at different latitudes. Man was coexistent with the pre-Flood plants and animals. Contrary to the catastrophist views of Buckland and Cuvier, there were no progressive creations over long ages before man.

71 Actually, the relationship of miracles to the uniformity of the laws of nature has been the focus of much scholarly discussion in both the 19th and the 20th centuries. So if Fairholme's articulation of his view, or my summary of it, is not perfectly clear or internally consistent to the mind of the reader, it may be understandable. See, for example, James H. Shea, "Twelve Fallacies of Uniformitarianism," *Geology*, vol. X (1982), p. 455–460; Martin J.S. Rudwick, "The Principle of Uniformity," *History of Science*, vol. I (1962), p. 82–86; Walter F. Cannon, "The Problem of Miracles in the 1830s," *Victorian Studies*, vol. IV (1960), p. 5–32; R. Hooykaas, "Catastrophism in Geology, Its Scientific Character in Relation to Actualism and Uniformitarianism," *Meded. Kon. Nederl. Akad. Wetenschappen*, deel 33, no. 7 (1970), p. 271–316.

4. On the basis of the worldwide traditions and other proofs, such as the origin of languages, we may conclude that the human race is descended from Noah's family in the Middle East.

5. All the evidence presented in support of these points corroborates the historical truth of Genesis 1–11 and other statements of Scripture. This evidence, along with the evidence of fulfilled prophecy, shows the Bible to be the product of divine inspiration.

In his *Mosaic Deluge* (1837), Fairholme stated that further personal study of the geological evidence convinced him that he had made some errors in his first book. The line of argument then in 1837 is quite different and more limited in scope, focusing completely on the Noachian flood, which he now believed, contrary to his earlier book, laid down virtually all the sedimentary fossiliferous rocks. First, he reviewed his previous arguments in favor of the global extent of the Flood (e.g., quadruped animal remains, especially mammoths in the diluvial deposits and in various caves). To this he added remarks about some recently discovered human fossils which he believed were strong evidence that the secondary strata were not all formed before the creation of man,[72] and he gave an overview of the traditional non-geological defense of the Flood account in Genesis. After this brief introduction, he turned his attention to arguing strictly from the phenomena of nature in proof of the following points.

1. As we look at the topographical features of the land masses all over the world, we observe systems of valleys draining in all directions from the summits to the present sea level. These valley systems were clearly formed by water, but, contrary to the ideas of Hutton, Playfair, and Lyell, they were not formed by the existing rivers over immense periods of time. The greatest evidence of this is the many dry valleys (no longer containing any river) in the valley systems, which connect into the drainage system at just the right level. These suggest that the carving, scooping waters which produced the valley systems are no longer seen on the continents.[73] As the valley systems end at the level of the present seas, so in a similar way the dry and wet valleys on the sides of lakes end at the present level of the lakes. These two points show that the whole network of valleys was formed contemporaneously, regardless of the length of the valleys. Since the valleys were not carved by the present streams but the latter merely flow down previously prepared valleys, a study of the additional erosion by the rivers leads us irresistibly to the fact of a commencement of their flow in a certain place.

2. By measuring the rate and amount of erosion of major waterfalls such as at Niagara Falls or at Schaffhausen on the Rhine, we can calculate the time of commencement of water flow to be, at most, 10,000 years, though additional consideration of the fact of constant power of the water coupled with a considerably smaller rock resistance in the past can reduce that date of commencement to about 4,000 to 5,000 years ago. Since the waters of Niagara represent the drainage of nearly half of North America and other river systems there are similar, even if they lack a falls, we can by analogy conclude that all the rivers started to flow and hence the continent became dry land, about 5,000 years ago.

3. Careful examination of the present sea-cliffs of Britain and Europe shows that they have eroded a relatively short distance. This leads us to a definite point in space and time where and when the present ceaseless activity of the waves commenced, which means that the continents rose at a definite period (contrary to Hutton, who saw no evidence of a beginning). The average coastal erosion in England and France is observed to be about one-half mile. Over 10,000 years this works out to an annual loss of

72 He had dealt with this at some length in *Geology of Scripture*, p. 377–420, and in his letter to the editor in *Christian Observer*, vol. XXXV (1835), p. 346–350.

73 Buckland argued in a very similar way in his *Reliquiae Diluvianae* (1823), p. 239–258. Although by the time of his 1836 *Bridgewater Treatise* he had abandoned the Flood as the cause of these valleys, he never, as far as I could discover, explicitly refuted his 1823 reasoning.

three inches, which is too little, given certain observed facts about the coasts. Therefore, the commencement of the sea erosion, and with it the elevation of the present continents, began sometime between 10,000 years ago and the beginning of historic times (i.e., human histories, at that time reckoned to reach back about 5,000 years). We cannot at present get any nearer to the true age of the present continents, but since there are similar effects and causes on all sea coasts, we can conclude that there was a simultaneous birth of the continents.

4. The coincidence between the commencement of the existing state of the continents and the Genesis flood and the worldwide traditions of a global flood is obvious. To the biblical evidence for the uniqueness of the Flood may be added geological evidence that the sedimentary strata were laid down in relatively rapid succession (during the year of the Flood) on top of each other when the lower one was yet damp and soft. These evidences include fossil trees found frequently in the secondary and tertiary strata (though primarily in the coal formations), which are buried in an upright position (at various angles) and which traverse several strata.[74] Also, smooth gradual transitions (in terms of the mixture of rock type) from one strata to the next generally characterize the stratigraphic record. Ephemeral markings (e.g., ripple marks and animal tracks) at the transition boundaries between strata likewise indicate that the strata must have been buried before erosion could take place.[75] Finally, there is a general lack of vast erosional features between the geological formations such as the present surface valley systems, which are shown to be the result of the Flood.[76] Therefore, the geological record is not the result of many catastrophes over millions of years.

5. All these lines of evidence, Fairholme argued, prove the fact, the recency, and the uniqueness of the global Noachian flood, which was the goal stated in the title of the book, and corroborate the literal truthfulness of the biblical account.

Conclusion

By early 19th century standards, George Fairholme was quite competent to critically analyze old-earth geological theories. He attempted to contribute new observations and inferences to the bank of geological knowledge. He was most certainly not opposed to the study of geology, but only to old-earth geological theories, which he believed were contradictory to both Scripture and the scientific facts.

In his view, Genesis does not teach an entire system of natural philosophy or even of geology, but rather it provides trustworthy beacons to guide geological studies into a true understanding of earth history. He attempted to show from the geological and geographical evidence (e.g., valley systems, waterfalls, sea coast erosion, human fossils, polystrate fossil trees, insensible transitions between the strata, etc.) that the global Flood had formed the present surface of the land masses about 5,000 years ago and that the strata were not the result of modern processes operating over millions of years, but were associated primarily with the Flood.

Being a wealthy landed gentleman, he had plenty of money to travel and pursue his strong interest in the study of nature, especially geology. His two books on geology were motivated by a deep conviction about the historical, as well as theological and moral, truth of Scripture and the detrimental effects that old-earth reinterpretations of Genesis would have on faith in the rest of the Bible.

74 He had previously argued this point in *Geology of Scripture*, p. 328–340, and in his 1833 journal article on coal, p. 247–251.

75 This was also discussed in his *Geology of Scripture* (1833), p. 340–345.

76 Fairholme, *Mosaic Deluge*, p. 12, 80, 285, 392–405, 412–429.

JOHN MURRAY (1786?–1851)

John Murray is particularly significant for our consideration of the scriptural geologists because he has been completely overlooked by historians[1] and his works related to the Genesis-geology debate were largely ignored by contemporary old-earth proponents,[2] even though he was competent in geology and was a very well-known scientist and Christian.

In about 1786, John Murray was born in Stranraer, Scotland to Grace and James Murray, a sea captain, and from an early age he demonstrated a great interest in science. Though he eventually attained M.A. and PhD degrees, it was said by contemporaries who knew him that "he was literally self-taught" and therefore was a great example to young people placed in disadvantageous circumstances.[3] In 1815, at the age of 29, he published his first work, *The Elements of Chemical Science as Applied to the Arts and Manufactures and Natural Phenomena*, in which he described himself as "lecturer on the philosophy of physics and chemistry." For many years, starting in 1816, he gave an annual lecture course at the Surrey Institution and also became well-known through lectures (which generally included experiments) at mechanics institutes throughout the kingdom, which led Lord Brougham to describe Murray as "one of the best lecturers in the world." Though he traveled extensively, his writings indicate that he made Hull his primary residence from about 1824

Unless otherwise noted, this biographical section is based on the *DNB* article on Murray.

1 None of the leading historians on this subject (e.g., Gillispie, Yule, Millhauser, Rupke, Roberts) mention him.

2 Neither his 1838 nor 1840 books dealing with geology received a review in the scientific journals or in the Christian periodicals (except one, below), though his anonymously published *Portrait of Geology* was mentioned in one letter to the editor of *Christian Observer*. See "A Scriptural Geologist, No 'More Last Words' on Geology," *Christian Observer*, vol. XXXIX (1839), p. 471. *Evangelical Magazine* gave a positive review of Murray's *The Truth of Revelation* (1840) in N.S. vol. XVIII (1840), p. 486–487.

3 *DNB* on Murray; "Death of Dr. Murray, Ph.D.," *Galloway Advertiser and Wigtownshire Free Press* (July 3, 1851), and Murray's obituary in *The Mining Journal*, July 12, 1851, p. 336–337.

until 1850, when he moved back to Stranraer. Shortly after establishing residence there with his lifelong wife, severe illness reduced him to a helpless invalid at the same time that he faced great financial difficulties.[4] He died on June 28, 1851. The Stranraer magistrates attended the funeral, the shops in the whole town closed, church bells tolled, and the streets of the procession were lined with spectators.[5] Having been a loyal member of the Church of Scotland and a strong Calvinist[6] all his life, the local paper said of him at this time:

> His benevolent heart was a stranger to bigotry and sectarianism. He loved all who loved the Lord Jesus Christ. In the hours of sickness and of death he manifested the same meek, patient, and amiable spirit which had characterized his deportment through life.[7]

With great industry he developed an impressive breadth of knowledge in many subject areas of both science and literature. Not surprisingly, he did not gain great eminence in any single field, though he contributed much to chemistry and to mining. Between 1816 and 1835 he lectured, wrote several papers, and conducted many experiments in relation to the safety lamps used by miners. In the process, he developed a theory on the efficiency of the safety lamp which opposed the theory propounded by renown chemist Sir Humphry Davy, and which in 1835 led to an invitation to testify on safety lamps and mine ventilation before the Select Committee of the House of Commons on accidents in mines.[8]

His breadth and depth of knowledge and experience qualified him to become a Fellow of the Linnaean Society in 1819, the Society of Antiquities in 1822, the London Geological Society in 1823, and the London Horticultural Society in 1824. In 1837, he was an annual member of the British Association for the Advancement of Science.[9] His membership in the Geological Society continued throughout his career and his death was reported in the Society's council minutes in 1858.

Additionally, he was a member of the Meteorological Society of London, the Wernerian Natural History Society of Edinburgh (from 1819), and the mechanics institutes of Exeter, Devonport, Portsmouth, and Bristol. He was also an honorary member of the Medico-chirurgical Society of Hull, the Medical Society of Inverness, and the philosophical societies of Sheffield and Hull. Finally, he was a corresponding member of the Northern Institution, the Horticultural Society of Edinburgh, and other societies.[10]

Besides lecturing and doing experimental research, he also traveled extensively to do his own firsthand geological and archaeological fieldwork. We will return to this later when examining his two most important writings related to the Genesis-geology debate. Additionally, he was a prolific writer, publishing 28 books (varying in length from 20 to 380 pages) and at least 60 articles in scientific journals,[11] plus frequent correspondence to the *Mechanics Magazine* (from 1831 to 1844) and the *Mining Journal* (from 1841 to 1851). He had nearly 20 inventions which came into practical use.[12] His journal articles addressed

---

4 *The Mining Journal*, June 14, 1851, p. 288, made an appeal to its more wealthy readers to give Murray financial assistance at this time.

5 "Death of Dr. Murray, Ph.D.," *Galloway Advertiser and Wigtownshire Free Press* (July 3, 1851). Stranraer's population was about 3,900 at the time.

6 In the preface to *A Glance at Some of the Beauties and Sublimities of Switzerland* (1829), p. vi, he said that in the book he would frequently "wage war against Catholicism" though he had no personal hostility toward individual Catholics. He also lamented the defection of the Church of Geneva from its orthodox Calvinist roots (see pages vi and 176–177).

7 "Death of Dr. Murray, Ph.D.," *Galloway Advertiser and Wigtownshire Free Press* (July 3, 1851).

8 *Report from the Select Committee on Accidents in Mines,* September 4, 1835, p. 237–248. In spite of his much greater scientific accomplishments, particularly in chemistry and in this problem of safety lamps, Partington's definitive work on the history of chemistry gives Murray only a passing comment in comparison to much more about another John Murray (d. 1820), who was no more and probably less productive as a chemist. See J.R. Partington, *A History of Chemistry* (1961–70), IV: p. 65–66.

9 "Appendix," *Report of the BAAS* (1837), p. 34.

10 John Murray, *A Treatise on Pulmonary Consumption; Its Prevention and Remedy* (1830), title page.

11 *Catalogue of the Royal Society* (*CRS*). Four works listed in the *CRS* under the name of John Murray (d. 1820) were actually written by the John Murray (1786–1851) under discussion in this chapter. See *DNB* on John Murray (d. 1820).

12 *The Mining Journal*, June 14, 1851, p. 288.

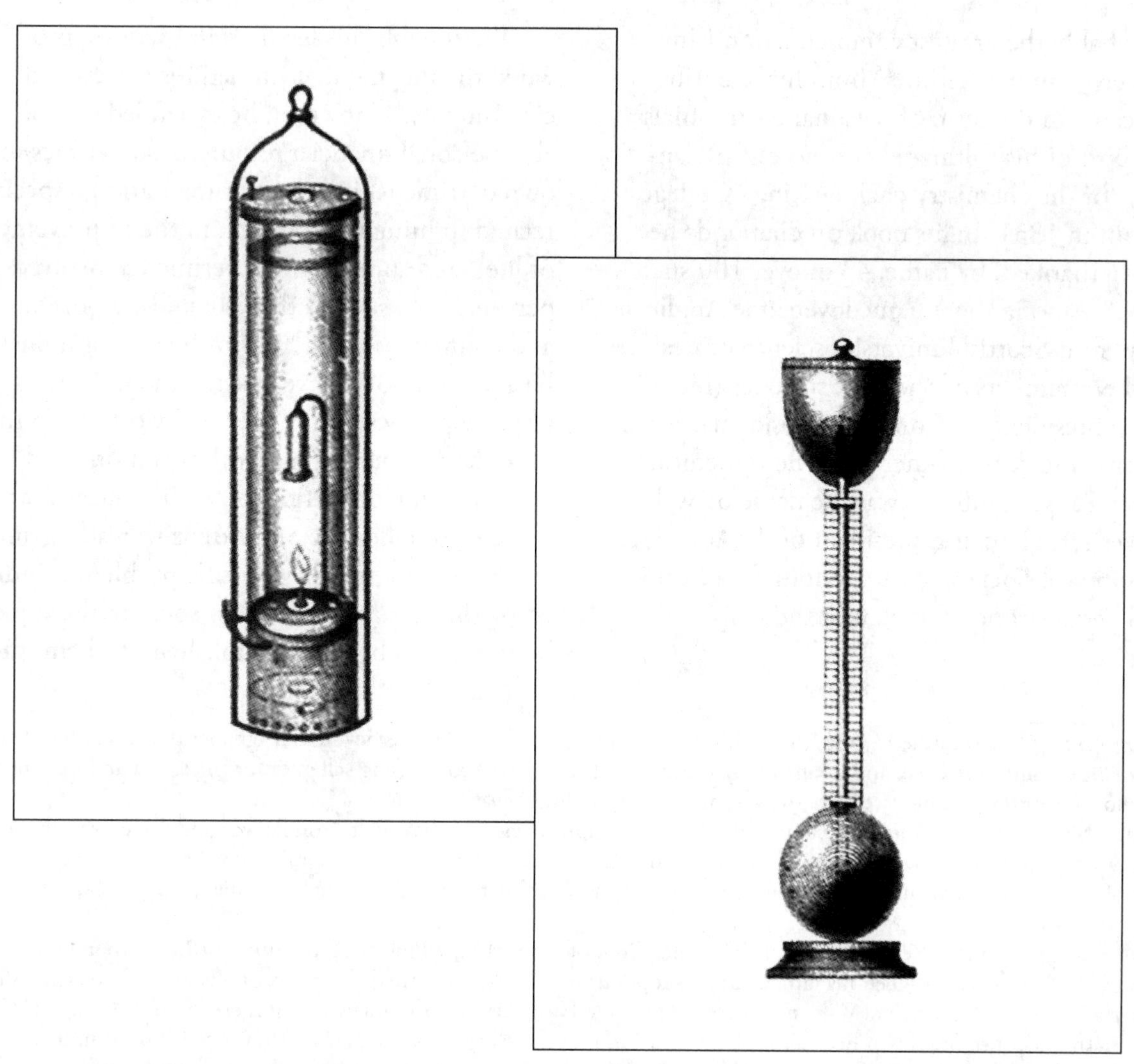

THE MINER'S SAFETY LAMP (LEFT) AND AETHRIOSCOPE (RIGHT) WERE TWO OF MURRAY'S NEARLY 20 INVENTIONS.

subjects in chemistry, physics, medicine, geology, natural history, and manufacturing. His books, some of which went through two or more editions, covered such diverse topics as the cultivation of the silkworm, illustrations of chemical experiments, modern paper, atmospherical electricity, pulmonary consumption (tuberculosis), hydrophobia (human rabies), plagues and quarantine, ventilation, disinfection and other sanitation measures, poisons, a shower bath and an artificial respirator (both of which he invented), diamonds, a method for forming an instantaneous contact with shore during a shipwreck, life boats, a lightning conductor, flax, glowworms, plant physiology, and the cow tree. He also wrote a passionate pamphlet calling for the end of slavery in the colonies, a book of minor poems, and a scientific/historical travel memoir of his three-month journey around Switzerland in 1825.[13] Many of his works contain in the back very positive reviews of his previous works.[14]

13 Most of these works are listed in the bibliography. A few are only known from advertisements in the back of Murray's extant works and do not appear in the catalogs of the Library of Congress or the British Library. Exact bibliographic data is wanting in these cases.

14 There is nothing in his writings or the reviews of others that would suggest that such advertising was a reflection of Murray's conceit or pride. Rather, it would appear to have been the understandable work of the publisher.

Probably the greatest commendation Murray received in his lifetime[15] from his scientific peers came in the form of personal testimonials in support of his (ultimately unsuccessful) candidacy for the chemistry chair at King's College, London, in 1831. In his book on diamonds he publicly thanked, by name, 43 of over 100 such people.[16] Among those named were one Anglican bishop, four Scottish university science professors, ten other members of scientific societies (including two presidents and one vice-president), seven surgeons, and several other prominent medical doctors. Most significant was the name of William Vernon Harcourt, president of the Yorkshire Philosophical Society, a leading founder of the BAAS and a strong opponent of the scriptural geologists.[17]

Presumably, his lectures and writing provided the income that funded his travels and experiments.[18] However, he expended considerable personal financial resources (sometimes to his own detriment) in his experimentation, especially related to human suffering and the improvement of life[19] and some of his experiments involved personal risk, such as those he did on poisons and counter-poisons.[20] As in the case of money, he appears also to have resisted the influences of party politics on his scientific work.[21] On the other hand, some of his work was motivated by a strong sense of patriotism.[22] His concern for thoughtful reflection and extensive reading and experimentation on a scientific problem is indicated by the years he devoted to some of the topics he researched before he published on them: the

15 *The Mining Journal*, June 14, 1851, p. 288, wrote just before he died: "He has devoted the greater portion of his life in the ardent pursuit of science, and in an almost unexampled earnestness to devising schemes for the safety and welfare of his fellow-creatures, without, we regret to add, any corresponding reward."

16 John Murray, *A Memoir on the Diamond* (1831), postscript. In the end the only reason he was not elected was that he was unwilling to leave his beloved Church of Scotland to become an Anglican, the denominational affiliation required of all professors by the new university's regulations. Murray wished his replacement, John F. Daniell, the great meteorologist, every success.

17 Murray listed him as "Rev. W.V. Vernon, FRS, etc., Pres. of the Yorkshire Phil. Soc." In January 1831 Vernon become William Vernon Harcourt when his father, Archbishop Vernon of York, inherited the Harcourt Estates. Thereafter, William Vernon was referred to as Mr. William Harcourt or Canon Harcourt (of York Minster), but more often as Reverend William Vernon Harcourt. See Susan F. Cannon, *Science in Culture: The Early Victorian Period* (1978), p. 196 (footnote 6).

18 This may be reflected in the fact that virtually all his books contained postscript advertisements for many of his other writings.

19 Murray, *A Treatise on Pulmonary Consumption; Its Prevention and Remedy*, p. vi, ix–x; *Descriptive Account of a New Shower Bath, Constructed on a Principle Not Hitherto Applied to That Machine; Also, an Apparatus for Restoring Suspended Animation* (1831), p. 3 and 5.

20 John Murray, "Researches on Hydrocyanic Acid and Opium, with Reference to Their Counter-poisons," *Edinburgh Philosophical Journal*, vol. VII, no. 13 (1822), p. 124–127.

21 Murray did not believe slavery was an issue of politics, but of morality. If it had been the former, he said he would not have gotten involved in the debate. See his *A Letter to the Right Honourable Earl Grey on Colonial Slavery* (1832), p. 3. Elsewhere he lamented what he perceived to be the intrusion of politics into the realm of science. See his *Practical Observations on the Phenomena of Flame and Safety Lamps* (1833), p. vii.

22 John Murray, *Remarks on the Cultivation of the Silk Worm, with Additional Observations, Made in Italy During the Summer of 1825* (1825), preface and p. 8; *The Natural History of the Silk Worm* (1838), preface. In these works he was seeking to encourage the cultivation of the silk worm with a view to creating jobs, especially for people in the poor houses, the elderly, the infirm, and negro wives and children when slavery ended.

In his *Practical Remarks on Modern Paper with an Introductory Account of Its Former Substitutes, Also Observations on Writing Inks, the Restoration of Illegible Manuscripts, and the Preservation of Important Deeds from the Destructive Effects of Damp* (1829), preface, Murray expressed the hope that his work would help to preserve documents of religion, literature, science, and government which were of great national importance, but were at risk of being lost due to paper and ink quality. Similar remarks were made in *Observations and Experiments on the Bad Composition of Modern Paper; with the Description of a Permanent Writing Ink, Which Cannot Be Discharged* (1824), p. vi. To the same end, he published the results of his research on flax in *An Account of the Phormium Tenax, or New Zealand Flax. Printed on Paper Made from Its Leaves, with a Postscript on Paper* (1836).

In *The Plague and Quarantine. Remarks on Some Epidemic and Endemic Diseases; (Including the Plague of the Levant,) and the Means of Disinfection; with a Description of the Preservative Phial. Also a Postscript on Dr. Bowring's Pamphlet Entitled "Observations on the Oriental Plague," Etc.* (1839), p. i, Murray stated that he wrote the book "with no other object in view but the public good."

safety lamp (15 years), hydrophobia (12 years), and pulmonary consumption (12 years).[23] He also had priority of discovery in four different areas of research: a cure for pulmonary consumption (by means of aerial clorine[24]), growth of New Zealand flax in Scotland (which was superior for making paper), a mining safety lamp, and fusing a diamond.[25]

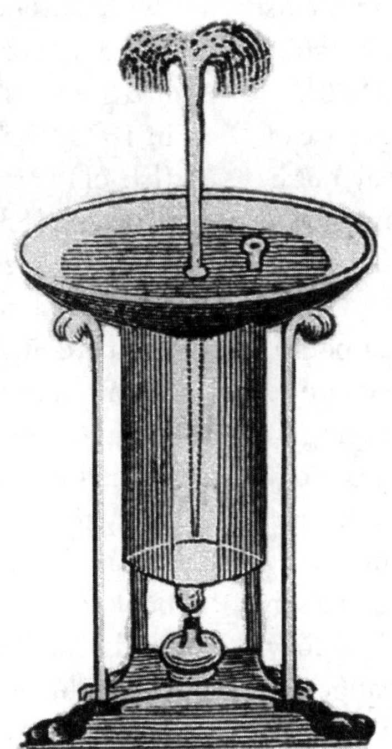

Murray's geyser apparatus.

Most important for this study were his two books directly related to geology and the Bible.[26] *The Truth of Revelation* (276 pages) was published anonymously in 1831, with a signed and greatly revised second edition (380 pages) appearing in 1840. In this book, Murray endeavored to demonstrate the truth and inspiration of the Bible by an appeal to the existing monuments, sculptures, gems, coins, and medals from ancient peoples of the Near East and elsewhere. Between these two editions, in 1838, his *Portrait of Geology* (214 pages) appeared anonymously.[27] This book was written to give proofs from geology of divine design in creation, and secondarily to add verification to the truth of Scripture. An examination of these two works reveals more about Murray's geological knowledge and experience, which provides a necessary context for understanding the views he expressed in these two books.[28]

Geological Competence

It is worthwhile to draw out in more detail from some of Murray's own writings the extent of his scientific, and especially geological, qualifications, in light of the common characterization that scriptural geologists were poorly informed in these areas.

Murray's up to date knowledge of mineralogy and geology is reflected in his description of the various rock types, definitions of geological terms, and the names of formations (in English, French, and German) associated with the work of Conybeare and Phillips, Murchison, De La Beche,

23 Murray, *Practical Observations on the Phenomena of Flame and Safety Lamps*, vi; *Remarks on the Disease Called Hydrophobia: Prophylactic and Curative* (1830), p. vii; *A Treatise on Pulmonary Consumption; Its Prevention and Remedy* (1830), p. vi.

24 However, he expressed his desire to find a less irritating treatment.

25 Murray, *A Treatise on Pulmonary Consumption; Its Prevention and Remedy* (1830), p. viii, xi; *Practical Observations on the Phenomena of Flame and Safety Lamps*, p. iii (on flax); *Practical Observations on the Phenomena of Flame and Safety Lamps*, p. 20–21 (this priority was acknowledged in a letter to Murray by Sir Humphry Davy; see also J.R. Partington, *A History of Chemistry* (1961–70), IV: p. 66); *A Memoir on the Diamond*, p. 61.

26 A summary of his published works up to 1839 is found in *The Plague and Quarantine*, p. 55–57. It lists (without a date) *Strictures on Modern Geological Speculations*, but I could not find this in any of the catalogs.

27 The title page says the book is written by "a Fellow of the Geological Society." Murray identified himself as the author of *Portrait of Geology* (1838) in his *The Truth of Revelation*, p. 143 (footnote). Why Murray wrote the former book anonymously is a puzzle. True, he was taking a position contrary to probably the vast majority of Fellows in the Geological Society. But throughout his life he never hesitated to challenge the dominant view, if he felt the scientific evidence was in his favor. A supreme (but not the only) example of this regarded his criticisms of Sir Humphry Davy's mining safety lamp and Michael Faraday's defense of Davy's lamp, and Murray's testimony to Parliament on the matter. See John Murray, *Practical Observations on the Phenomena of Flame and Safety Lamps*, p. vi–vii; John Murray, *Observations on Safety Lamps* (1836, second edition), p. 39–40; and his public testimony before the House of Commons in *Report from the Select Committee on Accidents in Mines,* September 4, 1835, p. 239. On the other hand, earlier in 1822 he was critical of someone who anonymously challenged his own research and charged him with fallacious experiments on the decomposition of metallic salts. Murray said that he would only engage in debate about the truth with a person who was willing to attach his name to his views. See John Murray, "Reply to B.M.," *Annals of Philosophy*, N.S. vol. III (1822), p. 121–123. It seems likely that Murray's anonymity with *Portrait of Geology* probably limited the number of readers and helps to explain why it was ignored by his geological opponents.

28 I have studied only the 1840 revised edition of *The Truth of Revelation* because it appeared after leading Christian geologists, such as Buckland, Conybeare, and Sedgwick, had recanted their belief in the Flood. It also reflects his most mature thoughts on the subject.

Sedgwick, Lyell, etc. However, in his comments about the great "Devonian controversy,"[29] which was drawing to completion in the late 1830s, Murray expressed dissatisfaction with the use of local names for rock formations that may not be strictly local and preferred instead a nomenclature of more universal application for the effective globalization of the study of geology.[30]

As noted earlier, in 1815 (in his first book) and in 1835 (before the parliamentary committee) he called himself a chemist. But judging from his writings in the latter part of his life, geology seems to have dominated his interests.[31] In the late 1830s he referred to himself as "a practical geologist"[32] and endeavored generally to stay out of the heated debates in theoretical geology, chiefly because it was his conviction that geology was still such a young science "in a state of constant revolution, and incessantly changing its aspect."[33] Obviously, he did not stay out of the debate completely.

As he stated, his "careful examination of geological phenomena, and observation of the facts consequent on the study of geology for many years" took him to such places as Switzerland, Italy, Germany, the Lyme Cliffs of Dorset, the Walker mine near Newcastle, and to the sites of erratic boulders all over the United Kingdom and Europe. He personally examined the immense collection of fossil bones in the possession of the man who diligently explored the cave near Torquay, called Kent's Hole, and he had investigated "with considerable attention" the rounded pebbles and bones of Kirkdale Cave, the analysis of which had greatly augmented William Buckland's fame in 1823,[34] as well as the cavernous crevice in the (Isle of) Portland Oolite, which by the time of Murray's 1838 book had almost been obliterated by quarrymen. He traveled to the British Museum in London and to a museum in Paris[35] to compare their collections of Gallibi (human fossil remains found in 1805 in calcareous rock on the island of Guadaloupe), also to the museum in the Birmingham Philosophical Institution to study toad fossils, and back again to the museum in Paris, just a few years before writing his 1838 book, to examine a footprint preserved in a clay-sandstone slab.[36]

In discussing his explorations in the Isle of Man, he described his careful observations of elk bones found in white shell marl under eight feet of peat: "On fracturing one of the antlers, I discovered a considerable quantity of the *earthy phosphate of iron*, filling the interior — fragments of flints evidently employed by man, and probably in the chase, were discovered in the marl, also a *styca of Ethelred*."

Another example of his careful field observations appears in his discussion of footprints found in the Dumfriesshire sandstone (and commented on by Buckland): "The impressions which I have examined, appear, at any rate, to belong to a three-toed animal, and the sand seems to have been raised behind the foot as is

---

29 As Murray noted, this controversy, which started a few years before his book, involved primarily De La Beche, Murchison, and Sedgwick. It resulted in the classification of the Silurian and Cambrian rock systems. See Martin J.S. Rudwick, *The Great Devonian Controversy* (Chicago, IL: University of Chicago Press, 1985).

30 Murray, *Portrait of Geology*, p. 26–52, 150–151.

31 In *Practical Observations on the Phenomena of Flame and Safety Lamps*, p. vii, he stated that due to the treatment he received from some influential fellow chemists to his work on safety lamps, "I have abandoned the field [of chemistry] in disgust, and thenceforth confined my exertions to the application of facts and principles to useful purposes in the economy of life — a task more pleasing to me than to be compelled to surrender the convictions of truth as the price of admission into the coteries of sect and party."

32 John Murray, "Dr. Buckland's Geological Sermon," *Christian Observer*, vol. XXXIX (1839), p. 401; Murray, *The Truth of Revelation*, p. 143.

33 Murray, *The Truth of Revelation*, p. 137–138, 142.

34 Murray concluded, on the basis of his own inspection of the bones and from the writings of other investigators (including George Young, another scriptural geologist), that Buckland's "extremely ingenious and interesting" theory faced "many and serious objections." See *Portrait of Geology*, p. 70–71.

35 He did not name the museum in this context, but on page 101 of *Portrait of Geology* he mentioned visiting the Musée d' Historie Naturelle Comparée in Paris.

36 Murray, *Portrait of Geology*, p. 37–43, 57, 71–72, 80, 82–83, 89, 99, 101, 197–198; *The Truth of Revelation* (1840), p. 132, 137.

the case in animals traversing the sand on the sea shore; small scales of mica, are seen more distinctly in the impress."[37]

Murray understood, and apparently accepted, the use of fossils in the identification and correlation of strata, for he said:

> The great importance of studying organic remains is evident in this, that it enables us to identify particular rocks, and refer them to their common group, or formation, however distant, and in whatever country found; and when the continuity is broken, it is our only guide, since the mineral structure may be altogether different from its associated member. Sometimes these organic remains have existing counterparts, or living analogues, occasionally both in genera and species; and at other times they are without their types in the present order of things.[38]

However, he did not consider this a fool-proof method, because some life forms are found all through the formations from the oldest to the most recent. And herein lay one of his objections to the catastrophism of Buckland, Cuvier, and other leading geologists of his day. So he wrote:

> This is a striking and memorable fact; and I do not see how it can be satisfactorily explained on the principles assumed by geologists — that is, repeatedly created, to be as repeatedly destroyed by succeeding cataclysms, for I believe it is the opinion of eminent geologists, that a new physical condition of things was constituted to meet the contingencies of the new order of being.[39]

Furthermore he stated:

> The prevalent views of geologists seem to be to attach an overweening confidence and undue importance to the character and condition of the organic remains found in rocks, while others lean almost exclusively to their mineral structure. It is evident, however, that just geological inferences can only be found in a happy combination of both, and in a proper line of distinction between general and continuous strata, and local deposits, or formations, together with the circumstances which have concurred to break the line of continuity.[40]

Murray "personally examined the subterranean recesses of Herculaneum[41] and its volcanic covering" and "especially examined, and with tolerable attention, the volcanic phenomena of the Neapolitan territory, in detail."[42] In 1818, at the risk of suffocation, he made observations and chemical experiments several hundred feet down in the crater of Mt. Vesuvius.[43] This was evidently not a unique experience for Murray, because in 1840 he commented that "I have been in both active and extinct volcanic craters."[44] He apparently always had with him the means for doing chemical analysis, as, for example, when he discovered in the waters of the Dead Sea several substances that had gone unnoticed by other investigators, and when he visited Stonehenge in 1839 and chemically compared the stones there with marbles he had examined in Greece.[45] But he also relied on the work of other scientists, as, for example, in his discussion of mineral veins he referred to R.W. Fox's laboratory and fieldwork,[46] especially using electricity, and noted that electrical action

37 Murray, *Portrait of Geology*, p. 95 and 100.
38 Ibid., p. 52.
39 Ibid., p. 53.
40 Ibid., p. 22.
41 This was a city buried along with Pompeii by the eruption of Mt. Vesuvius in A.D. 79.
42 Murray, *The Truth of Revelation*, p. 136–137.
43 Murray, *Portrait of Geology*, p. 173–174.
44 Murray, *The Truth of Revelation*, p. 77–79.
45 Ibid., p. 77–79 and 234.
46 Robert Were Fox's research received positive comment by William Whewell in his February 1839 presidential address to the Geological Society. See *Proceedings of the Geological Society*, Vol. III (1838–42), p. 95.

is associated with volcanoes.[47] In his extensive 14-page discussion of what he believed was good evidence of antediluvian human fossils he cited the analysis of some bones done by a surgeon and fossil collector, William Tyson.[48] Murray also collected rock specimens and fossils from such places as Kent's Hole near Torquay, a coal mine in Yorkshire, Mt. Sinai, the Isle of Portland, and from various locations in Cornwall, Devonshire, Derbyshire, and Bohemia.[49]

These data show that he traveled widely in the United Kingdom and in Europe, sometimes even at risk to his life, in pursuit of geological and other scientific knowledge. Certainly in this regard he was more qualified as a geologist than either Hutton or Werner and, at the time, nearly as well-traveled as Buckland, Lyell, Macculloch, and other respected geologists.

His more-than-superficial knowledge of conchology, a subject so important for identifying and correlating rock strata, is reflected in these words:

> Thus, in *conchology*, shells, generally, are the habitations of testaceae; but, this is, by no means, always the case: for the reverse of this happens in some instances. In the latter, instead of the animal inhabiting the shell, the shell inhabits the animal: thus, the *dolabella* of Lamarck, and the *bulla aperta*, and *helix haliotoida* of Linneus [*sic*], afford examples wherein the shell is embedded in the animal, and the animal is wrapped like a mantle round it. Sometimes the shell is a mere plate or escutcheon, as in the *limax* or slug; and in the beautiful *argonauta vitrea*, it is a case or pouch which contains some of the organs. Again, in almost every case, we find the spires of shells in one determinate direction, their mouths opening to the left hand; but, though extremely rare, there are remarkable exceptions to this rule: in these contrarieties, the whirls are *reversed*, and the involutions are to the right — for example, the *murex perversus* and *fusus contrarius*. We also find instances of this kind among the Linnaean genera of *helix*, *strombus*, and others. On the other hand, the *reversed* variety of the *citrina* is LESS RARE than the usual form. When the chank shell, *turbinella* of Lamarck, is found to possess this very curious character, it is highly prized by the natives of India. A chank shell, with an opening to the right, is, indeed, rarely obtained; but when found, always sells for its weight in gold.[50]

He read widely and in several languages: Latin, Italian, French, German, and some Hebrew.[51] In addition to geological writers already mentioned, he indicated that he had read works by Cuvier, Buckland, Mantell, Hitchcock, Werner, Hutton, Playfair, Buffon, Demaillet, Lamarck, Burnet, Woodward, and Whiston. He was conversant with the writings of leading 18th and 19th century philologists, physicians, explorers, travelers, antiquaries, and Bible scholars.[52] Additionally,

---

47 Murray, *Portrait of Geology*, p. 152 and 170–171.

48 Ibid., p. 90–93.

49 Ibid., p. 54, 90, 99, 149; *The Truth of Revelation*, p. 143, 146, 273.

50 Ibid., p. 315–316. In *Physiology of Plants* (1833), p. 299, Murray noted that a book on the physiology of shells was in process at the time. But no extant copy exists, as far as I could discover.

51 He frequently quoted from Latin authors such as Pliny, Chalcidius, Suetonius, Phlegon, Lucretius, Ovid, Lucian, and Plutarch and cited the Latin works of the German theologian Weissenborn: e.g., *The Truth of Revelation*, p. 142, 206–207, 328–329, 332, 353–356 and *Portrait of Geology*, p. 97. Once he translated a small French book into English with the title of *Napoleon Never Existed*. It was a work which responded to another that considered Christianity a mythological fable. See *The Truth of Revelation*, p. 374 and 316. His knowledge of Italian is inferred from both the description of his travels in Italy and the fact that in *The Truth of Revelation*, p. 262–263, he gave an English quote from an Italian chemistry book published in 1793, which according to the British Museum Catalogue does not appear to have been translated into English. His knowledge of German is inferred from remarks about his travels in Switzerland and his awareness of German biblical criticism. See his *A Glance at Some of the Beauties and Sublimities of Switzerland*, especially p. 202–203, and *The Truth of Revelation*, p. xxvii and 357. He referred to his modest knowledge of Hebrew in *The Truth of Revelation*, p. 351.

Murray interacted with David Hume (*Enquiry Concerning Human Understanding*, 1758), Charles Babbage (*Ninth Bridgewater Treatise*, 1837), Henry Milman (*History of the Jews*, 1829), and Sir Charles Bell.[53]

He only referred to the writings of three other scriptural geologists: Andrew Ure, Granville Penn, and George Young. He described Ure's book (*New System of Geology*) as betraying "no very accurate knowledge of the principles of geology." In discussing animals entombed in caves, he respectfully disagreed with Penn's explanation, but he also rejected Buckland's hyena den hypothesis on the Kirkdale cave in Yorkshire and instead "generally coincides" with "Mr. Young's judicious remarks," from which he quoted six pages out of Young's *A Geological Survey of Yorkshire* (1828).[54]

General View of Geology

Murray loved geology for it "charms and instructs the reflective mind" and has a very practical utility in wise and profitable mining, farming, well-drilling, and the construction of buildings, roads, canals, and railways.[55] Furthermore, it is an aid to natural theology in that it reveals aspects of God's creative power and wisdom, as well as serving as a support of scriptural revelation.

> My object in this little volume has been to consider geological phenomena as a collection of curious facts, at once novel and rare, and affording decisive proofs of wise and beneficent design. The interest of geology is therefore of a sterling cast, as it ministers important aid to the student in natural theology. The science will also be found tributary, and that in no mystic or unintelligible form, to the cause of Revealed Truth, and thus "put to silence the ignorance of foolish men."[56]

But Murray also believed that geology poses dangers.

> Modern geology is the very *beau idéal* of romance; and it cannot be denied that, in many instances, bold assumptions and reckless speculation have usurped the throne of reason and reality. No marvel indeed, for it must be candidly admitted, that it requires no slight effort of the mind to curb the reins of imagination, when wandering among the wonders of a world destroyed.[57]

He believed that "geologists are generally a skeptical race; but whether such skepticism rests on a philosophical basis, we may well question."[58] In comparing the geology of the past to that in his own times he expressed his own attitudes to

52 Such writers included philologists such as Sir William Jones (1746–94), Professor Samuel Lee (1783–1852), Dr. Alexander Murray (1775–1813) and Claudius James Rich (1787–1820); eminent physicians such as Dr. John Farre (1775–1862); famous travelers and writers such as James Bruce (1730–94), Thomas Shaw (1694–1751), Dr. Edward D. Clarke (1769–1821, also a fellow geologist and antiquary), Fredrick Hasselquist (Swedish), James Silk Buckingham (1786–1855), Sir Robert Ker Porter (1777–1842), Capt. Charles Leonard Irby (1789–1845), Capt. James Mangles (1786–1867), Dr. Robert Richardson (1779–1847) and Dr. Richard Pococke (1704–65); world-renowned Egyptologists such as Sir John Garner Wilkinson (1797–1875), Dr. Thomas Young (1773–1829) and Jean Francois Champollion (1790–1832); noted geographers such as Strabo (Greek, 64/63 B.C.–A.D. 25) and Major James Rennell (1742–1830); highly regarded meteorologist John F. Daniell (1790–1845); and Old Testament scholars and textual critics such as Dr. Benjamin Kennicott (1718–83). Numerous references to these are sprinkled throughout his 1840 book. Most of these men appear in *DNB*.

53 Murray, *The Truth of Revelation*, p. 145, 262–263, 274, 308–309.

54 Murray, *Portrait of Geology*, p. 21, 62–63, 73. He gave no evidence of having personally known these men, though it seems likely that he did have personal contact with Young since they both were members of the Hull Philosophical Society. Young was still alive and writing on the Genesis-geology debate at the same time as Murray was, and on more than one occasion Murray lectured in Whitby, where Young lived. See "Death of Dr. John Murray," *Galloway Advertiser and Wigtownshire Free Press*, July 3, 1851.

55 Murray, *Portrait of Geology*, p. 4–7.

56 Ibid., p. vii; similar remarks on the value of geology to natural theology (showing "the beneficence of a prospective Providence") appear on pages 192 and 201–203. He said the same about the study of plants in *Physiology of Plants*, p. ix; *A Descriptive Account of the Palo de Vaco or Cow-Tree of the Caracos with a Chemical Analysis of the Milk and Bark* (1837), p. 1; and *Economy of Vegetation* (1838), p. v–vi.

57 Murray, *Portrait of Geology*, p. v.

58 Murray, *The Truth of Revelation*, p. 21.

the dominant theories of the catastrophists and uniformitarians. While he disagreed with them at the theoretical level, he did not employ *ad hominem* attacks.

> Modern geology differs materially from the speculative hypotheses which in former times amused the fancy and ministered to the imagination, while they left the mind as uninformed and uninstructed as it was before. It was formerly subordinated and tributary to mineralogy, though essentially distinct, and was thus defined, what geology is *en masse*, mineralogy is in detail. The geology of modern times, when *legitimately* engaged, is more busied in collecting and combining facts, than anxious to display its argumentative powers in rearing worlds, and bewildering its imagination, and beclouding its reason in labyrinths of perplexity and error. I do not say that all modern geologists are free from the charge of rash, intemperate, and even presumptuous speculations: of clysmic action there is no lack, and of cataclysms and what may well suffice — much more we think, than the book of nature teaches, or the sister volume warrants. There is, it is but too true, much dogmatism in modern times, and many conclusions formed in defiance of the principles of inductive logic; assertions are made to supplant facts, and inferences formed unwarranted by the premises. This indeed is the great difficulty with which the student has to contend. The facts are of the most sterling and interesting kind, and at once novel and instructive; but to separate the chaff from the wheat, and the grain from the tares "hic labor — hoc opus" [Latin for: This is the toil, this is the task]. While I therefore feel in common with all the students engaged in gleaning the fields of truth, the liveliest gratitude for the practical fruits developed in the assiduous researches of those excellent geologists, Messrs. Buckland, Lyell, Sedgwick, De la Beche, Conybeare, and others, I cannot subscribe to many of their opinions, and must remain a conscientious dissentient.[59]

Murray then went on in the next 14 pages to draw the readers attention to what he believed to be some of the erroneous speculations of Kepler, Demaillet, Lamarck, Leibnitz, Hooke, Woodward, Burnet, Whiston, Buffon, Werner, Hutton,[60] Knight, Lyell,[61] Buckland,[62] Ure, Macculloch, and Mantell.

On the Laws of Nature

Murray did not provide us with a sustained discussion of his view of the "laws of nature." Regarding Lyell's radical uniformitarianism he wrote, "Mr. Lyell stands out in solitary relief from his fellows, and endeavors to explain the former changes which have supervened on the earth's surface, by referring them to causes that are now in operation."[63] In such a comment, Murray was distancing

59 Murray, *Portrait of Geology*, p. 8–9.

60 Though not rejecting all aspects of Hutton's theory, Murray criticized Hutton for being "more a cabinet or a closet geologist than a practical student of the great mountain features of the globe" (ibid., p. 16; This was similar to Buckland's criticism of Hutton. See William Buckland, *Vindiciae Diluvianae* [1820], p. 22). Murray called Werner an "eloquent and eminent teacher," who "raised up a multitude of zealous cultivators in the field of geology," and "a genius of no ordinary stamp," but, "Werner had not visited distant countries, and he was no peripatetic" and so erred as he "generalized from his own little Saxon 'Goshen' " (Murray, *Portrait of Geology*, p. 16–18). This assessment of these two geologists has been confirmed by Alexander M. Ospovat, "The Distortion of Werner in Lyell's *Principles of Geology*." *British Journal for the History of Science*, vol. IX, no. 32, pt. 2 (1976), p. 191–192.

61 While criticizing Lyell's extreme uniformitarianism, "self-contradictions," "gratuitous assumptions," "obvious low regard for Scripture," and "compromised theism," Murray nevertheless acknowledged Lyell's "multitudinous mass of valuable and truly interesting facts, collected with much industry, and the fruits of considerable research." (Murray, *Portrait of Geology)*, p. 20.

62 Although Murray regretted Buckland's recantation of his previous belief in the global Noachian flood, Murray nevertheless considered Buckland "an eminent geologist" (ibid., p. 60) "of high character" (ibid., p. 199), "whose opinions must ever claim deference and respect" (ibid., p. 62), because his investigations were conducted "with great industry and indefatigable assiduity" and were described "with remarkable precision" (ibid., p. 68).

63 Ibid., p. 19.

himself from uniformitarianism while not denying the principle of uniformity (or actualism, as it was called on the continent), which is the principle that undergirds all modern scientific investigation.[64]

Murray's commitment to the principle of uniformity is seen in his rejection of Sir Charles Bell's conclusion that man could not have existed contemporaneously with the ichthyosaurus because the physical constitution of the earth was significantly different in the past. Murray stated:

> I entirely repudiate the assumption that there was a physical change, as he [Bell] has assumed, and sufficient to impose such a negation of being [extinction of ichthyosaurus]; though I am prepared to admit mutations to a minor extent in the density of the atmosphere, and of course the concurrent hygrometric and thermometric relations; but there is abundant evidence to neutralize the sweeping conclusion [of Bell] referred to.
>
> In the ripple marks, etc., on the forest marble, and on sandstone, I read the important lesson, that the flux and reflux of the tides, and the agency of the winds, were just the same then as now;[65] the laws of gravitation, and the dynamics of the atmosphere, operated then precisely as they do in our own times. In the structure of the lenses which compose the eye of the trilobite, and are constructed precisely like the eyes of living crustacea, I see the same laws of light and vision then operating as now, and I therefore infer the same physical condition of light and the atmosphere; and I have trilobites in specimens of *grauwache* (transition) both from Devonshire, etc., and Bohemia. I find, too, that the bone was subject to the same diseases then as now prevail, such as *caries*, *mollities* and *necrosis*, and when fractured, it was healed by the same process of a callus. I have a specimen of silicified lignite, from the chalk, pierced by the *teredo navalis*, an event which occurs before our eyes. Similar facts might be indefinitely multiplied; and not only has the cheriotherium walked over the sands, not then indurated, nor consolidated into sandstone, but man himself has impressed his footsteps.[66]

Murray did refer to significant physical change related to the Flood.[67] In contrast to Bell's notion, however, that change was associated with an event resulting from a unique judgment of God which in certain ways disrupted the normal laws (or course) of nature. Here, then, Murray expressed his belief in the general laws of nature and criticized Bell's view that such drastic physical change in the earth could be a normal characteristic of nature (rather than a unique intervention of God).

Earlier, he stated that the original various forms of life were created instantaneously in a mature state during the six days of creation, as recorded in Genesis.[68] Here, he argued that the "laws of ossification" would not explain the bones of the first created man, any more than the "laws of lignification" would explain the origin of the first created trees. Likewise, he said, the laws of lithifaction would lead the geologist to erroneous conclusions about the origin of the non-fossiliferous primitive rocks.[69] In a similar discussion in his 1838 book he put it this way:

> I do not believe that this science [geology] has a legitimate right to exercise its "cunning" on the forms of rocks

64 In modern parlance, Murray was distinguishing between methodological uniformity and substantive uniformity. Compare R. Hooykaas, "Catastrophism in Geology, Its Scientific Character in Relation to Actualism and Uniformitarianism." *Meded. Kon. Nederl. Akad. Wetenschappen*, Afd. Let., Nieuwe Reeks, deel 33, no. 7 (1970), p. 271–316, and Stephen J. Gould, "Catastrophes and Steady State Earth," *Natural History*, vol. 84, no. 2 (1975), p. 14–18.

65 See a similar comment in his *Portrait of Geology*, p. 99.

66 Murray, *The Truth of Revelation*, p. 145–146.

67 This will be discussed later.

68 Murray, *The Truth of Revelation*, p. 128–130. His line of reasoning is similar to that put forth by Philip Gosse in *Omphalos* (1857), though Murray did not use the argument to explain fossils, as Gosse mistakenly did.

69 Today these are known as the Precambrian and have been found in some cases to contain fossils of single-celled algae and bacteria.

developed in the creation of being, and to reason on their phenomena as if *time* and its infinitesimal and successional series were an essential element in the fiat of Almighty power — No! "He spake and it was done," and "commanded and all things stood fast." [Ps. 33:6, 9] At this point, I must assume modern geologists have greatly erred. Crystallizations, precipitations, and other processes belong to the chemist and the laboratory, but the "ways" of the Author of these existencies [*sic*], and the "creator of the ends of the earth," are not "as our ways." If this point be not readily conceded, I frankly confess that there is much force in an observation made by an able writer on geology, namely, that "the mineral geology, considered as a science, can do as well without GOD (though in a question concerning the origin of the earth) as Lucretius did." For my own part, I will have nothing to do with a Cosmogonal chaos. I acknowledge no authentic record of creation, except the chronicles of revelation.

The simplest intellect, and the soundest judgment, must equally discern that the same process of reasoning which we now apply to the phenomena of ossification and lignification, in determining the age of a man, or that of a tree, would fail as a *metre* in relation to the prototype of humanity, or the primitive tree. In the dawn of existence they were severally mature; had man not been so, as well as other links in palaeontology, then death would have instantly supervened on creation, and his cradle been his sepulchre. In like manner the "Master-builder" laid the foundations of the world; they were summoned into existence, and instantly "stood confessed," complete in form and structure. This seems a reasonable, and I will add, philosophical view of the act of creation, and it is corroborated by the only appropriate standard of appeal. What has supervened since, however, becomes the legitimate province of geological science.[70]

Clearly, in Murray's mind, there was a difference between the way God originally created the world and the way He now sustains it.[71] In stressing the general consistency and continuity of the laws of nature, Murray followed on from the above quote to say that "two great evils" of modern geological theories (i.e., of catastrophists and uniformitarians) were:

1. We reduce the present system of being to the dilemma of an *imperfect series*, and not a beautiful gradation of "shade softening into shade," but rather one composed of dislocated joints, a chain of broken links — *per saltum*, oft repeated. And 2. In the assumed antecedent systems, how many we are not informed, there is "confusion worse confounded," *exceptions* without rules of reference; unconnected and insulated joints, and no continuity or chain. On the principles of a sound theism, I demur, and cannot but think that Newton's maxim is a safe guide in our investigations — "We must not admit more causes of natural things than those which are true, and sufficiently account for natural things."[72]

Again, on the continuous chain of life he stated:

From infusoria [microscopic organisms] up to man, the terraqueous system of being seems to be connected with a continuous chain. In this chain the continuity is here and there broken; the extinct genera and species, whose organic remains are revealed to us, supply the vacant links, and complete the concatenation; and we therefore infer, on the soundest principles of inductive logic,

70 Murray, *Portrait of Geology*, p. 24–25. Murray's argument here is very similar to Penn's, as discussed earlier.

71 I will return to this distinction at the end of the book, under "the problematic nature of geology."

72 Murray, *The Truth of Revelation*, p. 146–147.

that they necessarily belong to the same order of existing being; and farther, that the same physical laws must have been in incessant operation in all periods of the past; and hence deduce, as a natural inference, the same CREATOR AND ALMIGHTY LAWGIVER — "the same yesterday, today, and forever."[73]

These statements on the continuity of the life chain could be interpreted to mean that he believed in some kind of theistic evolution. But we must balance our understanding of him on this point with these words:

> Further, the rhapsodies of Lamarck, and his atheistical speculations, which have neither common sense nor the deductions of reason to recommend them, as well as the successive developements [sic] of some modern geologists, which seem to have originated in the same eccentricities and aberrations, are once for all nullified, and must be repudiated on the inductive basis of scientific truth. The discovery of mammiferous remains in the Stonesfield slate, as well as those of quadrumana, in the miocene period of tertiary strata, with many other corresponding phenomena, are entirely conclusive on this part of the argument. The laws of hybridism seem clearly to be the imposition of that INFINITE INTELLIGENCE, who is the "God of order and not of confusion." These laws also most distinctly prove the extreme absurdity, at once of spontaneous production and successive developements [sic].[74]

In a brief section on miracles, Murray rejected both Hume's definition (in his *Essay on Miracles*) of a miracle as a transgression of the laws of nature and Hume's notion that miracles cannot be proven by testimony. Murray contended:

> Nature determines the existence of a power superior to itself. Testimony can determine no fact whatever, it simply testifies the individual's belief concerning it, and no more; and none but an infinite mind can determine the limits of nature's laws, or set bounds to their operations. There is within and over these mystic wheels, a living principle — the plastic powers of which no finite mind can fathom. Are these laws so inelastic that they will refuse the impress of their author's seal? Are they so inflexible that they will not bend to contingencies when their maker wills it? Was the omniscient eye of the Almighty lawgiver, bounded by the dim horizon of definite periods, and limited measures of time; and are the physical laws of physical phenomena not to be subordinate to the Almighty's will, when specific purposes are to be consummated in the great moral and mental drama of which time is the theatre, and when such purposes cannot be fulfilled without such control or ordinance?
>
> In order to illustrate our views on this subject, we may refer to a few of the miracles recorded in the Old Testament, without at all impugning the better counsel of those who may believe, that miracles may be a counteraction of the laws of nature in all cases: our views have to do with *infidels*; and it is to contest the question on *their* assumptions, that we take up our position. As we defy them to prove, that a miracle does, in its very nature, imply a contradiction of the laws of nature, or something contrary to them and cannot imply any thing else; we have ventured an opinion, that a miracle does not necessarily and essentially imply this. *For aught they can tell*, the original laws of creation may remain precisely as they were and now are; and a miracle may be altogether independent of those laws, and involve the question of a new law superadded to the previously natural course of events, and provided in the councils of heaven for

73 Murray, *Portrait of Geology*, p. 193.
74 Murray, *The Truth of Revelation*, p. 140–141; similar comments appear in *Portrait of Geology*, p. 192–193.

> the contingencies of time: that GOD, who "made a decree for the rain, and prepared a way for the lightning of the thunder," (which laws were, in all probability, imposed *after* the deluge,) has many other laws in store, of which we know nothing.[75]

In other words, Murray seems to be arguing that the laws of nature are not so determinative that God cannot alter them if His purposes require it. The laws of nature are descriptive of God's providential activity, or customary behavior, in the creation, not prescriptive of how God must act at all times. Miracles involve God's uncustomary imposition of higher laws at particular points for particular reasons.

He then proceeded to illustrate this line of reasoning in his explanations, based on his scientific knowledge, of the miracles of meteoric stones falling from heaven on the enemies of Israel (Josh. 10:11), Joshua's long day (Josh. 10:12), the apparent backward movement of the sun on Hezekiah's stairs (2 Kings 20:11), and the ravens feeding Elijah (1 Kings 17:6). He concluded:

> Apart from these considerations, a very natural inquiry may arise: Are we fully acquainted with these *laws*, so as to be able to sit in judgment on them, and define them accurately? We hold it to be an axiom, that there is no such thing as an *anomaly* in the sight of GOD, however convenient the term may be to us, who use it, to conceal an ignorance we are unwilling to confess.[76]

He gave three examples of anomalies which are the exceptions to the general laws of nature and said that such examples could be found in every department of nature. The examples were 1) the then recent discovery that two of the moons of Uranus moved in a direction contrary to the movement of all other bodies in the solar system, 2) certain plants that "violate" the laws of vegetable physiology, and 3) some creatures whose shells have features contrary to the normal laws of shell physiology.

So Murray viewed the "laws of nature" to be valid generalizations of the way God providentially sustains His creation (with some of those laws instituted at the time of the Flood), but that they are not descriptive of the processes God used to bring into existence the original perfect and mature creation. Furthermore, God has suspended or overridden these laws to perform miracles, and the Noachian flood was definitely an unparalleled disruption in the normal course of nature.

On Scripture

As noted earlier, Murray was a Calvinist. He did not believe Calvin's *Institutes* were free from error, but that most Protestants considered them to be "the most happy compendium of the doctrines of Christianity that was ever conceived by the mind of man." Nevertheless, he believed that they must always be tested against the highest authority, which is Scripture.[77] He only made passing comments in *Portrait of Geology* on his view of Scripture, though the ones he made are clear and consistent with a more thorough discussion in *Truth of Revelation*. In the preface to the *Portrait* he stated:

> In has been my earnest endeavor to stand aloof from the hostile array of conflicting opinions [in theoretical geology]. There is only ONE authentic record of the primordial history of the globe, and of its tenants; that ancient book may be safely referred to, and in the question of geology, is the only legitimate standard of appeal. The facts of our science corroborate its evidence; and its relation of physical events has survived intact and undisturbed [*sic*] the progress of discovery. Hypotheses have indeed warred with, and may continue to assail the solemn and sublime dicta of Revelation, but it may fearlessly be asserted, that its INTEGRITY will "flourish in immortal youth."[78]

75 Murray, *Truth of Revelation*, p. 310–311.
76 Ibid., p. 313–314.
77 Murray, *A Glance at Some of the Beauties and Sublimities of Switzerland*, p. 176–177.
78 Murray, *Portrait of Geology*, p. v–vi.

In *Truth of Revelation* Murray began in the preface by stating that the Scriptures had been and were being fully vindicated regarding their historical reliability.

> The mass of evidence which the researches of modern times have accumulated, in verification of the Scriptures of Truth, is so overwhelming in magnitude and variety, as to put infidelity to the blush, and leave its benighted votaries without excuse. . . . the recent accessions of new and unexpected facts, warrant us in asserting, that there is not an historical fact within the precincts of the Inspired Volume, unsubstantiated by some existing and tangible monument, which time wither has not already, or may not hereafter reveal.[79]

The chapters of the book lay out some of the evidence he gathered to support this claim. After some general remarks on atheism in chapter 1, he went on in chapter 2 to discuss how the present-day Jews, Samaritans, Arabs, and Gypsies, as well as the permanence of many Oriental, near-Eastern customs and habits all are living evidences of the truth of Scripture. In chapter 3 he cited examples of monuments to the truth of the Bible in the topographical features of the Holy Land. Chapter 4 treats the necessity of revelation from God, and chapter 5 deals with Genesis 1–11 in the light of recent geological theory. More about this will come later.

In chapter 6, Murray considered the relation of the Bible to Egyptian and Indian chronology. He criticized the views expressed by Playfair in his *Astronomy of the Brahmins* (1822)[80] and concluded, in the words of the famous 18th century Oriental scholar, Sir William Jones,[81] that the early chapters of Genesis were not borrowed from Israel's neighbors, but composed the oldest history of the world we have.

> There is no shadow, then, of a foundation for an opinion, that Moses borrowed the first nine or ten chapters from the literature of Egypt; still less can the adamantine pillars of our Christian faith be moved by the result of any debates on the comparative antiquity of the Hindoos and Egyptians or of any inquiries into the Indian theology.[82]

His defense of the historicity of the fall of man by reference to ancient coins and the remnants of truth, which he believed are contained in the pagan mythologies of antiquity, appears in the seventh chapter.

In chapter 8, he dealt with the Noachian deluge. We will look later at his views related to geology. Here I only note his conclusion based on the historical evidence he presented from Sir William Jones, Cuvier, Mr. Rich, and Dr. Wiseman, as well as ancient writers like Josephus, Lucian, Plutarch, Juvenal, and Ovid, that the Flood was a historical fact.

> We may therefore state, that the evidence on this question is universal and conclusive. The Chaldeans, Phoenicians, Assyrians, Greeks, Romans, Goths, and Druids, Persians, Hindoos, Burmese, Chinese, Mexicans, Peruvians, Brazilians, Nicaraguans, the inhabitants of Western Caledonia, the Otakeitan and Sandwich Islanders, all have recorded the event of the Deluge, and it is incorporated in our annals. This universal testimony is wonderful, and we should think amply sufficient to satisfy the most skeptical mind.[83]

79 Murray, *Truth of Revelation*, p. xxii–xxiii.

80 This was the same John Playfair who wrote *Illustrations of the Huttonian Theory of the Earth* (1802).

81 Jones (1746–94) was considered the greatest oriental scholar of the 18th century and was the first to master Sanskrit. He was appointed judge of the high court in Calcutta in 1784, but his main love was his studies. Fluent in 13 languages and reasonably able in another 28, he became a prolific writer on anything pertaining to the Hindus, as well as on the botany and zoology of India. See *DNB* article on him.

82 Murray, *The Truth of Revelation*, p. 173.

83 Ibid., p. 211.

Chapters 9 through 12 present historical evidence in support of the veracity of various biblical accounts, such as the Tower of Babel, Abraham, Moses and the Exodus, the giving of the Ten Commandments, the serpent in the wilderness, Samson, and the Babylonian captivity. The historicity of the New Testament is defended in chapters 13 through 15. The book closes with quotes from Matthew Hale, John Milton, John Locke, Lord Bacon, Robert Boyle, and others affirming the truth of the Bible. Sir William Jones seemed to express Murray's views best when Jones wrote on the last leaf of his Bible:

> I have regularly and attentively read the Holy Scriptures, and am of [the] opinion that this volume, independently of its divine origin, contains more sublimity and beauty, more pure morality, more important history, and finer strains of poetry and eloquence, than can be collected from all other books, in whatever age or language they may have been composed.[84]

Murray devoted several pages to the extraordinary care the Jews gave to the copying and preservation of the Scriptures and confirmed the Mosaic authorship of the Pentateuch, saying:

> Its style, its careful transmission from age to age, the numerous independent authorities which corroborate this, such as the Samaritans, the Jews of the eastern hemisphere — ancient and modern — separated by barriers that have remained impassable for many centuries — Pagan evidence — all proclaim the authenticity of the sacred code of the Jews, beyond doubt or appeal.[85]

In holding this view he was not ignorant of the skeptical biblical criticism developing on the continent, particularly in Germany. In the preface he stated that "the neologists of Germany" are "worse than infidel" and are "left without excuse" and in a discussion of the death of Christ he wrote, "The *reality* of the Savior's *death* has been denied by the infidel German school, though the reality of our Savior's *life* has not been questioned."[86]

Regarding the interpretation and clarity of Scripture, he stated that "in beneficent condescension to our feeble intellect and limited reason, the Supreme Being has, in the Revelation he has sent us from heaven, used no unintelligible symbols. Deity speaks to us in our own tongue. . . . It applies to all nations of the world alike."[87] When discussing the Fall of man he was more explicit.

> The fall of man is a terrible event in the history of the species. It is related with affecting brevity, and with all the simple emphasis of truth. . . . I am perfectly aware that this fearful transaction has been considered *metaphorical* or figurative — a flourish of orientalism; but the Bible no where deceives us, and the event detailed is perspicuous and palpable. . . . The Jews understood it as a literal event, do now receive it as such, and it was so understood in the apostolic age.[88]

To Murray, the account of the Noachian flood was similarly perspicuous. He wrote, "This description of a catastrophe, which is attested by universal consent of mankind, and confirmed by the testimony of geological phenomena, is though brief, a very circumstantial and explicit account."[89] And in general he viewed the relation between the interpretation of the geological record and the interpretation of the scriptural record this way:

> I may premise, however, that though creations antecedent to MAN may *possibly* not affect the philological argument and

84 Ibid., p. 277.
85 Ibid., p. 319–320.
86 Ibid., p. xxvii, 357. He obviously was not yet aware of David Strauss's *Leben Jesu*, which appeared in 1835 in Germany and declared the gospel accounts of Jesus to be mythical. It was not translated into English until 1846 by George Elliot (under the pseudonym of Mary Ann Evans).
87 Ibid., p. 37.
88 Ibid., p. 175–178.
89 Ibid., p. 214–215.

the language of Scripture, yet, irrespective of its testimony, I confess, after a careful examination of geological phenomena, and observation of facts consequent on the study of geology for many years, I can find nothing to disturb the generally received recognition; and I confess, too, that my opinion can only be changed by a different class of facts to what has yet been adduced, and very different elements of reasoning to any I have yet met with. There cannot be a position more fixed and determinate than this — namely, that the right meaning of a Hebrew word is to be determined by the canons of philology, and not by the elements of geology. The Scripture narrative existed before the science of geology had an existence among men, and as geology is in a state of constant revolution, and incessantly changing its aspect, and moreover, is yet in an incipient state; if the Scripture is to be determined by such a versatile and ever-changing reference, there can be no standard whatever, and the pillar of our security is shaken to its foundation. Geologists were wont to convert the demiurgic days into periods of indefinite and indeterminate length, but this untenable position is now abandoned by all geologists, and the mode or scene of attack is shifted, being transferred to the Hebrew word BARA, in the first paragraph of the Genesis [sic], and the *conjunction* which links the first and second verses. . . . As modern geologists have abandoned this error [making the days of creation long ages], I advert to it because, on a former occasion, I had already insisted that it could not be reasonably or consistently maintained; and it moreover proves how dangerous it is to tamper with sacred truth, which sooner or later must always triumph.[90]

It is clear from Murray's defense of the historicity of Scripture in his *Truth of Revelation* that he believed that Scripture conveyed more than just religious and moral truth. He was convinced that the Bible also is completely accurate (though not exhaustively detailed) in its historical parts, which included the first 11 chapters of Genesis.

As far as the Galileo affair was concerned, Murray felt that it had no comparison to the Genesis-geology debate.

> The statics and formularies of astronomical science are nowhere taught in the sacred narrative; but the creation of the world at a specific period of past time, the fall of man, and the infliction of death as the penalty due to his transgression, together with an universal deluge, (certainly not a local inundation) — these facts are clearly and unequivocally taught in the records of Revelation, and no man may contravene them; and yet they are virtually repudiated by modern geological speculations. "If the foundations be destroyed, what can the righteous do?" [Ps. 11:3] Are the Protean forms and chameleon hues of a constantly changing science, to be made the test and touchstone of immutable truth? It is quite true, Weissenborn of Weimar talks about a "shortsighted interpretation of a symbolical tradition," quite upon a par with a *metaphorical* flood and a *moral* deluge. I cannot think, however, that though modern geologists are making rapid advances to these infidel conclusions, they are as yet quite prepared to go so far.[91]

Creation and the Age of the Earth

Murray strongly believed that the accounts of creation, Noah's flood and the biblical chronology are generally written in clear understandable language and are literally and historically accurate.[92] He stated in the preface to his 1840 book:

90 Ibid., p. 137–139. It might be argued that this statement reflects a lack of understanding of the evangelical old-earth geologists' Galileon-Baconian principles. But this would be debatable. It may only show a difference of perspective on the correct principles for the interpretation of Scripture.

91 John Murray, "Dr. Buckland's Geological Sermon," *Christian Observer*, vol. XXXIX, no. 19 (1839), p. 400–401.

92 The only exception to this view was his uncertainty about whether the sun was created on day 1 or day 4 of creation week. Discussion of this follows.

> I have also in these pages abandoned the geological argument, except in so far as geological monuments substantiate and confirm the doctrine of an UNIVERSAL DELUGE, entirely repudiated by modern geologists, though its summary rejection assails the authenticity of the Mosaic narrative in an essential point. If language has any meaning, its universality is clearly and unequivocally propounded for our belief, and no man may contravene its high authority or challenge its testimony; and I trust I have clearly proven that the phenomena of geology corroborate the announcement of the catastrophe of the Hebrew prophet.
>
> While I feel satisfied that in the facts revealed in modern geological research, startling and astonishing though they be, there is nothing to disturb the sacred history of creation, yet there are many difficulties and perplexities connected with arrangement and classification [of the geological phenomena]; and facts, on which there can be no misunderstanding, are better separated, in a work like the present, from conflicting speculations, and what is allowed by the dispassionate observer to be ad hoc subjudice.[93]

In chapter 5, when he discussed creation, chronology, and geology, he opened with these words:

> The opening drama of the history of time is introduced by the Hebrew prophet, under the influence of inspiration, with inimitable majesty and magnificence; and there is a grandeur and a glory about it, which stamps upon it the image and superscription of heaven. When we examine it with a philosophic eye, we discover such traces of integrity, and such elements of truth, as prove incontestibly [sic] its source and origin to be divine.[94]

Murray was clearly of the conviction that God's acts of creation were instantaneous in their effects, though spread over six 24-hour days. He wrote that "No one can read the record of creation without being impressed with the conviction, that matter and motion were instantaneous products of Almighty Power."[95] Quoting an unnamed author he reasoned:

> Common sense discerns that creation alone can give origin to existence; or first formation, to that which before did not exist; it discerns, that there can be no intermediate stage or degree between non-existence and existence, and therefore no graduality in passing from the one state to the other. To the mode of creation, we cannot therefore ascribe that mode of succession to which we give the name of time. The action of creation, was therefore effected without the mediation of time, and consequently, in that mode which we express when we exclude all notion of the mediation of time; namely, immediately, that is instantaneously, or suddenly.[96]

His view of terrestrial bodies applied no less to the celestial bodies, and was a conclusion he drew from Scripture as well as from his knowledge of astronomy.

> By reading attentively the sacred narrative of creation of Genesis, it seems quite clear that the *entire solar system* was created simultaneously and contemporaneously with this earth, and physical astronomy clearly teaches that this must have been the case. Let us remember that the various members of the solar system reciprocally depend upon each other — act and react, and are thus relatively equipoised. The sun and moon influence the earth, and are influenced by it. Were one member to be withdrawn from the solar system, all the other members would suffer; nor

93 Murray, *The Truth of Revelation*, p. xxii.
94 Ibid., p. 112.
95 Ibid., p. 127.
96 Ibid., p. 128.

is it possible for us to calculate the confusion and ruin that might be entailed on the whole, if even the least important of the number were extinguished from the system in which these spheres revolve.[97]

As a general statement he could then conclude, "When we survey the act of creation, it seem [sic] obvious, that the creative fiat was followed by instant obedience; matter started into being when the voice of the CREATOR vibrated on the TOHU BOHU; and became conscious from the infusion of living principles; distinct and definite periods marked the succession of creation."[98]

At the end of creation week the perfect universe "stood a finished monument, erected to the glory of the Creator."[99] From then on the procreation of plant and animal life and the changes to the inanimate creation proceeded according to the "laws of nature." Though in God's wise providence some creatures became extinct, no new forms of life were being created to replace them.

> There is not the slightest evidence to suppose that their places [i.e., that of extinct forms of life] have been supplied; it would be most unphilosophical, and even rash, to assume any thing of the kind — certainly unwarranted by Scripture; for we read that "God rested from his work" at the termination of the demiurgic days, and the observation and experience of ages concur in a similar conclusion.[100]

This biblical teaching, as he understood it, along with his geological knowledge led him, as we would expect, to reject the catastrophist notion of many revolutions, each followed by new acts of creation.

Though he stressed the instantaneous nature of the original creative acts of God, he also made it clear that the days of creation were normal 24-hour days. He rejected the day-age theory because 1) the context of Genesis 1 "sufficiently defined" the Hebrew word *YOM* (day), 2) the sabbath command of Exodus 20:11 ruled out any notion of an indefinite time period, and 3) ancient heathen writers also believed in a six-day creation. He rejected the gap theory because, while the Hebrew word *BARA* elsewhere in Scripture meant "adorn," "array," or "set in order," the narrative of Genesis 1 demanded the highest meaning of "create out of nothing," as Hebrews 11:3 indicated, and if it did not mean this in Genesis 1, then the Hebrews had no word to speak of creation out of nothing. The use of the conjunction at the beginning of Genesis 1:2, said Murray, cannot be so flexible and elastic in meaning to imply millions of years, for this negates the continuity of the passage.[101]

Murray devoted considerable attention to the question of the creation of light on the first day and the sun (and moon and stars) on the fourth day. At the beginning of his discussion he appeared to believe that the sun was created on the first day (as the source of the light) and only became visible on the fourth day. But after discussing this for three pages, he entertained the possibility that:

> In some localized form, apart from the orb of the sun, light might have arisen over the axal [*sic*] revolution of the earth, divided the day from the night in periodic times, and not have been transferred to the splendid station of one of the foci of the ellipsis until the fourth diurnal revolution. It was the opinion of the Greeks and

97 Ibid., p. 117–118. Nowhere did he write specifically of the creation of the distant stars, but there seems to be nothing in his writings that would lead us to any other conclusion than that he believed they were created at the same time as the solar system and earth.

98 Ibid., p. 119.

99 Ibid., p. 118.

100 Murray, *Portrait of Geology*, p. 194.

101 Murray, *The Truth of Revelation*, p. 138–140. The ancients he referred to were Ovid and Lucretius (whom he cited on pages 119–120). On the meaning of *YOM*, Murray made no mention of any of the early church fathers. To support his view of the Hebrew conjunction, *"waw,"* he noted the work of Professor M. Steuart, whom he did not identify clearly. He may have been the American Old Testament scholar, Moses Stewart.

Romans, indeed, that the sun was created on the *fourth* day.[102]

In the end he did not commit himself to either interpretation, but left open the question of when the sun was created (day 1 or day 4).[103]

Murray also did not commit himself on the precise age of the earth, though clearly it was only thousands of years old. He discussed the dates of Ussher (4004 B.C.), Dr. Hales (5411 B.C.), the Samaritans (6084 B.C.) and the Septuagint (7229 B.C.), as well as the efforts of Halley and Newton to reconcile the discrepancies between these chronologies and concluded:

> When the complexity of the question is estimated, and its liability to fallacy, with the independent sources which must be reconciled, it is rather remarkable that the error is not of wider extent.[104]

Regarding the determination of the age of the earth by a study of the strata and fossils he said:

> To natural chronometers I shall again refer, as concurring to validate the date of the deluge. But to claim a high antiquity for our globe from the extraordinary premises which some have assumed, is quite sufficient to excite our astonishment. We particularly allude to an attempt to determine the age of the world from the process of petrifaction in the piles of Trajan's Bridge, and Brydone's story about the alternations of lava and earth on the flanks of [Mount] Etna.[105]

Elsewhere he stated:

> As for the *questio vexata* of systems antecedent to man, with "millions of ages," and "creations and destructions innumerable," I confess I have strong objections to these dogmas. The phenomena of geology do not, in my mind, warrant or require such deductions. There are difficulties, no doubt, but to fly off from the orbit of induction to the eccentric regions of speculation, is not a procedure best calculated to solve them. . . . . Let it be remembered that there is no *absolute* CHRONOMETER in geology, and I very much doubt whether there yet be a fixed *relative* one among fossiliferous rocks, because there are FOSSIL REMAINS COMMON TO THEM ALL; and again, fossils innumerable are common both to *tertiary* and *secondary* strata; a fact that repudiates the assumed distinction.[106] The statics of a sound chronology being absent, prudence would require us to be cautious and less dogmatical in a science confessedly of intense interest, but comparatively young in age. Besides, fossiliferous rocks are *local*, not circumambient.
>
> It is quite true, numerous animals that once have walked the earth, and lived as well as we, are extinguished from the map of existence, and sealed up in the cerements of the solid rock, to remain an evidence in after times, in order to confront the atheist; and the only question therefore, in those that have no living analogues, is, *first*, whether they belong to antecedent systems of being, anterior to man, or to the present and existing chain of being; and, *second*,

---

102 Ibid., p. 116.

103 He had lived with this uncertainty for a long time, for he expressed the same two possibilities (without expressing preference) in his discussion on luminous matter in his *Experimental Researches on the Light and Luminous Matter of the Glowworm, the Luminosity of the Sea, the Phenomena of the Chameleon, the Ascent of the Spider into the Atmosphere, and the Torpidity of the Tortoise, Etc.* (1826).

104 Murray, *The Truth of Revelation*, p. 130.

105 Ibid., p. 130–132. In the next five pages Murray gave his geological reasons for rejecting these two dating methods. Later, on page 218, he stated, "It must never be forgotten, that geology can lay claim to no *positive chronometer* in its chronology."

106 After a discussion of some of the fossils found associated with Murchison's "Silurian rocks," Murray similarly remarked in *Portrait of Geology*, p. 150, "From the preceding summary it must, I think, be sufficiently obvious that the predilection for subdivision tends very much to fetter the science and perplex the student. It is, in fact, making a distinction without a difference: for neither in mineralogical character, nor in that of their organic remains, can some of the 'silurian rocks' be disassociated from their congeners *grauwacke*, and clay slate."

whether their disappearance or extinction, is any evidence whatever of a different physical condition of the globe in former assumed revolutions.

I can only, in this place, refer cursorily to the general facts, and have elsewhere considered the phenomena of this science, as a practical geologist, more in detail.[107] In the existing chain of being, there are links wanting, here and there, in the line of continuity, and it does happen that the extinct animals, whose organic remains have been discovered, do, in many instances, if not in all, fill up these absent links, and perfect the chain of continuity. The dinotherium, for instance, supplies the hiatus between pachydermata and cetacea; the habits and habitats of the dinotherium, as deduced from its organic remains, precisely correspond with those of the *behemoth* of scripture, and he is a bolder philosopher than I pretend to be, who would venture to assert that the Dinotherium was *not* contemporaneous with the patriarch of Uz — "Behemoth, whom I made with thee"[Job 40:15].

Again, there are many organic remains found interspersed among *all* the strata; and some, the Terebratula, for instance, found in the supposed *earliest*, or lowest of these, and yet exist in living analogues; of this description are the nautilus, echinus, gryphea, trigonia, etc.[108]

In summary then, Murray was convinced, both on the basis of his study of the Scriptures and geology, that Genesis 1 was a historical account of a supernatural creation in six 24-hour days a few thousand years ago (though he was not adamant about the precise year of the first day of creation or the precise day of the creation of the sun). This creation included all the life forms represented in the fossil record (including dinosaurs) and in modern times. The procreation of life forms and resultant variation within the original created kinds has been according to laws different from those by which God created the prototypes.

The Flood

In *Portrait of Geology*, Murray addressed the relation of the Bible and geology primarily with reference to the Flood. He stressed several times that this unique flood was "penal," and not just one of many natural disasters in the normal course of nature.[109] Unlike any other natural catastrophes, this Flood drastically changed the world.

> There is a fact stated in Scripture of considerable importance when considered in this relation: "the fountains of the great deep were broken up" — this unequivocally implies the issue of torrents from the bosom of the globe; and it seems, to us, more likely that the nucleus of the earth is an *abyss of water* than a lake of fire, however the latter view of it might coalesce with Buffon's notion, of which that of Hutton was a more elaborate transcript. The synchronous mention of the fountains of the great deep, along with the floodgates of heaven, is very remarkable, and seems to refer the effect to a *uniform cause*. The SUPREME BEING, if we may be permitted to hazard an opinion, seems to have accomplished this great event, by affecting a vast change in the density of the atmoshpere [*sic*]; to this circumstance we are inclined to refer, as a secondary agent in the fiat of deity, the rush of the waters from the recesses of the earth, "when they brake forth as if they had issued out of the womb." This increased density, in the first creation, might be the "bars and doors" referred to in the Book of Job [38:10]. In pursuing our inquiries, we shall perceive that this greater density of the atmosphere, in the antediluvian world, will account for an increased temperature in climate; and perhaps, too, be connected with the extended term of human life in the antediluvian

107Here in a footnote he identified himself as the author of his anonymous 1838 work, *Portrait of Geology*.
108 Murray, *Truth of Revelation*, p. 141–143; *Portrait of Geology*, p. 195.
109 Murray, *Portrait of Geology*, p. 81 and 97–98.

> world; since a diminished density, would be accompanied with not only a change of *temperature*, but a change in the *hygrometic* [*sic*] character of the atmosphere.[110]

From these thoughts and other details stated in Genesis, Murray reasoned that there would have been no rain, clouds, or rainbow before the Deluge. Rather, the earth was watered by very copious and uniform dew. And where did the waters of the Flood go? He answered that, "For any thing we know to the contrary, the diluvial waters may have retreated into the profound abysses of the earth; besides, much would disappear as water of crystallization, in crystalline rocks, and much, also, as water of composition, in sedimentary rocks."[111] Many who rejected the notion of a global Flood asserted that the Flood was too brief to be able to account for the geological record. Murray, on the other hand, thought that although the Flood lasted only for a year, the earth did not reach a state anything like its present state of relative climatic and geological equilibrium until many years or even centuries later.

> Though the waters only "prevailed on the earth for one hundred and fifty days," it by no means follows, that when they were "assuaged," or began "to abate," they were so soon reduced to their present limits. Centuries might have rolled away before they had contracted their bounds to the dimensions that now restrain them.[112]

Murray acknowledged that the geological record is in many ways "perplexing and complicated" to interpret properly. He took this as the expected result of the combined work of the normal course of nature and the great and singularly abnormal Deluge. He stated:

> No doubt there have been local catastrophes of greater or less extent, both in antediluvian and postdiluvian times, and these combined with a *universal deluge*, seem to me quite adequate to the solution of geological phenomena, without the assumption of "an age of reptiles and a reign of saurians."[113]

In discussing the biblical account of the Flood, Murray quoted Genesis 7:10–24 and italicized the following words to emphasize the violent and global nature of the Flood: *were all the fountains of the great deep broken up* and the *windows (or floodgates) of heaven were opened* (v. 11), *all the high hills that were under the whole heaven were covered* (v. 19), *the mountains were covered* (v. 20), *all flesh died that moved upon the earth, both of fowl, and of cattle, and of beast, and of every creeping thing that creepeth upon the earth, and every man* (v. 21), *of all that was in the dry land, died* (v. 22), *every living substance was destroyed, both man and cattle, and the creeping things, and the fowl of heaven* (v. 23). He described this account as "though brief, a very circumstantial and explicit account."[114] Given his conviction that the account of the Flood, indeed the whole first 11 chapters of Genesis, could hardly be more perspicuous, Murray's reaction to the interpretations of the Scriptures by De la Beche, Phillips, Lyell, and others who denied the Flood, by reinterpreting it as a tranquil local affair, is understandable.

> "If," says Mr. De la Beche, "the existence of man and those extinct animals should ever be satisfactorily proved, it would become a curious question whether his so found remains are those of an extinct species!" How this speculation is to be reconciled with the Mosaic narrative I have yet to learn. . . . Mr. John Phillips has boldly, though I think indiscreetly, promulgated the following assumption and speculation — "If it should be generally admitted by theologians that the

110 Murray, *The Truth of Revelation*, p. 215–216.
111 Ibid., p. 216–217.
112 Ibid., p. 217. He made no mention of Genesis 8:13–14, 21–22, and 9:7–17, which seem to indicate that at the end of the Flood year the oceans were essentially established at their permanent limits.
113 Ibid., p. 144; John Murray, *Portrait of Geology*, p. 81–82.
114 Murray, *The Truth of Revelation*, p. 214–215.

Noachian flood, though general with respect to the area over which the early races of mankind had spread, was not an *universal* deluge, some one of the repeated geological deluges, which could not be universal, though some of them were every extensive, may perhaps be successfully compared with that event!"[115] If language has any meaning, this is a direct impeachment of the sacred records. This author [Phillips] elsewhere calls the "diluvial hypothesis" "a seducing error," "a monstrous violation of the laws of nature," and "a narrow and unreasonable interpretation of the Mosaic narrative." Weissenborn of Weimar, terms it "a short sighted interpretation of a symbolical tradition." Mr. Lyell accounts for "an event related in Scripture," by the overflow of an inland lake elevated above the level of the sea, or the depression of the land below that plane! Some say, indeed, that the account of the deluge, though recorded as an historical event, is "metaphorical" — a mere oriental flourish of speech: others again, that it is "elliptical in the extreme;" and another party that a "moral" event was meant, and not a physical catastrophe. Most extraordinary assumptions and interpretations I must needs say.[116]

In addition to the written and oral traditions of peoples around the world concerning a "universal and penal flood,"[117] Murray presented what he believed to be "conclusive and irresistible" geological evidences for a global flood. The most important line of evidences included the global distribution of erratic boulders, gravels, valleys of denudation, and limestone caves, which he believed doubtlessly were contemporaneous in formation. Though some erratic boulders were the result of local causes, he reasoned, only a universal flood could satisfactorily explain their global distribution.[118]

Murray also believed that there was compelling fossil evidence for antediluvian man and that this evidence had been neatly ignored or unjustifiably discarded by most geologists. He devotes 14 pages[119] to a discussion of some of the evidence from Guadaloupe (reported to the Royal Society in 1814) and the limestone caves near Köstritz, Germany (found in 1820);[120] near Bize, Pondre, and Sommières, France (reported to the French Academy of Sciences in 1829); near Liège, Belgium (found in 1833–34); and several other locations. Several times Murray complained that the leading geologists seemed anxious to overlook or explain away this evidence.[121]

Murray also presented historic evidence of rapid mountain building to show that G. Poulett Scrope's assumption of tens of thousands of years needed for the formation of the Auvergne region in France was illegitimate.[122] He answered the alleged difficulty of harmonizing the great thickness of the stratified rocks with the scriptural narrative of the Flood by citing known examples of very rapid deposition of limestone.[123] Although he presumed that some coal was the product of lacustrine deposits of plant material, such as possibly in his day in peat bogs in France, he also cited evidence for a marine origin, believing it to be the

115 As we saw earlier, the local flood view was not the *dominant* view among the most respected Bible commentators at the time Phillips wrote this statement. Even in 1840, when Murray wrote his criticism, the highly and broadly respected commentators such as Horne, Scott, and Clarke were still arguing that Genesis was describing a global flood.
116 Murray, *Portrait of Geology*, p. 96–98.
117 Ibid., p. 98; Murray, *The Truth of Revelation*, 203–215. Murray emphasized the penal nature of the Flood; in other words, it was not an accidental event in the natural course of the world.
118 Murray, *Portrait of Geology*, p. 56–81, 199–201; Murray, *The Truth of Revelation*, p. 218–222.
119 Murray, *Portrait of Geology*, p. 82–96.
120 This evidence, as we've seen, was also referred to by Fairholme. Murray gave no evidence of knowing Fairholme or of having visited Köstritz personally, but their arguments are similar in their rejection of the interpretations of the fossil evidence given by Schlotheim, the original discoverer, and later by Buckland.
121 Murray, *Portrait of Geology*, p. 82–83.
122 Ibid., p. 176–177.
123 Ibid., p. 195–198.

better explanation for the vast coal beds found throughout the world.[124]

As to the date of the Deluge, he gave the following geological argument in support of the biblical chronology.

> That the chronometric period of the universal Deluge cannot have been anterior to the date assigned to it by the Hebrew cosmogonist can be clearly determined by an appeal to *natural chronometers*, such as the phenomena of the advance and formation of *glaciers*, and those of the *talus* or debris of rocks, accumulated at the base of mountains. To these may be added the advance of the sand-flood on the land, and the entire formation and progress of *dunes*, on the sea coast. The L'landes of France and some parts of Ireland and of Cornwall, exemplify what we refer to, and to these united testimonies may be added the formation of *deltas* at the mouths of rivers — the deposition of the alluvion transported by their waters.[125]

From all these lines of evidence he concluded:

> The evidence in favor of a UNIVERSAL DELUGE, identical with that recorded in the inspired narrative, becomes thus as complete, when combined with the unequivocal traditional testimony of a world; on the aggregate principles of an inductive generalization, as any problem in Euclid. This general and universal testimony cannot be disturbed by any *apparent* partial and limited discrepancy, if that seeming exception can be explained by any local or casual circumstance that may have occurred subsequent to the event.[126]

Therefore he considered as "rash" Sedgwick's statement in 1831 that there is no geological evidence of the Flood. To Dr. Kidd's remarks in his *Bridgewater Treatise* (1833) that any potential geological evidence for the Flood was obliterated by God so as to better try our faith, Murray replied, "I, on the contrary believe that we might reasonably expect the very reverse, in order that our faith might be strengthened and confirmed, and that a perennial monument of the penal infliction should remain till the end of time."[127]

On the Fall of Man

I have already shown that Murray understood the account of the fall of man in Genesis 3 in a literal historical sense. Buckland preached his sermon at the Cathedral of Christ Church in Oxford on January 27, 1839, in which he discussed several passages of Scripture to justify his view that there had been animal death and catastrophic extinctions before the Fall.[128] Murray voiced his objection to Buckland's position in the *Christian Observer* magazine. He viewed Buckland's interpretation of the biblical texts (which applied the Fall only to man) to be unique and concluded that the old-earth idea

124 Ibid., p. 140–142.

125 Murray, *The Truth of Revelation*, p. 222.

126 Murray, *Portrait of Geology*, p. 201.

127 Ibid., p. 96–97. An interesting contrast to Murray's sentiments about the remaining effects of the Flood are the words of an old-earth opponent, James Smithson, later founder of the Smithsonian Institution in Washington, D.C., in "Some Observations on Mr. Penn's Theory Concerning the Formation of the Kirkdale Cave," *Annals of Philosophy*, vol. VIII (1824), p. 60. Smithson wrote, "Under the impression of these [God's] paternal feelings, to obliterate every trace of the dreadful scourge, remove every remnant of the frightful havoc, seem the natural effects of his benevolence and power. As a lesson to the races which were to issue from the loins of the few who had been spared — races which were to be wicked indeed as those which had preceded them, but which were promised exemption from a like punishment, to have preserved an memento of them would have been useless. To a miracle then which swept away all that could recall that day of death when 'the windows of heaven were opened' upon mankind, must we refer what no natural means are adequate to explain."

128 William Buckland, *An Inquiry Whether the Sentence of Death Pronounced at the Fall of Man Included the Whole Animal Creation or Was Restricted to the Human Race* (1839). The passages Buckland analyzed were: Romans 5:12, 17–18, and 8:19–23; 1 Corinthians 15:21; Colossians 1:23; Mark 16:15; Genesis 3:17–19; Isaiah. 11:6–9. Buckland's conclusion was that the Fall only affected man, not the rest of creation.

129 John Murray, "Dr. Buckland's Geological Sermon," *Christian Observer*, vol. XXXIX (1839), p. 401.

that pain, suffering, and death were a part of the original created order stripped them of any penal character.[129]

Conclusion

Contrary to the general charges leveled against the 19th century scriptural geologists, Murray was a highly qualified and respected scientist with a competent knowledge of geology who believed, because of both the biblical teaching and the geological evidence, that God created the world in six literal days a few thousand years ago and that He judged the world in a unique, global Flood. While his understanding of and belief in the Scriptures guided his interpretation of the rocks, he was not ignorant of the rock strata and fossils. He traveled widely to study geological formations, observed carefully the rocks and fossils, used chemical analysis, and relied on the work of other experts as he interpreted the geological evidence from a broad and recognized knowledge of many scientific disciplines.

Murray never developed an "anti-geology" attitude. During his entire life he was enthusiastic about the practical benefits of geology and contributed constructively to this end. He did not make *ad hominem* attacks against those geologists with whom he disagreed, but showed respect for their knowledge and accomplishments in science and geology. Also, he did not deny all geological facts, which the geologists had commendably gathered. Rather, he believed that not everything the old-earth geologists called "facts" were facts indeed. Many of them were, in his opinion, disputable speculative inferences from the indisputable facts, and he gave his geological and biblical reasons for firmly rejecting those inferences.

While he held firmly to Scripture, he did not have a blind faith that refused to look at challenging objections. He admitted that there were as yet unsolved geological problems for his young-earth view, but because of what he believed to be the infant state of geology and the multifarious evidences that the Bible is the inspired and infallible Word of God, he was confident that these geological problems would eventually be solved and the literal historical accuracy of the early chapters of Genesis would be vindicated, just as other criticized parts of the Scriptures had been previously substantiated.

GEORGE YOUNG (1777–1848)

George Young was born on July 25, 1777, the fourth of ten children of John and Jean Young, at their small farm in the parish of Kirk-Newton, southwest of Edinburgh. Since George was born with only a right hand (the left forearm ended in a stump), agriculture was ruled out as a future vocation. His pious parents therefore educated him with a view to Christian ministry, a course consistent with his own spiritual convictions which developed early in his life.

To fulfil the requirements for ordination in the Church of Scotland, to which he and his family belonged, he commenced in 1792 four years of literary and philosophical studies at the University of Edinburgh. He distinguished himself especially in mathematics and natural philosophy, being a favorite student of Professor John Playfair, who was in the process of becoming the articulate interpreter of James Hutton's uniformitarian geological theory.[1] Young completed his degree with high honors and then began a five-year course in theology at Selkirk, under the tutelage of Dr. George Lawson (1749–1820), a famous Scottish divine who was well read in philosophy, history, and natural science.[2] In 1801 he was licensed to preach by the presbytery of Edinburgh.

After a brief visit in the summer of 1805 to Whitby, North Yorkshire, the following year he became the pastor of Whitby Chapel, a congregation he served for 42 years until his death. In 1819 the University of Edinburgh conferred on him the degree of M.A., and in 1838 he received

Unless otherwise stated, this biographical section is based on Gideon Smales, *Whitby Authors and Their Publications* (1867), p. 64–71, and the *DNB* article on Young.

1 Playfair published his *Illustrations of the Huttonian Theory of the Earth* in 1802 based on Hutton's earlier work of 1795, which was the penultimate year of Young's university studies. It is quite likely therefore that Young gained a thorough knowledge of the Huttonian theory.

2 *DNB* on Lawson. Lawson was professor of theology at Divinity Hall, Selkirk, where he also pastored. Known as the "Scottish Socrates," he was admired for his vast erudition and apparently infallible memory. He trained many notable Presbyterian, Independent, and Church of Scotland ministers. See also Nigel M. de S. Cameron, editor, *Dictionary of Scottish History and Theology* (1993), p. 474.

George Young (1777–1848)

an honorary degree of Doctor of Divinity from Miami College (Oxford, Ohio).[3] In 1826 he married Margaret, a daughter of prominent Robert Hunter of Whitby and a woman known for her piety and ministry to women.[4] They had a happy marriage until her death in 1846,[5] but they had no children.[6]

Young faithfully discharged his responsibilities as a pastor and was respected for his concern for the poor and his generous, self-denying, Christian spirit, because of which he delighted to unite with Christians of other Protestant denominations in joint efforts of witness and service.[7] His congregation fixed a monument over the pulpit of the church after his death, which honored Young for having "preached the Word of God within these walls with unabated zeal for 42 years, actuated and sustained throughout solely by a sense of duty, and an anxious desire for the salvation of souls."[8]

Beyond this, his scholarly attainments were also considerable. He had a more than common knowledge of Hebrew, Greek, Latin, French, and Italian, as well as an acquaintance with Arabic, Chaldee, and Syriac, and was considered quite an authority on the Anglo-Saxon language. He also developed his own shorthand, which he used for writing his sermons and which no one yet has been able to translate. His extensive knowledge of antiquities and numismatics enabled him to decipher ancient manuscripts, coins, and inscriptions with great skill.

In 1823 he became a founding member and the first secretary of the Whitby Literary and Philosophical Society, a position he held until his death, and which also included the establishment of the Whitby Museum.[9] He was also a corresponding member of the Wernerian Natural History Society and the Northern Institution and an honorary member of the Yorkshire, Newcastle, Leeds, and Hull literary and philosophical societies.[10] Although only an honorary member of the Yorkshire Philosophical Society, Young served as an advisor to the Society and, as a series of ten letters from Young to the Society during the years 1823–27 shows,[11] he served as

3 Thomas H. English, *Whitby Prints* (1931), I: p. F.6.
4 Anonymous, "Memoir of the late Rev. George Young, D.D.," *The United Presbyterian Magazine*, vol. III (1849), p. 102.
5 Anonymous, "Brief Notice of the Late Rev. George Young, D.D.," *Evangelical Magazine*, vol. XXVII (1849), p. 114.
6 Personal conversation on September 22, 1995, with Mr. Harold Brown, honorary librarian of the Whitby Museum.
7 Anonymous, "Brief Notice of the Late Rev. George Young, D.D.," *Evangelical Magazine*, vol. XXVII (1849), p. 114; Anonymous, "Memoir of the late Rev. George Young, D.D.," *The United Presbyterian Magazine*, vol. III (1849), p. 101–102.
8 Francis K. Robinson, *Whitby* (1860), p. 145.
9 Anonymous, "Whitby Literary and Philosophical Society: A Retrospect (1823–1948)," *Whitby Gazette* (January 16, 1948).
10 The requirements for such membership was the same as for ordinary members of these societies. The difference was related to a member's place of residence and his degree of involvement in a society's activities. See Abraham Hume, *Learned Societies and Printing Clubs* (1847), p. 143–144, 146, 149–150, 175–176.
11 S. Melmore, "Letters in the Possession of the Yorkshire Philosophical Society," *North Western Naturalist*, vol. XVII (1942), p. 325–332.

Whitby, Yorkshire, England.

the coastal representative procuring fossil and mineral collections for the Society.[12]

His published books numbered 21. Eleven were 30–40 pages long and contained sermons addressed to such topics as the experiences of seamen, compassion for British prisoners in France during Napoleon's rule, the downfall of Napoleon, the unity of the Church, the deaths of Queen Charlotte and King George III, and the great solar eclipse of 1836. His longer works included a series of lectures on the Book of Jonah, a two-volume *The History of Whitby*,[13] a treatise vindicating the evangelical principles of religion, a catalog of hardy plants for the garden,[14] and a highly acclaimed biography of Captain James Cook.[15]

On the subject of geology, Young wrote six scientific journal articles and three books. *A Geological Survey of the Yorkshire Coast* (236 pages), written with the assistance of John Bird, first appeared in 1822, with a greatly revised edition (356 pages) coming out in 1828.[16] Ten years later he published *Scriptural Geology* (1838, 78 pages), followed shortly thereafter by *Appendix to Scriptural Geology* (1840, 31 pages), in which he responded to John Pye Smith's theory that Genesis described merely a local creation and local Noachian flood, both in the Mesopotamian Valley.[17]

12 Barbara J. Pyrah, *The History of the Yorkshire Museum* (York, England: W. Sessions, 1988), p. 33.

13 This appeared in 1817 and contained 33 pages of information on the geology of the area. It was republished in 1976.

14 George Young, *A Catalogue of Hardy Ornamental Flowering Shrubs, Forest and Fruit Trees, Etc.* (1834). Alexander Willison, a much-respected Scottish gardener in Whitby, assisted Young in this work.

15 In *The Life and Voyages of Captain James Cook* (1836), Young sought not only to give an accurate history, but also to teach moral lessons from Cook's character, conduct, and life experiences with the hope of inciting virtue and piety in his readers. See the preface to the book. The 275 pre-publication subscribers for the book included Louis Agassiz and William Buckland.

16 Hereafter, this work is cited as *Geological Survey*. John Bird, who did the illustrations for this book, was curator of the Whitby Museum and member of the Whitby Literary and Philosophical Society, as well as an honorary member of the similar societies of Hull and Yorkshire.

17 These two were published in a combined second edition, also in 1840.

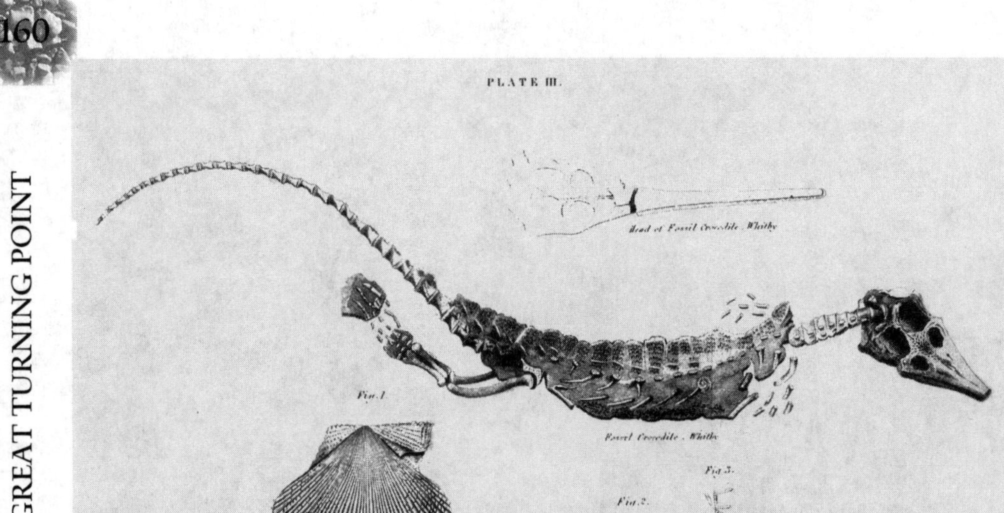

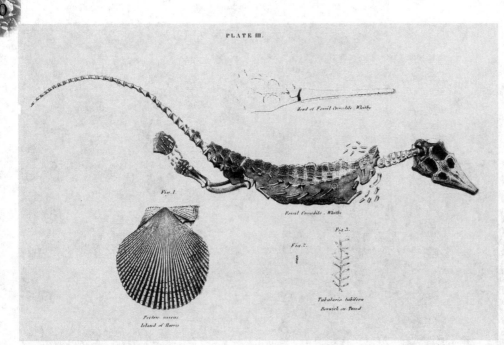

Fossil crocodile found near Whitby around 1825 about which Young wrote a scientific article

He hoped that his efforts would have a practical benefit for the manufacturer and businessman to know where the valuable minerals were, for the landed proprietor to know the nature of the strata under his soils, for the miners not to waste money searching for coal in the wrong places, and for "the admirers of the works of God" to be stimulated in their devotion to God.[20]

In addition to his scientific training at the university, his writings show that he kept himself current in his reading on geology and related fields in books and science journals, both British and foreign. But he also had extensive geological field experience. In his introduction to the *Survey*, Young stated that he and his co-author, Bird, had completed their study of the geology of Yorkshire.

> . . . with no small labor; exploring the whole line of coast, and visiting every part of the interior likely to throw light on the objects of their research. Scarcely a hill or a valley, a cliff or a chasm, remains unexamined; scarcely an alum-work, a coal-pit, a quarry, or any other remarkable opening in the strata, has been left unvisited; so that, if the result should not come up to their wishes, or the expectations of their friends, they cannot well charge themselves with want of diligence, patience, and perseverance.[21]

After contracting influenza in early 1848, he died on May 8 (two years after his wife), which brought deep and general grief to the residents of Whitby. One contemporary biographer wrote of his death, "As in health, so also in affliction, he showed a child-like simplicity and confidence in the verities of religion; and his last words were: 'Jesus is precious — exceedingly precious — whether we are living or dying.' "[18]

View of Geology and Geological Competence

Young had an obvious love for the study of geology and saw it not as a threat, but as an aid to faith. He wrote:

> The researches of the geologist are far from being unworthy of the Christian, or the philosopher: for, while they enlarge the bounds of our knowledge, and present a wide field for intellectual employment and innocent pleasure, they may serve to conduct us to the glorious Being.[19]

18 Smales, *Whitby Authors and Their Publications*, p. 68.
19 George Young, *Geological Survey* (1828), p. 2.
20 Ibid., p. 12.
21 Ibid., p. 9.

Young more than once examined the geological formations around Edinburgh.[22] He continued his geological field research and reading up to the time of his writings in 1840, for he said, "For many years I have paid particular attention to the courses of rivers, and have invariably found that these courses are connected with breaks, faults, denudations, or other irregularities in the strata through which they pass."[23] He also mentioned his discovery of a fossil fish in limestone rocks near South Shields, early in 1840, at the age of 63.[24]

A very important test, however, of his geological acumen must be the reviews of his geological writings by contemporary geologists. Of Young's *The History of Whitby* (1817) the contemporary Whitby geologist Martin Simpson wrote:

> . . . a work of high literary character and antiquarian research, in which he gave a very luminous and correct exposition of the rocks and organick remains of the district, [which] immediately produced a general revolution in publick opinion respecting the fossil remains of the district, and excited great zeal for further discovery.[25]

Young's *Geological Survey of Yorkshire* (1822) received positive reviews from the *Philosophical Magazine* and the *Edinburgh Philosophical Journal.* Most of the former review, rather than giving an analysis of the book, is a lengthy quote from the *Geological Survey* giving some of Young's argument against the old-earth theory of multiple catastrophes. However, the geologically informed, anonymous reviewer wrote generally:

> Such has been the labor of the two gentlemen who have undertaken the task, that they have with unremitting ardour explored the whole line of the Yorkshire coast, from the Humber to the Tees, visiting every part of the interior likely to throw light on the objects of their research. Scarcely a hill or a valley, a cliff or a chasm, remains unexamined; scarcely an alum rock, a coal pit or a quarry, or any other remarkable opening in the strata, has been left unvisited,[26] and the result of their labors is now laid before the public in a well-written memoir, illustrated by such engravings as fully explain the subjects referred to in the text. . . . The limits of a magazine are much too narrow to do justice to a work of this nature, either in the way of analysis or extract: we shall therefore content ourselves with quoting from the facts and inferences some observations of the authors on the hypothesis of successive creations or formations of strata, contended for by some geologists, but to which they are opposed.[27]

In an 1825 article on diluvial formations, Adam Sedgwick (the esteemed Cambridge geology professor), who likely knew Young personally, described the *Survey* as containing "some excellent observations."[28] The next year, in an article on the classification of the strata of the Yorkshire coast, Sedgwick again commended the work of Young and Bird, whose "information induced me to shorten the task

22 George Young, *Appendix* (1840), p. 27. Here he was responding to Smith's objections to William Rhind's views on the geology of Edinburgh. See John Pye Smith, *Relation Between the Holy Scriptures and the Geological Sciences* (1839), p. 299.

23 Young, *Appendix*, p. 21.

24 Ibid., p. 22.

25 Martin Simpson, *The Fossils of the Yorkshire Lias* (1884), p. iv. Simpson was appointed lecturer in natural science for the Whitby Literary and Philosophical Society and curator of the Whitby Museum in 1837, positions he held up to the time of his book in 1884. So he was personally acquainted with Young and Bird; the latter he described as "an artist, and a man of a philosophical turn of mind." Simpson wrote several books on geology and on the fossils of the Lias formation in Yorkshire, and late in life he was recognized by the Geological Society of London for his lifelong research in paleontology. The above information about him comes from the preface to his book.

26 These last few lines are obviously almost verbatim from page 9 of Young's *Geological Survey*, as noted above.

27 *Philosophical Magazine*, vol. LIX (Jan.–June 1822), p. 294.

28 Adam Sedgwick, "On Diluvial Formations," *Annals of Philosophy*, N.S. vol. X (1825), p. 19. Young and Sedgwick possibly met when the latter was in Whitby for a long weekend during his own study of the Yorkshire coast in September 1821, though he did not specifically mention Young in a letter about the trip written to his friend, William Ainger. See J.W. Clark and T.M. Hughes, *Life and Letters of Adam Sedgwick* (1890), I: p. 226–227.

which I had proposed to myself." This was because "with many excellent details" the relations of the geological phenomena had been "elaborately and faithfully described" to give an accurate history of the structure of the whole Yorkshire coast.[29]

In light of the fact that readers already knew something of the nature of Young's work from his 1822 edition of the *Geological Survey*, it is noteworthy that the pre-publication subscribers to the 1828 revised edition numbered 113, including 33 members of scientific societies, even though the theoretical part III of this edition was virtually unchanged from the first edition. Four of the latter subscribers were members of the Geological Society of London, one of whom was Reverend William Vernon (Harcourt), president of the Yorkshire Philosophical Society and one of the leading founders of the BAAS in 1831.[30] Another subscriber was Mrs. Gideon Mantell, wife of the doctor and well-known old-earth geologist from Sussex.[31]

Young and Bird were quick to admit and correct previous errors as their geological studies progressed. In the introduction to the second edition of *Geological Survey* they wrote of themselves:

> They are far from supposing that the work is free from mistakes, or that nothing more can be done for elucidating the geology of the district; on the contrary, their own experience has served to convince them, that a work of this nature is susceptible of progressive improvement; for as, in making this extended survey, they have been enabled to detect some mistakes in the sketch of the strata contained in the *History of Whitby* and the Vicinity; so, in the prosecution of this undertaking, they have been able, in various instances, on repeating their visits to the same spots, to correct inaccuracies in their first observations, and every new journey has supplied them with additional illustrations of the objects of their pursuit. It is natural, therefore, to expect, that such as may trace their steps, will detect other errors into which they have fallen, and discover new facts which have escaped their notice.[32]

The work was divided into three parts. Part 1 (172 pages) is a geological description of all the strata of the coast. Part 2 (126 pages, plus 37 pages of plates) is a description of the various fossils found, arranged into classes and identified according to the locations where they were found. This section contained a 17-page discussion of the famous Kirkdale Cave, which included a refutation of Buckland's post-diluvian hyena den theory of the cave. Young especially pointed out a number of factual errors in Buckland's description of the cave. He also gave his reasons for concluding that the cave and its fossil remains were deposited by the Noachian flood. Young's argument was based on his own first-hand research of the cave, commenced within a week of its discovery, and on his personal discussions with the workmen who cleared the cave of fossils (sometimes while he was watching them), as well as conversations with William Salmond (FGS) and William Eastmead, the

29 Adam Sedgwick, "On the Classification of the Strata which Appear on the Yorkshire Coast." *Annals of Philosophy*, N.S. vol. II (1826), p. 339, 341.

30 Vernon was also an old-earth creationist and, in a somewhat veiled manner, spoke out against the scriptural geologists. See William Vernon Harcourt, "Address of the Presidency of the BAAS," *Atheneum*, No. 618 (August 31, 1839), p. 653–654.

31 Gideon Mantell expressed his old-earth creationist views through an introduction, written by an anonymous clergyman, attached to his *Fossils of the South Downs: Geology of Sussex* (1822). At that time Mantell believed both that there was a gap of untold ages before Genesis 1:3 and that the first three "days" (at least) of creation were long ages of time.

The first edition of Young's *Geological Survey* had a total of 269 pre-publication subscribers. Eighteen of these were members of scientific societies, including six fellows of the Geological Society of London and six members of the Edinburgh Wernerian Society. Buckland ordered six copies. Other subscribers were E.D. Clarke (professor of mineralogy, Cambridge), Adam Sedgwick, Dr. Williams (professor of botany at Oxford), Alexander Tilloch (editor of *Philosophical Magazine*), William Scoresby (master mariner, arctic explorer, and expert on earth magnetism), Robert Jameson (president of the Edinburgh Wernerian Society), George Greenough (prominent member of the Geological Society of London), and William Eastmead (one of the leading explorers of the Kirkdale Cave).

32 Young, *Geological Survey*, p. 9–10. This is very similar to Henry De la Beche's comments about his own geological efforts in his *A Geological Manual* (1831), p. vii.

two geologists most involved in the analysis of the cave and its fossils. A number of the fossils were deposited in the Whitby Museum, which Young and Bird managed. In *Historia Reivallensis* (1824), Eastmead concluded that the cave was an antediluvian deposit. This discussion was a revised form of Young's two journal articles on Kirkdale written in 1822 and mysteriously published much later in the *Memoirs of the Wernerian Natural History Society*.[33]

In Part 3 (46 pages) Young and Bird presented their theoretical inferences from these facts. They realized that there would be opposition to the latter part and addressed their critics:

> As the hints here thrown out are chiefly suggested by existing phenomena, it is hoped that they may be serviceable to the studious enquirer. Where the views adopted by the authors militate against the favorite theory of any of their readers, they expect from the reader that candor and indulgence which he himself has a right to claim from others. On subjects involved in so many difficulties, mutual forbearance is indispensable.[34]

Young was cautious in his theoretical interpretations of the geological phenomena, because of what he perceived to be the still rather infant state of geology. In 1828 he wrote:

> It is within the last twenty or thirty years, that geology has begun to assume her proper rank among the sciences. . . . Within these few years, the collection of geological facts has been rapidly accumulating. Still, if we may judge from the jarring opinions held on the subject, we have not obtained sufficient data, for establishing a general theory of the earth; in other words, we cannot satisfactorily explain the natural causes employed by the Creator to bring our globe into its present state; which, as all agree, is widely different from its original state. The chief thing to be done, therefore, in the present stage of the science, is to enrich it with ample stores derived from actual observation. . . . Every addition to these stores, will serve to enlarge and consolidate the basis on which a true theory of the earth, if such can be found, must necessarily rest.[35]

Even in 1838 he explicitly claimed that he was not offering a complete theory.[36] Therefore, he preferred to focus his attention on the careful gathering and integrating of geological facts. In the summary of his 1838 *Scriptural Geology* he wrote:

> Upon the whole, let us learn, in the pursuits of geology, to guard against

33 There are some interesting facts to be noted in regard to these. The first article, read to the Wernerian Society in May 1822, was published in 1822 (*Memoirs of the Wernerian Society*, vol. IV, 262–270) and was a purely descriptive account of caves and the fossils found in them. The second article, which gave Young's *theoretical* interpretations of this geological data (in terms of Noah's flood) and gave a critique of Buckland's den theory, was read to the Society on November 30, 1822. However, it was not published until about four years later in 1826 (*Memoirs*, vol. VI, 171–183), long after Buckland's theory was established in people's minds.

It also should be noted that in this second article Young said that he waited to publish his theoretical interpretations until Buckland had published his in the *Philosophical Transactions of the Royal Society*. According to Young's second journal article (p. 172), Buckland's views were already known to Young as a result of earlier personal correspondence and personal conversation in Whitby between the two. So why did the Wernerian Society wait so many years before publishing Young's objections to Buckland's ideas, especially since Young had more firsthand knowledge of Kirkdale Cave and its fossils than Buckland did?

This may have been a case of deliberate suppression (under Jameson's influence) of Young's article. Robert Jameson was the founder and director of the Edinburgh Wernerian Society and editor of its *Memoirs*. He secretly encouraged John Fleming, who advocated a tranquil Noachian flood which left no geological effects, to oppose Buckland's views on the Flood (*DSB* on Fleming, p. 32). Fleming did so in the *Edinburgh Philosophical Journal* (co-edited by Jameson and David Brewster) in 1826 (vol. XIV, no. 28, 205–239). Could it be that Jameson intentionally delayed publication of Young's article until after Fleming's, because of Jameson's own drift from catastrophism to uniformitarianism, which was in progress at the time?

34 Young, *Geological Survey*, p. 11–12. Young also expressed his caution regarding theoretical interpretation and speculation on pages iv and 311. His third part is therefore labeled "general observations" and broken into two sections: "facts and inferences," which he said could be regarded as "certain," and "hints and conjectures," which comprise "what is only probable."

35 Ibid., p. 2–3. He further stresses the infant state of geological knowledge on pages 8–9.

36 George Young, *Scriptural Geology*, (1838), p. iv.

launching into wild imaginations, alike unfavorable to science and religion. Let every phenomenon be attentively surveyed, let every fact be duly investigated, let facts be accumulated, and diligently compared; and, instead of indulging in flights of fancy, let sober reason and sound judgment determine the results.[37]

Nevertheless, more than any of the other geologically informed scriptural geologists, Young presented the most thorough explanation at his time of how the whole geological record could be harmonized with a literal reading of the Genesis account of creation and the Noachian flood. Therefore, we should consider his arguments carefully.

Attitude toward His Geological Opponents

While not hesitating to challenge the theories of the most famous geologists, Young was respectful of their knowledge, research, and accomplishments. For example, he described his former professor, Playfair, as "one of the most learned" authors.[38] Though critical of Cuvier and Brongniart's theory of the Paris basin, Young nevertheless said that they were authors "to whom science is otherwise much indebted."[39] In spite of his strong refutation of Buckland's theory of Kirkdale Cave, Young wrote, "We are sensible of the value of his researches into this subject," and he described Buckland's *Bridgewater Treatise* as generally "valuable" and "admirable," the work of "my learned friend."[40] John Phillips's writings were also "valuable."[41] Lyell, though even more hostile to Young's views, was respected as an "indefatigable" collector of geological facts, and in several places Young used some of the ideas which Lyell had "advanced and ably maintained."[42]

In return for such respectful disagreement, Young hoped for a similar kind of hearing from his critics. After stating in the *Survey* his reasons for rejecting the day-age theory he commented:

> Aware that our sentiments on this subject differ materially from those of a great proportion of our literary friends, we would beg of them a patient hearing; that they may not condemn our remarks, till they have candidly weighed them.[43]

He obviously did not feel that he had received that kind of treatment from his geological opponents, for ten years later he introduced his *Scriptural Geology* by saying:

> These geologists [his critics] complain, and have a right to complain, of those who stigmatize them as atheists, infidels, and enemies to revelation: yet they ought to remember, that they have no right, on their part, to denounce their opponents as bigots, fanatics, ignorant, and illiberal. It is not by hard names, but by strong arguments, that the cause of truth is to be established.[44]

Without apology, he used information and arguments from his geological opponents to refute their own theories, but he expressed his effort not to misrepresent them in any way.

Reference to Other Scriptural Geologists

The only work of a fellow scriptural geologist that Young particularly commended to his readers in 1828 was Granville Penn's *Comparative Estimate of the Mineral and Mosaical Geologies* (1825),

37 Ibid., p. 77.
38 Young, *Geological Survey*, p. 327.
39 Ibid., p. 328.
40 Ibid., p. 302–307; Young, *Scriptural Geology*, p. 37, 41, 75; "On the fossil remains of quadrupeds, etc. discovered in the cavern at Kirkdale, in Yorkshire, and in other cavities or seams in Limestone Rocks," *Memoirs of the Wernerian Society of Edinburgh*, vol. VI, (1822), p. 172. As noted earlier, Young knew Buckland personally through face-to-face conversation and correspondence.
41 Young, *Scriptural Geology*, p. 11.
42 Ibid., p. iii, 31, 34, 55.
43 Young, *Geological Survey*, p. 343.
44 Young, *Scriptural Geology*, p. iv.

which Young felt had opposed the contemporary old-earth theories with "much force of argument." He continued, "We are not prepared to admit all that Mr. Penn has advanced; but his theoretical views appear to us, on the whole, much more judicious than those which he combats."[45]

In the introduction to his *Scriptural Geology* (1838), he indicated that he knew of other works being prepared for publication, but that he did not know their contents and so was unable to comment on their arguments. However, he did make a positive remark about Leveson Vernon Harcourt's *Doctrine of the Deluge* (Vol. 3, 1838), and in his 1840 appendix he supported his argument with information from John Murray's *Portrait of Geology* (1838) and William Rhind's *Age of the Earth* (1838). Young gave no indication of personally knowing any of these other scriptural geologists.[46]

View of the Relationship of Scripture and Science

Young did not discuss at length the relation between Scripture and science, but he was clearly sensitive to the common objection raised against the scriptural geologists in light of the Galileo affair.

> An appeal to Scripture on geological questions, is regarded by many as altogether inappropriate; because, from the superior nature of its objects, we cannot expect it to be occupied with matters of science. And it is true that the Bible is not intended to teach us geology any more than astronomy: its statements relating to nature are not expressed in scientific language, but are set forth in the simplest form; being in accordance with the appearances of things, and the views most generally received among men. Yet we are sure, that the facts of science may be reconciled with the sacred page; and we may be permitted to doubt the truth of any theory, which makes that reconciliation impossible. The volume of creation, the volume of providence, and the volume of inspiration, have all one author; and whatever apparent discrepances [*sic*] there may be between them, there can be no real opposition. It is an interesting fact that the progress of science has, in more than one case, illustrated the truth of the sacred records.[47]

Young never explained in detail how the interpretation of the Bible and the interpretation of the physical world should be harmonized. Nor did he explain on what basis he could rely on the Bible for his understanding of earth history, while at the same time agreeing with his opponents that the Bible is not intended to teach geology. However, he clearly believed that with regard to the origin and history of the earth, the plain teaching of Genesis (as he saw it) should guide the interpretation of geological phenomena, not vice versa. And he certainly did attempt to explain many geological phenomena in light of his biblical framework of a recent creation and global Flood.

View of the Laws of Nature

Young rejected Lyell's uniformitarianism which maintained "that the strata have been formed in the same gradual way in which sediment is now being deposited" in the ocean and that all geological phenomena "may be accounted for by existing causes still in operation."[48] But he thereby was not constantly invoking miracles to explain what he observed. Although he clearly believed that the Flood was a unique event, he was also convinced that the rocks and fossils could be explained by causes similar to those observed in the present, which during the Flood had operated at abnormally and vastly magnified levels of intensity, frequency, and geographical extent as a result of special divine decree in judgment.[49]

45 Young, *Geological Survey*, p. 356.
46 Young, *Scriptural Geology*, p. iii; *Appendix* (1840), p. 19, 20, 27.
47 Young, *Scriptural Geology*, p. 39–40. After this he gave one example of the vindication of the Bible from archaeology.
48 Ibid., p. 21–22.
49 Ibid., p. 46.

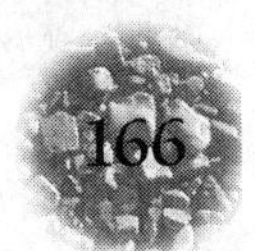

The tranquil flood view came under severe criticism precisely because, from Young's perspective, it must invoke numerous unnecessary miracles which were not justified by the biblical narrative. In defense of the global Flood view he said the following:

> An effusion of waters over the whole earth, so still as not to destroy the vegetation, is the kind of deluge fancied by some geologists; but such a deluge could not take place without the most extraordinary miracles — miracles uncalled for, and of which Moses gives not the slightest hint. . . . But there was no occasion [during the Flood] for such miracles: existing causes, directed and controlled by the great First Cause, were sufficient to produce the deluge, without any new creation, or any violation of the laws of nature.[50]

The chief natural causes God used were, he believed, spelled out in the Genesis narrative: the 40 days of rain and the breaking up of the "fountains of the deep," which included massive volcanic activity.[51]

The Argument of *Geological Survey* (1828)

I will focus on Young's later writings of 1838–40, because they represent his most seasoned reflections on geology and the Bible, and because they appeared after the recantations of Buckland and Sedgwick and at a time when the contemporary and modern critics of the scriptural geologists stated or implied that no competent geologists still argued that the Flood was global and deposited the secondary and tertiary formations. Nevertheless, a summary of the arguments in the theoretical part of his 1828 *Survey* will provide a valuable context, especially since they were ignored by the reviewers of his day. As noted earlier, Young divided this third part into two sections: "facts and inferences" and "hints and conjectures." The former he considered to be "certain," whereas the truth of the latter was "only probable."[52]

From his geological research of the Yorkshire coast he drew out 20 facts and inferences, which are as follows.[53]

1. All the strata (except whinstone dikes) were formed by aqueous deposition.
2. They were deposited horizontally or nearly so.
3. Some powerful force inclined and dislocated the strata.[54]
4. A denudation of the strata (seen in the topography of the present continents) has occurred by a force other than existing rivers.
5. Alluvial beds of gravel and sand were deposited after the sedimentary strata and as a result of the dislocation and denudation of the strata.
6. Valleys were formed by faulting and denudation, not by the rivers in them presently.[55]
7. In many places, subsidence has caused basins, which are not limited to the coal measures, contrary to the impression given by many geological writers at the time.
8. None of the strata are universal over the earth, like an onion skin, but rather are scale-like and many, if not all, of these strata thin out at the edges, many of which were obliterated by the denudation of the strata.[56]
9. As a result, we should not expect the same strata series everywhere in the world, as indeed

50 Ibid., p. 43–44.

51 Ibid., p. 44–45. Again in 1840 he stressed the unnecessary and unscriptural miracles involved in the tranquil flood theory: *Appendix* (1840), p. 12.

52 Young, *Geological Survey*, p. 311.

53 Ibid., p. 311–340.

54 He did not argue here that the force was volcanic. That was proposed later under his "hints and conjectures."

55 This is one of his longer points, occupying five pages, as he refuted the Huttonian theory adopted by Scrope and Lyell. One of his reasons for rejecting the river theory was the existence of dry valleys, where no river presently flowed, an idea that George Fairholme discussed at length a decade later as a result of his study of the plains of France.

56 Lyell described and illustrated this thinning out of the strata in his *Manual of Elementary Geology* (1855), p. 16, 98, 102.

we find examples of missing strata[57] and strata in the wrong order.[58]

10. Often one stratum makes an insensible or gradual transition into another stratum of a different mineralogical character, making it difficult to define the dividing line.

11. Seams or secretions sometimes are imbedded within (and therefore are subordinate to) another stratum.

12. Strata are in different states of induration (i.e., lower strata are often softer than upper strata)[59] and organic remains are in different states of preservation irrespective of the order of succession of the strata.

13. The strata were not formed gradually at the bottom of the ocean in the way that modern rivers and ocean currents deposit material.[60]

14. The varying plentitude of fossils in the strata is in no relation to the order of succession of the strata.

15. Some strata have marine fossils, some land fossils, but most contain a mixture of the two, which implies that when the strata were deposited land and sea life were blended together.[61]

16. Some fossils are well-preserved, while others are mutilated and compressed and none show evidence of having lived where they died.[62]

17. The use of fossils to identify the strata is very limited to local areas, since so many fossils are extensively diffused and intermixed through the whole geological record.[63]

18. Fossilized creatures with living analogues and those without (i.e., apparently extinct) are so intermixed in the strata as to make it impossible to label some as more ancient than others.[64]

19. From the above facts and inferences it is reasonable to conclude that all the strata had a nearly contemporaneous deposition.[65]

---

57 Today these are known as paraconformities. T. Sheppard has a tabular illustration of this from the work of William Smith. See his "William Smith, His Maps and Memoirs," *Proceedings of the Yorkshire Geological and Polytechnic Society*, N.S. vol. XIX (1914–22), p. 139–141.

58 Here he cited an example from Greenough's *A Critical Examination of the First Principles of Geology* (1819).

59 This he attributed to the fact that the cause of induration is primarily, if not exclusively, intrinsic to the nature of the stratified deposit, rather than simply being an effect of time.

60 Here, in rejecting the uniformitarian theory, which in 1828 was in the process of being recast by Scrope and Lyell, Young gave a rebuttal to an argument used by his former professor, John Playfair, in his defense of Hutton.

61 Here he argued against the theory of alternating sea beds and lake bottoms put forth by Cuvier and Brongniart to explain the Paris Basin. One reason he cited was that land and sea shells, by which the French geologists distinguished their lacustrine and marine environments, are often difficult to distinguish. In a footnote, he cited supporting evidence from James Sowerby's *Mineral Conchology* (1812–29) and F.S. Beudant's article, "Extract from a Memoir Read to the Institute on the 13th of May 1816 on the Possibility of Making the Molluscae of Fresh Water Live in Salt Water, and Vice Versa," *Philosophical Magazine*, vol. XLVIII, no. 22 (1816), p. 223–227.

62 Here he argued for the allochthonous (ie., transported) origin of upright trees and plant stems and of shell-fish preserved in the strata.

63 This statement is consistent with the table in William Smith's representation of the stratigraphic record. See William Smith, *Stratigraphical System of Organized Fossils* (1817), unpaginated chart facing page 137. Young named ostracites, ammonites, belemnites (all of which feature prominently in Smith's chart), and terebratulae as particular examples of shells that pervade almost all the strata.

Young repeated this point in his *Scriptural Geology* (p. 9), to which John Pye Smith vociferously replied that it was "an assertion full of extreme inaccuracies." See John Pye Smith, *Relation between Holy Scriptures and the Geological Sciences*, p. 388. However, the prominent conchologist Sowerby agreed with Young regarding ammonites and terebratulae. See James Sowerby, *The Genera of Recent and Fossil Shells* (1820–25), pages (unnumbered) on these creatures. Buckland also confirmed Young's statement. See William Buckland, *Bridgewater Treatise* (1836), I: p. 292, 312–313, 333.

64 Here he argued against the idea, then popularized by some leading geologists, that the lower one goes in the strata the more dissimilar creatures are from the present. No such gradation exists in the actual strata, he said, citing zoophytes in the chalk and oolite strata well above the lowest strata which contained oysters and other shells virtually identical to living species. See Young, *Geological Survey*, p. 334.

65 This is confirmed, he wrote, by the facts that 1) breaks (or faults) and denudations in a given location generally affect all the strata of that location, 2) the bending of the strata associated with the breaks indicate that at the time of such modifications the strata were still only partially consolidated, and 3) the insensible transitions and lack of evidence of erosion (i.e., conformity) between the strata belie any long stretches of time between deposition of strata.

20. The basaltic dyke (in Yorkshire) was produced by the same agent that elevated the continents.

For these 20 reasons, Young concluded that the old-earth "formation system [of multiple creations and revolutions before the creation of man] may please the imagination, and give scope to the fancy, but it will not stand the test of an appeal to facts."[66]

Having discussed the facts and inferences that he considered to be "certain," Young then proceeded to his "probable" hints and conjectures as to the time and the manner of the deposition of the strata. In defense of a literal interpretation of Genesis 1–11, he first dealt with the day-age theory for harmonizing Genesis with old-earth geological theory, which insisted that the strata had been deposited before the creation of man. He presented five reasons for rejecting this:

1. The order of events in Genesis 1 do not coincide with the order of fossil remains in the strata.
2. A creation over long ages detracts from the honor of God.
3. The goodness of creation (as stated in Genesis 1:31) militates against the notion of long ages of death and destruction before man.
4. There is strong evidence that the days were literal.[67]
5. Having ages of catastrophes resulting in the misery and destruction of creatures before man's fall in sin and even before his creation is incongruous.[68]

After giving his reasons for rejecting the notion of a tranquil Noachian flood (which we will consider later), Young concluded his theoretical discussions by responding to nine geological objections to his theory of a recent creation and a global catastrophic Noachian flood.[69] These were presented in a question and answer format and covered such issues as the extent to which the antediluvian strata were demolished by the Flood, how the Flood could dissolve so much of the earth's crust, how the pre-Flood world could have supplied all the animal and vegetable matter that we find in the strata, how the violent Flood could produce such a regular series of strata and, in many cases, homogeneous strata, how it could transport the quantity of matter necessary to produce the strata, what the cause of the breakup of the crust was, how plant life could survive the Flood and be so quickly restored after the Flood, and why more quadrupeds and humans were not found in the fossil record. In each case he endeavored to answer the objection based on known facts of natural science.

The Argument of *Scriptural Geology* (1838)

We now turn our attention to the arguments in Young's *Scriptural Geology* and subsequent *Appendix*. The former (composed of two parts) was initially communicated to the geological section of the BAAS at their annual meeting in Newcastle in 1838. Only the first half of it was admitted to the meeting, and then only read in abstract, which was followed by a reply from Sedgwick. Before Young presented it to the public, it was enlarged.[70]

Like the original draft submitted to the BAAS, the published edition also was divided into two parts. In the first part he sought to prove from the geological evidence that the strata were laid down not over long ages but primarily in one period, the Flood. He then dealt with objections to this conclusion. In the second part he argued against the gap theory, and local and tranquil flood theories, by going into great detail about the effects of the Flood in relation to the geological phenomena. The 1840 *Appendix*, serving as a rebuttal to John

66 Young, *Geological Survey*, p. 338.
67 His evidences were the use of morning and evening in Genesis 1, the parallel use of "day" in the sabbath commandment of Exodus 20:11, and the impossibility of having an ages-long seventh day within the total days of Adam's life.
68 Young, *Geological Survey*, p. 341–342.
69 Ibid., p. 346–355.
70 Young, *Scriptural Geology*, p. iii. The BAAS Report for 1838 does not refer to Sedgwick's reply. It was briefly remarked on in a footnote in James Smith, "On the last changes in the relative levels of the land and sea in the British Islands," *Memoirs of the Wernerian Natural History Society*, vol. VIII (1838), p. 63.

Reverend John Pye Smith (1774–1851), whose local flood and local creation view was opposed by Young.

Pye Smith's criticisms and theories, added to his arguments against a local or tranquil flood. It also responded to Smith's notion of a local creation.

To refute the old-earth theory, Young first briefly (in three pages) dealt with two common arguments. First, the regularity of the stratified deposits, the thinness of some of those strata, and the ripple marks on the upper boundary of some strata were interpreted by old-earth geologists as evidence of slow deposition over many years. But Young contended that this was not a justified inference because all these features can be observed as they form on present-day ocean beaches in a matter of days. Second, the claimed fact of different fossils occurring in different layers was interpreted by old-earth geologists to imply progressive creations over a long period, with different creatures "reigning" in each "age." But Young countered that the complexity of creatures does not gradually increase as one proceeds up through the strata and, in fact, many fossils in the lowest strata are more analogous to living forms than some fossils in higher strata.

But the primary focus of Young's rebuttal (p. 10–23) was on the idea that the fossils buried in the strata were situated in the place where the plants and animals had lived, died, and were later buried. He instead argued that the evidence pointed to the conclusion that these creatures had been transported by flood waters and deposited with the sediments of the strata.

He rejected the *in situ* theory for plants because, first, no existing peat bog was thick enough to produce the vast coal seams, which were also interspersed with ocean-deposited sediments. He cited evidence and arguments from Lyell and Phillips to support his contention that upright fossil trees and stems, so often associated with the coal, had been transported to their positions before being buried. In response to the claim that such trees often showed evidence of the work of boring insects on the surface, which was interpreted to have taken place while the tree grew, Young said that it was marine creatures that did this work as the tree floated and he referred to a log with such markings that had been retrieved recently from the sea and was in the Whitby Museum.[71]

The *in situ* theory to explain fossil animals was also problematic in Young's view. The beds loaded with shells generally lie conformably above or below the coal formations, which were clearly transported deposits. Also, there is often the mixture of marine and terrestrial creatures in a single stratum. Further, a four to five inch thick seam (in the Lias formation) extends for many miles on the coast and is primarily composed of oyster shells. The shells give every indication of having been transported and the bed is far more extensive than any modern oyster bed. Similarly, he argued, the upper oolite strata abounding in corals and shells are unlike the arrangement of modern coral reefs and must have been transported.[72] He argued that the proven proliferation of animalcules, insects,

71 Young, *Scriptural Geology*, p. 10–14.

72 He cited John Phillips, *Treatise on Geology* (1837), I: p. 218, in support of the transport theory of the oolite.

and sea-life in the present world[73] would have been even greater in the generally tropical climate of the pre-Flood world, which could provide all the material necessary to form the chalk by the depositing currents of the Flood. When we come to the tertiary, Young said, these deposits are too limited in extent and thickness to be assigned whole ages of time. Finally, the highly preserved fossils are not proof of the *in situ* theory, for ocean currents are known to carry glass bottles with messages inside all the way across the Atlantic without causing any damage.[74] Thus, Young concluded, the great epochs of geological history are only fanciful products of the imagination.[75]

As proof that the sedimentary rock record is largely the result of one depositional event, the Noachian flood, Young gave five reasons.[76] First is the general conformity; each stratum insensibly or gradually transitions into the one above with no erosional inequalities at the boundary to suggest long ages before the next was deposited. Second, though there are also some unconformities, no doubt caused by volcanic force from below (which is a sudden, not a gradual, event in any case), these show evidence of rapid deposition, not slow deposition over thousands of years. This is because the breaks or faults affect the whole rock mass of many strata[77] and also in cases where the breaks are small, the strata (from the lower to the upper) are bent, indicating that all the strata were only partially consolidated at the time of movement. Third, the denudation of the strata, again affecting many strata in a location to produce the valleys and alluvial detritus, must have occurred also when the strata were only semi-consolidated. Furthermore, there is no evidence of the denudation of the surface of past "worlds" at different levels in the stratigraphic record. Fourth, highly preserved and flattened fossils (e.g., of fish and reptiles) point to rapid deposition of the strata with accumulating pressure on the lower, still soft, layers. Many such fossils showed evidence of crushed bones and contorted bodies, suggesting that they were violently entombed alive.[78] Finally, the evidence of tropical climate throughout the geological record was strong evidence to Young that it had all been laid down in one short period.

In the remaining pages of Part I,[79] Young dealt with two geological objections and one theological objection to his view. The evidence for a global tropical climate in the past[80] helps to explain the existence of tropical plants and animals in the strata as well as the prodigious quantity of fossils generally. Secondly, to the fact that many fossils are peculiar to particular strata and different from living forms, Young responded that the rich variety of creatures in the present world would have been greatly augmented in the antediluvian world and, as today, would not have been equally distributed on the earth.[81] In addition, the currents of the Deluge would have been in many different directions carrying different creatures from different locations.[82] Theologically, it was objected that a 6,000-year old creation limits the display of God's glory; also, there was no clear reason why God waited so long to create the world. But Young countered that as mere humans we are in no position to judge God's choice of

73 He referred to the research done by Professor M. Ehrenberg. For a brief summary of some of his work over many years, see M. Ehrenberg, "Observations on the Disseminations of Minute Organic Bodies," *Edinburgh New Philosophical Journal*, vol. XXXVI, no. 71 (1844), p. 201–202.

74 Lyell also argued that in spite of the perfect state of preservation of shells in the strata, the intermingling of freshwater and marine shells indicated transport from a distance by agitated water currents. See Charles Lyell, *Principles of Geology* (1830–33), III: p. 245.

75 Young, *Scriptural Geology*, p. 14–21.

76 Ibid., p. 23–30.

77 He gave two extensive examples. One of them, taken from Phillips, *Treatise on Geology*, I: p. 182, was a fault 1,000–2,000 feet deep and running for 110 miles.

78 He cited many examples, some of which were in the Whitby Museum.

79 Young, *Scriptural Geology*, p. 31–38.

80 He relied on Lyell's argument for a different geographical arrangement of the land masses in the past, which would have produced such a universal climate. See Lyell, *Principles of Geology*, I: p. 125–143.

81 He gave many examples of this and also cited the research of Lyell and Darwin.

82 Again, he cited Phillips in support of this idea.

when He created the world. As far as God's glory is concerned, Young felt that creation in six days demonstrates more of God's power and skill than creation in six years or six ages of untold years. Furthermore, the amount of glory ascribed to God is not determined by the length of time used to create something, but rather by the evident wisdom of its design and adaptation to the purposes for which it was created.

In Part II, Young turned his attention to the various attempts to harmonize the creation account with old-earth theories. He spent no time on the day-age theory because it "seems now to be abandoned as utterly untenable."[83]

Rather, he presented four reasons for rejecting the gap theory. First, even if one conceded that there is life on other planets[84] and many creations before Genesis 1:3, out of the wreck of which this present world was created (as Gen. 1:2 might suggest), such a scenario was not the pre-adamite theory of the leading geologists. That theory did not end with a wrecked chaos before the present state of the world, but with a good world of marvelous creatures, continents, oceans, rivers, etc.[85] Second, there was a theological problem. All the thousands or millions of years of pre-adamite worlds supposedly passed without any rational beings on earth (i.e., man) to praise God for His works. How could there be so many ages with no provision for such an important task? Third, another theological objection, which Young had raised in 1828 against the day-age theory, was the fact that:

> According to scripture, it was man's disobedience that brought death into the world, with all our woe; but, according to this geological system, death had reigned and triumphed on the globe, in the destruction of numerous races of creatures, thousands of years before man existed.[86]

The final and, to Young, the strongest reason for rejecting the gap theory was that the theory "leaves no room for the deluge, that great catastrophe so distinctly recorded in sacred history."[87] In other words, Young felt that by either tranquilizing or localizing the Flood, the gap theory trivialized (and effectively denied) the biblical description of the Flood.

Since a discussion of the Flood occupied most of this second part of his book, we will look at it in more depth shortly. Before that I will briefly summarize how Young responded, in his 1840 *Appendix*, to John Pye Smith's idea of a local creation (i.e., Gen. 1 only describes the creation of a portion of central Asia). Young agreed with Smith that God used figurative language to describe himself, that in "matters of science" He accommodated the descriptions to the knowledge of the Jews and early Christians, and that universal terms in the Bible were also used in a limited sense. But these facts could not be used to reject a universal creation for several reasons. The ancient Israelites were not nearly as ignorant as Smith portrayed them, argued Young. And at the time Moses wrote Genesis, they knew of larger portions of the globe

83 Certainly by 1838 the day-age theory would not have been the dominant view of the leading Christian geologists. Even Christian periodicals which accepted the antiquity of the earth, such as the *Christian Observer* and *Christian Remembrancer*, no longer favored it as a solution to the apparent conflict between Genesis and geological theories.

84 This was an increasingly popular speculation at the time and one that Young did not think was necessarily contrary to Scripture. But "plurality of worlds" had two meanings at this time: the successive creations dominating different "ages" during earth history or the existence of life on other planets. For the former meaning of the phrase, see Nicolaas A. Rupke, *The Great Chain of History* (1983), p. 130, William Buckland, *Vindiciae Geologicae* (1820), p. 26–27, and William Conybeare and William Phillips, *Outlines of the Geology of England and Wales* (1822), p. lxi. On the other hand, Rupke, ibid., p. 214, and John Dillenberger, *Protestant Thought and Natural Science* (1960), p. 133–134, briefly discuss the prevalence of the latter meaning in the 1840s and 1850s as well as earlier in the 17th century.

85 A clear summary of this pre-adamite theory was provided by Mantell just a few months after Young published this criticism. Mantell wrote, "Thus geology reveals to us the sublime truth — *that for innumerable ages our globe was the abode of myriads of living forms of happiness, enjoying all the blessings of existence, and which at the same time were accumulating materials to render the earth, in after ages, a fit, temporary abode, for intellectual and immortal beings!*" See Gideon Mantell, *The Wonders of Geology* (1839), II: p. 504.

86 Young, *Scriptural Geology*, p. 41–42; Young, *Geological Survey*, p. 342.

87 Young, *Scriptural Geology*, p. 42.

than just the area outlined by Smith, so that there was no need to use universal terms to describe a local creation, if it indeed had been only local. Furthermore, Genesis 1–11 professes to describe the early history of the whole world, not just central Asia, which became the focus after the Flood.[88]

Defense of a Global Flood

By combining the arguments of his 1838 and 1840 books, we get a total picture of why he rejected the local flood and tranquil flood views and instead contended that the secondary and tertiary formations were attributable to the Flood. First, let us consider the local flood theory.

Young presented his reasons for believing that the antediluvian human population was at least as great and as widely dispersed over the earth's surface as in the 19th century, so that a local flood would be inadequate to destroy that ungodly race of men.[89] Then there was the plain and repeated use of universal terms to describe the Flood (such as "all," "every," and "under heaven"). Also, the local flood would involve a number of miracles, which, as noted earlier, Young deemed unnecessary and unjustified. Such miracles would have been: 1) while the sea level was raised over the mountains locally in Mesopotamia, it would have had to be kept constant at the normal level generally on the earth; 2) the flux of the waters that flooded the local area would have had to be restrained from producing a natural reflux; 3) this action of the water would have needed to be maintained for 150 days, with no water slipping out through the many mountain passes on the edge of this local area; and 4) the diurnal and annual motion of the earth could not have been affected by this watery bulge. Another problem was the lack of any surviving landmarks to identify this local area of creation and flood which Pye Smith envisaged. Furthermore, Young asked, why was the ark needed at all, if Noah, his family, and the animals could easily migrate out of the area? The building of the ark and a year's confinement in it were unnecessary hardships on them. Finally, Young argued, 2 Peter 3 draws a tight parallel between the Flood and the coming universal conflagration.[90]

The notion of a tranquil flood was equally problematic to Young. The purpose of the Flood was to destroy the earth, not just man, according to Genesis 6:13. The year-long duration of the Flood intimates that much more than the drowning of earth's inhabitants was its object. Young thought it reasonable to assume, from the description in Genesis, that "many years might revolve before the ocean subsided to its present level." Also, like the local flood theory, a tranquil flood would necessitate miracles "uncalled for, and of which Moses gives not the slightest hint," such as the creation and annihilation of the flood waters and the suspension of the laws of water erosion by flooding rivers and tempestuous seas (which would naturally accompany 40 days of rain and the volcanic activity that produced the rupturing of the fountains of the deep). For these reasons, the notion of a tranquil flood was quite unbelievable to Young.[91]

In arguing that God directed and controlled existing causes to accomplish the judgment of the Flood, Young challenged his geological opponents by saying:

> Is it, then, unreasonable or unphilosophical to suppose that when the Almighty resolved to destroy an ungodly world, he might employ the energies of this great expansive force [volcanic activity] to heave up the bottom of the sea, and to shake, dissolve, and depress the land? We cannot easily conceive how the fountains of the great deep could be broken up, in any other way, so as to co-operate with the rains in overflowing the world. In this way, the object could be accomplished by the supreme Ruler, without forming any new matter; and as, at the creation, one day only was occupied in raising up

88 Young, *Appendix*, p. 4–7.
89 Young, *Scriptural Geology*, p. 42; Young, *Appendix*, p. 8–12.
90 Young, *Scriptural Geology*, p. 42–43; Young, *Appendix*, p. 12–14, 18.
91 Young, *Scriptural Geology*, p. 43–46.

the dry land from the sea, even so at the Deluge, a single day might have sufficed for submerging the dry land beneath the waters. But, instead of being the work of a day, this mighty revolution was in progress during several weeks; the earth sinking, and the sea rising, in a gradual and comparatively tranquil manner; so that the safety of the ark and its inmates was not endangered, and time was allowed for effecting, in a more orderly way, the changes now made in the crust of the earth. There was not one great terrific convulsion to complete the work at once; but a series of smaller convulsions, carrying it forward by successive stages. Now, may we not trace, in the different formations of the stratified rocks, a correspondence with these successive convulsions; and on this principle, explain the diversified phenomena of the present strata? Let us inquire, then, into the effects, which volcanic agency thus operating, would naturally produce.[92]

Over the course of the next 30 pages, Young endeavored to demonstrate this by describing in some detail his conception of the year-long progression of the Flood's work in relation to the present state of the stratigraphic record and by answering the most common objections to this view, of which he was aware.[93]

Among other things in his description of the progress of the Flood, he explained how the earth could have been so quickly prepared for human and animal life after the Deluge. The consolidation of the strata, providing an adequate base for the new post-diluvian soils, was much faster than was supposed by the old-earth geologists since the chief agent of induration was not time but rather several factors: chemical action, the pressure of the rapidly accumulating strata, and the heat and electricity associated with the volcanic activity. Though much of the pre-Flood vegetation would have been buried in the strata to form coal seams, Young reasoned, a considerable portion of seeds, roots, and even whole plants would still be floating on the receding waters and take root in the rich moist alluvial soils left by the Flood. In the weeks that Noah waited for the earth to sufficiently dry, this would have produced a lush mantle of vegetation for the earth, in which the dove found a fresh olive leaf. Likewise, some still-floating carrion would have provided food for the raven Noah had sent out earlier.[94]

Young contended that the alternating fresh water and marine formations were better explained by the complex vicissitudes of the Flood than by a long series of multiple catastrophes gradually raising and then lowering the land. The different kinds of rocks were formed by the sorting power of water, igneous intrusions, and post-depositional chemical modification.[95] Faulting and aqueous denudation associated with the recession of the floodwaters resulted in cliffs, caverns, and valleys, the detritus from which the alluvial sands, gravels, and erratic boulders were formed.[96]

Another issue Young addressed, as he had in 1828, was why fossil bones of man and quadrupeds were so rarely found and then only in the top strata and alluvium. He replied that quadrupeds would naturally escape the Flood longer, because of mobility. But he also cautioned against concluding the non-existence of creatures on the basis of the lack of fossil evidence, because quadruped footprints in lower strata proved that they had existed at the time those strata were being deposited, even though their bones had not been found in them. Also, bird and monkey prints occasionally had been found, but bones of both were a much rarer discovery.[97]

As far as human remains are concerned, the main reason we do not find many in the rock

92 Ibid., p. 46–47.

93 He attributed the *primary* and *transition* stratified rocks to the antediluvian period: ibid., p. 47. His ideas on this point were similar to those expressed by Thomas Gisborne, *Considerations on Geology* (1837), p. 28–30. See my article on Gisborne at <www.answersingenesis.org>.

94 Young, *Scriptural Geology*, p. 52, 56–57, 59, 65.

95 Ibid., p. 53–55.

96 Ibid., p. 60–61. Here he particularly rejected Lyell's iceberg theory for explaining the erratic boulders.

97 Ibid., p. 62–65. The infrequency of finding monkey bones in the strata was also particularly noted by Robert Bakewell in his *Introduction to Geology* (1833, fourth edition), p. 37.

strata is that, for the most part, the pre-Flood land and sea changed places during the Deluge so that most human remains would be buried under the ocean bottom beyond the reach of geologists. Still Young contended that some relics had been found in ancient deposits, such as the caves in Gailenreuth (Germany), in Bixe, Pondres, and Souvignargues (France), and in Liege (Belgium).[98]

He asserted that human remains had not only been found in caves, but also in solid rock, such as the limestone on the island of Guadaloupe. This too had been firmly rejected by the old-earth geologists,[99] so Young remarked:

> It is to be regretted that further researches have not been made into that interesting deposit; especially as most geologists roundly assert, that the stone is a mere modern concretion. This notion, now so generally adopted, is quite at variance with the plain facts of the case as detailed by Mr. Konig, in the *Philosophical Transactions* for 1814; and the valuable specimen in the British Museum gives it no countenance whatever. The stone, which I carefully examined, greatly resembles some varieties of oolite limestone; like which, it contains fragments of shells and of corals; the latter, as in the oolite, sometimes retaining their original red color. The bones are entirely fossilized and have no appearance of recent bones accidentally incrusted with stalactite or travertine. Nothing but a fixed determination to set up theory against fact can resist the evidence arising from this discovery. The strange idea, that these imbedded human remains are the result of a battle and massacre, of so late a date as 1710, may be believed, when once another petrified field of battle can be pointed out; but it is far more likely, that we shall first discover other fossil specimens of the human race in secondary rocks, affording such irresistible evidence, as will at once annihilate the whole system of pre-adamite creations.[100]

The last six pages of *Scriptural Geology* and the bulk of the *Appendix* were devoted to answering ten objections to the Flood being the cause of most of the stratigraphic record.

1) It was asserted by Young's opponents that the fact of extinct creatures was inconsistent with Noah's mandate to save two of every living thing. Young replied that in the Bible "all" does not always mean all, but often only denotes very many so that what Genesis means is that Noah was to take either all the animals within his reach in that part of the world where he lived, or all the animals which God thought necessary to replenish the earth.[101]

2) Closely related to this was the objection that the ark was far too small for the purpose of carrying the number of creatures envisaged by the global flood view. Young insisted that critics calculated on far too many species, since, for example, most insects and reptiles (or their eggs) could survive outside the ark on floating vegetation.[102]

3) The thickness of the strata are too great to be produced by the Noachian flood, objected the critics. Again, Young charged them with gross exaggeration as a result of adding together the measurements of the *extreme* thickness, rather than the *mean* thickness, of each strata. This was erroneous, because the strata were not of uniform thickness throughout, but rather lens-shaped

---

98 Young, *Scriptural Geology*, p. 69–71. Murray and Fairholme had referred to these, also.

99 Mantell, just a few months later, supplied a drawing of the area where the bones were discovered along the coast, attributing the remains to the massacre of a tribe about 120 years earlier. He said, "This being the only known undoubted instance of the occurrence of human bones in solid limestone, has excited great attention; and the fact, simple and self-evident as is its history, has been made the foundation of many vague and absurd hypotheses." See Mantell, *The Wonders of Geology*, I: p. 71–75. No reference was made to Young's remarks.

100 Young, *Scriptural Geology*, p. 70–71.

101 Ibid., p. 72. Young did not explain why he could take "all" here in a limited sense, but not interpret in a similarly limited sense the universal terms describing the extent of the Flood. But in his response to John Pye Smith in the 1840 *Appendix* (p. 6–11) he did explain why the Flood must be seen as global (as discussed earlier).

102 Young, *Appendix*, p. 16.

(thick in the middle and tapering at the edges),[103] and were not of universal extent over the face of the globe. Therefore, instead of the geological column being ten miles deep, as some old-earth geologists supposed, Young thought two miles was closer to reality and a credible production of the Noachian flood.[104]

4) Critics asserted that a flood as violent as the scriptural geologists supposed could not produce such distinct, homogeneous strata as we find. Young had briefly responded to this in 1828 by referring to the sorting action of oceanic tides observed on modern beaches.[105] In 1838 he argued that, in reality, these characteristics of the strata militate far more against the theories of his critics. He thought it inconceivable that there could have been a purely oolitiferous ocean depositing its homogeneous stratum for thousands of years followed by a purely cretaceous ocean depositing the evidence of its reign for another epoch of thousands of years, and so on. On the other hand:

> We shall shew a disposition to be "willingly ignorant,"[106] if we shut our eyes against evidences everywhere visible, indicating that the earth has experienced convulsions inconceivably greater than any now felt, and that the stratified rocks have been deposited at a rate incomparably more rapid than the present depositions of mud in the ocean. Professor Buckland himself, though he attempts to neutralize the effect of his own testimony, shews in his [Bridgewater] Treatise ([Vol. 1] p. 307), by indubitable tokens, that the lias at Lyme Regis must have been deposited with a rapidity a thousand times greater than the sediment now accumulating in the sea; for the fossil cuttle-fish found there, must have been killed and imbedded in the strata almost in a moment of time, being prevented from discharging the contents of their ink-bags. "I might register the proofs of instantaneous death, detected in these ink-bags, for they contain the fluid which the living sepia emits in the moment of alarm; and might detail further evidence of their immediate burial, in the retention of the forms of these distended membranes; since they would speedily have decayed, and have spilt their ink, had they been exposed by a few hours to decomposition in the water. The animals must therefore have died *suddenly*, and been *quickly* buried in the sediment that formed the strata, in which their petrified ink and ink-bags are thus preserved." It is strange, that the learned author of these valuable remarks, should ever advocate the system of gradual deposition, during countless ages. The difficulties attending that system are vastly greater, than any that can be started [*sic*] against the diluvian theory.[107]

Young's final criticism against the old-earth interpretation of the homogeneous strata was its ambiguity; his opponents never explained "in what way these destructions can have taken place, or in what form the new creations followed them." It appeared to Young from their expressions that they might be resurrecting the old notions of the frequent spontaneous generation and gradual evolution of life and that the world is eternal.[108]

The remaining objections against the Flood to which Young responded were specifically raised by Smith. 5) Smith supposed that a global flood would necessitate a miraculously created supply

103 Lyell made similar remarks about this horizontal thinning of the strata in his *Manual of Elementary Geology*, p. 16, 98, 102.

104 Young, *Scriptural Geology*, p. 72–73. The lens-shaped nature of the strata had been discussed in more detail on pages 50–51.

105 Young, *Geological Survey*, p. 48–49.

106 A reference to 2 Peter 3:5; KJV.

107 Young, *Scriptural Geology*, p. 74–75.

108 Ibid., p. 76–77; *Appendix*, p. 29–30. Young used the word "generated." Although the terms "spontaneous generation" and "evolution" are mine, I think any reader would agree that they accurately reflect Young's discussion on this point.

of water five miles deep to encircle the globe and cover all the high mountains. Young countered that no such miracle was required since the present oceans had enough water; all that was needed was for the ocean beds to rise by volcanic force and the land would correspondingly sink. Furthermore, it was not essential, or even legitimate, to assume that the pre-Flood mountains were as high as at present.[109]

6) To the question of post-diluvian animal distribution, Young responded that the antediluvian universal tropical climate only gradually changed to the present varied climatic conditions. This process of climatic change would have allowed time for the migrations to take place.

7) To another of Smith's objections, Young responded that fresh and saltwater fish and their spawn could survive in the waters of the Flood, because there would not have been a completely homogeneous mixture of these two kinds of water.[110]

8) Regarding the refurbishment of the earth at the end of the Flood to make a suitable habitation for Noah's family and the animals, Young wrote:

> Hence, Dr. Smith's remarks (p. 162–163) about the perils of descending Mount Ararat, on the wet and slippery faces of naked rocks, and the necessity of a miracle, to save Noah and his family and cattle from breaking their necks in attempting to get down, are rather puerile.[111]

This was because the volcanic activity during the Flood would have sustained the tropical climate for some time after the Flood, thereby aiding the drying and solidification of the surface sediments and the rapid growth of lush vegetation during the several months of receding waters between the time of the landing of the ark and disembarkation from it.

9) The dating of extinct volcanoes in southern France and of some trees (by the tree-ring method) to be much older than the supposed date of the Flood led Smith to reject its universality. But Young rebutted that the ages of trees and lavas were equally difficult to determine.[112] He also cited examples, taken from Murray's *Portrait of Geology*, of the rapid formation of volcanic cones. Based on his own observations, he rejected the notion that existing rivers cut the valleys through the lava; rather they only slightly modified valleys formed by faults and denudation of the Flood waters.

10) Finally, adding to the answer he had already given in 1838, Young explained how the Flood could have produced the thinly laminated layers in the strata. He objected that Smith had no proof for his assertion that a 1/25-inch thin layer represented one year's deposition. On the contrary, flatly crushed and highly preserved fish, which naturally decay in hours, were frequently found fossilized in such laminated strata, which was a clear proof of very rapid deposition and lamination.[113]

Young summed up his defense of the Flood as the chief cause of the geological record by saying that all the current old-earth views miserably failed to explain the phenomena. He said:

> It is acknowledged, in a quotation from Dr. Macculloch,[114] "that the accumulation of materials at the bottom of the ocean, is a work *infinitely slow*." Can

---

109 Young, *Appendix*, p. 14–15.

110 In other words, some parts of the universal Flood would have been saltier than others and would have only gradually changed from one kind to the other.

111 Young, *Appendix*, p. 17.

112 Ibid., p. 18–21. In rejecting tree-ring dating he cited *Physiology of Plants* (1833), the work by his fellow scriptural geologist, John Murray. The difficulty of dating lavas in the early 19th century, has been noted by Martin Rudwick, "Poulett Scrope on the Volcanoes of Auvergne: Lyellian Time and Political Economy," *British Journal of the History of Science.* vol VII, no. 27 (1974), p. 216. In a footnote, Rudwick discussed the error of Scrope (a leading expert on volcanoes in the 1830s) in dating the volcanoes of southern France as being much older than Daubeny (Scrope's contemporary) and modern geologists have dated them.

113 Young, *Appendix*, p. 21–25; Young, *Scriptural Geology*, p. 7–8. He cited examples of such fossils found in several locations of Europe and Britain.

114 John Macculloch, *A System of Geology* (1831), II: p. 397.

this infinitely slow deposition account for the phenomena presented by our present rocks? The materials washed down by the rivers, or abraded from the coasts by the sea itself, are deposited, partly along the shores of the ocean, and partly in hollows in its bed. In this manner, banks of mud, sand, and gravel are formed in various spots; and a few organic substances, chiefly shells, may be found mixed up with such materials. But what ground have we to believe that these banks are future rocks in embryo? Is there any portion of them that can be called an incipient bed of red sandstone, or of magnesian limestone or of oolite or of lias or of chalk? At the mouth of one or two great rivers are found masses of drifted trees, covered with mud, illustrating in some degree, the origin of coal beds; but where do we find any carboniferous strata now forming; any incipient beds of sandstone, shale, ironstone, and coal? It is plain that the existing rocks, composed in so many instances of homogeneous materials, have been deposited under very different circumstances, and with far more rapidity, than any of those accumulations of sand, gravel, or mud now going on.[115]

Furthermore the notion of a long series of elevations and submersions of the crust lacked any real supporting evidence. He continued:

"In the majority of cases," adds Dr. Smith, "it is shown by physical evidences of the most decisive kind, that each of those successive conditions was of extremely long duration; a duration which it would be presumptuous to put into any estimate of years or centuries, etc." But where are these decisive evidences — where is there any evidence at all that such successive conditions, such seesaw motions, such dippings and redippings of the earth's crust, have ever taken place? The *evidences* exist only in the wild imaginations of some modern geologists. It is true that in countries where earthquakes and volcanoes prevail, coasts have been elevated, or have subsided; and in a few instances, the same spots that have sunk at one time, may have risen at another: but can the occurrence of one or two isolated facts of this kind authorize us to set up a system of alternate elevation and subsidence as a general law of nature, prevailing throughout the globe during countless ages? Dr. S. objects to my ascribing the phenomena of unconformable strata "to the elevating force of volcanic agency" (p. 390); but surely it is more rational to suppose, that in such cases, volcanic agency has thrown one set of strata out of their natural position before the next set began to be deposited over them, than to attempt an explanation of such phenomena on the principle of alternate elevation and subsidence.[116]

Conclusion

The contemporary descriptions of Young's character as a non-conformist pastor in a small town, the nature of his geological and non-geological writings and the peer reviews of his scientific work and writings indicate that he was a very competent geologist who was motivated to write on the subject of geology out of a sincere passion for truth, both scientific and biblical.

He sought to explain the Flood and the geological record by natural processes analogous to those operating in the present, though greatly magnified during the Noachian flood. In this regard he argued in a manner very similar to how all the old-earth catastrophists contested the uniformitarian interpretations of the geological data. Cleevely stated that Young "questioned many of the facts concerning fossils, sedimentation and geological time."[117] But the evidence here presented shows that it is more accurate to say that

115 Young, *Appendix*, p. 23.
116 Ibid., p. 24–25.
117 R.J. Cleevely, *World Palaeontological Collections* (1983), p. 320.

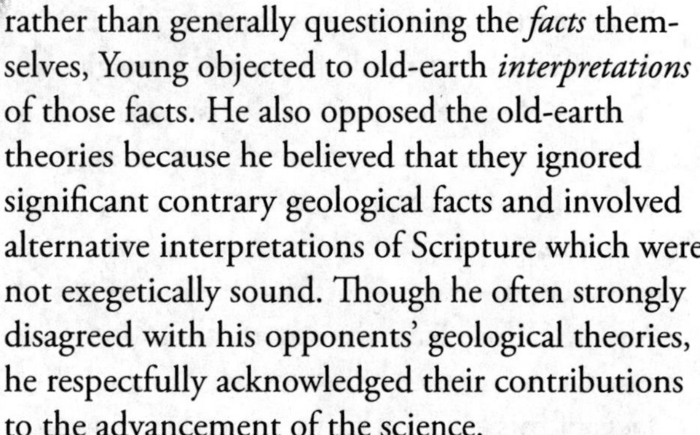

rather than generally questioning the *facts* themselves, Young objected to old-earth *interpretations* of those facts. He also opposed the old-earth theories because he believed that they ignored significant contrary geological facts and involved alternative interpretations of Scripture which were not exegetically sound. Though he often strongly disagreed with his opponents' geological theories, he respectfully acknowledged their contributions to the advancement of the science.

Using both geological and scriptural arguments, he attempted to provide a brief answer to every difficulty and objection to the biblical view of earth history of which he was aware. He believed that new discoveries would throw much additional light on the subject. But he hoped that his research and writings would assist future geologists to arrive at a more accurate knowledge of the structure and history of the globe.

WILLIAM RHIND (1797–1874)

Like John Murray, William Rhind[1] is virtually unknown in historical discussions of the scriptural geologists. But he is important to consider because of his geological qualifications to debate the issues of his day.

He was born on November 30, 1797, in Inverlochty, in the parish of Elgin, Scotland.[2] He was one of the many children (having at least three brothers) of Margaret and William Rhind, who was a farmer.[3] By then his family's ancestors had been resident in the county of Moray, Scotland, for many centuries. Rhind received his early education first at the parish school of Duffus and later at the Elgin Academy.

In 1812 he commenced his university studies at Marischal College, Aberdeen. After two years there[4] he took up an apprenticeship with a well-known Elgin physician, Dr. James Stephens. He continued his medical training in Edinburgh, becoming a licentiate of the Royal College of Surgeons of Edinburgh in September 1818.[5] Upon completion of his medical studies, he moved to London to gain further experience and instruction, and hopefully a comfortable living.

He stayed in London only a couple of years, having found it difficult to earn the kind of living he desired. Upon his return to Elgin he began a medical practice in a shop where he also sold medicines. Although he became quite successful in these endeavors, his mind was really bent in the direction of literature and scientific research. He became a leading member of the Elgin Literary Association, and in 1822 helped to publish a periodical called *Ephemera*, which only ran for one year.

He soon found that Elgin was not a suitable location for his literary and scientific studies and so moved in the mid-1820s to Edinburgh, where he spent nearly 40 years of his life writing and

1 Pronounced like the "rind" of a fruit.

2 Unless otherwise noted, this biographical sketch is based on Robert Douglas, *Sons of Moray* (1930).

3 Mormon *International Genealogical Index* for Elgin, Morayshire.

4 Peter John Anderson, *Fasti Academiae Mariscballanae Aberdonensis* (1898), p. 414.

5 Personal correspondence (December 21, 1994) from the archivist of the RCSE, Miss A.M. Stevenson.

lecturing on various subjects of natural science, primarily botany, zoology, and geology. He did not completely give up medicine, however. In 1832, he wrote the section on diseases of India in a multi-author work about that land,[6] and in 1841 he was still doing surgery and publishing articles about it.[7] Neither did he ever lose his love for Moray. From Edinburgh he traveled back to Elgin on several occasions to give lectures on natural history in the museum there. He also wrote a historical sketch of Moray in 1839.

In April 1854, he became a lecturer in botany in the medical faculty at Marischal College in Aberdeen.[8] How long he remained in this position is not known, but he was no longer on the staff list in 1860 when Marischal and King's colleges united to become Aberdeen University.[9] He evidently returned to Edinburgh for a short while, but in 1866 his declining health inclined him to move in with the family of his older brother Alexander, a retired corn merchant, who lived in Woodhaven, near Newport, Fife. Little is known of his activities in these later years of his life,[10] though he did revise some of his previous writings on botany.[11] At the age of 76, he died peacefully of natural physical exhaustion on March 15, 1874, in Woodhaven.[12]

Rhind, like George Young, suffered from a physical disability all his life; he was somewhat lame in both legs, a fact which makes his geological field research more remarkable. His church affiliation remains unknown, though he was likely a member of the Church of Scotland. In any case, his writings reflect a strong commitment to the Scriptures. And according to one biographer, "he was universally loved for his character and bearing, and a most amiable man. He was unassuming and retiring in his manner, but a most agreeable and interesting member of society."[13]

Scientific and Geological Competence

In addition to his early membership in the Royal College of Surgeons of Edinburgh, by 1830 he also had become a member of the Royal Medical Society and Royal Physical Society of Edinburgh,[14] and some time before 1858 he became an honorary member of the Natural History Society of Manchester.[15] In 1835 he was an annual member of the BAAS.[16]

He was a voluminous writer on many subjects. His non-scientific works included the historical work on the county of Moray (1839, 144 pages) and three tourist guides of Scotland (one going through nine editions). Of his scientific writings, a number reflected his strong commitment to see good textbooks available for the education of children, aged 10–18 years. Many of these books went through several editions and included class books on the natural history of the earth (1832, 69 pages), botany (1833, 76 pages), geology and physical geography (1837, 104 pages),[17] zoology

6 Hugh Murray, editor, *Historical and Descriptive Account of British India* (1832), 3 volumes. In the preface to the first volume (p. 5) Rhind is described as one of the contributing "gentlemen whose abilities and acquirements have raised them to the first eminence in their respective departments of literature and science."

7 William Rhind, *Cases Illustrative of the Division of Tendons* (1841). This little tract first appeared as an article, by the same title, in the *Edinburgh Medical and Surgical Journal*, vol. LV, no. 146 (1841), p. 126–135. It shows that he was performing surgery alone and in cooperation with other doctors at the time.

8 Anderson, *Fasti Academiae Marischallanae Aberdonensis*, p. 70.

9 Personal correspondence (November 30, 1994) from Mrs. Jane Pirie, library assistant in the Department of Special Collections and Archives of the Aberdeen University Library.

10 After much effort, it was surprising to me, several librarians, and the head of the Fife Family Historical Society, that no obituary for such a prominent citizen as Rhind could be located in any of a number of local newspapers, or in scientific journals which had published his articles.

11 His last revision of his massive *History of the Vegetable Kingdom* was published in 1868. Two more unrevised editions appeared before his death.

12 The precise date of death was obtained from the Scottish Records Office in Edinburgh.

13 Douglas, *Sons of Moray*, p. 6.

14 William Rhind, *Studies in Natural History* (1830), title page.

15 William Rhind, *Elementary Geography* (1858), title page.

16 "Appendix," *Report of the BAAS* (1835), p. 31.

17 William Rhind, *Elements of Geology and Physical Geography* (1837). Further editions appeared in 1838 and 1844. At the end of this book Rhind gave a list of useful works on geology, many of which he had consulted in preparing the book. They

(1839, 119 pages),[18] meteorology (1840?),[19] physical geography (1850, 88 pages, and 1851, 96 pages), and elementary geography (1858, 112 pages). In 1829 he published the first thorough work on the the nature and cure of intestinal worms in the human body. He also produced for the general public *Studies in Natural History* (1830, 247 pages)[20] and *The Feline Species* (1834, 183 pages).[21]

His magnum opus was his 711-page *A History of the Vegetable Kingdom*, which appeared in about 1841 and went through eight later editions up to 1877.[22] Written for both the general reader and the systematic student of botany, it embraced "the physiology, classification and culture of plants [both living and fossil], with their various uses to man and the lower animals, and their application in the arts, manufactures, and domestic economy."[23]

In addition to his books, Rhind published several scientific journal articles on various topics: a species of worm in sheep (1830), the spontaneous generation of living creatures (1830, an idea he rejected), the geological arrangement of the strata (1844),[24] the hydrology of the British Isles (1855), and coal found in Seil Island, Argyleshire (1858).[25]

His books dealing directly with geology at an adult level were three. In 1833, he produced a book of excursions around Edinburgh which illustrated the geology and natural history of the area. A review of the 1836 second edition in the *Magazine of Natural History* said, "There is much and various interesting information in this volume: the greater portion relates to geology."[26] The *Edinburgh Journal of Natural History and Physical Sciences* "confidently recommended" the 1833 edition, particularly for its "lucid" geological descriptions.[27] When the second edition, which was twice as long and described double the number of locations, appeared in 1836, the same journal remarked:

> Mr. Rhind has most judiciously availed himself of all that has been written, while he has himself visited every corner which he describes, and has added many interesting observations. Mr. Rhind's remarks on the Coal Fields of this district are very judicious, and give a clear view of the subject. . . . several well-engraved woodcuts of all the fossils have been introduced.[28]

In 1842 he published *The Geology of Scotland and Its Islands* (168 pages). As was the case with all of his writings on geology so far mentioned, this was a purely descriptive work which he hoped would stimulate further geological research by local students. While he relied on the work of at least 21 other local and national geologists, he also

included the recent editions of works by Macculloch, Conybeare, Jameson, Phillips, Bakewell, de la Beche, Lyell, Buckland, Playfair, Daubeny, Sowerby, Woodward, Parkinson, Murchison, Sedgwick, Mantell, William Smith, Greenough, and Silliman. He likely knew French and German as he cited French titles by Cuvier, Daubuisson, Boué, Agassiz, and Brongniart, and German works by Sternberg and Goldfuss.

18 A positive review appeared in *Athenaeum*, no. 620 (Sept. 14, 1839), p. 696. A second edition was published in 1845.

19 I could not find this in any major library catalogs but it was advertised in the back of his *Elements of Zoology* (1839) as "in preparation for publication."

20 This received rather negative reviews in *Athenaeum*, no. 109 (Nov. 25, 1829), p. 738, and in *Magazine of Natural History*, vol. III, no 11 (Jan. 1830), p. 79, because, the reviewers said, the scientific information was not current enough and too shallowly treated.

21 These works are listed in the bibliography.

22 The title page of the work has no date. The publication date comes from Benjamin Jackson's *Guide to the Literature of Botany* (1881), which lists Rhind's book as a very worthy contribution to botanical studies. The 1868 edition was a complete revision by Rhind to bring it up to date with current knowledge, though the changes were small and the new edition was only 727 pages, compared with the original 711.

23 William Rhind, *A History of the Vegetable Kingdom* (1841), title page, i.

24 This article was republished in a German science journal in 1844.

25 See the bibliography for full details.

26 *Magazine of Natural History*, vol. IX, no. 65 (1836), p. 504.

27 *Edinburgh Journal of Natural History and Physical Sciences*, vol. I, no. 3 (1835), p. 12.

28 Ibid., vol. I (1836), p. 60.

based his writings on his own field work. In the preface he wrote:

> Notwithstanding the researches of several eminent geologists in detached districts, much of the particular and local geology of Scotland remains yet to be explored. Of the labors of his predecessors, the author, as will be seen in the marginal references of these pages, has frequently availed himself, more particularly of the descriptions of some few localities which he has not himself personally inspected.[29]

As already noted,[30] Rhind showed evidence of being well-read in all the leading geological literature of his day.[31] But he was also committed to field work. His concern for careful geological exploration is reflected in his preface to *Elements of Geology and Physical Geography* (1837), a work written for 12–14 year-old students.

> Geology is one of those sciences which cannot be learnt by books alone, or studied in the closet. All that has been attempted here, then is a class book to aid verbal instruction and the actual inspection of nature. . . . In geological excursions, all that is generally necessary is a strong hammer and bag, a pocket compass, and notebook. Specimens should always be taken from the rocks *in situ*, and a few inches below the exposed surface, which is always more or less changed from the action of the weather. These specimens should be from three to five inches long and two to three broad, and formed by the chipping hammer into an oblong square. Crystals, minerals, and fossils, should be carefully wrapped in paper. On returning home, the whole should be labeled, and put up in drawers, for habits of accurate arrangement and neatness are among the necessary consequences of scientific training.[32]

The work in which Rhind discussed geological theory, and which therefore will be the focus of our study, was *The Age of the Earth*, published in 1838. In it he further alluded to his own geological field work, when he observed carefully the contact point between mica schist and granite, found and collected fossils, and studied waterfall erosion at several locations in Scotland.[33]

Attitude Toward Geology and His Geological Opponents

It is obvious from the books he wrote that Rhind was anything but anti-geology. He considered few fields of study "of greater interest" than geology, and far from being harmful, the facts of geology, better than most information, could be "usefully employed" in "the promotion of the arts and conveniences of life."[34] But geological

29 William Rhind, *Geology of Scotland* (1842), p. v.

30 See Footnote 17.

31 Besides the many books published by geologists, the leading journals were also part of his reading, such as the *Edinburgh Philosophical Journal, American Journal of Science, Transactions of the Wernerian Society, Asiatic Journal, Transactions of the Philosophical Society* (of both London and Edinburgh), *Philosophical Magazine*, and *Transactions of the Geological Society* of London.

Since Rhind also responded to theological arguments for an old earth, it needs to be noted that his accurate knowledge of opposing views is reflected in several very long quotes in *The Age of the Earth* (1838), p. 171–194, by Thomas Chalmers, John B. Sumner, William Buckland, Baden Powell, and John Fleming, which accurately conveyed their current positions on the subject.

32 Rhind, *Elements of Geology and Physical Geography*, p. iii–v. The second edition of this work received a positive review in *Athenaeum*, no. 549 (May 5, 1838), p. 322. The reviewer wrote, "Mr. Rhind deserves the thanks of the class of students for whose use this treatise is intended. The facts are arranged in a concise and systematic form. . . . His work may be safely recommended to the friends of that comprehensive system of education now generally pursued."

33 Rhind, *The Age of the Earth*, p. v, 144, 153, 166, 171. Since none of Rhind's geological notebooks are known to survive, we cannot know with certainty if in his field work he noted such geological features as dips, strikes, and cleavage (as were frequently noted in the notebooks of old-earth geologists). However, the positive reviews of his 1833 book on the geology around Edinburgh (quoted earlier) and the content of his other books and journal articles on geology suggest that he was a careful observer of all kinds of geological phenomena.

34 Ibid., p. vi.

theories about earth history were another matter all together.

> In no department of science has [sic] the vague speculations of theorists, both ancient and modern, excited more contention or ridicule than this. Most of these theories have been hastily formed, and without a due regard to facts and observations; or when these have been partially made, such facts have often been perverted; hence such theorists have exposed themselves to the lash of the Satirist. . . . We cannot look upon the visionary speculations of some of these philosophers without surprise, mingled also with regret at the dogmatism and self sufficiency with which they are propounded.[35]

For this reason it is not surprising that Rhind considered his own theoretical considerations of geological phenomena as "very incomplete."[36] In several places he emphasized that geology was still very much in its infant state with much controversy in interpreting the geological data.[37] He did not believe, for example, that even the diluvial deposits had been adequately investigated, much less the strata they covered. And as noted above, in 1842 he asserted that the geology of Scotland still was largely unknown.[38] He wondered, given the nature of the subject matter, whether geologists would ever be able to gather enough facts to conclusively prove a general theory of history based solely on the geological evidence. For these reasons, Rhind hoped his readers would not think him presumptuous to publish his own opinions on the history of the earth, to stimulate thought.

Regarding those geologists who were proposing theories contrary to the literal interpretation of Scripture, Rhind was always respectful, crediting them with a "comprehensive intellect" and "acute and patient" investigation of facts and the publication of "a mass of valuable practical knowledge."[39] In alluding to the recent changes of opinions of Buckland and Greenough regarding the Flood he said, "We by no means presume to hold them up to censure. The avowal of them, on the contrary, indicates a true nobleness of mind."[40]

Rhind referred briefly to only three other scriptural geologists. In his endnote discussion of waterfall erosion, he had one sentence on Fairholme's calculations on the recession of Niagara Falls, describing them as "interesting."[41] He cited Granville Penn's view that Genesis 2:11–14 is a textual gloss as a possible (though not the most probable) explanation for this passage in light of a world-destroying flood.[42] But he made no comment on Penn's geological theory. In his conclusion, he quoted at length from Sharon Turner's *Sacred History of the World* (1837) to express his conviction that he would stick with Scripture and wait for time to expose the errors of the geological theories that contradicted its plain teaching on creation and the Flood.[43]

The Relationship Between Scripture and Science

More clearly than the other geologically informed scriptural geologists we have considered, Rhind remarked on the relation of Genesis and geology, particularly in light of the Galileo affair.

As far as Scripture was concerned, he believed that its meaning was generally very clear and its teaching authoritative.

> I must also here, in the outset, state that I may be reckoned by some not an unprejudiced judge of the questions before me; for, entertaining such a belief in the

35 Rhind, *Studies in Natural History*, p. 29–30.
36 Rhind, *The Age of the Earth*, p. iv.
37 Ibid., p. iii–iv, 10 and 109–112.
38 The great Scottish geologist Hugh Miller would have agreed with Rhind in relation to the deep and extensive Old Red Sandstone. See Miller's *Old Red Sandstone* (1841), p. 40–49.
39 Rhind, *The Age of the Earth*, p. 138–141.
40 Ibid., p. 196.
41 Ibid., p. 171.
42 Ibid., p. 196–197.
43 Ibid., p. 121–122.

Sacred Writings as makes me confident that their general import was intended to be as readily understood by the mass of mankind as by the critical inquirer, I am disposed to give implicit credence to the narrative of creation, to the whole extent that it goes; and wherever discrepancies present themselves, to await the issue of the approximation of geological knowledge to the sacred history, instead of attempting to torture this latter into a conformity with the former.[44]

The historical reliability of the Bible was confirmed in his mind by, among other things, the growing archaeological evidence for biblical statements about such ancient cities as Nineveh and Babylon.[45] Rhind viewed geology, a science concerned about history, as being very similar to archaeology and therefore a subject to which Genesis had relevance.

> If a stranger were to visit, for the first time, the ruins of Pompeii, without any knowledge of its previous history, he would view with interest the numerous fragments of most elaborate architecture strewed in ruins, and, struck with the still and silent antiquity of the scene before him, compared to the lively and luxuriant country around, his first impulse would be to inquire whether any tradition of this catastrophe existed. And thus it is, that the geologist turns from the contemplation of vast creative power, and of destruction and desolation everywhere around him, to ask of history, if it can throw any gleam of light on his perplexing meditations. With the exception of national traditions and legends, which are all traceable to one common source, the Book of Genesis contains the only record of creation given to man. We do not deem it necessary here to enter into any proof of the authenticity of the Mosaical history; but assume the fact as granted, that this account, brief as it is, is a genuine detail of the creation of the world.[46]

But, it was objected, the Bible is not intended to teach science. To this Rhind responded:

> But if the Mosaical account of creation be not strictly and exclusively a statement of physical facts, it is nothing; and if the facts of geology and the statements of Moses, when brought to bear upon each other, be not found to coincide, one of them must be false, or there must be something wrong in the mode of their conception, or the manner of their application. Two circumstances, however, are necessary, before a perfect and harmonious coincidence of both can be acquired. We must, first, have a complete and accurate collection of the facts of geology, and we must have a precise and definite conception of the statements of Moses.[47]

We will consider his reflection on the facts and theories of geology shortly, but first we will follow his remarks about the correct interpretation of Genesis.

> In perusing the simple but sublime commencement of the Holy Scriptures, where the successive acts of creation are recorded, what is the natural and obvious conception of the passages by the general reader, unsophisticated by preconceived notions or critical propensities? As these records were most certainly penned for the general mass of mankind, and delivered, no doubt, with the view that they should be universally and easily understood, we conceive this is the question by which their true meaning should be tried, and

44 Ibid., p. iv–v.
45 Ibid., p. 88.
46 Ibid., p. 71–72. This remark was similar to one made by Kirwan and, as noted earlier, quoted by Penn. In a footnote, Rhind said it was uncertain, but also immaterial to the historicity of Genesis, whether Moses wrote Genesis from direct revelation or on the basis of traditions passed down from Noah.
47 Ibid., p. 73.

not by verbal criticism, and forced constructions of half sentences, and isolated passages.[48]

In response to Baden Powell's view that Genesis 1 was a figurative, theological myth which taught truth about creation, Rhind added:

> But this is an extremely loose mode of reasoning indeed. The Scriptures must be held to contain matters of fact applicable to all men, of all intellects, otherwise they must lead only to error and delusion; and if we can conceive that it was the pleasure of the Divine Being to reveal to man so much of the origin of the world which he inhabits, as was deemed necessary, it is reasonable to suppose that it was just as easy to give that revelation simply and unequivocally as to clothe it in mystery and allegory. Nor indeed does [*sic*] the other parts of the Book of Genesis partake of this character. It is, throughout, a plain, simple, and matter of fact history, with the names and dates given to a scrupulous nicety.[49]

But still, what about the Galileo affair? Rhind was well aware that old-earth geologists frequently used this to attempt to silence their critics. Rhind, however, saw a significant difference between that 16th century astronomical debate and the geological debate of his day.

> When a check is offered to his [the old-earth geologist's] crude and inconclusive conceptions, he fancies himself another Galileo, and glories in his imagined martyrdom. Yet no case was ever more exaggerated than that of Galileo; and even assuming it in its worst phase, it was rather the fault of the age than of the individuals engaged in it. How many really wicked attacks have been leveled at sacred things from the days of Galileo to the present, and successfully refuted by divines, laudably on the watch to preserve the purity of that faith which has been intrusted to them, and yet how small praise has been awarded them, compared to the opprobrium of this one case of exaggerated oppression! Even our modern cosmogonists triumphantly appeal to this, although the Galileon heresy has nothing in common with their objectionable theories in thus far — that the most remote revelation of astronomical truths would have been foreign to the very purpose of our limited and probationary state, while, on the other hand, a distinct revelation, so far, of the origin of the world and its physical history, was necessary to the understanding of man's moral condition and prospects. In the former case, the common language, descriptive of phenomena as they are seen, was necessarily made use of; in the latter, language expressly descriptive of the actual facts was indispensable.[50]

So, for Rhind, Genesis gives us plain straightforward history of the creation, which is indispensable for a correct interpretation of the geological evidence.

His Geological Arguments Against an Old Earth

Rhind divided his book, *The Age of the Earth*, into three parts. First, he evaluated some of the main geological arguments for an old earth (p. 10–70). Next, he gave his objections to the various attempts to harmonize old-earth geological theories with the Genesis accounts of creation and the Flood (p. 71–124). And finally, he gave a sketch of the history of geology, from the times of the ancient Greeks to the present, and its theories of the earth (p. 125–152). These three

48 Ibid., p. 73–74.

49 Ibid., p. 84.

50 Ibid., p. 117–118. It was not just in geology that Scripture had a bearing. Rhind saw other connections. In a footnote he said, "Nor can we allow that revelation does not, in many important questions, bear upon physical science. Can science, for instance, demonstrate the immortality of the soul? Is this conception innate? Or without revelation could unassisted reason have ever dreamt of a future state of existence? Let us only think what would have been the state of this question without the aid of revelation, where all the physical facts are decidedly in favor of the materialist."

sections were supported by lengthy endnotes (p. 153–202). We will carefully consider only the first two sections, since the historical sketch was really an extended note that supplemented his earlier arguments without adding anything substantially new.

Rhind did not attempt to give a detailed theory of how Genesis and the geological record fit together, because of the infant state of geology, as noted above. Rather, he simply gave some of his reasons for rejecting the arguments in favor of an old earth.

After some introductory remarks about the tendency of geological speculation to transgress the "sober boundaries of facts,"[51] he considered the thickness of the stratigraphic record. Old-earth geologists were convinced that the total thickness was far too great to be harmonized with a literal interpretation of the Mosaic chronology. But Rhind questioned this conclusion because of the difficulties involved in determining that thickness. For one thing, the whole geological column was not known then to exist in any single location on the earth.[52] Furthermore, the strata were not the same thickness through their horizontal extent, so that the average thickness was considerably less than the maximum.[53] A succession of stratified rocks having a continuous inclination to each other, which may imply enormous thickness, might instead:

> . . . only be a bed of very moderate dimensions, broken up by repeated wave-like eruptions of igneous rocks from below, which may not always make their appearance on the surface. The sedimentary matter may have originally been deposited by a current of water flowing over a sloping channel, by which means a succession of inclined strata may have been formed, extending for a long space horizontally, although of no very considerable depth — a mode of deposition which may be witnessed daily in many river currents, and which has been so well illustrated by M. De la Beche.[54]

Finally, Rhind argued, it was difficult in many instances to determine the actual depth of the original deposition because, in the schistose strata and other slate masses, lines of cleavage could be mistaken for those of stratification and their lamination and stratification may have resulted from a process of crystallization.

Added to the problem of measuring the actual total thickness of the strata,[55] Rhind believed there was evidence that the sediments had been deposited more rapidly than geologists generally assumed. Starting with the uniformitarian assumption of the present rate of deposition by rivers and ocean currents, he cited several measured examples of large rivers to show that the stratigraphic record could have been produced in thousands of years rather than millions. But he felt it was very likely that these processes would have been accelerated in the past because the primitive rocks, which provided the materials for the secondary sedimentary strata, would have been softer and more exposed than in his day, resulting in more rapid erosion. Also, contemporary geologists generally agreed that early in earth history the climate was essentially tropical everywhere. This would have meant a higher rate of evaporation producing more rain and consequently more and larger rivers again leading to greater erosion. Such a climate also naturally would have produced a more luxuriant vegetation, which as transported debris would have been the source for the production of the vast coal measures.[56]

---

51 Ibid., p. 12.

52 This is still true. See Derek Ager, *The Nature of the Stratigraphical Record* (1981), p. 35.

53 Rhind, *The Age of the Earth*, p. 17–18. He argued in the same way as George Young did. But there is no reason to believe that he was dependent on Young for this conclusion.

54 Ibid., p. 19. Here he footnoted the work of old-earth proponent, Henry De la Beche, *Researches in Theoretical Geology* (1834).

55 His fellow Scottish geologist, Hugh Miller, did not venture to estimate the depth of the Old Red Sandstone in Scotland, because "there are no calculations more doubtful than those of the geologist." See Miller, *Old Red Sandstone*, p. 54.

56 Rhind, *The Age of the Earth*, p. 20–30.

He also believed there was evidence for the contemporaneous deposit of formations. Certainly some strata were deposited in the order that they were found in a local area. But he did not think that this could be proved to be the case generally. So, for example, he argued that the last great change by which the British strata were elevated out of the ocean took place at basically one period, which, if so, would mean that the carboniferous formation would have been roughly contemporaneous with at least parts of the lias and oolite (which in the old-earth view were deposited millions of years apart).[57]

For Rhind, one of the strongest evidences of rapid diluvial deposition of formations, even hundreds of feet thick, was the many examples of polystrate trees. He discussed in some detail the famous fossil tree found in a 200-feet thick mass of alternating sandstone and shale in Craigleith Quarry, near Edinburgh, in 1830.[58] His residence in Edinburgh at the time and his detailed description strongly suggests that he had investigated this matter personally, in addition to reading journal articles about it. Besides the evidence that the sand of the sandstone had been drifted into place by impetuous currents of water, the fact that this tree, and others frequently found in the coal measures, traversed many strata firmly persuaded him that the sediments had accumulated rapidly (in less than a few months) so as to preserve the trees as found. And this applied whether the trees were buried where they grew or had been transported by water to the burial place, the latter view being more probable in his opinion. From this he concluded, "If we thus, then, have proofs of strata, two hundred feet in depth, having been formed suddenly, may we not apply the same analogy to other strata, where proofs of the fact are not now so evident?"[59] In his endnote (p. 158–160) on the Craigleith fossil he discussed the history of the identification of this tree: first it was declared by Brongniart to be an extinct fern, then it was renamed as a new species of extinct tree, and finally it was proved to be identical to a living species in the islands of the South Seas. To Rhind's mind, the fossil remains of this living species in the geologically low formation of the coal measures militated against the idea that the coal measures were from a world existing long ages before the creation of man.

Rhind believed that the elevation of the strata to form dry land was the result of volcanic action, similar to that which geologists then observed. However, he argued that:

> [the extent of the] ancient mountain chains, the manner in which they appear to have elevated the strata of whole islands and large portions of continents, by one continuous and uninterrupted process, seem to indicate, that though the causes were similar to volcanic, yet the amount of the forces and the extent of the operations were in an infinitely greater degree, and much more general, than any witnessed in modern times.[60]

Another reason that leading geologists believed the earth was much older than traditionally believed was the alleged fact of the successive series of organic remains in the different formations. While Rhind agreed that it was generally true that each formation was characterized by peculiar fossils, he added that new discoveries were constantly necessitating revisions in the classification of species and rocks. Furthermore, he considered several factors that militated against the notion that such an organic progression in the geological record represented long ages of time marked by periods of extinction and creation. Extinctions were a fact of life, but looking at existing nature he saw no means for life to be formed from inorganic matter and the lowest strata of geological record showed well-organized life forms to have appeared on the scene suddenly. Likewise, the observed laws of nature opposed the idea that new species could arise

57 Ibid., p. 31–35.

58 Ibid., p. 36–37, 158–160.

59 Ibid., p. 37.

60 Ibid., p. 39. He elaborated on his view of greater and more general volcanic activity in the past on pages 148–151, where he discussed Lyell's theory of igneous rocks and metallic veins.

from existing forms. If nature had the ability in itself to produce life or new forms of life, it would do so continually, he reasoned. The fact that we do not see this tendency in nature, he said, was not overcome by adding millions of years to earth history.[61] We should not interpret Rhind here to be denying biological variation of any kind, for he later remarked, "Among the extinct animals there are no such diversities from the present as to render the creation of new classes or orders necessary, they are only so far different as to constitute new genera and species of old established classes."[62]

One more factor opposing the idea of a long succession of creations and extinctions was the fact that many creatures range through the whole, or large portions, of the fossiliferous strata.

> Now, although each of these formations. generally speaking, contains a certain amount of distinctive species, yet there are some tribes of animals which range throughout the whole. Thus, various species of coral zoophytes are found in all the strata; terebratulae also are common through the whole; ammonites extend throughout all the strata, except the tertiary; spirifers and productae extend through all the series to the oolite; while belemnites only appear in the lias, oolite, and chalk; and the echinae in the chalk alone. In short, these fossil animals appear to have strictly conformed in their habits to recent species. They had certain localities which they frequented as being suited to their organization; some inhabited deep seas; some littoral situations, and others the shallow estuaries of rivers.[63]

By analogy with the present diverse distribution of plants and animals, it was more reasonable in Rhind's mind to assume that creatures in different formations were living at the same time on the earth, though in different environments, which affected where the creatures were deposited in the strata.

But Rhind's opponents objected that a great many of the plants and animals in the lower formations differed markedly from those in the upper strata and those still existing, a fact which surely must imply multiple creations and extinctions over long ages in a pre-Adamite world. He replied:

> Now, this is undoubtedly a fact not readily accounted for. But we must consider, first, that the ancient marine strata, in which the greater part of these remains are found, were at one period, in all probability, under a tropical climate, and formed, moreover, the outskirts of a region under the process of progressive organization. Second, that organized beings suited to such circumstances first took possession of the strata. Third, that we are still ignorant of perhaps one-third of the forms of animals and vegetables existing on the earth, and, consequently, cannot pronounce the fossil ones to be of an exclusive

61 Ibid., p. 41–44.

62 Ibid., p. 57. On page 163 he added, "The idea of spontaneous production has long ago been scouted from science, and the no less illogical one of equivocal generation is fast going. We see no analogy in nature to lead us to suppose that such a law exists — we see no provision for such operations, and no trace of such having ever occurred — we can predicate that the earth will produce certain plants after we have deposited certain seeds, but that if such seeds are carefully excluded, that no species of vegetation will follow — we can predicate that a lupin seed will produce a certain flower, followed by a seed similar to the parent one; and we may speculate freely on certain varieties of these, but we know to a certainty, from experience and analogy, that the lupin can never produce a rose, and that the soil alone will never bring forth a new species of plant."

Earlier he had made similar remarks against the idea of spontaneous generation, concluding that matter had no inherent creative property. In his rejection of evolution *between* the various kinds of creatures, he did not deny variation *within* divinely ordained biological groupings. He wrote, "Some First Cause must have given a determinate form, and prescribed to such creations regular and definite limits." See William Rhind, "An Examination of the Opinions of Bremser and Others on the Equivocal Production of Animals," *Edinburgh Journal of Natural and Geographical Science*, vol. II (1830), p. 391–397 (the quotation is on 397).

63 Rhind, *The Age of the Earth*, p. 44–45.

kind; and that as proof of this, every year is adding new living genera and species as analogues of the fossil kinds. Lastly, that peculiarities of climate, modifications of the saline portions of the ocean, and other local changes, may have so far influenced the external forms of many testaceous mollusca, as to deceive the most practiced conchologist with regard to the species; and that, indeed, in many instances, it is impossible from the fossil shell positively to decide on the species of many genera.[64] . . . Another important circumstance has to be noticed, that as yet only about seven thousand fossil animals and plants have been discovered. It can never be supposed that this number sufficed for the ancient system of things, and filled a world which now contains thirty times the number — nay, probably three times this proportion. A mere fraction, then, of the organic remains of former strata, has yet become familiar to us, and it would be absurd to form any sweeping conclusions under our present ignorance.[65]

Added to this was the fact that in the diluvial clay and gravel and in caves and rock fissures were found a mixture of extinct and existing species and genera of animals, of which cases Rhind documented several examples.

He conceded that no well-authenticated ancient fossil men had been discovered, but accounted for this by several facts. Geologists had not yet studied the lands where it was most likely to find such remains. The pre-Flood human population was undoubtedly much smaller in proportion to animals, and so human fossils would naturally be much rarer. But also, concurring with Cuvier, he thought it very probable that the continents of early man's habitation had become part of the ocean bottom. Lastly, he believed that the modern theories "render geologists now averse to believe the possibility of finding a true fossil man."[66] Actually, Rhind reasoned, the fact that there was no physical proof of man before the Deluge, strengthened one's belief that the Flood was a global catastrophe.[67]

The theory of a progressively cooling earth was popular among many old-earth geologists. But Rhind argued that if it was true, it actually would refute the notion of long ages having transpired in the history of life and the formation of strata. For example, plants and mollusca at the top and bottom of the coal measures were the same. But this would be impossible if, as some old-earth geologists believed, the coal measures represented at least one million years of gradual cooling of the earth.

Rejecting the theory of central heat, Rhind thought it more likely that Lyell was right in suggesting that the former, generally tropical climate was attributable to a change of position and proportions of land and sea. In contrast to Lyell, however, he believed this change was abrupt and global because there was no trace of intermediate vegetation between the system of extinct plants and existing species and because the fossil plants of the carboniferous formation and the animals in fossil beds and the diluvium "extending over many regions of the globe, exhibiting one era of existence, all indicate a similarity of climate."[68]

Virtually all geologists agreed at the time that the commencement of the present system of life and natural processes on the surface of the earth was quite recent. Though the combined operations of biological, chemical, and mechanical forces at work over long ages in the inorganic world must have left traces of their effects on the earth, especially more so in the ocean than on land, it was astonishing, said Rhind, how little

64 Ibid., p. 49–50. Rhind made a similar comment about shells being effected by water depth and temperature, thus making species classification (and therefore strata identification) difficult. See his "The Geological Arrangement of Ancient Strata, Deduced from the Condition of the Present Oceanic Beds," *Edinburgh New Philosophical Journal*, vol. XXXVI, (1844), p. 333.

65 Rhind, *The Age of the Earth*, p. 50–51. He supported this with a table in the footnote comparing the numbers of living and extinct species of plants and animals in the different classes.

66 Ibid., p. 54–55.

67 Ibid., p. 96–97.

68 Ibid., p. 60.

change had occurred in the last 4,000 years. To use such processes to calculate the relative ages of the countries was possible to some extent, but Rhind cautioned against the wholesale uniformitarian extrapolations.

> Yet, in making calculations of this nature, we must bear in mind, that the amount of disintegration will be in proportion to the impetus and constancy of the forces at work, and to the degree of hardness of the materials acted upon. Thus, some shores are of very soft materials, easily yielding to the waves, while others are so hard as to resist in a great measure any very extensive destruction. The ocean, too, after having acted with considerable force and effect on some shores for a long period, at last throws up a barrier of loose debris which shuts out its waves, and completely excludes their farther operations; tides and currents, also, interfere with the regular deposition of deltas, and circumstances take place in the course of ages which may materially modify the impetus of rivers. Thus, the constant effect of flowing streams is to lower the level line of their courses, and consequently to lessen the velocity and force of their currents. All rivers exhibit this to a greater or less extent; the gradual lowering of the height of many waterfalls is evidently caused by the abrading force of the currents on the sides of the rocks, now many feet above the commencement of their present descents. Under these modifications, however, this subject of inquiry is an interesting one, and deserving of further prosecution. If a collection of accurate data of this description were made, it would then be seen how far these may tend to throw light on the actual age of particular countries, or that period when the surface of the strata first became dry land, as also on the relative ages of different continents. For it is still an important desideratum to ascertain whether the great leading outlines of the continents of the earth have had a simultaneous formation, and have been afterwards partially modified and filled up by successive operations, or whether they are of very different ages, and owe their origins to causes acting at remote intervals of epochs.[69]

These, then, were the main objections he had to geological theories of an old earth. Next he turned to a consideration of the various attempts to harmonize the Bible with such theories.

Creation and the Flood

As already noted, Rhind considered the traditional literal interpretation of the early chapters of Genesis to be correct. Therefore, he rejected the three alternative theories: the day-age theory, the gap theory, and theological framework theory.

The day-age theory, most recently promulgated by the Reverend George Faber,[70] was problematical because in Genesis 1 Moses so clearly defined "day" in reference to morning and evening and light and darkness.[71] Furthermore, the fourth commandment in Exodus 20:8–11 would have only been understood by Jews to be speaking of literal days, though Rhind allowed that, because the sun was only created on day 4, it was possible that the first three days may have been more indefinite.[72] But even in this case, there were geological objections to this theory, since the fossil record did not reflect the order of events in Genesis 1. In fact, he argued, contrary to what some geologists believed, there was no progression from simple to more complex forms of life as we move up through the strata.[73]

69 Ibid., p. 63–64. The last part of this quote would suggest that Rhind had not read George Fairholme's *Mosaic Deluge* (1837), which was devoted to just such an analysis and age calculation.

70 Rhind quoted Faber's view at length in the endnotes, ibid., p. 171–173. Faber's work appeared in 1823.

71 Of the few scriptural geologists who explicitly argued against the day-age theory, only Rhind, here (ibid., p. 74), referred to some of the early church fathers (Origin, Augustine, and Bede) who had proposed this interpretation.

72 Such an interpretation, however, could be seen as a compromise of his belief that Genesis 1 is "a plain, simple, and matter of fact history" that all men of any intelligence could understand (ibid., p. 84).

73 This was precisely what Lyell argued in his *Principles of Geology* (1830–33), especially Volume II.

Rhind rejected the more popular gap theory, propounded by Chalmers, Sumner, Buckland,[74] and some of the most eminent geologists in England and Europe because he was not convinced by their arguments that any interval of time between Genesis 1:1 and 1:2 was even remotely suggested by the language. Nor, in his opinion, would Moses' predecessors or contemporaries have ever dreamt of such an interpretation. But in addition to the geological objections to an old earth which he had earlier discussed, the fact of many examples of existing species having been found buried in strata with extinct ones also militated against the notion of many pre-Adamite worlds. Furthermore, in light of the perfect state of preservation of delicate leaves, shells, and animal tissue lying almost on the surface of the uppermost strata:

> We would require strong facts and powerful reasonings to persuade us that these have survived through "millions of millions of ages," the wreck of ancient worlds, the dark period of chaos, and the various commotions incident to the formation of an entirely new world.[75]

As noted earlier, Baden Powell[76] and other commentators viewed Genesis 1 as a figurative, pictorial framework for teaching us some theology. Rhind rejected this notion because of the clear indications in Genesis that the whole book was "plain, simple, and matter of fact history."[77]

In his mind, the utmost latitude in interpretation of Genesis 1 was that possibly there had been an indefinite period of time between the creation of the earth and the first day when light appeared and that maybe the first three days were not exactly the same length as the latter three. But even if we became convinced that such interpretations did no violence to the Mosaic narrative, it would not help harmonize the Bible with the dominant geological theories. At best, it could explain the formation of the primary, non-fossiliferous strata, but not the secondary strata, for reasons previously cited. Nevertheless, Rhind thought the general tenor of Genesis 1 implied a consecutive, uninterrupted process of creation in six literal days (i.e., with no time gap at Genesis 1:2).

He believed that the Noachian deluge was a unique, year-long, global catastrophe. The flood traditions among the nations of the world, the detailed description in Genesis (especially 7:11–12, 19–21, 24 and the use of universal terms), the general belief of the Jews (as ascertained from Josephus and Philo), and the references to the Flood in the rest of the Bible convinced him of this. Furthermore, if it had only been a local flood, the ark would have been unnecessary to save the animals, which could have escaped to the adjacent countries. The notion of a tranquil flood, suggested by Linnaeus and promoted by Fleming and Buckland, was totally out of harmony with a text like Genesis 6:13, he asserted.

Rhind devoted several pages to considering historical and contemporary answers to the question of whether geology afforded proof of the Flood. Though he did not think it necessary for geology to do so, he gave two main geological factors which strengthened his belief in the biblical account. One was the fact that no remains of antediluvian man had yet been found, even though the pre-Flood population would have been large, due to the longevity and reproductivity of the antediluvian people over a period of nearly 2,000 years, and their technology was advanced, according to Genesis.[78]

Secondly, the secondary strata seemed not to be the remains of an anterior world but part of the present creation. These geological phenomena indicated to him that there had been a sudden change of climate, the extinction of a considerable portion of plant and animal life on the earth, and the sudden deposition of diluvial matter over the

74 Ibid. He quoted these men extensively in the notes, p. 180–188.
75 Ibid., p. 81.
76 Ibid., p. 188. Rhind quoted him at length.
77 Ibid., p. 84.
78 Ibid., p. 88–89 and 96–97. Rhind was not dogmatic about the length of the antediluvian period. He compared the Hebrew, Samaritan, and Septuagint versions of Genesis without giving a firm conclusion about which one he believed was correct.

strata, which had been forcibly elevated from the ocean.

He did not think that the cause of the Flood could be determined with certainty. Doubtless, it was a mixture of natural and supernatural causes.

> The catastrophe may have been produced by natural operations, or a special cause — that is, the operations periodically taking place on the surface of the globe — such as the sudden overflow of rivers and bursting of lakes, of the sinking and submergence of dry land from volcanic action, may have acted both with increased intensity and enlarged extent of operation; or some special cause may have been employed for this specific purpose, which is not to be repeated, and which, therefore, remains a miracle unknown and inexplicable.[79]

Rain alone would have been an inadequate water supply. The Flood almost certainly would have involved volcanic activity, which would have heated the oceans (thereby increasing evaporation and precipitation) and produced more tumultuous seas. He gave several reasons for ruling out a change in the tilt of the earth's axis as a cause.

In any case, the Flood was completely different from an ordinary event of nature and never to be repeated. Therefore, trying to explain it from man's present knowledge was nigh impossible.

> In speculating on the deluge, however, we must bear in mind that it was a supernatural event, and though it may have been in a great measure caused by natural operations, yet we are entirely ignorant of the manner of its accomplishment. For this reason there are circumstances attending it which must be to us inexplicable — such as the reinvesting [*sic*] the new surface of the earth with plants — the verdant condition of the olive tree, immediately on the cessation of the waters — the miraculous preservation of every terrestrial animal, etc. As we have no facts or analogies in nature to guide us in such operations, any attempted explanation of them would be preposterous.[80]

Since the Flood was a unique global catastrophe, speculating about the past on the basis of the absolute uniformity of present-day processes would be faulty. So also it would lead to erroneous conclusions about the future. As Peter had written in 2 Peter 3:3–7, the Flood was a harbinger of things to come. Though Rhind would not presume to say exactly what kind of judgment this would be and to what extent the globe would be affected, he gave reasons why he did not think life would yet continue for millions of years.

Conclusion

In the first part of *The Age of the Earth,* Rhind attempted to show that the strata could have been formed in the time allotted by Moses. The thickness of the secondary strata was difficult to determine and usually exaggerated. The strata were clearly formed from the debris of primary rocks. While their relative ages could be determined in the case of physical superposition, there was no direct and convincing proof that widely separated strata were not formed and the continents were not raised above the sea at roughly the same time period. On the contrary, he saw positive reasons for believing that most of the geological record was deposited rapidly. Because of this fact and the analogy of present-day biological processes, he considered the idea of successive creations to be unphilosophical. Certainly, we ought not to introduce miraculous interventions without biblical justification, and dogmatism in geological theory was unwarranted, given the infant state of the science, he argued.

> The intellect of the present age has been characterized as acute, discriminating, active, and energetic, in the pursuit of facts; but loose, illogical, and inconclusive

79 Ibid., p. 99.
80 Ibid., p. 101–102.

in the application of them. If we glanced at the theoretical geologies of the day, these characteristics could not, perhaps, be more happily applied.[81]

As far as Scripture was concerned, he favored the traditional literal interpretation of Genesis. But he was not dogmatic about the time involved in Genesis 1. Regardless of how it was interpreted, it could not be made to harmonize with the dominant geological theories of his day. The imperfect state of geological knowledge, the ambiguities of Genesis 1, and the miraculous nature of the creation and the Flood hindered the complete harmonization of geological facts with Genesis. Rhind believed that although Scripture did not completely settle the question of the age of the earth, it did unmistakably teach the following:

> . . . that the world was created and furnished with plants and animals for the express habitation of man within a definite period; that, after a time, it suffered a partial destruction and change by some great catastrophe; and that ultimately, it will be totally destroyed, after it has ceased to be needed as the theater of moral probation for the human race.[82]

Rhind was neither ignorant of nor opposed to geology. Neither was he disrespectful of those he criticized. Confident that Genesis would be vindicated eventually, he simply sought in his book "to enter a caveat against hasty conclusions" made by contemporary geologists, rather than "to bring the reader to any secure and stable haven of certainty."[83]

81 Ibid., p. 112.
82 Ibid., p. 114–115.
83 Ibid., p. 122.

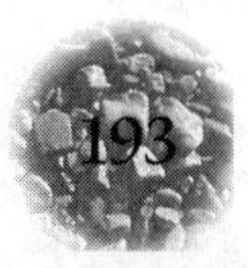

GENERALIZATIONS AND CONCLUSIONS

We have considered the historical context and individually examined seven of the scriptural geologists. We are now in a position to draw out some generalizations and conclusions. First, a summary is given of the similarities and differences between the scriptural geologists, which for accuracy of generalization will take into account also the writings (cited in the bibliography) of six other scriptural geologists (Cole, Cockburn, Gisborne, de Johnsone, Brown, and Best).[1] Then some of their common and most important theological and geological objections to old-earth theories will be set in the context of early 19th century debate on those particular topics. This then provides a basis for analyzing why they engaged in the debate, the overall reactions they received from their contemporaries, and what this reveals about the nature of the conflict.

COLLECTIVE PORTRAIT

Similarities of the Scriptural Geologists

Like most Christians in previous church history and in the early 19th century, all the scriptural geologists believed that Genesis 1–11 provided a divinely inspired and historically accurate account of the origin and early history of the world.[2] This was in contrast to the emerging view that Genesis was a semi-historical, poetical or mythical theological treatise written by pre-scientific and primitive people, like the cosmologies of the ancient Greeks, Egyptians, Hindus, and others.[3] In contrast to their old-earth opponents, many of whom also believed in the inspiration, infallibility, and historicity of Genesis 1–11, the scriptural geologists held to a literal six-day creation approximately 6,000 years ago. None of them,

1 I discussed these men in my Ph.D. thesis, but due to space constraints they were not included in this book. Articles (based on the thesis) on Cole, Gisborne, and Best are on the Web at www.answersingenesis.org. The others may be in the future.

2 Documentation for the views summarized and compared in this section is found in the individual chapter on each man.

3 The Babylonian *Gilgamesh Epic*, which is the most similar to the Genesis account, was not discovered until the mid-19th century and the first publication of a translation did not appear until 1872. See Alexander Heidel, *The Gilgamesh Epic and Old Testament Parallels* (Chicago, IL: University of Chicago Press, 1946).

however, contended strictly for Ussher's date of 4004 B.C. for the creation of the world. Certainly they believed that the early chapters of Genesis were more than just a record of historical events; they indeed taught theological truths. But in their minds these chapters were not less than historical. On the contrary, they believed, the theological truths depended on the literal historicity of the accounts. As a historical account, Genesis 1–11 could no more be rejected or ignored in reconstructing the history of the creation than the writings of Roman historians could be ignored, while only the ancient monuments and artifacts were studied, in reconstructing the history of the Roman empire.

As a result, they all explicitly or implicitly criticized their opponents for what they considered to be a superficial handling of Scriptures relevant to the debate, for making theoretical generalizations based on inadequate geological knowledge, for closing their minds to evidence contrary to their theory, and for faulty logic in reasoning from the geological phenomena they had accurately described. While the scriptural geologists may have been in error in some of their geological facts and theoretical interpretations, one thing is clear: none of them was opposed to the study of science in general or geology in particular, nor did they rely on *ad hominem* attacks in place of reasoned arguments. Most were respectful as they strongly disagreed with their opponents.

Virtually all of the scriptural geologists were repeatedly explicit that they opposed *old-earth* geological theories of the earth, rather than geological facts or even geological theorizing about secondary causes of the observed effects.[4] In fact, most of them theorized about the physical causes and time of geological effects. They generally accepted the geological facts as described by the leading geologists, but challenged the old-earth inferences made from the observed phenomena. Such inferences, they believed, were often erroneously termed "facts" by old-earth geologists, when in reality they were theory-laden interpretations of some of the facts. This, contended some of the scriptural geologists, was in contrast to the old-earth geologists' frequent assertion about themselves that they were just unbiased observers allowing the facts to speak for themselves.[5]

Those who particularly addressed the question of the origin of life and biological change (Bugg and Rhind) were opposed to the idea of evolution (unlimited transmutation) *between* the original, created kinds. (Given that Bugg [non-scientist] and Rhind [scientist] agreed on this point, it is virtually certain that the other scriptural geologists shared their view of variation only within the original created kinds.) Though they did not attempt to define a "kind" precisely, they clearly believed it was a larger biological classification than "species." They did not believe in the fixity of the species, but considered that the potential for species variation (due to various environmental factors), though limited, was greater than many of their old-earth opponents believed. In this regard, by excluding a third option such as Bugg and Rhind suggested, old-earth scientist and philosopher William Whewell created a false dichotomy when he wrote:

> The dilemma then presents itself to us anew — either we must accept the doctrine of the transmutation of species, and must suppose that the organized species of one geological epoch were transmuted into those of another by some long-continued agency of natural causes; or else, we must believe in many successive acts of creation and extinction of species, out of

4 The exceptions to this statement might be Cole, Brown, and de Johnsone. De Johnsone did not write enough for us to know his attitude to the study of geology. The comments of Cole and Brown are sufficiently ambiguous so that it is debatable whether in their minds the legitimate domain of geology included only the description of the position and mineral content of the strata, but not the inferring of causes and time sequences of geological effects.

5 For example, Gideon Mantell, in his *The Wonders of Geology* (1839), p. 4, said, "We must dismiss from our minds all prejudices, from whatsoever source they may arise. This mental purification becomes the more indispensable in a science like geology, in which we meet at the very threshold with facts so novel and astounding; teaching us, that although man and other living things be, as it were, but the creation of yesterday, the earth has teemed with numberless forms of animal and vegetable life, myriads of ages ere the existence of the human race."

the common course of nature; acts which, therefore, we may properly call miraculous.[6]

None of the scriptural geologists appeared to believe that anyone could properly (or should even attempt to) develop a whole "system of natural science" from the Bible. They were certainly not trying to do so, as their critics so often stated or implied.[7] Two of the non-scientists, Bugg and Penn, emphasized this explicitly and repeatedly. Ure, Murray, and Rhind gave no indication in any of their writings that they looked to the Bible as the source of an outline or system for chemistry, physics, botany, medicine, or even practical geology (e.g., mining). Based on what they wrote, this was presumably because they believed the Bible gave no such system or outline for these fields of science. Rather, to advance knowledge in these areas they advocated and participated in experimental and observational scientific research. In their opinion, geology was another matter, however. All the scriptural geologists were convinced that Genesis 1–11 did give an infallible[8] historical outline or framework for developing a history of the earth. Within this outline they believed there was much room, and need, for geological research and speculation, and biblical analysis. Just as their opponents were unanimous about a general outline of earth history but argued over the finer points, so the scriptural geologists differed in their interpretation of some of the minor details of the scriptural account and of the geological evidence, as will be noted shortly, while agreeing on the major points of the outline.

A final similarity among the scriptural geologists is that all of them appeared to believe in the general uniformity of the operation of the laws of nature, which were an expression of God's providence. They believed in the miracles recorded in Scripture, which were rare, local exceptions to the general uniformity of nature. But apart from the initial creation period and the Flood, times when, they believed, the Bible indicated that supernatural power was being exercised on a global scale, they did not invoke miraculous causes for physical phenomena, but rather sought to argue by analogy from present-day processes. They did not explicitly discuss the notion of God's continual, providential control and maintenance of the physical creation, but without a doubt they all believed in it, for the idea of divine providence was part of their world view as traditional orthodox Christians, and was not an issue of debate between them and their opponents.

So, it becomes quite clear that George P. Scrope, who was a budding uniformitarian and a close friend of Lyell, projected a false dichotomy when comparing his view of earth history with all others. In 1825 he said that the whole geological record of the earth is attributable to three primary modes of production: aqueous chemical precipitation, aqueous mechanical deposition, and volcanic uplift of either solid or liquid rocky matter. He claimed that this three-part theory of geological formation had "one immense advantage over most, perhaps over all, of the hypotheses that have as yet been brought forward to explain the same appearances; and which speaks volumes in [its] favor; and this is, that [these modes of production] *are still in operation* —with diminished energy, it is true."[9]

It should be clear from this study that apart from the initial supernatural creation of the earth with its primary rocks, the scriptural geologists (as well as the catastrophists) used the same three modes of production to explain the geological features of the earth. They only differed on the degree or rate of change in the energy, extent, and frequency of these processes in the past.[10]

6 William Whewell, *The History of the Inductive Sciences* (1837), III: p. 574–575. Whewell, like most old-earth scientists of his day, rejected the first option (evolution).

7 For example, Mantell, *The Wonders of Geology*, I: p. 6, and W. Vernon Harcourt, "Address of the President to the BAAS," *Athenaeum*, no. 618 (August 31, 1839), p. 654.

8 "Infallible" was the term they all used, though a few also used "unerring." In this they were following the terminology used by many of the leading contemporary Bible commentators, as shown earlier.

9 George P. Scrope, *Considerations on Volcanos* (1825), p. 241–242.

10 Several modern scholars have shown that the uniformitarians and catastrophists had the same view of the uniformity of processes, though disagreeing about the uniformity of rates of processes. See R. Hooykaas, *Catastrophism in Geology, Its*

Differences Between the Scriptural Geologists

The scriptural geologists we have studied were an eclectic group. Young, Fairholme, and Murray were Presbyterians and members of the Church of Scotland. Though I could not discover it, Rhind may have been also. The others were probably all members of the Church of England, though I am not sure about Ure, Penn, and de Johnsone. Fairholme, Murray, Young, Rhind, and Ure were Scottish; the rest were Englishmen. Fairholme, Murray, Ure, Rhind, and Penn were laymen; the rest were clergymen. Three (Murray, Ure, and Rhind) earned their livelihood from their scientific work; for the others it was an avocation, though in the case of Fairholme and Young, and to a lesser extent Gisborne, the study of nature consumed a very large portion of their time. Fairholme, Best, and Cockburn were wealthy, some were middle class, while others (Bugg and Cole) had quite limited financial resources.

Within the framework of a recent six-day creation and global Flood, they had many differences of opinion about the interpretation of some of the minor details of the geological and biblical records, and in a few instances openly disagreed with each other. For example, regarding geology, they did not all agree on the climatic, geographical, and geological effects of the Flood. Penn, Fairholme (in 1833), and Gisborne rejected the idea of a drastic global climatic change and Bugg was not sure, whereas Ure, Young, Murray, and Rhind all believed the pre-Flood world was generally tropical. Penn, Ure, and Fairholme (in 1833) attributed much of the secondary formations to the processes of nature operating during the roughly 1,600 years between creation and the Flood. On the other hand, Bugg, Young, Murray, Gisborne, Rhind, and Fairholme (in 1837) attributed most of the secondary and tertiary formations to the work of the Flood. Similarly, Penn, Bugg, Fairholme, and Young all rejected Buckland's theory of Kirkdale Cave, whereas Ure accepted it. Also, while most of the scriptural geologists were absolutely convinced of the recency of creation (i.e., approximately 6,000 years ago), Rhind and Best were somewhat hesitant in expressing that belief.

Although there was much overlap, they did not cover precisely the same ground in their arguments against the old-earth theories. Rather, many of them focussed on different aspects of the debate, though it does not appear that they consciously collaborated to any significant extent. They differed, too, on their interpretation of some of the details of Genesis; for example, whether the Septuagint or Hebrew Old Testament gives the correct chronology from Adam to Abraham, or whether the sun, moon, and stars were created on day 4 of creation week or on day 1 and only became visible on day 4. Further, they disagreed about whether Genesis 2:10–14 was a textual gloss, whether a new creation of plants, and even animals, after the Deluge was suggested by the text, or whether there had ever been rain and rainbows before the Flood. Also, some gave fairly detailed discussions of the creation and flood accounts, while others did not.

They also differed greatly in their geological competence and writing style, as illustrated in the graphs on the following page. I have added the names of the less important scriptural geologists on page 195, all of whom were clergy, in order to give a more representative view of this group of writers.

It is not surprising that these scriptural geologists, who with one accord believed the traditional literal interpretation of the six-day creation, Noah's flood, and the Genesis genealogies, would have some different ideas about how precisely this view could be reconciled with the strata of the geological record (e.g., where in the secondary formations was the pre-Flood/Flood boundary). Given the complex nature of the subject and the limits of any

---

Scientific Character in Relation to Actualism and Uniformitarianism (1970), and Martin J.S. Rudwick, "The Principle of Uniformity," *History of Science*, vol. I (1962), p. 82–86.

Also, the distinction between uniformitarians and catastrophists was blurred in the case of many. Nevertheless, they remained two competing schools of geological thought. See Walter Cannon, "The Uniformitarian-Catastrophist Debate," *ISIS*, vol. LI (1960), p. 38–55. By 1870, Lyell's uniformitarian view had become accepted by almost all geologists, at least in Britain. See Joseph Prestwich, *Collected Papers on Some Controverted Questions of Geology* (1895), preface and 1–18.

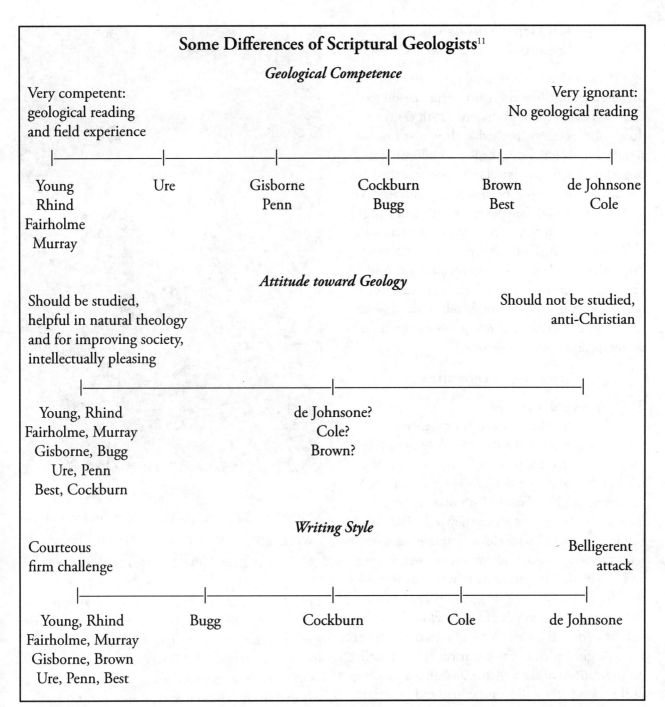

Some Differences of Scriptural Geologists[11]

Geological Competence

Very competent: geological reading and field experience — Very ignorant: No geological reading

Very competent					Very ignorant
Young Rhind Fairholme Murray	Ure	Gisborne Penn	Cockburn Bugg	Brown Best	de Johnsone Cole

Attitude toward Geology

Should be studied, helpful in natural theology and for improving society, intellectually pleasing — Should not be studied, anti-Christian

Should be studied		Should not be studied
Young, Rhind Fairholme, Murray Gisborne, Bugg Ure, Penn Best, Cockburn	de Johnsone? Cole? Brown?	

Writing Style

Courteous firm challenge — Belligerent attack

Courteous				Belligerent
Young, Rhind Fairholme, Murray Gisborne, Brown Ure, Penn, Best	Bugg	Cockburn	Cole	de Johnsone

one individual's knowledge, as well as the relatively small amount of collective geological knowledge at the time and the strong debates going on between the catastrophists and uniformitarians in the late 1820s and 1830s, such an imprecision of the scriptural geologists' theories is perfectly understandable. We should therefore not expect them to be any more monolithic in the details of their views than were their catastrophist or uniformitarian opponents, whether deist or Christian.

11 Attempting to plot these men on such graphs is admittedly a very subjective and rather dangerous exercise, but I think the benefit of the attempt outweigh the dangers. The extensive quotes used in this book (and in the thesis) serve as a partially objective control by which the reader can assess my interpretations. The definition of competance is based on contemporary 19th century standards, as discussed earlier in this book. On the question of whether geology should be studied or not, the study of geology means not only the classifying of minerals, strata, fossils, etc., but also the inferring of the physical causes and sequence of events which produced the rock layers and fossils.

Key Objections of the Scriptural Geologists

The fact that the scriptural geologists did not present a compelling alternative explanation to every old-earth claim in the early 19th century does not necessarily imply that they raised no significant objections or made no philosophical contributions to geological reasoning worthy of consideration. In spite of their many differences in argumentation, there were a number of major objections which several or many of the scriptural geologists raised. These objections fell into two categories: theological and geological. A consideration of these shows that these men were not quibbling over insignificant details or dead issues long before resolved, but were raising objections on important points of debate.

Theological Objections

The Ignoring of Scripture

All the scriptural geologists explicitly or implicitly complained about the old-earth geologists' superficial treatment or complete ignoring of relevant Scripture, particularly the Flood account in Genesis and the Fourth Commandment in Exodus 20:8–11, even when they (e.g., Buckland, Cuvier, Sedgwick) were clearly attempting to defend the Scriptures or were asserting that Scripture and old-earth geological theory were not incompatible. The scriptural geologists believed that a local Flood or a tranquil universal Flood, which left little (only the superficial diluvial deposits) or no geological effects, was inconsistent with biblical indications of the violence and global extent of the Flood. They also were convinced that the Bible clearly taught that the Flood was unique in its duration, extent, and divine purpose (to destroy not only almost all people, but also most plants and animals as well as the surface of the whole earth), rather than being one of a number of rare floods occurring in the natural course of earth history, as many of their geological opponents interpreted it to have been. While old-earth geologists may have thought the Flood was penal in some sense, they did not emphasize this fact, as the scriptural geologists did. Sedgwick's vague allusion to the Flood was typical of the old-earth geologists' view: "And what has happened, again and again, from the most ancient, up to the most modern periods in the natural history of the earth, may have happened once during the few thousand years that man has been living on its surface."[12] Furthermore, nearly all the scriptural geologists

Reverend Samuel Best (1802–1873), a scriptural geologist who compromised with millions of years after Darwin's book was published in 1859.

12 See Adam Sedgwick, "Address to the Geological Society," *Philosophical Magazine*, N.S. vol. IX, no. 52 (1831), p. 315. See also John Phillips, *Illustrations of the Geology of Yorkshire* (1829-36), I: p. 16–30 (especially p. 28–30), where Phillips discussed the Flood at length, but did not refer to God or judgment, nor did he distinguish it from other earlier major floods, except by the fact that the Flood was universal in extent.

In a similar approach, Lyell viewed the Flood as tranquil and doubted its universality. See Charles Lyell, *Principles of Geology* (1830–33), III: p. 271–274. In Vol. I, p. 89, he displays a most convoluted and bizarre logic about past and future geological events when he says, "If it could have been shown that a certain combination of circumstances would at some

contended that the Fourth Commandment in Exodus 20 severely militated against both the day-age theory and the gap theory, but this text was almost universally ignored by their opponents.

Regardless of the correctness of their own interpretations of relevant Scriptures, their criticisms were valid that their geological opponents completely ignored or superficially interpreted the relevant Scriptures when asserting the harmony between Genesis and geology. For example, in none of the editions of Cuvier's *Theory of the Earth* did he deal with the biblical text in any direct way, although he did refer to Scripture generally and defended the post-Flood biblical chronology against the exaggerated Hindu chronology. Likewise, Cuvier's Scottish commentator, Robert Jameson, did not refer to any scriptural texts in either his preface or his appendix to the English editions, even though he used Cuvier's theory in general support of the truth of Genesis.

Buckland, an ordained Anglican clergyman and Oxford geologist, only vaguely referred to Genesis 1–11 in discussing the Flood in his *Vindiciae Geologicae* (1820) and although briefly mentioning the gap theory and day-age theory he did not discuss Exodus 20:11.[13] In his *Reliquiae Diluvianae* (1823) he made virtually no mention of Scripture as he defended the Flood. Similarly, although he devoted the first chapter of volume one of his 1836 *Bridgewater Treatise* to the relation of geology to Scripture, he dismissed the Flood as geologically insignificant in just two separate paragraphs and without any reference to Scripture. In a paragraph treatment of Exodus 20:11 he discussed the meaning of *asah* (the Hebrew word for "made") but did not address the verse with reference to the meaning of "day" in Genesis 1, as virtually all the scriptural geologists did.[14]

In 1825, Sedgwick (also an ordained Anglican geologist) "carefully abstained from any allusion to the sacred records" when arguing that geological evidence of worldwide diluvial detritus demonstrated that a recent global Flood had engulfed the earth.[15] In his recantation of this view (after his conversion to Lyell's uniformitarianism) six years later, he likewise made no reference to scriptural texts.[16] Nor did he discuss the Genesis record in the geological section of his 1834 sermon with explanatory notes, *Discourse on the University*, where he discussed biblical issues and made some negative remarks about scriptural geologists. The same is true of the 1850 edition. In fact, Marston observed that during his entire lifetime Sedgwick never clearly explained his view of how geology could be harmonized with Genesis, though he was obviously confident that it did.[17]

Conybeare (yet another Anglican cleric and geologist) discussed the relation of geology to scriptural revelation in the introduction to *Outlines of the Geology of England and Wales* (1822), but he did not cite a single scriptural passage either in the text or the footnotes.[18] In his 1834

---

future period produce a crisis in the subterranean action, we should certainly have had no right to oppose our experience for the last three thousand years as an argument against the probability of such occurrences in past ages; but it is not pretended that such a combination can be foreseen. In speculating on catastrophes by water, we may certainly anticipate great floods in future, and we may therefore presume that they have happened again and again in past times. . . . Notwithstanding, therefore, that we have not witnessed within the last three thousand years the devastation by deluge of a large continent, yet, as we may predict the future occurrence of such catastrophes, we are authorized to regard them as part of the present order of Nature, and they may be introduced into geological speculations respecting the past, provided we do not imagine them to have been more frequent and general than we expect them to be in time to come."

13 William Buckland, *Vindiciae Geologicae* (1820), p. 22–31, 35–39.

14 On the Flood, see William Buckland, *Bridgewater Treatise* (1836), I: p. 16–17, 94–95 (footnote); on Exodus 20:11 see I: p. 32–33. Volume one (p. 22–26) also contained a lengthy footnote by Oxford Old Testament professor Edward Pusey, but this only focused on a few words and verses in Genesis 1, with likewise no reference to Genesis 6–9 or Exodus 20:8–11.

15 Adam Sedgwick, "On Diluvial Formations," *Annals of Philosophy*, N.S. vol. X (1825), p. 34.

16 Adam Sedgwick, "Address to the Geological Society," *Philosophical Magazine*, N.S. vol. IX, no. 52 (1831), p. 314–315.

17 V. Paul Marston, "Science and Meta-science in the Work of Adam Sedgwick" (1984, Open University Ph.D. Thesis), p. 528–543.

18 See William Conybeare and William Phillips, *Outlines of the Geology of England and Wales* (1822), p. l–lxi. Here he remarked on the gap theory, the day-age theory, the Flood, and the age of the earth, quoting heavily from Buckland, Cuvier, and Bishop Sumner in support of his views. At this time, Conybeare believed in a global catastrophic Flood, but one which did not produce the secondary sedimentary rock formations.

response in the *Christian Observer* to an anonymous layman who was defending the scriptural geology view, he likewise made no references to any particular biblical texts, all the while insisting that geology did not contradict Scripture.[19]

In asserting that creation was a continuing process lasting at least 600,000 years and that the Bible's plain language indicated a global tranquil Flood, Macculloch did not refer to a single verse of Scripture, even though the full title of his two-volume work on geology said that he would give an explanation of geology's connection with Scripture.[20]

Mantell had an anonymous Anglican clergyman write the 13-page introduction to his *Fossils of the South Downs: Geology of Sussex* (1822) to deal with the relation of geological theory and Genesis. But it referred only to some of the verses in Genesis 1, as he argued for a mixture of the day-age and gap theories, ignoring completely the Flood account and Exodus 20:8–11. Mantell devoted only three pages in *The Wonders of Geology* (1839) to the topic of the harmony of geology and Scripture and made no reference to Genesis.[21]

So the scriptural geologists were accurate in their complaint that their opponents, and especially those who professed to defend the idea of a global Flood and/or to harmonize geology and Scripture, generally failed to engage explicitly with the biblical text. Their opponents probably avoided this, at least in part, because of their conviction (to which most of them referred) that they were heeding the lessons of the Galileo affair and following the "two books" methodology advocated by Francis Bacon (i.e., to keep the study of the natural world separate from that of scriptural revelation). It is more likely that they avoided the text because they had no idea how to make the text fit their theories. Nevertheless, it was still inconsistent for them to tell their readers that their old-earth theories did not conflict with Scripture, when they never carefully looked at what the relevant Scripture passages said. While some Christian old-earth geologists may have thought (as Sedgwick definitely did) that it was too early to try to put scriptural truth together with geological theory, the scriptural geologists felt that because of the infant state of geology (to be discussed shortly) it was premature and, in fact, philosophically unsound to pull geology and Scripture apart in the first place.

The Problem of Evil

A second important and recurring theological objection to old-earth theories related to the problem of evil. The scriptural geologists believed that according to Scripture the whole creation was originally perfect, but then was cursed by God at the fall of man and judged again at the Flood. In their view, the notion of millions of years of revolutions and animal extinctions before the fall in sin (and even before the creation of man) was in direct contradiction to this plain teaching of Scripture.[22] Closely related to this, several scriptural geologists[23] also argued that a long process of gradual creation or creation followed by sporadic catastrophes with new acts of creation over the course of millions of years was contrary to the nature of God revealed in Scripture. If God created in such manners over long ages, it would reflect very poorly on His wisdom, power, and goodness, they contended.[24]

19 William Conybeare, "Rev. W.D. Conybeare in Reply to a Layman, on Geology," *Christian Observer*, vol. XXXIV (1834), p. 306–309. By this time Conybeare clearly no longer believed in a geologically significant, universal Flood.

20 John Macculloch, *A System of Geology with a Theory of the Earth and an Explanation of Its Connexion with the Sacred Records* (1831), 2 volumes. His idea of continuous creation appears on I: p. 505–507 and II: p. 460–461, and his views on the Noachian flood are on I: p. 408–409, I: p. 445–446 and II: p. 33–34.

21 Mantell, *The Wonders of Geology*, fourth edition), I: p. 5–7.

22 See James Mellor Brown, *Reflections on Geology* (1838), p. 43–48; George Young, *Scriptural Geology* (1838), p. 41–42 and George Young, *Geological Survey* (1828), p. 342; John Murray, *Portrait of Geology* (1838), p. 401–402; George Bugg, *Scriptural Geology* (1826), I: p. 143–147; Andrew Ure, *Geology* (1829), p. 505–506

23 See Granville Penn, *Comparative Estimate* (1825), I: p. 124–127; James Mellor Brown, *Reflections on Geology* (1838), p. 26; Ure, *Geology* (1829), p. 505–506; Cockburn *Remarks on the Geological Lectures* (1839), p. 9–10 and 13–14; Bugg, *Scriptural Geology*, I: p. 142 and 318–319.

24 Modern creationists are arguing the same thing. For a popular treatment, see these Web articles: <www.icr.org/pubs/imp/imp-191.htm> and <www.answersingenesis.org/docs/4126.asp>. For scholarly discussions see James Stambaugh, "Creation and the Problem of Evil" (paper given at the ETS national meeting, Nov. 17, 1995) and "Creation and the Curse" (paper given at the ETS Far West regional meeting, April 26, 1996). Both papers can be obtained from the author at Michigan Theological Seminary, 41550 Ann Arbor Tr., Plymouth, MI 48170.

Their opponents did not address this problem of evil in the non-human creation until the late 1830s (if they discussed it at all), long after the old-earth view had become dominant in geology and in the Church. Buckland first addressed it in his *Bridgewater Treatise* (1836), attributing the death (even mass extinction) of animals to God's wise plan of creation (i.e., a long series of revolutions, renovations, and creations).[25] Actually, he focused his discussion on the role of carnivores in maintaining the balance of nature and, by the elimination of the weak and sick, increasing animal enjoyment (of the survivors, that is). In defense of his view he made no mention of the Fall or of Scripture generally. Three years later, in response to the criticisms of scriptural geologists,[26] he preached a sermon at Oxford University in which he argued that there was no foundation in Scripture for believing that animals were included in the sentence of death at the Fall.[27] He defended this by proposing alternative interpretations to the passages most often cited by his opponents. He argued that Romans 5:12–18, 1 Corinthians 15:21, Romans 8:19–23 and Colossians 1:23 referred only to the death and suffering of man, and Genesis 3:17–19 referred only to man and plants. He interpreted Isaiah 11:6–9 figuratively, which in any case, he said, referred to the future and so was irrelevant to our understanding of the past.

In the same year, John Pye Smith responded to scriptural geologists on this topic. He primarily used philosophical arguments about the necessity of carnivores and animal death for the perpetuation of the present biological system. But he also gave some scriptural arguments similar to those of Buckland.[28]

With respect to how this death in the animal world over millions of years was consistent with the nature of God, the few old-earth proponents who even dealt with the issue focused on how the design features of the carnivores revealed the creative intelligence of God, but they ignored the ethical issues.[29]

So, the scriptural geologists were raising serious biblical and theological objections to the old-earth views, but these objections were largely ignored by those who insisted that there was no conflict between old-earth theories and the Bible.

Geological Objections

The geologically informed scriptural geologists also similarly cited several geological phenomena which, they argued, militated against the old-earth theories and supported their view that the stratigraphical record was consistent with a recent creation and global catastrophic Noachian flood. It is important to understand their interpretations of the geological evidence, if their role in the history of science is to be accurately assessed. However, to correctly understand why their young-earth arguments were ignored or rejected by their contemporaries, we need to see these key objections in the historical context of the geological understanding and debate at the time.

Insensible Transitions

Young and Fairholme especially, and to a lesser extent Gisborne,[30] argued that insensible transitions

25 Buckland, *Bridgewater Treatise*, I: p. 129–135. As noted earlier, several other authors of the *Bridgewater Treatises* also interpreted the apparent evil in the physical world as a good part of the creation as it was made by God. See John M. Robson, "The Fiat and Finger of God: The Bridgewater Treatises," in *Victorian Faith in Crisis* (Stanford, CA: Stanford University Press, 1990), edited by Richard J. Helmstadter and Bernard Lightman, especially pages 103–113.

26 Though Buckland mentioned no names, this probably included Brown's book, *Reflections on Geology*, which was largely devoted to criticisms of Buckland's writings.

27 William Buckland, *An Inquiry Whether the Sentence of Death Pronounced at the Fall of Man Included the Whole Animal Creation or Was Restricted to the Human Race* (1839).

28 John Pye Smith, *The Relation Between the Holy Scriptures and Geological Science* (1839), p. 96–100, 294–298, 361–375.

29 For a thorough historical analysis of this problem see Thane Hutcherson Ury, "The Evolving Face of God as Creator: Early Nineteenth-Century Traditionalist and Accommodationist Theodical Responses in British Religious Thought to Paleonatural Evil in the Fossil Record" (Ph.D. dissertation, Andrews University, 2001), which is presently being prepared for publication under the same title. A summary of this thesis was presented by Ury in a paper by the same title at the 2002 annual meeting of the Evangelical Theological Society, Nov. 20, 2002, in Toronto, Canada. Ury argues that the traditional Christian understanding of God's goodness and justice had to be redefined by those who sought to accommodate millions of years of animal death before Adam with the biblical teaching about God and creation.

30 Thomas Gisborne (a well-known and respected evangelical Anglican pastor who was well-read in geology but had no field experience), *Considerations on Geology* (1837), p. 16–18, 30, 50.

between the different mineralogical formations were a dominant feature of the geological record. This characteristic of one kind of mineral deposit gradually changing into another kind, without evidence of erosion or soil at the transition line, shows that the strata were deposited in rapid succession (as expected in a year-long global flood), while the subjacent strata were still rather soft and moist. Therefore, they reasoned, the notion of long ages during deposition of a single mineralogical layer (the uniformitarian view) or between deposition of two different strata (the catastrophist view) is erroneous.

Many geological writers recorded their observations of this geological feature. William Smith alluded to this fact many times in his 1816 work on identifying strata by their fossils. The mineralogical transitions were so smooth, said Smith, that frequently the fossils provided the only means of dividing them.[31] In describing the secondary formations from the transition rocks up through the Oolite found in Gloucestershire and Somerset, Thomas Weaver frequently remarked on the gradual intermingling, or "reciprocal incorporation," of different minerals at the contact boundary of two different adjacent formations.[32] Buckland and Conybeare described how the strata of the Greywacke up to the coal measures and the New Red Sandstone up to the Oolite "graduate so insensibly" into each other as to make it very difficult to assign the precise limits of each.[33] In 1832 Conybeare described how frequently the tertiary formations "pass insensibly into the subjacent secondaries."[34] In tracing the strata between the Primary and Oolite formations in northern Scotland, Sedgwick and Murchison often referred to the way the different formations generally graduated into each other so that it was impossible to draw a precise line between them.[35] Buckland wrote in 1836:

> [The strata] are arranged under the old divisions of primary, transition, secondary, and tertiary series, more from a sense of the convenience of this long received arrangement, than from the reality of any strongly defined boundaries by which the strata, on the confines of each series, are separated from one another.[36]

Lyell repeatedly remarked on these insensible transitions in his discussion and rejection of Cuvier's theory of the Paris Basin.[37] Whewell noted that this was an important line of evidence used by Lyell and other uniformitarians to ridicule and reject the catastrophist theory.[38]

These writers, however, made few, if any, inferences from this fact about the time involved in the depositional process. In contrast, some of the geologically knowledgeable scriptural geologists were attempting to improve or correct geological understanding by highlighting this generally

31 William Smith, *Strata Identified by Organized Fossils* (1816), p. 1, 9–11, 13, 15, 21, 27, 32.

32 Thomas Weaver, "Geological Observations on Part of Gloucestershire and Somersetshire," *Transactions of the Geological Society*, 2nd ser., vol. I, pt. 1 (1822), p. 323–324, 339, 343, 349, 360.

33 William Buckland and William Conybeare, "Observations on the Southwestern Coal District of England," *Transactions of the Geological Society*, 2nd ser., vol. I, pt. 1 (1822), p. 211–212, 242–243, 264–280, 306, 315.

34 William D. Conybeare, "Report on the Progress, Actual State, and Ulterior Prospects of Geological Science," *Report of the BAAS: 1831–32* (1833), p. 399.

35 Adam Sedgwick and Roderick I. Murchison, "On the Structure and Relation of the Deposits Contained Between the Primary Rocks and the Oolitic Series in the North of Scotland," *Transactions of the Geological Society*, 2nd ser., vol. III (1835), p. 130, 132, 141, 147, 150.

36 Buckland, *Bridgewater Treatise*, I: p. 38–39.

37 Lyell, *Principles of Geology*, III: p. 244–249.

38 Whewell, *The History of the Inductive Sciences*, III: p. 614–615. He wrote, "Thus, in the cases where there had appeared in one country a sudden and violent transition from one stratum to the next, it was found, that by tracing the formations into other countries, the chasm between them was filled up by intermediate strata; so that the passage became as gradual and gentle as any other step in the series. For example, though conglomerates, which in some parts of England overlie the coal-measures, appear to have been produced by a complete discontinuity in the series of changes; yet in the coal-fields of Yorkshire, Durham, and Cumberland, the transition is smoothed down in such a way that the two formations pass into each other. A similar passage is observed in central Germany, and in Thuringia is so complete that the coal-measures have sometimes been considered as subordinate to the *todtliegendes*."

observed fact and showing its relevance to the theoretical question of the age of the earth.

This famous polystrate fossil, found in a quarry in Craigleith, Scotland, in 1826, is imbedded in a 200-foot thick formation of alternating sandstone and shale.

Polystrate Fossil Trees

Young, Fairholme, and Rhind argued that fossil trees found in many places in the geological record, though most notably associated with coal formations, and generally traversing more than one stratum and often many strata, were evidence that the strata were formed by rapid deposition of transported mineral and organic debris. Since the formations where the polystrate trees were found were analogous in their alternating mineralogical content to other formations where no trees were found, the scriptural geologists saw these trees as strong evidence that most of the strata were formed by the Noachian flood, and were not the remains of successive forests that had grown where they had been gradually buried by successive submersions over many ages.

The interpretation of these polystrate fossils was much debated by naturalists and geologists in the 1820s and 1830s.[39] Some favored the allochthonous theory, which said that the trees had been ripped up, transported by water, deposited in their present positions and rapidly surrounded by sediments.[40] Nicholas Wood stated that most of the fossil trees found by 1831 seemed to demand this conclusion.[41]

Others argued for the autochthonous theory, that the trees had been buried where they grew, even as they grew.[42] Some proponents of this theory, however, believed the evidence did point to rapid burial.[43] Buckland stated in 1840 that the

39 Nicolaas A. Rupke, *The Great Chain of History: William Buckland and the English School of Geology 1814–1849* (1983), p. 195–196.

40 S.P. Hildreth, "Notice of Fossil Trees, Near Gallipolis, Ohio," *Philosophical Magazine*, N.S., vol. II, no. 10 (Oct. 1827), p. 311–313; H.L. Pattinson, "On the Fossil Trees Found in Jefferies Rake Vein at Derwent Lead Mine in the County of Durham," *Philosophical Magazine*, N.S., vol. VII, no. 39 (March 1830), p. 185–189; Phillips, *Illustrations of the Geology of Yorkshire*, I: p. 95; John Phillips, *Treatise on Geology* (1837–39), I: p. 160; John Lindley and William Hutton, *The Fossil Flora of Great Britain* (1831–37), II: p. xx–xxi; Henry Witham, "A Description of a Fossil Tree Discovered in the Quarry of Craigleith," *Transactions of the Royal Society of Edinburgh*, vol. XII, pt. 1 (1834), p. 147–52. Young, Fairholme, and Rhind all referred to this last discovery. Witham wrote as if the evidence pointed to transport by flood waters, but did not consider this conclusion proven.

41 Nicholas Wood, "Account of Some Fossil Stems of Trees," *Transactions of the Natural History Society of Northumberland*, vol. I (1831), p. 205–214, especially 205.

42 Henry Witham, "On the Vegetation of the First Period of an Ancient World," *Philosophical Magazine*, N.S., vol. VII, no. 37 (Jan. 1830), p. 23–31; James Smith, "Account of Fossil Trees in the Attitude of Growth in the Coal Measures Near Glasgow," *Philosophical Magazine*, 3rd ser., vol. VII, no. 42 (Dec. 1835), p. 487.

43 Robert Bakewell, *Introduction to Geology* (1838, fifth edition), p. 180–181.

debate was still continuing and that most fossil trees showed evidence of having been transported into their present positions; in his own experience, the number of cases of fossilized trees or smaller erect plants that appeared to have grown in their native place were "very few."[44] Apart from Bakewell, I could find no other old-earth geologist who noted the fact[45] that the trees often traversed many strata (even though old-earth geologists frequently included drawings showing this fact) and discussed the inferences and responded to a scriptural geologist's argument, such as Fairholme's in *Philosophical Magazine*.[46] Buckland, for example, devoted 27 pages in his 1836 *Bridgewater Treatise* to the subject of fossil trees, without referring to this polystrate feature of the fossils.[47] Mantell stated that such trees often traverse many strata, but he made no comment on any theoretical inferences regarding time.[48] Ultimately, the "growth *in situ*" theory prevailed, though modern old-earth neo-catastrophists and young-earth creationists are again arguing for the old allochthonous theory of catastrophic uprooting, transport, and rapid burial.[49]

Closely related to these fossil trees was coal, which the scriptural geologists, such as Young, Murray, Fairholme, and Rhind, attributed to the Flood. Although by the late 1820s the vegetable origin of coal was conclusively proven (and the scriptural geologists agreed), the mode of formation (either by buried debris which had been transported and deposited by water, or by buried peat-bogs and forests which grew *in situ)* was still an "obscure and difficult question" in the early 1840s, though the peat-bog theory was gaining dominance.[50]

Shells and Dating the Strata

Since shells made up the vast majority of fossils, they had a great, if not singular, importance for old-earth geologists in working out their history of the earth. For example, William Smith, the "Father of English stratigraphy," based his depiction of the geological column primarily on shells.[51] In 1828, Lyell worked out his

44 William Buckland, "Geological Society Anniversary Address of the Reverend Prof. Buckland, Pres., Feb. 21, 1840," *Philosophical Magazine*, 3rd ser., vol. XVII, no. 113 (Jan. 1841), p. 512–513.

45 Bakewell noted this fact in his *An Introduction to Geology*, p. 180–181.

46 George Fairholme, "Some Observations on the Nature of Coal," *Philosophical Magazine*, 3rd ser., vol. III, no. 16 (Oct. 1833), p. 245–252.

47 Buckland, *Bridgewater Treatise*, I: p. 469–496.

48 Mantell, *The Wonders of Geology*, II:p. 630–631.

49 Ager used these polystrate fossils as part of his argument for the rapid deposition of much of the stratigraphic record. See Derek Ager, *The Nature of the Stratigraphical Record* (New York: Wiley, 1981), p. 42–43, and *The New Catastrophism* (Cambridge; New York, NY: Cambridge University Press, 1993), p. 47–50. A similar view on these fossils is found in David Raup "Geology and Creationism," *Bulletin of the Field Museum of Natural History*, vol. 54 (1983), p. 17, 22. Both of these well-known geologists think the trees speak of rapid burial. However, they do not discuss the fact that the trees frequently transverse two or more strata, though they both include pictures of such trees which illustrate this fact.

Like their 19th century counterparts, modern young-earth geologists also consider these polystrate trees as key evidence in their view that the Flood caused most of the geological record. See, for example, John D. Morris, *The Young Earth* (Green Forest, AR: Master Books, 1994), p. 100–103, and Steven Austin's video *Mount St. Helens: Explosive Evidence for Catastrophe* (1994).

50 William Buckland, "Address Delivered on the Anniversary, 19 Feb. 1841," *Proceedings of the Geological Society*, vol. III, pt. 2, no. 81 (1841), p. 487–489.

51 William Smith, *Stratigraphical System of Organized Fossils* (1817), p. vi and "Geological Table" after page xi. This table is reproduced in T. Sheppard, *Proceedings of the Yorkshire Geological and Polytechnic Society*, N.S. vol. XIX (1914–22), opposite page 137.

interpretation of the tertiary (on which the first and later editions of his *Principles of Geology* depended) solely on the basis of shells.[52] Buckland stated that fossil shells were "of vast importance in investigating the records of the changes that have occurred upon the surface of our globe" and that "in fact without these [organic remains], the proofs of the lapse of such long periods as geology shows to have been occupied in the formation of the strata of the earth, would have been comparatively few and indecisive."[53] Geologist James Smith said in 1838 that judging the age of a deposit purely on conchological considerations was a sound rule of geological reasoning.[54] These so-called index fossils then, as now,[55] were of critical importance as evidence for the old-earth theories.[56]

To this use of fossil shells in dating the strata, Bugg, Young, Rhind, and Penn raised objections regarding both the uncertainties in taxonomic classification of shells and the ambiguities about the geological distribution of the shells. But they were not the only objectors. In both the 1812 and the 1831 editions of his *Theory of the Earth*, Cuvier rejected the use of shells as a means of reconstructing earth history, because differences in fossil species in the strata may have been the result of slight changes in salinity or temperature of the water or some other accidental causes, and testaceous animals were still too little known to confidently claim that some were extinct.[57] From 1808 to 1813, Beudant (to whose work George Young referred) had experimentally shown that marine shell creatures could adjust to life in fresh water and, similarly, freshwater shellfish could become accustomed to life in the sea if the change in salinity was gradual as in the brackish waters of river deltas.[58] Macculloch referred to this and other observations about fish and shell creatures when in 1824 he cautioned geologists about the use of these fossils to distinguish freshwater geological formations from those of marine origin.[59] Six years later, Macculloch said that the use of fossils to identify, correlate and date strata from different locations was "groundless" and "nearly, if not entirely, useless."[60]

In 1819, Greenough, then president of the Geological Society, conceived Cuvier's theory of the Paris Basin to be open to "insurmountable objections," one of which was the difficulty

52 Charles Lyell, *The Antiquity of Man* (1863), p. 3–5.

53 Buckland, *Bridgewater Treatise*, I: p. 110–112.

54 James Smith, "On the Last Changes in the Relative Levels of the Land and Sea in the British Islands," *Memoirs of the Wernerian Natural History Society*, vol. VIII (1838), p. 84–85.

55 John Thackray, *The Age of the Earth*, (London: Institute of Geological Science, 1980), p. 10, 13.

56 Other old-earth geologists who said the same were: R.C. Taylor, "Geological Arrangement of British Fossil Shells," *Magazine of Natural History*, vol. II, no. 6 (1829), p. 26–41; Buckland, *Bridgewater Treatise*, I: p. 110; Phillips, *Treatise on Geology*, I: p. 77–78; Mantell, *The Wonders of Geology*, I: p. 202.

On the continuing dominant use of shells in the arrangement and relative dating of the strata see Thackray, *The Age of the Earth*, p. 8–9, 10, 13. Referring to his figure 21 on p. 10 (showing only shell creatures) Thackray says (p. 8–9), "Two ideas form the basis of [time] correlation [of the strata] using fossils today: first that all members of a species evolve together over their whole geographical range, so that evolutionary changes can be regarded as taking place at the same time wherever they occur, and second that evolution is a process which does not repeat itself, so that once a species or fauna has gone, it will never reappear. For a fossil to be useful in time-correlation it must be widely distributed in a variety of rock types, reasonably common and easy to recognize, and a member of a well-defined, rapidly evolving lineage. No fossil satisfies all these requirements and all have their particular problems. The most useful are those like graptolites and ammonites which moved freely in the surface waters and are therefore found over wide areas in many different rock types. Less adequate are those like corals, gastropods, and bivalves, which evolved slowly and which were confined to a narrow range of environments. Widely used fossils, including some of the unfamiliar microscopic forms which are very important in borehole correlation, are shown in figure 21."

57 Georges Cuvier, *Theory of the Earth* (1813), p. 58–60; Georges Cuvier, *Researches on Fossil Bones* (1834), p. 46–47.

58 F.S. Beudant, "Extract from a Memoir Read to the Institute on the 13th of May 1816 on the Possibility of Making the Molluscae of Fresh Water Live in Salt Water, and Vice Versa," *Philosophical Magazine*, vol. XLVIII, no. 22 (1816), p. 223–227.

59 John Macculloch, "Hints on the Possibility of Changing the Residence of Certain Fishes from Salt Water to Fresh," *Quarterly Journal of Science*, vol. XVII, no. 34 (1824), p. 209–231 (especially 230–231).

60 John Macculloch, "Organic Remains," in *Edinburgh Encyclopaedia*, edited by David Brewster, Vol. XV (1830), p. 753–754. See also Macculloch, *A System of Geology*, I: p. 422–428, 453.

of confidently distinguishing fresh-water and marine shells.[61]

Charpentier, one of the leading geologists in Europe, argued in 1825 that only the relative position of strata could indicate the relative ages of the rocks, because knowledge of fossils and their distribution in the strata were not sufficiently precise to use them as an index for dating.[62] Also, in 1825 the conchologist William Wood decried the "extreme multiplication of the genera, rather to increase than remove the difficulty of determining the species."[63] In an article on *mollusca* in the *Edinburgh Encyclopaedia* (1830), John Fleming remarked on the persisting difficulties in classifications of shell creatures into species, genera, and even the correct orders.[64] The next year, De la Beche expressed strong caution in using shells to date strata, because of the considerable errors and confusion in the catalogs of fossil shells.[65]

In 1833, John Gray (1800–75), a leading conchologist at the British Museum, recorded the many difficulties and errors that had been made in classifying shell creatures based on the features of the shells, which far too often resulted in the creation of many different species and even genus names to identify what in nature was a single species.[66] Two years later, his further published observations were explicitly applied to geology. He stated that geologists had built their theories on much fallacious information about the species and genera of testaceous mollusca and he seriously called into question the propriety of using shells to distinguish and date strata.[67]

In the five editions of his *Introduction to Geology*, published and revised between 1815 and 1838, the respected geologist Robert Bakewell[68] repeatedly expressed his conviction that many of his fellow geologists relied too much on shells in their interpretations of the rocks; both in identifying distant, non-contiguous formations and in distinguishing fresh-water from marine deposits. This he deemed unwise because of the still too-limited knowledge of shell creatures and the continuing evidence of much erroneous classification of them, especially the multiplication of different species and genera.[69] One reviewer of Bakewell's 1828 third edition apparently agreed with him about the dangers in applying conchological knowledge to stratigraphy.[70]

---

61 George Greenough, *A Critical Examination of the First Principles of Geology* (1819), p. 302–304. This criticism of Cuvier was inaccurate, because, as noted above, Cuvier himself cited reasons why shells were not reliable indices and why he built his theory of the earth totally on the basis of quadruped fossils.

62 Jean de Charpentier, "On Fossil Organic Remains as a Means of Distinguishing Rock-formations," *Edinburgh Philosophical Journal*, vol. XII, no. 24 (1825), p. 320–321.

63 William Wood, *Index Testaceologicus; or a Catalogue of Shells, British and Foreign* (1825), p. iv.

64 John Fleming, "Mollusca," *Edinburgh Encyclopaedia* (1830), Vol. XIV, p. 599.

65 Henry De la Beche, *A Geological Manual* (1831), p. v–vi.

66 John E. Gray, "Some Observations on the Economy of Molluscous Animals, and on the Structure of their Shells," *Philosophical Transactions*, vol. CXXIII, pt. 2 (1833), p. 771–819.

67 John E. Gray, "Remarks on the Difficulty of Distinguishing Certain Genera of Testaceous Mollusca by Their Shells Alone, and on the Anomalies in Regard to Habitation Observed in Certain Species," *Philosophical Transactions*, pt. 2 (1835), p. 301–310. A one-page summary of this appeared under the same title in *Philosophical Magazine*, 3rd ser., vol. VII, no. 39 (1835), p. 210.

It is noteworthy that both Gideon Mantell, in his *Wonders of Geology* (1839, second edition), I: p. 202, and John Phillips, in his *Treatise on Geology*, I: p. 78, cited Gray's 1833 article, but not his 1835 article. William Buckland referred to neither article in the various discussions of shells in his *Bridgewater Treatise*.

68 Based on extensive geological field work in Britain, Ireland, and Europe, Bakewell published many geological articles in scientific journals. See *DNB* on Bakewell. His highly successful *Introduction to Geology* was translated into German after the second English edition (1815), and the leading American geologist, Benjamin Silliman, said of the third edition (1829), which became the first American edition, that it was "the most intelligible, attractive, and readable work on geology in the English language." See *Magazine of Natural History*, vol. II, no. 9 (1829), p. 366. Woodward said it was considered to be "undoubtedly the best of the early textbooks" on geology. See Horace B. Woodward, *History of the Geological Society of London* (1907), p. 84.

69 Robert Bakewell, *An Introduction to Geology* (1828, 3rd ed.), p. 44–45 (in this edition he quotes from his 1815 second edition without giving the page numbers therein); (1833, 4th ed.), p. iv–v, 42–43, 565; (1838, 5th ed.), p. 46–47, 397–404, 635.

70 T., Anonymous review of Robert Bakewell's *An Introduction to Geology* (third edition), *Magazine of Natural History*, vol. 1, no. 4 (1829), p. 355–356.

So, the scriptural geologists were raising a serious objection against old-earth theories when they contested the use of shells to date the rocks, either in the catastrophist or uniformitarian view.

Human Fossils

A significant reason that the majority of geologists believed that most of the geological record was deposited long before the creation of man was their conviction that no fossil human bones had been found except in recently formed deposits, and never with extinct animals.[71] Buckland said that "no conclusion is more fully established than the important fact of the total absence of any vestiges of the human species throughout the entire series of geological formations."[72]

Fairholme, Murray, Young, Penn, and Bugg argued that there were several instances which refuted this generally accepted opinion and therefore militated against the old-earth theory. Those instances were fossil human bones found in Guadaloupe; in Kent's Hole (near Torquay, England); near Köstritz (Germany); near Bize, Pondre, Souvignargues, and several other places in France; and near Liège (Belgium). The scriptural geologists reasoned that if fossil man was found with any extinct creatures, it would falsify the idea that any other extinct fossil creatures were necessarily in existence and became extinct before the creation of man.

In other words, just because the dodo bird is now extinct (becoming so in the 18th century) does not mean that dodo birds became extinct before man was created.

At the time, these objections were ignored or dismissed on the contention that the above-mentioned fossils had been erroneously interpreted by the men who discovered them (or by the scriptural geologists who read their published reports).

However, not many years later Lyell argued, in the cases of Kent's Hole and Liège (just as Phillips asserted in the cases of Bize, Durfort, Pondres, and Souvignargues), that the original discoverers (whom the scriptural geologists cited) had indeed been correct about man living, dying, and being buried contemporaneously with now extinct animals.[73] Lyell and Phillips used the evidence of the contemporaneity of man and extinct creatures to prove the great antiquity of man (beyond the biblical chronology), an idea many old-earth proponents in the first half of the century had strenuously resisted.[74] In contrast, the scriptural geologists had used the same evidence earlier to argue against the antiquity of the earth. Lyell was not able to examine all of the physical evidence which had been reported three decades earlier because some of the sites had been destroyed by quarrying. But what he did investigate convinced him that the original investigators had provided "ample evidence" for their conclusions. He explained that the reason geologists back then (including himself) had not been willing to believe the conclusions was that the discoveries "contradict[ed] the general tenor of previous investigations."[75] The scriptural geologists, however, had contended that the reason for unbelief was that the findings contradicted the old-earth *theories*.

In addition, several scriptural geologists (Ure, Rhind, Gisborne[76]) emphasized that the argument for the non-existence of man (or indeed any other creatures) in earlier times, based on the absence of fossil evidence, was philosophically unsound. For

71 See, for example, Conybeare and Phillips, *Outlines of the Geology of England and Wales*, p. lix; Charles Lyell, *Principles of Geology*, I: p. 153–154.

72 Buckland, *Bridgewater Treatise*, I: p. 103.

73 Lyell, *The Antiquity of Man*, p. 62–69, 96–98; John Phillips, *Manual of Geology* (1855), p. 438 (quoted in Anonymous, *Voices from the Rocks* (1857), p. 83–85).

74 This seems to have been for at least two reasons. First, most old-earth geologists in the early 1800s apparently still accepted as literal the Old Testament chronology from Adam to Abraham (though they never explained why this part of Genesis, but not the rest of Genesis 1–11, was to be taken as literal and authoritative). Second, to them considerable evidence indicated that Hindu, Chinese, Egyptian, and other ancient writings (which gave a greater antiquity to man than the Bible did) were not historically reliable and that many other pagan traditions did confirm the Bible. See, for example, Georges Cuvier, *Theory of the Earth*, p. 152–165, and Buckland, *Vindiciae Geologicae*, p. 23.

75 Lyell, *The Antiquity of Man*, p. 68.

76 Gisborne, *Considerations on Geology*, p. 52.

one thing, they argued that since all contemporary creatures do not live in the same ecological habitat, it is unreasonable to expect them to be buried together. Also, geologists had only examined a very small portion of the earth's strata. Furthermore, if during the Flood much of the antediluvian continents had been submerged to become post-diluvian ocean bottoms, most humans would have been buried out of the reach of geological investigation.

But some old-earth geologists also found the argument for non-existence of creatures based on the absence of fossil evidence to be problematic. Phillips said it led to erroneous conclusions about the history of birds.[77] Smith remarked that it would result in false inferences about the history of man in the British Isles.[78] Lyell argued that erroneous conclusions about the history of fishes were produced by such reasoning, and in 1855 he provided a table documenting the previous 100-year history of the gradual discovery of different classes of fossil vertebrates in lower (i.e., older) formations than had been previously expected. He ended the discussion by saying:

> In conclusion, I shall simply express my own conviction that we are still on the mere threshold of our inquiries; and that, as in the last fifty years, so in the next half-century, we shall be called upon repeatedly to modify our first opinions respecting the range in time of the various classes of fossil vertebrata. It would therefore be premature to generalize at the present on the non-existence, or even on the scarcity of vertebrata, whether terrestrial or aquatic, at periods of high antiquity, such as the Silurian or Cambrian.[79]

This is a significant revelation given Buckland's confident assertion in 1836:

> The deeper we descend into the strata of the earth, the higher do we ascend into the archaeological history of past ages of creation. We find successive stages marked by varying forms of animal and vegetable life, and these generally differ more and more widely from existing species, as we go further downwards into the receptacles of the wreck of more ancient creations. When we discover a constant and regular assemblage of organic remains, commencing with one series of strata, and ending with another, which contains a different assemblage, we have herein the surest grounds where on to establish those divisions which are called geological formations, and we find many such divisions succeeding one another, when we investigate the mineral deposits on the surface of the earth.[80]

Lyell's observation seems to be confirmed on a regular basis in our own time. For example, recently paleontologists digging in China and Mongolia have unearthed literally thousands of well-preserved salamanders in rocks supposedly 165 million years old, although previously the earliest they had been found was in rocks estimated to be 65 million years. And they resemble salamanders found today in North America and Asia.[81] Many other such examples could be cited of living creatures with essentially identical fossil counterparts being found lower in the rocks than previously thought.

Infant State of Geology

Lyell's remark above leads us lastly to consider an important contention of many scriptural geologists (e.g., Young, Gisborne,[82] Murray, Bugg, Rhind), namely, that geological knowledge was far too limited in the early 19th century to justify a

---

77 Phillips, *Treatise on Geology*, I: p. 96.

78 James Smith, "On the Last Changes in the Relative Levels of the Land and Sea in the British Islands," *Memoirs of the Wernerian Natural History Society*, vol. VIII (1838), p. 84.

79 Charles Lyell, *Manual of Elementary Geology* (1855), p. 458–463. The quote is from page 463. Lyell, of course, had his own agenda in saying this. At the time he was still very much opposed to the idea of progression (or evolution) in terms of plant and animal history, favoring instead a cyclical uniformity to life. See Stephen J. Gould, *Time's Arrow, Time's Cycle* (1987), p. 132–142, and Ager, *The New Catastrophism*, p. xvii.

80 William Buckland, *Geological and Mineralogical Considerations* (1836), I: p. 113.

81 Jonathan Amos, "Earliest Salamanders Discovered," *BBC News*, March 28, 2003, <news.bbc.co.uk/1/hi/sci/tech/2896407.stm>.

82 Gisborne, *Considerations on Geology*, p. 28–43.

theory of the earth based solely on the geological data. As we have repeatedly seen, they also had a theory of earth history, but the difference was that it was founded on Scripture, which, they believed, provided the infallible historical framework or outline for geology and was well corroborated by many geological facts and indisputably contradicted by none. Although only Penn and Ure discussed Bacon's ideas in any detail, a few others expressed agreement with Penn's argument on first formations, where he dealt with Bacon's ideas. Also, the scriptural geologists contended for Bacon's methodology with respect to the need for a wealth of observational particulars as an inductive basis for sound theoretical generalizations.[83] They felt that the observational data of geology were still exceedingly insufficient.

Again, however, they were not the only ones who were saying that geological science was too young to confidently advance a particular theory of the earth. Many people who were not scriptural geologists remarked on this in the 1820s and 1830s.[84] Conybeare said in his report to the geological section of the BAAS in 1832:

> The great branches of the comparative geology, and comparative palaeontology (or study of fossil remains) of distant countries, much as they have recently advanced, have as yet even a still wider interval to pass over than that which they may have already accomplished, before they shall have obtained that degree of completeness which alone can qualify them to serve as sound bases in any geological theory.
>
> First, as to comparative geology. The very introductory question is yet inadequately answered, Is there or is there not anything like such a general uniformity of type in the series of rock formations in distant countries, that we must conceive them to have resulted from general causes, of almost universal prevalence at the same geological aeras? . . . Two conditions obviously enter into this problem — first, the contemporaneous prevalence and extent of similar geological causes; and secondly, how far these causes, even where active, may have been modified by varying local circumstances. Now, at present, our materials for answering these questions accurately are confined to Europe.[85]

Five years later, in his discussion of the history of geology, the leading historian and philosopher of science in the early 19th century and old-earth creationist, William Whewell, wrote (and was quoted by Rhind):

> While so large a portion of the globe is geologically unexplored — while all the general views which are to extend our classifications satisfactorily, from one hemisphere to another, from one zone to another, are still unformed — while the *organic fossils of the tropics are almost unknown*, and their general relations to the existing state of things has not even been conjectured, how can we expect to speculate rightly and securely respecting the history of the whole of our globe? And if geological classification and description are thus imperfect, the knowledge of geological causes is still more so. As we have seen, the necessity and the method of constructing a science of such causes are only just beginning to be perceived. Here, then, is the point where the labors

83 See the earlier discussion on Bacon. Fairholme made only a passing comment on Bacon in this regard in his *Geology of Scripture* (1833), p. 22 (footnote).

84 For example, anonymous review of Young's *A Geological Survey of the Yorkshire Coast*, *Philosophical Magazine*, vol. LIX, no. 288 (1822), p. 293–294; P., anonymous review of *Conversations of Geology*, *Magazine of Natural History*, vol. I (1829), p. 466.; T., anonymous review of Bakewell's *Introduction to Geology* (third edition), *Magazine of Natural History*, vol. I (1829), p. 250–251; anonymous review of Higgins' *Mosaical and Mineral Geologies Illustrated* and Fairholme's *Geology of Scripture*, *Christian Remembrancer*, vol. XV (1833), p. 391–392, 397; Phillips, *Treatise on Geology*, II: p. 243–247; anonymous review of Rhind's *Age of the Earth*, *Athenaeum*, no. 549 (May 5, 1838), p. 321.

85 William Conybeare, "Report on the Progress, Actual State, and Ulterior Prospects of Geological Science," *Report of the BAAS: 1831–32* (1833), p. 410–411, also 413.

WILLIAM WHEWELL (1794–1866)

of geologists may be usefully applied, and not in premature attempts to decide the wisest and abstrusest questions which the human mind can propose to itself.

It has been stated, that when the Geological Society of London was formed, their professed object was to multiply and record observations, and patiently to await the result at some future time: and their favorite maxim was, it is added, that the time was not yet come for a general system of geology. This was a wise and philosophical temper, and a due appreciation of their position. And even now their task is not yet finished — their mission is not yet accomplished: they have still much to do in the way of collecting facts, and in entering upon the exact estimation of causes — they have only just thrown open the door of a vast labyrinth which it may employ many generations to traverse, but which they must needs explore before they can penetrate to the oracular chamber of Truth.[86]

In 1863, Lyell, commenting on the "imperfections of the geological record," also sounded remarkably like the scriptural geologists three decades earlier. Then, as a uniformitarian evolutionist, Lyell wrote:

> When we reflect, therefore on the fractional state of the annals which are handed down to us, and how little even these have as yet been studied, we may wonder that so many geologists would attribute every break in the series of strata, and every gap in the past history of the organic world, to catastrophes and convulsions of the earth's crust, or to leaps made by the creational force from species to species, or from class to class.[87]

So, this fact of the still infant state of geology, which in 1863 was useful to Lyell as a repudiation of catastrophism and defense of the antiquity and evolution of man, was essentially denied by the leading geologists in the 1820s and 1830s when the fact was used by virtually all the scriptural geologists as an objection to theories about the great antiquity of the earth.

In this regard, while the old-earth geologists may have been Baconian in separating Scripture from their geological investigations, the scriptural geologists believed their opponents were not following Bacon in a different respect. Bacon argued that sound scientific theories could only be established after an accumulation of vast amounts of data comparable to the scope of the theory which was designed to give a generalized interpretation of those data. In the case of geology, a sound theory of the earth would, in

86 Whewell, *The History of the Inductive Sciences*, III: p. 621–622. Rhind quoted this in his *Age of the Earth*, p. 113–114. Whewell had made a similar remark in his 1832 review of Lyell's *Principles of Geology*. See *Quarterly Review*, vol. XLVII, no. 93 (1832), p. 126–127.

87 Lyell, *The Antiquity of Man*, p. 449.

the opinion of the scriptural geologists, need to be based on a thorough study of all areas of the earth's surface, which in the early 19th century was far from accomplishment. Of course, we now know that Bacon's strictly inductive approach is not the way science and theory development often works, but that was the stated assumption of the Geological Society and others in the 1820s and 1830s.

This review of the historical context of the biblical and geological objections of the scriptural geologists does not prove that their view of a relatively recent beginning of creation and global Flood was correct. But it does show that all of their major objections were substantive and important and therefore worthy of a response from their opponents. They were not scientific or geological ignoramuses raising petty irrelevant objections as their antagonists charged. So we must conclude that the reason that the criticisms of the most well-informed scriptural geologists were ignored was elsewhere to be found. To the important question of the true nature of the debate we now turn.

THE NATURE OF THE DEBATE

Having considered the similarities and differences of the scriptural geologists and having shown that many of them raised the same theological and geological objections to the old-earth theories on important and debatable points, we now have a better context in which to assess the nature of the debate. To do this, we must consider why the scriptural geologists wrote on this subject, summarize the contemporary reactions to their writings, and then analyze the reasons for the reactions of their opponents.

Motivations of the Scriptural Geologists

We cannot assume that the scriptural geologists' stated reasons for writing on geological theories were their only, or most important, motivations. There may well have been others. But it is proper historiography to assume the sincerity of a writer's own stated motivations, unless there is strong historical evidence to the contrary.[88] The following considerations would indicate that such strong contrary evidence is lacking.[89]

Certainly, Young, Rhind, Fairholme, and Murray demonstrated genuine interest in geological science by their purely scientific journal articles or books. In particular, Young stated in his first geology book that he hoped his geological research would contribute to more effective and profitable mining and farming and industrial applications of minerals. Especially in his second book, Fairholme was attempting also to contribute to geological knowledge by making new observations and interpretations and advancing new arguments for the Flood. Similarly, Murray was concerned about practical, applied geology, evidenced in his numerous contributions to the *Mining Journal* and his invention of a safety lamp. Rhind wrote several purely geological or geographical books designed to stimulate further geological research by others.

But they also wrote on the subject out of the conviction that the old-earth theories were leading the geologists into a bewildering labyrinth that would impede the progress of true geological knowledge, by locking observations and interpretations into a false theoretical framework, thereby blinding geologists from seeing what they might otherwise see.[90]

88 In defending the sincerity of Lyell's expressed views on natural theology, Rudwick has said, "It is surely an important historiographical rule that one should assume sincerity unless there is strong evidence against it." See Martin J.S. Rudwick, "Charles Lyell, F.R.S. (1797–1875) and His London Lectures on Geology, 1832–33," *Notes and Records of the Royal Society of London*, vol. XXIX, no. 2 (1975), p. 244–245.

89 Again, documentation for this section can be found in the individual chapters on each scriptural geologist.

90 Interestingly, Derek Ager, a leading 20th century neo-catastrophist, remarked on this with reference to contemporary geologists: "So it was — as Steve Gould put it — that Charles Lyell 'managed to convince future generations of geologists that their science had begun with him.' In other words, we have allowed ourselves to be brain-washed into avoiding any interpretation of the past that involves extreme and what might be termed 'catastrophic' processes." See Ager's *The Nature of the Stratigraphical Record*, p. 46. Neo-catastrophists are contemporary evolutionary geologists who have largely rejected uniformitarianism and rather think that the early 19th century catastrophists, such as Cuvier, were on the right track in interpreting the rocks.

Closely related to the study of science is the teaching of it. Ure, Murray, and Rhind had strong interests and involvement in education. They believed that education in science contributed to improving man's standard of living, sharpening the mind and deepening a person's reverence for the Creator. By his lecturing and writing, Ure wanted to raise the level of general scientific knowledge of artisans and industrial workers. Murray was a nationally known lecturer, especially in mechanics' institutes, and many of his pamphlets were written to help spread scientific knowledge among the general public. Similarly, Rhind lectured and wrote to contribute to the education of secondary school students as well as the general public.

Obviously, the scriptural geologists were also motivated by their Christian faith. But I see little support for Rudwick's assertion:

> . . . more was involved than simple religious and social conservatism. The geologist's startling assertions about earth history were indeed derived from increasingly esoteric inferences that the ordinary person could no longer follow easily. Mosaic geology was, therefore, in part a cultural reaction to social and cognitive exclusion of all but self-styled experts from an area of speculation that, in the heyday of theories of the earth, had been open to all.[91]

As we have seen, however, the scriptural geologists were not "ordinary people." Most (including the ones not discussed in this book) were highly educated clergymen or scientists, who were quite able to analyze the logic of inductive conclusions from the stated facts in old-earth arguments, and some of them were fully competent to engage in the geological debate of their day about the old-earth theories and the stated supporting evidence. Furthermore, some of the most influential works by old-earth geologists were not so esoteric, for they were deliberately published for a general readership and in fact gained wide circulation.[92] Also, it was not "simple religious and social conservatism" which was driving the scriptural geologists, but their convictions about the divine inspiration of Scripture. Rudwick acknowledges this conviction about Scripture, but belittles it by equating "simple religious and social conservatism" with pre-critical biblical scholarship. However, from the widely known writings of T.H. Horne and others on the inspiration and authenticity of Scripture,[93] evangelicals and high churchmen had well-reasoned arguments against the new critical biblical scholarship.

In light of all these considerations, it seems right to conclude that the *primary* motivation behind the scriptural geologists' defense of a biblically based view of earth history was their expressed unshakeable conviction that the Scriptures were the inspired, infallible, and historically accurate Word of God. This dominating conviction was not unlike that which motivated the contemporary Clapham Sect to be such agents of social change.[94]

All the scriptural geologists agreed about the grave importance of the controversy. Ultimately, they saw this as a part of a cosmic spiritual conflict between Satan and God, and those who rejected the plain teaching of Scripture (which, in their thinking, included the literal historical interpretation of Genesis 1–11) were unwitting enemies of the truth and of God. George Bugg, Henry Cole, and James Mellor Brown expressed their view of this spiritual conflict more explicitly than other

91 Martin J.S. Rudwick, "The Shape and Meaning of Earth History," in *God and Nature* (Berkeley, CA: University of California Press, 1986), edited by David C. Lindberg and Ronald L. Numbers, p. 312.

92 The many editions of Cuvier's *Theory of the Earth*, Buckland's *Vindiciae Geologicae*, *Reliquiae Diluvianae*, and *Bridgewater Treatise*, and Lyell's *Principles of Geology* are good, but by no means the only, examples.

93 See the earlier section on biblical interpretation.

94 For a discussion of how the convictions of the evangelical Clapham Sect contributed to their social and political impact, see Ernest M. Howse, *Saints in Politics: The "Clapham Sect" and the Growth of Freedom* (London: Allen & Unwin, 1976), especially p. 134–135. This is not to say that all the Clapham Sect necessarily favored the young-earth view of the scriptural geologists, though many of them probably did, given the fact that Gisborne was so closely connected to and highly respected by the Clapham leadership.

scriptural geologists,[95] but given their common conviction about the literal interpretation of Scripture, they all undoubtedly shared the same conviction that the undermining of Scripture was a part of a spiritual conflict.

They believed that with the rejection of the plain teaching of Genesis, the proper interpretation and authority of the rest of Scripture would be undermined so that faith in other important biblical doctrines, including the origin of evil, the gospel, and the second coming of Christ, would slowly be eroded. These erosions of faith in turn would have a devastating effect on the life of the Church, the social and moral condition of the nation, and the spread of the gospel at home and abroad. As well-read Christians, the scriptural geologists were aware of the skepticism pervading continental theology and biblical scholarship[96] and perceived that it was slowly affecting the British churches and contributing, along with old-earth geological theories, to the weakening of the Church.

Contemporary Reactions to the Scriptural Geologists

The reactions to the scriptural geologists were three-fold. Many appreciated their works and generally agreed with their view of earth history, though not necessarily accepting their conclusions on every detail. For the most part, their opponents either mischaracterized and rejected the scriptural geologists collectively as a group or, more often, completely ignored their arguments, especially of those who were the most geologically competent to criticize the old-earth theories.

Appreciation

Many Britons must have appreciated the writings of the scriptural geologists, judging from the fact that some of the writings went through more than one edition and many of the works received positive reviews. This was especially the case in the Christian periodicals, but also in several scientific journals.[97] The expressed reasons for their appreciation generally centered on (1) the scriptural geologist's soundness of philosophical (or logical) reasoning (though the reviewers sometimes disagreed with minor points), (2) the reviewer's shared view of Scripture as supremely authoritative divine truth in matters of history as well as theology and morality, and (3) his shared conviction that the then-infant state of geology gave old-earth geologists no basis for dogmatism about earth history, and therefore there was no compelling reason to make Scripture harmonize with their old-earth theories.

Misrepresentation

Among their opponents, a very common response was a general misrepresentation of the scriptural geologists as a group. One of the most popular forms of this misrepresentation was the frequently encountered statement to the effect that, as Phillips put it in 1838, it was "universally admitted among geologists, that the earth is of vast antiquity."[98] The clear implication, of course,

95 Both Cole and Brown were Anglican pastors and neither was very informed on the technicalities of geology. Their criticisms of old-earth geological theories were biblical and theological. Cole wrote in his 1834 book, *Popular Geology Subversive to Divine Revelation* (London: Hatchard & Son, 1834), p. 44–45 that the church's compromise with old-earth reinterpretations of Genesis would lead to great moral and spiritual harm to the church and to society. He said, "What the consequences of such things must be to a revelation-possessing land, time will rapidly and awfully unfold in its opening pages of national skepticism, infidelity, and apostacy [*sic*], and of God's righteous vengeance on the same!" In *Reflections on Geology* (London: James Nisbet, 1838), p. 24, Brown likened the spiritual battle to the ancient battle for the city of Troy: "This affords another illustration of men who pull down the bulwark, but disclaim any intention of endangering the citadel. The Trojan Horse, drawn within the walls of the devoted city by friendly hands, is a standing emblem of men acting under the unsuspecting guidance of the Evil One."

96 Murray, Bugg, Ure, Fairholme, and Penn (along with Brown and Gisborne) were most explicit in regard to their acquaintance with skeptical biblical criticism emanating from the continent.

97 For documentation, see Terry Mortenson, "British Scriptural Geologists in the First Half of the Nineteenth Century," Ph.D. thesis, Coventry University, 1996, p. 440–443.

98 John Phillips, "Geology," in *The Penny Encyclopaedia*, Vol. XI (1838), p. 147. Similarly, in his *Bridgewater Treatise*, I: p. 13, William Buckland said, "The truth is, that *all observers*, however various may be their speculations respecting the secondary causes by which geological phenomena have been brought about, *are now agreed* in admitting the lapse of very long periods of time to have been an essential condition to the production of these phenomena" (emphasis added).

was that anyone who disputed the great ages was simply not a geologist. However, by early 19th century standards, it is clear that at least Young and Rhind were geologists who did not believe in an old earth. Also, within a year of Phillips' comment, four books appeared from geologically competent scriptural geologists (Young, Murray, Rhind, and Fairholme) and two of them (Young and Fairholme) had published their reasons for rejecting the old-earth view several years before Phillips' generalization. This general misrepresentation of the scriptural geologists as a group was seldom followed by the mention of any specific names or the differentiation between those who were geologically ignorant (and admitted it) and those who were well informed both by reading and fieldwork. But in the minds of many, they would all have been tarred with the same brush stroke.

For example, in 1834, after Ure, Young, Murray, and Fairholme had published on the subject, Sedgwick made the sweeping generalization that the scriptural geologists were controlled by "bigotry and ignorance" and that they believed "the pursuits of natural science are hostile to religion."[99] Two years later, Buckland implied that they were among those who "regard with jealousy and suspicion the study of any natural phenomena" and who "look for a detailed account of geological phenomena in the Bible."[100] In 1839, Mantell, in his brief comments on geology and Scripture, wrote that they had a "prejudice against the study of geology" and were authors who "falsely styling themselves as geologists" had attempted to "found a system of natural philosophy on the inspired record."[101] Certainly, none of the men I considered here or in my thesis fit this description, and especially not George Young, whose 1828 *Geological Survey of the Yorkshire Coast* was undoubtedly known to Mantell, since his wife had purchased a copy.[102] Whewell similarly charged that they sought "a geological narrative in a theological record."[103] The prominent evangelical Scottish Presbyterian theologian, Thomas Chalmers, was very influential in the popularization of the gap theory, and yet like many scriptural geologists had no geological experience or qualifications. He wrote in 1835 (and was quoted in 1837) that he regretted "that Penn, or Gisborne, or *any other* of our scriptural geologists, should have entered upon this controversy without sufficient preparation of natural science."[104] It seems difficult to believe that Chalmers was ignorant of the writings of Young, Ure, and Fairholme prior to this statement, given the high visibility of their writings and the fact that Young and Fairholme were also Scottish evangelical Presbyterians.

Two years later (1839), an old-earth geologist, who nevertheless identified himself as a "scriptural geologist," said that "the opponents of geology have not grappled with the actual phenomena, and shewn how they can reconcile them with their interpretations of Scripture." In particular, he criticized the author of *A Portrait of Geology*. Although he admitted that he had not even read the book, he confidently asserted that the anonymous author (who, he evidently did not know, was John Murray) "has not advanced one syllable of argument to refute" the old-earth geologists, "much less shewn how he can reconcile facts and Scripture," and that the author did not really know much about the geological

99 Adam Sedgwick, *Discourse on Studies of the University* (1834), p. 148, 150–151.

100 Buckland, *Bridgewater Treatise*, I: p. 8, 14.

101 Mantell, *Wonders of Geology*, I: p. 5–6. The 1848 edition contained the same remarks (I: p. 27–28). He also misrepresented the scriptural geologists when he said (1848, I: p. 26–27), "To the mind that is unacquainted with the nature and results of geological inquiries and which has been led to believe that the globe we inhabit is in the state in which it was first created, and that with the exception of the effects of a general deluge, its surface has undergone no material change. . . ."

102 See Young's list of subscribers in his 1828 book, *Geological Survey*, p. 365–366.

103 Whewell, *History of the Inductive Sciences*, III: p. 587. He also said they adhered to an "arbitrary mode of understanding scriptural expressions" (I: p. 403).

104 F.F., "Dr. Chalmers on Scriptural Geology," *Christian Observer*, vol. 37 (1837), p. 446–448, quoting from Chalmers' *Natural Theology* (1835); emphasis added.

Similar charges of the geological ignorance of the scriptural geologists can be found in Charles Babbage, *The Ninth Bridgewater Treatise: A Fragment* (1837), p. 66–68, 70–71, 79; Baden Powell, *The Connexion of Natural and Divine Truth* (1838), p. 279–281; and Frederick J. Francis, *A Brief Survey of Physical and Fossil Geology* (1839), p. 92–93.

facts.[105] It seems doubtful that, had he actually read Murray's book first, his criticism would have been so scathing.

This misrepresentation of the scriptural geologists continued after they had laid down their pens (on this subject) in *The Testimony of the Rocks* (1857), written by Hugh Miller, one of the leading Scottish geologists and an influential evangelical. He had accepted Chalmers' gap theory for much of his life, but geological fieldwork in the upper secondary and tertiary formations in the years 1847–56 had convinced him that this view was no longer tenable, and so he changed to the day-age theory as the preferred harmonization of geology with Scripture.[106] In this book, Miller devoted a chapter to "the geology of the anti-geologists," in which he exposed the geological "errors and nonsense" of "our modern decriers of scientific fact and inference."[107] In harmony with the approach of other old-earth Christian geologists, Miller criticized seven writers, most of whose views were not representative of the scriptural geologists considered in this book and none of whom was geologically competent.

Disregard

Besides a general and serious misrepresentation of the scriptural geologists as a group, most of their opponents ignored the more geologically competent writers, even though their works were referred to or reviewed in many Christian and secular periodicals and a number of them wrote many scientific journal articles. For example, in 1825 Sedgwick mentioned that most objectors to Buckland's *Reliquiae Diluvianae* appeared "entirely ignorant of the very elements of geology." He only referred to one exception to this general criticism: John Fleming, a leading Scottish clergyman and zoologist who accepted the great antiquity of the earth. Of him, Sedgwick wrote, "Yet I willingly allow that his arguments are adduced with a sincere love of truth, and that his facts and inferences are entitled to a candid examination."[108] Sedgwick never extended the same allowance to Young, even though Young was also known as a sincere lover of truth, Young was geologically more qualified than Fleming to raise objections to Buckland's theory, and Sedgwick surely knew of Young's objections.[109] In his *Discourse on the University* (in both the 1834 and the greatly revised 1850 editions) Sedgwick referred by name only to Bugg, Penn, Nolan, and Forman, none of whom was a competent geologist.[110] He made no mention of Young, even though he had praised Young's 1822 work on Yorkshire geology, probably knew Young personally from his stop in Whitby on his own study of the Yorkshire coast, and reportedly gave a rebuttal at the BAAS meeting in 1838 when an abstract of the first part of Young's *Scriptural Geology* (1838) was read.[111]

105 "A Scriptural Geologist, No 'More Last Words' on Geology," *Christian Observer*, vol. XXXIX (1839), p. 471–472. This geologist also gave no evidence of being aware of, much less reading, the works of Fairholme, Young, or Rhind.

106 It was the presence of fossils of existing mammals with extinct mammals in strata below those containing man and the presence of fossils of living mollusk species in still lower strata of the upper formations, which convinced Miller that the day in which man was created had to have been a long age extending "over mayhap millenniums of centuries." Hugh Miller, *The Testimony of the Rocks* (1857), p. x–xi.

107 Ibid., p. 351–352.

108 Adam Sedgwick, "On the Origin of Alluvial and Diluvial Formations," *Annals of Philosophy*, N.S. vol. IX (1825), p. 241–242.

109 Sedgwick most certainly knew about Young's objections to Buckland's theoretical interpretation of Kirkdale Cave. Although Young's 1822 journal article criticizing Buckland's Kirkdale theory was not published in the *Memoirs of the Wernerian Natural History Society* until volume VI (1826–31), Young had written about Kirkdale Cave in his 1822 edition of *Geological Survey of the Yorkshire Coast* (which Sedgwick had praised in 1825 but undoubtedly read long before that since he had been a pre-publication subscriber to that edition). Young also had corresponded about Kirkdale with Buckland, Sedgwick's good friend, from the earliest days of discovery andinvestigation.

110 Sedgwick, *Discourse on the University* (1834), p. 150–152; (1850), p. 11–16. The first three wrote much on the Genesis-geology debate. Sedgwick did not give Forman's first name or the name of Forman's work to which he referred. My conclusion is that it was Walter Forman, who was a captain in the Royal Navy. But Forman wrote only seven pages on geology in his 117-page *Treatises on Several Very Important Subjects in Natural Philosophy* (1832), a work otherwise devoted to physics and astronomy. Forman objected to Cuvier's theory of multiple floods and instead believed the global Noachian flood had been unique.

111 A brief reference to Sedgwick's rebuttal appeared in *Athenaeum*, no. 567 (Sept. 8, 1838), p. 652. But the *Report of the BAAS* on the 1838 meeting contains no mention of this and I was not able to locate a detailed report of what Sedgwick said.

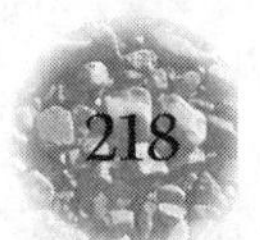

Similarly, Buckland ignored Young's work on the Yorkshire coast, even though Buckland had purchased six copies of the first edition in which Young presented reasons for rejecting Buckland's interpretation of Kirkdale cave.[112] Young wrote two scientific journal articles on the same subject, and he and Buckland exchanged correspondence on their personal investigations of the cave. Neither Buckland's 1836 *Bridgewater Treatise* nor the 1858 edition made any explicit reference to any particular scriptural geologists, though Buckland discussed the relation of geology and Genesis, as well as human fossils and polystrate fossil trees, two key issues for the scriptural geologists, as already noted. Ironically, in the only instance where Buckland named a scriptural geologist, he vaguely remarked on the "geological errors" in Gisborne's *Testimony of Natural Theology* (1818).[113] For the details of these errors, however, Buckland, a geologist writing in a geological work, referred the reader to a review in a non-scientific journal written by an anonymous author, who was not a geologist and who did not cite one explicit geological error.[114] Buckland's ignoring of opponents, regardless of their geological competence, was apparently intentional. A contemporary said of him, clearly with scriptural geologists in view, that "he very wisely determines not to attempt to reason with those who shut their eyes and say that the geologists invent facts."[115]

Although Fairholme, who was reasonably well known through his several scientific journal articles, invited a geologist's response to his journal articles on the important issues of coal, polystrate fossil trees, and human fossils in Köstritz, Germany, no geologist replied.[116] In an 1834 issue of the *Christian Observer*,[117] Conybeare answered an anonymous layman, who favored the scriptural geologists' view and made no claims to geological knowledge, but neither Conybeare nor any other old-earth geologist made any response to Fairholme on Köstritz the next year. In 1842, Lyell wrote on Niagara Falls. But although Lyell's view on how the falls were formed was similar to Fairholme's and Lyell referred to Henry Rogers' article, who wrote in response to Fairholme's article and had a different interpretation of the falls from that of Lyell and Fairholme, Lyell made no mention of Fairholme's article.[118]

Lyell was very concerned to sever the connection between Scripture and geology and he did not completely hide his opposition to orthodox Christianity.[119] Evidently, after his scathing but general remarks about the scriptural geologists in his 1827 review of Scrope's work on the geology of France,[120] he felt that the best way to oppose them

112 Young's discussion of Kirkdale in the *Geological Survey of the Yorkshire Coast* was on p. 68–69, 270–278, and 323 in the first edition (1822) and p. 294–310 in the second edition (1828).

113 Buckland, *Vindiciae Geologicae*, p. 35.

114 *Quarterly Review*, vol. XXI (1819), p. 41–63. The author was Reverend Thomas Dunham Whitaker, according to Leroy Page, "Diluvialism and Its Critics in Great Britain in the Early Nineteenth Century" in *Toward a History of Geology* (Cambridge, MA: M.I.T. Press, 1969), edited by Cecil J. Schneer, p. 265. According to *DNB*, Whitaker (1759–1821) was an Anglican clergyman and respected topographer, but no indication is given that he was particularly knowledgeable in geology. Whitaker wrote no books or scientific journal articles on geology according to the Royal Society or National Union catalogs.

115 Mary Carpenter quoted, without giving the source, by A.D. Orange, *Philosophers and Provincials: The Yorkshire Philosophical Society from 1822 to 1844* (Museum Gardens, York: Yorkshire Philosophical Society, 1973), p. 67.

116 Possibly, no leading British geologist had personally investigated the Köstritz fossil location as Fairholme had in 1834. I could find no evidence that any had done so since Weaver had reported Schlotheim's original discovery in Thomas Weaver, "On Fossil Human Bones and other Animal Remains Recently Found in Germany," *Annals of Philosophy*, N.S., vol. V (1823), p. 17–34.

117 William Conybeare, "Rev. W.D. Conybeare in Reply to a Layman, on Geology," *Christian Observer*, vol. XXXIV (1834), p. 306–309.

118 Charles Lyell, "A Memoir on the Recession of the Falls of Niagara," *Proceedings of the Geological Society*, vol. III, pt. 2 (1838–42), p. 595–602; Henry D. Rogers, "On the Falls of Niagara and the Reasonings of Some Authors Respecting Them," *Edinburgh New Philosophical Journal*, vol. XIX (1835), p. 281–292, originally published in *American Journal of Science and Arts*, vol. XXVII (1835), p. 326–335.

119 See Lyell's statements quoted on pages 225–226. Also, some contemporaries, even some old-earth geologists, perceived in Lyell's public writings a covert hostility towards orthodox Christianity. See Edward Hitchcock, "The Historical and Geological Deluges Compared," *The American Biblical Repository*, vol. IX, no. 25 (1837), p. 129.

was to ignore them. Furthermore, when only an abstract of the first part of George Young's essay on the antiquity of organic remains[121] was read in the geological section of the 1838 BAAS meeting in Newcastle, the official reason was that too many other long essays were submitted to the section.[122] It seems at least questionable, however, whether Lyell, who was president of the section, and Buckland, who was vice-president, had a reason other than quantity in view in the selection of essays.

This disregard of the objections of the scriptural geologists, especially those who were most geologically competent, cannot have been because of an abrasive writing style, for most of them wrote respectfully.[123] Nor was it because of excessive geological errors in their writings, for it has been shown that in many cases the accusation of error was false or too vague to be validated.[124] Furthermore, their opponents sometimes accused each other of being very ignorant of the relevant facts and of erroneously interpreting the facts, yet they nevertheless engaged in respectful debate.[125] Finally, Buckland, Sedgwick, and Greenough all recanted previous geological interpretations (related to the Flood), and De la Beche excused his own inevitable mistakes in his work, by saying that even erroneous ideas serve to advance science as they are exposed and corrected.[126]

Sedgwick said that even if all that the scriptural geologists had done was to point out old-earth geologists' errors of logic and fallacious inductions they "might, perhaps, have done us some service."[127] Since even some of the criticisms that Bugg, one of the least geologically informed scriptural geologists, made of Cuvier's logic and inferences were shared by Lyell and Fleming, it seems contrary to the evidence to conclude that all the scriptural geologists, even the most geologically competent, utterly failed even in this regard, as Sedgwick's statement implied.

Marginalization: Contributing Factors

Why then were the scriptural geologists misrepresented and ignored by their opponents? Earlier discussion has shown that the scriptural geologists were not just challenging minor debatable points, but rather points that were critical to the defense of the old-earth theories. These included the theological issues of the origin of evil and biblical interpretation and the geological issues of insensible transitions between strata, polystrate fossils, using shells to date rocks, fossil humans, and the infant state of geology. This marginalization by their opponents, therefore, was not because the scriptural geologists' arguments completely lacked any geological or

120 Charles Lyell, Review of *Memoir on the Geology of Central France*, by G.P. Scrope, *Quarterly Review*, vol. XXXVI, no. 72 (1827), p. 482..

121 This was published as part of his *Scriptural Geology*.

122 Young, *Scriptural Geology*, p. iii. The six-line abstract was recorded in the *Report of the BAAS* (1839), part II, p. 95.

123 Even in the case where scriptural geologists suspected and even accused their opponents of infidelity, it is noteworthy that some of their opponents did the same. The old-earth American geologist Hitchcock expressed his suspicions that Lyell's infidel creed affected his geological theory. See Edward Hitchcock, "The Historical and Geological Deluges Compared," *The American Biblical Repository*, vol. IX, no. 25 (1837), p. 129–130.

In language reminiscent of the scriptural geologist James Mellor Brown, the old-earth proponent John Pye Smith described Baden Powell's view that Gen. 1–11 is mythological poetry, not history, as "rash and harsh . . . deeply injurious to the cause of Christianity" which "cannot but be revolting to the calm judgment of any man; as well as to the enlightened piety of a reflecting Christian." See John Pye Smith, *On the Relation Between the Holy Scriptures and Some Parts of Geological Science* (1839), p. 203–204.

124 Examples include Sedgwick's criticisms of Ure, Buckland's criticisms of Gisborne, and John Pye Smith's criticisms of Young.

125 A classic example of this is the rather heated journal debate between John Fleming and William Conybeare in 1829–30. See Fleming, "On the Value of the Evidence from the Animal Kingdom, Tending to Prove That the Arctic Regions Formerly Enjoyed a Milder Climate Than at Present," *Edinburgh New Philosophical Journal*, vol. VI (1829), p. 277–286; Conybeare, "Answer to Dr Fleming's View of the Evidence from the Animal Kingdom, as to the Former Temperature of the Northern Regions," *Edinburgh New Philosophical Journal*, vol. VII (1829), p. 142–152; Fleming, "Additional Remarks on the Climate of the Arctic Regions, in Answer to Mr Conybeare," *Edinburgh New Philosophical Journal*, vol. VIII (1830), p. 65–74.

126 Henry De la Beche, *A Geological Manual* (1831), p. vii.

127 Adam Sedgwick, "Presidential Address at the Annual General Meeting of the Geological Society," *Philosophical Magazine*, N.S. vol. VII, no. 40 (1830), p. 310.

theological substance, nor was it the result of a reasoned critique of their most geologically informed arguments.

Having cleared away some of the supposed and frequently stated reasons why the writings of at least the geologically competent scriptural geologists were not considered in the geological debates, we are now prepared to consider what I believe were the real reasons.

Social Problems

In the light of religious controversy and frequently attending violence, especially in Europe during the previous centuries, religious tolerance was becoming a highly important value. Technological advancement, a rising general standard of living, and political reformation (especially in the wake of the French revolution) toward more representative democracy all contributed to a sense of progress. Yet at the same time, industrialization and urbanization were also stimulating economic deprivation, crime, and other unrest.

Science was increasingly viewed as a social and political peacemaker and stabilizer, as well as the means of successful industrialization.[128] The founding of the Geological Society was motivated in part by a desire to maintain a civil society.[129] As noted earlier, the mechanics' institutes generally avoided controversial subjects (such as geology) in their teaching of science. The BAAS was very influential in this regard as it consciously sought to be politically and religiously neutral and tolerant of all views.[130]

Many felt the necessity of avoiding all needless controversy that might contribute to political and social instability in Britain. The old-earth leaders of the scientific establishment obviously believed that the age-of-the-earth debate was a needless controversy, and so marginalized the scriptural geologists. The biblical convictions of the scriptural geologists would doubtless have led them to agree with efforts to avoid needless controversy. But the perceived threat of the old-earth geological theories to the Christian faith and biblical authority absolutely required their opposition. It was not a needless controversy in their estimation. They gave no evidence of desiring to use political or ecclesiastical power to stop what they viewed as dangerous ideas. Instead, they sought to fight with reasoned arguments in the marketplace of ideas.

The scriptural geologists were also probably ignored, in part, because they evidently acted as lone individuals rather than banding together to speak with a united voice.[131] Had they formed a society of some kind to share their ideas and to strategize about how to influence others they might have received more attention, but this would have only delayed their marginalization, given the reasons discussed below. That they did not join together is surprising, given the facts that none of them was a social recluse and several of them (for example, Ure, Young, Murray, and Rhind) were members of scientific societies. Also, the influential Anglican theologian/pastor and scriptural geologist Thomas Gisborne knew from his association with the evangelical "Clapham Sect" the power of collective action. This lack of collaboration could reflect an excessive individualism. But this does not seem to fit the character of these men, as revealed in their writings and the reputation they had among their contemporaries. Alternatively, it could indicate merely that their other responsibilities and interests, and in some cases poor health, along with difficulties in travel and communication in those days between such

128 In the case of geology, however, Porter has shown that the leading geologists had very little concern for practical geology and its application to mining and the industrial revolution. Rather, they pursued geology primarily for its intellectual, religious, and moral benefits. See Roy Porter, "The Industrial Revolution and the Rise of the Science of Geology," in *Changing Perspectives in the History of Science* (London: Heinemann Educational, 1973), edited by M. Teich and R. Young, p. 320–343.

129 Paul J. Weindling, "Geological Controversy and Its Historiography: The Prehistory of the Geological Society of London," in *Images of the Earth* (Chalfont St. Giles: British Society for the History of Science, 1979), edited by L.J. Jordanova and Roy S. Porter, p. 256.

130 Jack Morrell and Arnold Thackray, editors, *Gentlemen of Science: Early Years of the British Association for the Advancement of Science* (Oxford: Clarendon Press; New York: Oxford University Press, 1981), p. 224.

131 Although some of them referred to the writings of other scriptural geologists, there is no evidence that they collaborated in their work.

a few men so widely scattered geographically,[132] prevented them from contributing any more to the defense of their beliefs than the books they were able to write.

Furthermore, although Rupke has shown that the process of university reform (i.e., the movement away from the study of classics and history toward that of natural science) had a strong influence on some of the old-earth geologists, the evidence in this book indicates that he goes too far in saying that the Genesis-geology debate was first and foremost a chapter in the history of university reform.[133] Certainly, one general result of the focus on the study of the present by the methods of experimental science was the growing disregard of the writings of antiquity. With technological advancement came the notion that the ancients were pre-scientific and therefore primitive and bound by superstition. This undoubtedly affected many people's view of Scripture and other ancient writings such as non-biblical testimonies to a great Flood. Since from the very early 1800s university geology courses were all taught within the old-earth paradigm, and by the late 1830s geology was rapidly on its way to becoming a full-time vocation and institutionally trained profession,[134] it is little wonder that, as far as I could ascertain, no new geologically competent scriptural geologist arose in the 1840s and 1850s to continue to defend the view after the most geologically informed defenders died[135] or were focused on other fields of study.[136] Some men did write in opposition to old-earth theories, but they were clergymen, laymen, or scientists in non-geological fields.[137]

Finally, the ignoring of the geologically competent scriptural geologists, especially in the 1830s, was probably also influenced by the dominance of Charles Lyell. He was largely responsible for moving Sedgwick, Buckland, Conybeare, Greenough, and others away from catastrophism and from any connection between the Bible and geology. This had a tremendous effect on what was deemed acceptable in geological research, journal publications, and scientific societies.[138] Sedgwick was president of the Geological Society from 1829 to 1831, Greenough from 1833–35, and Lyell from 1835–37. Lyell was also president of the geological section of the BAAS in 1838. Yet the years 1837–38 were when the most geologically competent scriptural geologists presented their most seasoned thoughts on the subject.

World View Conflict

These social and political factors, however, were only symptomatic of what I believe was a more fundamental reason for ignoring and rejecting the arguments of the scriptural geologists. It was primarily a conflict of philosophical paradigms or world views, which included assumptions about the nature of science (especially geology), the nature of Scripture and the nature of God's relationship to His creation.[139] It was not a conflict between science and religion, or scientific facts and religious obscurantism, but between the scientific theories of one religious group and the scientific theories of another, or alternatively said,

132 Their homes included Ramsgate, Andover, London, Glasgow, Edinburgh, York, Hull, Kettering, Yoxall, and Whitby. Also, several of them often traveled for long periods on the continent or around the United Kingdom.

133 Rupke, *The Great Chain of History: William Buckland and the English School of Geology 1814–1849*, especially p. 62.

134 Colin A. Russell, *Science and Social Change: 1700–1900* (New York: St. Martin's Press, 1983), p. 195–202.

135 Fairholme died in 1846, Young in 1848, and Murray in 1851.

136 Rhind focused on botany and zoology and Ure on chemistry and industry.

137 For example, Anonymous, *Scriptural Evidences of Creation* (1846); Anonymous (possibly Reverend Charles Williams), *Voices from the Rocks*; Philip Gosse, *Omphalos: An Attempt to Untie the Geological Knot* (1857); James A. Smith, *The Atheisms of Geology* (1857).

138 In the late 19th century, Prestwich, a prominent geologist of his day, stated that Lyell's uniformitarian ideas about time and change (which Prestwich said formed the creed of most geologists in 1895) "have probably done as much to impede the exercise of free inquiry and discussion as did the catastrophist theories which formerly prevailed." See Prestwich, *Collected Papers on Some Controverted Questions of Geology*, p. 14. More recently, Ager has gone as far as describing the influence of Lyell's gradualistic uniformitarianism as "brain-washing" geologists for 150 years into avoiding any catastrophic interpretations of the rocks. See Ager, *The New Catastrophism*, p. xi.

139 Dillenberger has argued that since the Reformation the "fundamental problem underlying all the issues [of science and religion] is the relative authority and interpretation of nature and Scripture in theological matters." See John Dillenberger, *Protestant Thought and Natural Science* (1960), p. 14.

between the religious convictions of one group of scientists and non-scientists and the religious convictions of another group of scientists and non-scientists. But this conflict was not defined by denomination or church party, for there were both Anglicans and non-Anglicans, and evangelicals and high churchmen on both sides.

The growing scientific establishment in early 19th century Britain was controlled by an elite group of men who either embraced or in varying degrees were influenced by the theologically liberal, "Broad Church" view of Christianity. This group of scientists, which included the leading geologists, comprised the dominant influence in the BAAS and the Geological Society, two of the most powerful scientific bodies at the time.[140] The BAAS was becoming the new "Church of Science" and its elite "gentlemen of science" were the new clerisy, who perceived themselves to be "the anointed interpreters of God's truth about the natural, and hence the moral, world."[141] Brooke has argued that Morrell and Thackray make an exaggerated claim when they say that the liberal Anglicans in the BAAS worshiped at the shrine of science rather than truly worshiping the biblical God. But he did admit that there "was undoubtedly a *tendency*" of this kind in the BAAS, even though some (such as Whewell) were opposed to it.[142]

The BAAS's theology was influenced by deistic thinking, in part as a result of the influence of skeptical German biblical criticism, which as we have seen was slowly penetrating the British church through the "Cambridge Network" and others, reaching its full expression in the seven articles in *Essays and Reviews* (1860) published the year after Darwin's *Origin of Species*.[143] This is not to say that all these scientists were deists. Many no doubt were deists, unitarians, agnostics, or atheists, even if covertly so because of the social stigma attached to such "faiths" in early 19th century Christian Britain. On the other hand, some of these elite scientists were quite orthodox in their beliefs. Brooke has shown from Whewell's sermons that he was far more evangelical in his theology than has been previously supposed, and that in an 1827 sermon he expressed his concern about the irreligious sentiments prevalent among many men of science.[144] Likewise, Hilton has noted that Vernon Harcourt, the first president of the BAAS, had a "moderate evangelical eschatology."[145] In the fifth edition of his *Discourse on the University*, Sedgwick expressed a very evangelical view of salvation and spoke out against the pantheistic rationalism of *Life of Jesus*, written by the German radical theologian, David Strauss.[146] But the compromise of orthodoxy is generally gradual and subtle, and in such a changing environment there are always new possibilities for perceived unorthodoxy. For example, Whewell's connection with the Cambridge network led him to believe that "German biblical scholarship could lead to a

---

140 The link between the two was very close. The council of the BAAS met in London, usually at the Geological Society. See J.B. Morrell, "London Institutions and Lyell's Career: 1820–41," *British Journal for the History of Science*, vol. IX (1976), p. 135.

141 Morrell and Thackray, *Gentlemen of Science: Early Years of the British Association for the Advancement of Science*, p. 19–29, 228–229, 244–245. See also A.D. Orange, "The Idols of the Theatre: The British Association and Its Early Critics," *Annals of Science*, vol. 32 (1975), p. 277–294; A.D. Orange, "The Beginnings of the British Association, 1831–1851," in *The Parliament of Science* (Northwood Midx: Science Reviews, 1981), edited by Roy MacLeod and Peter Collins, p. 43–65.

142 See John H. Brooke, "Indications of a Creator: Whewell as Apologist and Priest," in Menachem Fisch and Simon Schaffer, editors, *William Whewell: A Composite Portrait* (Oxford, England: Clarendon Press; New York: Oxford University Press, 1991), p. 165.

143 Walter F. Cannon, "Scientists and Broad Churchmen: An Early Victorian Intellectual Network," *Journal of British Studies*, vol. IV, no. 1 (1964), p. 65–88. On the connection of biblical criticism to the early 19th century scientific establishment and especially geology, see also John H. Brooke, *Science and Religion* (1991), p. 263–274 and Martin J.S. Rudwick, "The Shape and Meaning of Earth History," in *God and Nature* (1986), edited by David C. Lindberg and Ronald L. Numbers, p. 311–312.

144 Brooke, "Indications of a Creator: Whewell as Apologist and Priest," in Fisch and Schaffer, *William Whewell: A Composite Portrait*, p. 149–173.

145 Boyd Hilton, *The Age of Atonement* (Oxford, England: Clarendon Press; New York: Oxford University Press, 1991), p. 31.

146 Adam Sedgwick, *A Discourse on Studies of the University* (1855), p. 135 and ccix.

deeper understanding of how God spoke to men than was enshrined in the newly conventional notion of verbal inerrancy."[147]

In this connection, what constitutes faithfulness to "orthodox Christianity" or "evangelicalism" is very frequently open to debate since the beliefs of individuals, churches, or other groups within the Church often change and orthodoxy has to be constantly redefined, clarified, and defended.

The scriptural geologists were concerned about this very issue, believing that the boundaries of orthodox Christianity were being slowly widened to include dangerously false ideas. It was their conviction that they were contending for the faith, not against total paganism so much as against a small, subtle, but polluting compromise of orthodox Christianity with potentially great consequences. They believed this compromise was being accomplished by Christian geologists and non-geologists whom they regarded as pious and orthodox in all, or most, other aspects of their faith. Quoting Psalm 11:3,[148] Murray did not decry that the superstructure was completely unsound but instead was concerned that the foundations were being attacked by the old-earth theories. Penn contended that through old-earth geologists, Greek atomist philosophy was infecting the Church. Cole was convinced that old-earth geological theory had the direct and inevitable tendency to subvert the Word of God, even though he was sure that neither Sedgwick nor any other Christian geologist had that intention.[149]

Brown compared the situation to the fall of the city of Troy:

> This affords another illustration of men who pull down the bulwark, but disclaim any intention of endangering the citadel. The Trojan horse, drawn within the walls of the devoted city by friendly hands, is a standing emblem of men acting under the unsuspecting guidance of the Evil One.[150]

As Cannon, Morrell, and Thackray argue, the god of the BAAS was not the God of the Bible, but the more tolerant and vaguely defined "author of nature," a god who did not care much about doctrinal precision. In the natural theology of some of these "gentlemen of science" the focus was on a god of power, wisdom, and goodness.[151] In contrast, the scriptural geologists emphasized (in addition to these other attributes) God's holiness, justice, and wrath, attributes which their opponents seldom, if ever, mentioned in this context. The scriptural geologists drew attention to these latter attributes most notably when they emphasized that the global Flood was a unique, penal intervention of God, and that the curse at the fall of man had affected the whole physical creation, not just man.

As far as Scripture was concerned, many of the opponents of the scriptural geologists generally accepted the infallibility and authority of Scripture only in matters of theology and morality,[152] but not necessarily also in historical matters.

147 Brooke, "Indications of a Creator: Whewell as Apologist and Priest," in Fisch and Schaffer, *William Whewell: A Composite Portrait*, p. 162. The quotation is of Brooke's words, not Whewell's. In light of the earlier discussion of early 19th century orthodox views of inspiration, infallibility, and inerrancy in the section on biblical interpretation, Brooke's assessment that verbal inerrancy was a "newly conventional notion" in orthodox Christianity is mistaken.

148 "If the foundations are destroyed, what can the righteous do?"

149 Cole, *Popular Geology Subversive of Divine Revelation*, p. 8–9, and 129. Cole was primarily responding to the views of Adam Sedgwick.

150 Brown, *Reflections on Geology*, p. 24.

151 So, for example, the full title of Buckland's *Bridgewater Treatise* reads, "On the Power, Wisdom and Goodness of God as Manifested in the Creation: Geology and Mineralogy Considered with Reference to Natural Theology." Buckland was more orthodox than many old-earthers, but his view of God and Scriptures was lower than that of the scriptural geologists.

152 This latter view was also rejected by some who favored the old-earth view, such as the editors of the evangelical *Christian Observer*, who wrote, "A more daring and absurd proposition was never invented, than that a Divine revelation is to be credited in its moral but not in its physical statements; and we do not believe that any man who so asserts has the slightest faith in the Bible as a Divine revelation in either department. A large number of geologists, as well as of other scientific and unscientific men, are, we fear, infidels — or at least skeptics — either avowed or concealed." See *Christian Observer*, vol. XXXIV (1834), p. 207 (footnote). Given this perspective, it is ironic that the *Christian Observer* supported the old-earth view.

The scriptural geologists, along with a great many contemporary and earlier Christians, believed that the theology and morality of the Bible were inseparably linked to its historical accuracy and they believed that the gap and day-age theories, as well as the tranquil and local flood views were subtle ways of denying that accuracy (even though the old-earth proponents claimed to be defending it).

Relying on Francis Bacon and the experience of Galileo, the old-earth proponents also increasingly insisted on a bifurcation of the study of nature and of Scripture. By this means they hoped to avoid the errors of the Church in Galileo's day and engage in an unbiased, objective, strictly empirical analysis of the physical world. But as we have seen, the scriptural geologists contended that this unbiased objective analysis, or "cosmological neutrality" (as Rudwick called it[153]), was not what actually happened. They believed their old-earth opponents were controlled by unbiblical religious and philosophical ideas which affected their selection and interpretation of the facts of geology, just as strongly as their opponents believed the scriptural geologists were biased by traditional literal interpretations of the Bible. Secord has noted:

> Most significantly, recent work in cultural anthropology and the sociology of knowledge has shown that the conceptual framework that brings the natural world into a comprehensible form becomes especially evident when a scientist constructs a classification [of rock strata]. Previous experience, early training, institutional loyalties, personal temperament, and theoretical outlook are all brought to bear in defining particular boundaries as "natural."[154]

It would be misleading to think that all these factors influenced all scientists to the same degree. Furthermore, a major component of anyone's theoretical outlook is his religious world view (which could include atheism or agnosticism). I would argue that world view had a far more significant influence on the Genesis-geology debate than has previously been perceived or acknowledged. The different religious orientations, or world views, of the scriptural geologists and their opponents influenced how these scientists and non-scientists interpreted the "two books" of God: creation and Scripture.

Consider the men most influential in the development of the old-earth theory. Buffon was probably a deist or atheist.[155] Laplace was an open atheist.[156] Lamarek straddled the fence between deism and theism.[157] Werner was a deist[158] or possibly an atheist.[159] Historians have concluded the same about Hutton.[160] William Smith was a vague sort of theist.[161] Cuvier was a nominal Lutheran, but recent research has shown that he was an irreverent deist.[162] As the following quotes will suggest, Lyell was probably a deist (or Unitarian, which is essentially the same).[163] Many of the other leading geologists of the 1820s and 1830s were the same. These men were hardly unbiased, objective pursuers of truth, as they would have wanted their contemporaries to believe.

Russell is generally right about scientists and non-scientists: "Men often perceive what they

153 Rudwick, "The Shape and Meaning of Earth History," in *God and Nature*, Lindberg and Numbers, editors, p. 311.

154 James A. Secord, *Controversy in Victorian Geology* (Princeton, NJ: Princeton University Press, 1986), p. 6.

155 See "Buffon, Georges-Louis LeClerc, Comte de," *DSB*, p. 577–578.

156 John H. Brooke, *Science and Religion* (Cambridge; New York: Cambridge University Press, 1991), p. 238–240.

157 Ibid., p. 243.

158 Leroy E. Page, "Diluvialism and Its Critics in Great Britain in the Early Nineteenth Century," in Cecil J. Schneer, editor, *Toward a History of Geology* (Cambridge, MA: M.I.T. Press, 1969), p. 257.

159 A. Hallam, *Great Geological Controversies* (Oxford: Oxford University Press, 1992), p. 23.

160 Dennis R. Dean, "James Hutton on Religion and Geology: The Unpublished Preface to His *Theory of the Earth* (1788)," *Annals of Science*, 32 (1975): p. 187–193.

161 Smith's own writings reveal this vague theism, as do comments by geologist John Phillips, Smith's nephew and geology student. See John Phillips, *Memoirs of William Smith* (London, 1844), p. 25. It is safe to say that Smith was definitely *not* a committed Christian.

162 Brooke, *Science and Religion*, p. 247–248.

163 Colin A. Russell, *Cross-currents: Interactions Between Science and Faith* (Leicester: IVPress, 1985), p. 136.

expect, and overlook what they do not wish to see."[164] In describing the controversy in the late 1830s over the identification of the Devonian formation, Rudwick wrote:

> Furthermore, most of their recorded field observations that related to the Devonian controversy were not only more or less "theory laden," in the straightforward sense that most scientists as well as historians and philosophers of science now accept as a matter of course, but also "controversy laden." The particular observations made, and their immediate ordering in the field, were often manifestly directed toward finding empirical evidence that would be not merely relevant to the controversy but also *persuasive*. Many of the most innocently "factual" observations can be seen from their context to have been sought, selected, and recorded in order to reinforce the observer's interpretation and to undermine the plausibility of that of his opponents.[165]

In his covert promotion of Scrope's uniformitarian interpretations of the geology of central France, Lyell had similarly said in 1827, "It is almost superfluous to remind the reader that they who have a theory to establish, may easily overlook facts which bear against them, and, unconscious of their own partiality, dwell exclusively on what tends to support their opinions."[166] However, many geologists, then and now, would say that Lyell was blind to his doing precisely these things in his own geological interpretations. In fact, Lyell's own words indict him. In a lecture at King's College London in 1832 he stated, "I have always been strongly impressed with the weight of an observation of an excellent writer and skillful geologist who said that 'for the sake of revelation

Charles Lyell (1797–1875)

as well as of science — of truth in every form — the physical part of geological inquiry ought to be conducted as if the Scriptures were not in existence.' "[167] In private correspondence around the same time, Lyell revealed his consciously devious and anti-biblical agenda. He was certainly not the unbiased objective geologist that he thought and led others to think he was. In an 1829 letter to Roderick Murchison just months before the publication of the first volume of Lyell's *Principles of Geology*, he candidly wrote:

> I trust I shall make my sketch of the progress of geology popular. Old Fleming is frightened and thinks the age will not stand my anti-Mosaical conclusions and at least that the subject will for a time

164 Colin A. Russell, "The Conflict Metaphor and Its Social Origins," *Science and Christian Belief*, vol. I, no. 1 (1989): p. 25.

165 Martin J.S. Rudwick, *The Great Devonian Controversy* (Chicago, IL: University of Chicago Press, 1985), p. 431–432.

166 Charles Lyell, Review of Scrope's *Memoir on the Geology of Central France, Quarterly Review*, vol. XXXVI, no. 72 (1827): p. 480.

167 Charles Lyell, Lecture II at King's College London on May 4, 1832, quoted in Martin J.S. Rudwick, "Charles Lyell Speaks in the Lecture Theatre," *The British Journal for the History of Science*, vol. IX, pt. 2, no. 32 (July 1976), p. 150. Rudwick thinks the quote is from Reverend John Fleming (though he was a zoologist, not a geologist), but Rudwick could not locate the original quote.

> become unpopular and awkward for the clergy, but I am not afraid. I shall out with the whole but in as conciliatory a manner as possible.[168]

Ironically, Reverend John Fleming, a professing evangelical Scottish Presbyterian minister and tranquil Flood proponent, was more supportive of Lyell's uniformitarianism than the truth of Genesis 1–11.

Writing in 1831 to fellow old-earther, Gideon Mantall, Lyell revealed:

> My dear Mantell — I have been within this last week talked of and invited to be professor of geology at King's College [London], an appointment in the hands entirely of the Bishop of London, Archbishop of Canterbury, Bishop of Llandaff, and two strictly orthodox doctors [of theology], D'Oyley and Lonsdale. Llandaff alone demurred, but as Conybeare sent him (volunteered) a declaration most warm and cordial in favor of me, as safe and orthodox, he must give in, or be in a minority of one. The prelates declared "that they considered some of my doctrines startling enough, but could not find that they were come by otherwise than in a straightforward manner, and (as I appeared to think) logically deducible from the facts, so that whether the facts were true or not, or my conclusions logical or otherwise, there was no reason to infer that I had made my theory from any hostile feeling towards revelation." Such were nearly their words, yet Featherstonhaugh tells Murchison in a letter, that in the United States he should hardly dare in a review to approve of my doctrines, such a storm would the orthodox raise against him![169]

Lyell must have been relishing this lack of spiritual and doctrinal discernment exhibited by leading churchmen. He wrote the previous June 14 (1830) to another good friend, fellow uniformitarian, and member of Parliament, George Poulett Scrope:

> I am sure you may get into Q.R. *[Quarterly Review]* what will free the science [of geology] from Moses, for if treated seriously, the [church] party are quite prepared for it. A bishop, Buckland ascertained (we suppose Sumner), gave Ure a dressing in the "British Critic and Theological Review." They see at last the mischief and scandal brought on them by Mosaic systems. . . . Probably there was a beginning — it is a metaphysical question, worthy of a theologian — probably there will be an end. Species, as you say, have begun and ended — but the analogy is faint and distant. Perhaps it is an analogy, but all I say is, there are, as Hutton said, "no signs of a beginning, no prospect of an end." Herschel thought the nebulae became worlds. Davy said in his last book, "It is always more probable that the new stars become visible and then invisible, and pre-existed, than that they are created and extinguished." So I think. All I ask is, that at any given period of the past, don't stop inquiry when puzzled by refuge to a "beginning," which is all one with "another state of nature," as it appears to me. But there is no harm in your attacking me, provided you point out that it is the proof I deny, not the probability of a beginning. . . . I was afraid to point the moral, as much as you can do in the Q.R. about Moses. Perhaps I should have been tenderer about the Koran. Don't meddle much with that, if at all. If we don't irritate, which I fear that we may (though mere history), we shall carry all with us. If you don't triumph over them, but compliment the liberality and candor of the present age,

---

168 Quoted in John H. Brooke, "The Natural Theology of the Geologists: Some Theological Strata," in L.J. Jordanova and Roy S. Porter, editors, *Images of the Earth* (British Society for the History of Science, Monograph 1, 1979), p. 45.

169 Taken from Lyell's full letter in Katharine Lyell (Lyell's sister-in-law), *Life, Letters and Journals of Sir Charles Lyell, Bart.* (London: Murray, 1881), I: p. 316–317.

> the bishops and enlightened saints will join us in despising both the ancient and modern physico-theologians. It is just the time to strike, so rejoice that, sinner as you are, the Q.R. is open to you. P.S. . . . I conceived the idea five or six years ago [1824–25], that if ever the Mosaic geology could be set down without giving offense, it would be in an historical sketch, and you must abstract mine, in order to have as little to say as possible yourself. Let them feel it, and point the moral.[170]

James Hutton similarly had a philosophically naturalistic world view that was hostile to the Genesis account of creation and the Flood. He insisted in 1785, "The past history of our globe must be explained by what can be seen to be happening now. . . . No powers are to be employed that are not natural to the globe, no action to be admitted except those of which we know the principle."[171] Obviously, this axiom of geological interpretation ruled out *a priori* any consideration of the biblical testimony to earth history and especially God's judgments at the Fall and the Flood.

So, the influence of world view on the observation, selection, and interpretation of the facts was considerable, especially given the limited knowledge of people individually and collectively in the still infant stage of early 19th century geology. As Kuhn has noted:

> Philosophers of science have repeatedly demonstrated that more than one theoretical construction can always be placed upon a given collection of data. History of science indicates that, particularly in the early developmental stages of a new paradigm, it is not even very difficult to invent such alternatives.[172]

Just as the catastrophist felt irresistibly driven by the "obvious" evidence to believe in great regional or global catastrophes separated by long ages of time, so the uniformitarian "saw" equally undeniable evidence that they had never happened. In the same way, scriptural geologists, like a Cole (with virtually no geological knowledge) or a Young (with a very high level of geological competence), felt that all the opposing geologists were "blind" to the plain evidences for a recent supernatural creation and a unique global Flood.[173]

One example of the influence of world view on the selection and interpretation of the facts is the case of polystrate fossils. The fact that trees were often found fossilized in an upright position in the rocks was agreed by all. The old-earth geologists overlooked or minimized the additional fact, and the theoretical implications of that fact, that the trees very often cut through several different strata. On the other hand, the scriptural geologists seized on this additional fact as one strong piece of evidence that much, if not most, of the geological record was very rapidly deposited during the year-long Noachian flood.

So the scriptural geologists were fighting against a major paradigm shift transpiring in both theology and geology (and generally in science and society) during the late 18th and early 19th centuries. Another way this new world view was expressed was in the increasing insistence both by liberal theologians and scientists that all things must be explained only by the laws of nature. This meant that miraculous interruptions of the normal course of nature were ruled out *a priori*. Miraculous activities in Scripture were then seen as mythical (i.e., historically untrue or inaccurate) accounts of events which occurred according to the laws of nature but which pre-scientific people did not understand. From such a deistic world view it was only a short step to atheistic naturalism. All that was necessary was to show philosophically that the apparent intelligent design in nature is an illusion — the accidents of a purposeless non-created cosmos.

170 Katharine Lyell, *Life, Letters and Journals of Sir Charles Lyell, Bart.*, I: p. 268–271.
171 James Hutton, "Theory of the Earth," *Transactions of the Royal Society of Edinburgh* (1785); quoted in A. Holmes, *Principles of Physical Geology* (United Kingdom: Thomas Nelson and Sons, 1965), p. 43–44.
172 Thomas S. Kuhn, *The Structure of Scientific Revolutions* (1970), p. 76.
173 Young, *Scriptural Geology*, p. 74; Cole, *Popular Geology Subversive to Divine Revelation*, p. 31.

Clearly, as the century progressed toward the acceptance of Darwin's theory, scientists were increasingly embracing this naturalistic world view, though certainly many old-earth geologists (e.g., Sedgwick, Buckland, Conybeare) and non-geologists (Whewell, Sumner, Pye Smith, Chalmers, etc.) firmly rejected it as a world view. Nevertheless, the controlling paradigm in science was shifting in this direction and many church opponents of naturalism were knowingly or unknowingly imbibing some of the naturalist presuppositions. The scriptural geologists felt that these Christian men were abetting that world view shift, in spite of their sincere intentions to the contrary.

The scriptural geologists' assumptions about the nature of Scripture (especially the early chapters of Genesis) and about the relationship of God to His creation and the "laws of nature" (i.e., the definition and relation of miracles and providence) were contrary to the assumptions of their opponents. The geologically competent scriptural geologists were observing the rocks with an eye for evidences that confirmed what they assumed (because of belief in the inspiration of Scripture) to be the historically accurate biblical account of the origin and early history of the earth. They also clearly had the philosophical assumption that the Word of God, the Bible, was more perspicuous, and therefore easier to interpret correctly than were the works of God, the physical creation. Their opponents, whether uniformitarian or catastrophist, were likewise looking for evidences of their theories of earth history. Their theories contained the assumptions that the Bible was not relevant to their science and they operated from the philosophical assumption that the works of God were more perspicuous and easier to interpret than was the Word of God.

The Problematic Nature of Geological Science

So what about the Galileon/Baconian dictum that the study of nature and of Scripture should be kept strictly separate, or the corollary that science should interpret Scripture but Scripture should never be allowed to interpret the natural world or judge scientific theories? This question is an important element in one's world view, but it is an issue which needs to be elaborated. The old-earth proponents insisted that maintaining this separation was the only way to do true science, especially geology, and the only way to avoid a repeat of the Galileo affair, which was deemed to have been detrimental to science and Christianity.

Most of the scriptural geologists did not develop an explicit and thorough answer to this Baconian-Galileon bifurcation, and surely this was another significant reason that they were marginalized. But Penn argued at some length (and other scriptural geologists apparently agreed) that the old-earth geologists had a faulty definition of what it meant to be Baconian, because they did not take into account Bacon's distinction between the supernatural initial creation of a perfect, fully functioning cosmos suitable for man and the subsequent commencement (on the seventh day of creation or after the fall of man) of the presently operative laws of nature.[174] Bugg, Rhind, Brown, and Murray referred to the Galileo affair, but their responses were brief and shallow. They objected that while the reinterpretations of the biblical texts relevant to the Copernican theory were exegetically convincing and in harmony with the rest of the teaching of Scripture, the old-earth reinterpretations of Genesis were exegetically unconvincing and contradicted (or undermined) other important teachings of Scripture. They believed also that the Copernican view had been tested and confirmed over a long time, whereas geology was still in its infancy and frequently was changing its interpretations of the geological data, thereby disqualifying it as a solid basis for reinterpreting Scripture. In any case, most of the scriptural geologists clearly believed there was a difference between scientific explanations about the origin and history of the earth, on the one hand, and

174 It has been the apparent assumption of historians generally that the 19th century old-earth proponents infallibly interpreted and applied Bacon's philosophy to the science of geology. But since Bacon formulated his ideas long before the Genesis-geology debate, it is suggested here that, given Penn's lengthy argument on this point and other geologically competent scriptural geologists' insistence that they were being Baconian, the validity of this historical assumption is open to question and that more analysis of both Bacon's diverse statements (related to creation and scientific study of creation) and the old-earth geologists' and scriptural geologists' interpretations of those statements would be worthwhile.

scientific explanations about the present state and operation of the creation, on the other. Rudwick remarked on this different character of geological science when he wrote:

> Even at the opening of its "heroic age" [ca. 1790–1830], geology was recognized as belonging to an altogether new kind of science, which posed problems of a kind that had never arisen before. It was the first science to be concerned with the reconstruction of the past development of the natural world, rather than the description and analysis of its present condition. The tools of the other sciences were therefore inadequate. The processes that shaped the world in the past were beyond either experiment or simple observation. Observation revealed only their end-products; experimental results could only be applied to them analogically. Somehow the past had to be interpreted in terms of the present. The main conceptual tool in that task was, and is, the principle of uniformity.[175]

We have seen, however, that the scriptural geologists argued analogically on the basis of the principle of uniformity, just as much as their opponents did.[176] An important difference between the scriptural geologists and their opponents then seems to have related to this distinction between sciences dealing with the origin and history of the creation and those dealing with its present condition and functioning.

Some of their old-earth opponents alluded to this difference also. For example, in his 1830 response to Lyell's *Principles of Geology*, Conybeare distinguished between "descriptive geology" and "theoretical geology," preferring to work at the former for the present because the data to support a theoretical system was then insufficient.[177] John Herschel observed that astronomy was quite mature in explaining how the present heavens operate, but that "the researches of physical astronomy are confessedly incompetent to carry us back to the origin of our system, or to a period when its state was, in any great essential, different from what it is at present."[178] These statements indicate that in his mind there was a distinction between astronomical theories about the past origins and astronomical knowledge of the present operations of the celestial bodies.

However, by far the most thorough discussion of this distinction between the origin and operation of the physical world came from the leading philosopher and historian of science of that time, William Whewell, who devoted 70 pages to the philosophy of that branch of science

175 Martin J.S. Rudwick, "The Principle of Uniformity," *History of Science*, vol. I (1962), p. 82. Similarly, David M. Raup, in "Geology and Creationism," *Bulletin of the Field Museum of Natural History*, vol. LIV (1983), p. 20, noted that geology is categorically different from some other sciences: "The creationists are fond of claiming that in order to be scientifically demonstrable, something must (1) be amenable to proof by experiment and (2) without exceptions. These requirements are probably valid in certain areas of science, particularly in parts of physics and chemistry and in certain areas of engineering. What the creationists seem to miss is the fact that geology and paleontology are historical sciences and therefore experimental testing of predictions is difficult if not impossible and that these sciences rely largely on statistical inference; that is, on the building of a general case which accepts exceptions as tolerable." Raup missed the fact that creationists do see the difference between experimental science and historical science.

Stephen J. Gould, in "Balzan Prize to Ernst Mayr," *Science*, vol. 223 (January 20, 1984), p. 255, likewise wrote in reference to the historical sciences of geology and evolutionary biology: "The Nobel prizes focus on quantitative, nonhistorical, deductively oriented fields with their methodology of perturbation by experiment and establishment of repeatable chains of relatively simple cause and effect. An entire set of disciplines, different though equal in scope and status, but often subjected to ridicule because they do not follow this pathway of 'hard' science, is thereby ignored: the historical sciences, treating immensely complex and nonrepeatable events (and therefore eschewing prediction while seeking explanation for what has happened) and using methods of observation and comparison."

176 To cite just two examples, Penn used the present flux and reflux of the ocean currents to help explain how tropical creatures could have drifted into northern latitudes before burial and fossilization during the Flood. Fairholme used the present erosional power of the ocean on coastlines and rivers on waterfalls to explain the formation of coastal cliffs and valley systems on the land masses since the Flood retreated.

177 William Conybeare, "Letter from the Rev. W.D. Conybeare, on Mr. Lyell's *Principles of Geology*," *Philosophical Magazine*, N.S. vol. VIII, no. 45 (1830), p. 215–217.

178 John Herschel, *A Preliminary Discourse on the Study of Natural Philosophy* (1840), p. 78 and 281.

for which he coined the term "palaetiology."[179] This branch of science attempts to identify the causes of past historical events whose effects we observe in the present, or, "to trace back the history and discover the origin of the present state of things."[180] These historical sciences, Whewell said, are notably different from the experimental sciences that deal with present causes and effects (or with "the general relations which permanently prevail and constantly recur among the objects around us").[181] He devoted attention to three examples of palaetiological science: geology (the history of the earth), comparative philology (the history of languages), and comparative archaeology (the history of arts). Before any of these sciences is prepared to erect a theory of the actual facts, said Whewell, it requires a systematic description of the facts (which he called "phenomenology") and a rigorous analysis of the causes (which he called "aetiology"). He argued that no sound palaetiological theory (in any of these three sciences) was yet extant, and concluded in 1840 that:

> . . . geological theory has not advanced beyond a few conjectures, and that its cultivators are at present mainly occupied with a controversy in which the two extreme hypotheses[182] which first offer themselves to men's minds are opposed to each other. And if we have no theoretical history of the earth which merits any confidence, still less have we any theoretical history of language, or of the arts, which we can consider as satisfactory. The theoretical history of the vegetable and animal kingdoms is closely connected with that of the earth on which they subsist, and must follow the fortunes of geology. And thus we may venture to say that no palaetiological science, as yet possesses all its three members. Indeed most of them are very far from having completed and systematized their phenomenology: in all, the cultivation of aetiology is but just begun, or is not begun; in all, the theory must reward the exertions of future, probably of distant, generations.[183]

The irony of this conclusion is that while Whewell insisted that geology was very far from being ready to erect a theory of the earth, he appeared certain that the two mainstream old-earth theories were the only options. The scriptural geologists' view of a 6,000-year-old earth was eliminated from consideration, even though Whewell did not explicitly name any scriptural geologists, gave no evidence of having read their most geologically informed books (most of which were published in the three years leading up to Whewell's book),[184]

---

179 William Whewell, *The Philosophy of the Inductive Sciences* (1840), II: p. 95–165.

180 Ibid., II: p. 109.

181 Ibid., II: p. 94. More recently, Whewell's word, palaetiology, has been replaced, while the category of science has been retained. Norman Geisler and J. Kerby Anderson, in *Origin Science: A Proposal for the Creation-Evolution Controversy* (Grand Rapids, MI: Baker Book House, 1987), similarly argue for two branches of science: operation science and origin science. They define operation sciences to be those which use observation of repeatable experiments in a controlled environment to discover patterns of regular behavior in the present physical universe. On the other hand, origin sciences (which include geology, paleontology, and archaeology) use present circumstantial evidence and reliable eyewitness testimony (when available) to ascertain the cause(s) of some past singular (non-repeatable) event. They contend that fruitful discussions about the history and origin of the physical world will be inhibited unless this distinction in the sciences is taken into account.

Several others have also recently remarked on the importance of this distinction: Stephen C. Meyer, "Of Clues and Causes: A Methodological Interpretation of Origin of Life Studies" (1990, Ph.D. thesis, Cambridge University); Stephen C. Meyer, "The Methodological Equivalence of Design and Descent: Can There be a Scientific 'Theory of Creation'?," in *The Creation Hypothesis* (Downers Grove, IL: InterVarsity Press, 1994), edited by J.P. Moreland, p. 67–112; Charles B. Thaxton, Walter L. Bradley, and Roger L. Olsen, *The Mystery of Life's Origin: Reassessing Current Theories* (1992), p. 200–208; J.P. Moreland, *Christianity and the Nature of Science: A Philosophical Investigation* (Grand Rapids, MI: Baker Book House, 1989), p. 225–226.

182 He meant catastrophism and uniformitarianism.

183 Whewell, *The Philosophy of the Inductive Sciences*, II: p. 122–123. Whewell had made similar remarks at the end of his 1839 presidential address to the Geological Society. See William Whewell, "Address to the Geological Society, Delivered at the Anniversary, on the 15th of Feb. 1839," *Proceedings of the Geological Society*, vol. III (1838–43), p. 95–97.

184 These were the books by Fairholme (1837), Murray (1838 and 1840), Young (1822, 1828, 1838, and 1840), and Rhind (1838).

and provided no examples of erroneous arguments for a recent creation.[185] Yet nowhere in this 70-page discussion, or anywhere else in these two volumes, or in his discussion of geology in *The History of the Inductive Sciences* (1837) did he summarize or refer to the evidence that to him ruled out a recent creation and global Flood.

This inconsistent conclusion led to others when later Whewell addressed the relation of these palaetiological sciences to Scripture. For example, he repeatedly used the Galileo affair (which dealt with the present operation, not the origin and history, of the heavens) in order to essentially sever Genesis from the development of a palaetiological theory of the earth. And this was after saying that the current leading theory of the origin of the solar system, the nebular hypothesis (which he classified as part of "cosmical palaetiology"),[186] was "many ages of observation and thought" away from verification.[187] It would appear that his somewhat liberal views of Scripture and the contradictions in his thinking about palaetiological sciences predisposed him against considering the arguments of the most competent scriptural geologists, who wrote their best works on the subject just prior to Whewell publishing his thoughts on palaetiology.

Nevertheless, he did argue that because the palaetiological sciences were concerned with reconstructing past events, human historical records (including the Scriptures) "must have an important bearing upon these sciences," and that with respect to geology in particular, these records "have the strongest claim to our respect."[188] Furthermore, like many other old-earth proponents, he believed that Genesis was crystal clear and literal in meaning when it explained the supernatural and recent creation of man.[189]

In the end, however, Whewell asserted (without reference to any particular texts of Scripture) that Genesis was too obscure in meaning to be relevant to geological theory.[190] But that was a theological and exegetical (not scientific or geological) conclusion, which the scriptural geologists disputed. Nevertheless, sounding very much like the scriptural geologist Granville Penn 15 years earlier, Whewell said:

> Thus we are led by our reasonings to this view, that the present order of things was commenced by an act of creative power entirely different to any agency which has been exerted since. None of the influences which have modified the present races of animals and plants since they were placed in their habitations on the earth's surface can have had any efficacy in producing them at first.[191]

With regard to the nebular hypothesis for the origin of the solar system, he continued, "Here

---

185 The irony of his certainty that the antiquity of the earth was proven and yet that both the catastrophist and the uniformitarian old-earth theories were far from verified is further reflected when he wrote, "While I have been speaking of this supposed series of events, including in its course the formation of the earth, the introduction of animal and vegetable life, and the revolutions by which one collection of species has succeeded another, it must not be forgotten, that though I have thus hypothetically spoken of these events as occurring by force of natural causes, this has been done only that the true efficacy of such causes might be brought under our consideration and made the subject of scientific examination. It may be found that such occurrences as these are quite inexplicable by the aid of any natural causes with which we are acquainted; and thus the result of our investigations, conducted with strict regard to scientific principles, may be that we must either contemplate supernatural influences as part of the past series of events, or declare ourselves altogether unable to form this series into a connected chain." See William Whewell, *The Philosophy of the Inductive Sciences* (1840), II: p. 115–116). The scriptural geologists were arguing that an earth history based solely on natural causes did fail to explain the phenomena.

186 Whewell, *The History of the Inductive Sciences*, III: p. 485. The nebular hypothesis was in contrast to the Copernican theory of the operation of the universe, which he discussed in volume I of *The Philosophy of the Inductive Sciences*, under the non-palaetiological "mechanical sciences" of mechanics, hydrostatics, and physical astronomy.

187 Whewell, *The Philosophy of the Inductive Sciences*, II: p. 105.

188 Ibid., II: p. 137–138.

189 See M.J.S. Hodge, "The History of the Earth, Life, and Man: Whewell and Palaetiological Science," in Fisch and Schaffer *William Whewell: A Composite Portrait*, p. 286–287.

190 Whewell, *The Philosophy of the Inductive Sciences*, II: p. 141–144.

191 Ibid., II: p. 134 (see also II: p. 137, 145, 157).

again, therefore, we are led to regard the present order of the world as pointing towards an origin altogether of a different kind from anything which our material science can grasp."[192] Three years earlier Whewell had written similarly:

> Geology and astronomy are, of themselves, incapable of giving us any distinct and satisfactory account of the origin of the universe, or of its parts. We need not wonder, then, at any particular instance of this incapacity; as for example, that of which we have been speaking, the impossibility of accounting by any natural means for the production of all the successive tribes of plants and animals which have peopled the world in the various stages of its progress, as geology teaches us . . . but when we inquire when they came into this our world, geology is silent. The mystery of creation is not within the range of her legitimate territory; she says nothing, but she points upward.[193]

So although the scriptural geologists never worked out a philosophical defense of their methodology, their conviction that geology was different from other sciences, because it dealt with history and origins, and their insistence that Genesis should not be severed from the interpretation of geological phenomena were philosophically and methodologically sound, according to Whewell's reasoning.

A statement which well conveys a sense of both the conflict of world views and the confusion about the nature of experimental sciences (or operation sciences) compared to palaetiological sciences (or origin sciences) is one made by Sedgwick to the Geological Society as he was introducing his scathing criticism of Ure's *New System of Geology* (1829). Sedgwick wrote:

> Laws for the government of intellectual beings, and laws by which material things are held together, have not one common element to connect them. And to seek for an exposition of the phenomena of the natural world among the records of the moral destinies of mankind, would be as unwise as to look for rules of moral government among the laws of chemical combination. From the unnatural union of things so utterly incongruous, there has from time to time sprung up in this country a deformed progeny of heretical and fantastical conclusions, by which sober philosophy has been put to open shame, and sometimes even the charities of life have been exposed to violation.[194]

Contrary to what Sedgwick implied in this statement, no scriptural geologist (including Ure, the chemist, whom Sedgwick was criticizing) argued that the Bible teaches or was intended to teach what operation science is to discover, namely, in Sedgwick's words, 1) "the laws by which material things are held together," 2) "an exposition of the phenomena of the natural world," and 3) "the laws of chemical combination." Rather, as I have repeatedly stated for emphasis, they argued that the Bible gave an outline of the origin and early history of the creation.

None of Sedgwick's phrases above dealt with the origin of the world or any rare divine interruption of the normal course of nature (i.e., the Fall or the Noachian flood), unless those phrases contained a built-in philosophical/theological assumption that the laws of nature describe the only way God has ever worked in the world. But that would have been assuming one of the very points of debate. So in this passage, Sedgwick was attacking a straw-man opponent. He was implying that Ure and the other scriptural geologists believed that the Bible taught how the world operates (i.e., the laws of nature), but they did not. They believed that scientific research should be done to figure that out, and Ure, Murray, Fairholme, Rhind, and several other scriptural geologists were very involved in that kind of scientific research.

192 Ibid., II: p. 135.

193 Whewell, *History of the Inductive Sciences* (1837), III: p. 687-88 (see also III: p. 580–587 and 620).

194 Adam Sedgwick, "Annual General Meeting of the Geological Society, Presidential Address," *Philosophical Magazine*, N.S. vol. VII, no. 40 (1830), p. 310.

One more point needs to be made in this regard. Although old-earth geologists generally insisted on keeping the Bible and geology separate, some of them, in fact, did not do this all the time. For example, Sedgwick stated, "The Bible instructs us that man, and other living things, have been placed but a few years upon the earth; and the physical monuments of the world bear witness to the same truth."[195] So Sedgwick started with the biblical teaching about the origin of man and believed he had found confirmation of this in geology.[196] Methodologically, this was precisely what the scriptural geologists did, when they believed they had found geological evidence in support of the biblical teaching on the Flood and a supernatural creation week. Sedgwick was taking the genealogies of Genesis quite literally, but he did not explain here or anywhere else on what basis he was correct to take this part of Genesis literally but the scriptural geologists were wrong to take the rest of Genesis 1–11 literally. Other old-earth proponents, who reasoned from the Bible and geology about the recency of man, just as Sedgwick did, included Conybeare, Mantell, Harcourt, and Babbage.[197] But they never gave criteria to distinguish when it was permissible (even desirable) to keep the Bible and science together and when we must separate them. So the old-earth proponents had a very arbitrary methodology.

The scriptural geologists insisted that Genesis had a direct bearing on the development of a geological theory of the earth; in fact, they said, it should be used as a framework in which to interpret the geological phenomena, just as ancient historical documents should be used to interpret the monuments and artifacts of an ancient nation. But their opponents increasingly severed the connection of Scripture to geology, except with regard to the recent creation of man, or insisted that geology should always determine the correct interpretation of related Scriptures. This historical nature of geology was linked to a theological perspective on how God began the creation, as well as how He has related to His creation over the course of time, which had a profound influence on the interpretation of geological phenomena and significantly contributed to confusion and misunderstanding in the debate between the scriptural geologists and their opponents.

Conclusion

From a closer examination of the historical evidence, several weaknesses in previous scholarly analysis of the early 19th century Genesis-geology debate have been exposed. This research has demonstrated that the scriptural geologists have been misrepresented both by their contemporaries and most later historians.

First, some scriptural geologists were admittedly geologically ignorant, but even many of these were generally well-read and obviously capable of interacting with serious minds over the validity of logical arguments (i.e., whether conclusions drawn from stated premises were logically valid). Others were very competent in geology, demonstrated especially in the case of two well-known men (Young and Fairholme) and two others who have been virtually unknown to historians (Murray and Rhind). These writers raised important geological objections to the old-earth theories and did so in a respectful manner.

Second, the frequent assertion that the scriptural geologists were "anti-geology" is very inaccurate and therefore misleading in our attempts to understand the debate. The great majority of them strongly advocated the study of science in general, and of geology in particular. If there is any sense that the scriptural geologists could be regarded

195 Sedgwick, *Discourse on the Studies of the University*, p. 148.

196 However by 1868, when many geologists, with the help of Darwin, increasingly insisted on the vastly greater antiquity of man, Sedgwick (then age 83) discarded this formerly confirmed truth of the recency of man, saying that man was "of a far higher antiquity than that which I have hitherto assigned to him." See John W. Clark and Thomas M. Hughes, editors, *The Life and Letters of the Reverend Adam Sedgwick* (1890), II: p. 440.

197 William Conybeare, "Rev. W.D. Conybeare in Reply to a Layman, on Geology," *Christian Observer*, vol. XXXIV (1834), p. 308; Mantell, *The Wonders of Geology*, I: p. 7 and II: p. 785; William Vernon Harcourt, "Address of the Presidency of the BAAS," *Athenaeum*, No. 618 (August 31, 1839), p. 653–654. Babbage, *The Ninth Bridgewater Treatise: A Fragment*, p. 64–67; also see the anonymous review of William M. Higgins's *The Mosaical and Mineral Geologies, Illustrated and Compared*, in *Christian Observer*, vol. 32 (1832), p. 743.

as "anti-geology," it would only be in the sense in which geology was defined by their opponents, namely that geology as a science *included* the assumption that the earth was of very great age, and therefore any challenge to the age of the earth was *ipso facto* opposition to the science of geology. All the scriptural geologists opposed the *old-earth* interpretations of the geological phenomena, primarily on biblical grounds. But the geologically competent and well-informed writers also presented important geological reasons for rejecting the old-earth theories of earth history and accepting the biblical account of a relatively young earth.

Third, contrary to the accusation of most of their contemporary opponents, the scriptural geologists were not trying to construct a "whole system of natural philosophy" from the Bible in place of doing scientific research, but only insisted on using the Bible as a framework for developing a geological theory of earth history (and also cosmic history). By equating these two different categories of scientific investigation (origin science and operation science), opponents and later historians have obscured the true nature of the debate.

Furthermore, the evidence indicates that their firm biblical convictions (rather than a vague "social conservatism" or "rigid obscurantist traditionalism") and genuine concern for the advancement of true scientific knowledge were far more important as motivations for their writing on geology than has previously been recognized. Though in some cases there were other motivations (e.g., socio-political, financial, educational or professional), the scriptural geologists' political, social, financial, vocational, and denominational diversity, coupled with their unity of opinion about earth history, indicates that these other motivations were not the *primary* ones, or even very significant.

But why did these and other scriptural geologists almost explode onto the scene of British history and then vanish nearly as quickly?[198] Some probable reasons are as follows. These men wrote at a time of great turbulence in British society. The Industrial Revolution was transforming the economy, the use of natural resources, the production of goods and services, the distribution of the population, the structure of the family, the availability and curriculum of schools, and the standard of living of everyone. These changes, coupled with the abolition of slavery, challenges to the establishment of the Church of England, and the horrifying results of the French Revolution were threatening social and political stability.

Added to this, atheism, deism, and other anti-biblical philosophies of the Enlightenment were gaining in popularity all over Europe and penetrating the Church with ideas rooted in the supreme authority of human reason. Such rationalism insisted on explaining everything (including not only the present function of the creation but also its original state and subsequent history) by the supposedly inviolable laws of nature, which was a view often accompanied by a total denial of miracles. It also insisted on a completely natural (i.e., only human), rather than supernatural-natural (i.e., divine-human) origin of the Scriptures. This in turn affected how the Scriptures were interpreted. The Bible was believed by some to contain either historical errors or only theological and moral truths conveyed through myth or some other symbolic literary genre, just as other ancient religious literature contained.

Certainly, very many of the opponents of the scriptural geologists did not absorb all these ideas. In fact, a number of them opposed many of these unorthodox ideas. But the changing views of Scripture in general and Genesis in particular form an important background to the controversy. The scriptural geologists did not reject these ideas out of ignorance, but were well-read in the writings of contemporary orthodox biblical scholarship in Britain, where many of the skeptical objections of continental biblical critics were answered.

Also, increasingly in the 19th century, science was being viewed as the dominant (and, in many minds, the only) source of truth, and thus the

198 As noted in the introduction, during the years 1820 to 1845 at least 29 authors published one or more books or pamphlets in which they defended the traditional interpretation of Genesis. The greatest intensity of publication appears to have been the period from 1833 to 1840.

teaching of science could promote social stability. Since the early 19th century also saw the rapid rise in the number of scientific journals and magazines, books and pamphlets on scientific topics, public scientific lectures, and scientific associations and educational institutions (such as philosophical societies and the mechanics' instititutes), this view of science was permeating all classes of the general public.

All of this was contributing to a gradual, but profound, shift in world view in society and a radical redefinition of Christianity in many parts of the Church in Europe and America. Up to this point in history, seldom, if ever, had there been so much simultaneous change, and the scriptural geologists were very conscious of these revolutions.

Unlike the European continent, Britain (along with America) was still experiencing the effects of the 18th century evangelical awakenings. As a result, it was the strongest center of orthodox biblical Christianity and produced many intellectually rigorous and devout people who sought to be influential in society (e.g., the evangelical Clapham Sect who led the fight against slavery and other social problems). Added to this was the long tradition of English writers who sought to relate the study of geological phenomena to the Genesis flood[199] and the early 19th century tradition of writings on natural theology,[200] in which science was seen as an ally in defending orthodox Christianity.

Finally, in the period 1820 to 1845, the scriptural geologists were writing toward the end of a debate among geologists about the physical effects of Noah's flood. Some, such as Hutton and Lyell, were saying that it was geologically irrelevant. Others, such as Cuvier, Buckland, Sedgwick, and Jameson, were insisting for a time that the Flood was responsible for at least some of the geological phenomena. The scriptural geologists' most intense reaction came in the wake of the recantations (of belief in the Flood) of Buckland, Sedgwick, and others, and the publication of Lyell's *Principles of Geology*.

In this context, the scriptural geologists felt compelled to write. They believed that the old-earth theories and the resulting reinterpretations of Scripture would have long-term catastrophic effects on the theological and spiritual health of the Church and her evangelistic mission and subsequently on the social and political life of the nation. But this was precisely because they believed these issues were related to a person's response to the inspired and infallible Word of God. As Cole put it:

> Many reverend geologists, however, would evince their reverence for the divine Revelation by making a distinction between its historical and its moral portions; and maintaining, that the latter only is inspired and absolute Truth; but that the former is not so; and therefore is open to any latitude of philosophic and scientific interpretation, modification or denial! . . . According to these impious and infidel modifiers and separators, there is not one-third of the Word of God that is inspired; for not more, nor perhaps so much, of that Word, is occupied in abstract moral revelation, instruction, and precept. The other two-thirds, therefore, are open to any scientific modification and interpretation; or (if scientifically required) to a total denial! It may, however, be safely asserted, that whoever professedly, before men, disbelieves the inspiration of any part of Revelation, disbelieves, in the sight of God, its inspiration altogether. If such principles were permitted of the most High to proceed to their ultimate drifts and tendencies, how long would they be sweeping all faith in revealed and inspired veracity from off the face of the earth? . . . What the consequences of such things must be to a revelation-possessing land, time will rapidly and awfully unfold in its opening pages of national skepticism, infidelity, and apostacy [sic], and of God's righteous vengeance on the same![201]

199 Burnet, Woodward, Whiston, Catcott, etc.

200 Paley, *Natural Theology* (1802); the *Bridgewater Treatises*; etc.

201 Cole, *Popular Geology Subversive to Divine Revelation*, p. ix–x, 44–45 (footnote).

It would appear that subsequent developments in the church and society in Britain (and in other so-called Christian lands of Europe and North America) over the last 170 years has confirmed the scriptural geologists' worst fears.

So it was the undermining of the Scriptures, far more than the undermining of the political and social status quo or their own personal positions in society, that was their shared concern. Also, as scientific knowledge was rapidly expanding and leading geologists and other scientists were claiming massive evidence in favor of an old earth, the scriptural geologists felt compelled to defend the traditional interpretation of Genesis, in part by attempting to show that much of what was being claimed as "evidences" of an old earth were really theory-laden inferences from the geological facts, with the theory being rooted in anti-biblical philosophical assumptions.

Having suggested some of the probable reasons for the sudden rise of the scriptural geologists, the following seem to be some of the reasons for their abrupt decline. From at least the 1810s, the control of the most influential scientific and educational institutions and scientific journals was held either by liberal Christians or moderate evangelicals or, as the century progressed, by men who were subtly or openly hostile to Christianity altogether. This inhibited the development of a new generation of geologically competent scriptural geologists. Closely related to this was the fact that in the 1830s and 1840s, geology was rapidly changing from a gentleman's avocation into a specialized profession. This specialization made full-time geologists sensitive to what they perceived as intrusions into their private domain by part-time geologists, such as some of the scriptural geologists. If the scriptural geologists had collaborated more and first published when they were in their twenties, they might have fought longer and succeeded in encouraging younger men to join them. Also, if they had held some prominent positions in the power centers of education and science, they might not have been ignored and rejected by their contemporary opponents without much, if any, serious engagement with their arguments. Furthermore, semi-deistic, liberal theology was gradually replacing orthodox theology as the dominating influence in the Church. All of these factors contributed to the marginalization and rapid near-extinction of the young-earth proponents.

Finally, the scriptural geologists and their opponents also collided in their views on the very nature of geology. It was not an experimental science, such as chemistry or physics, seeking to discover how the present creation operates, but a science concerned with the historical question of origins. All of the scriptural geologists recognized, and some of their opponents attempted to articulate, this special characteristic of geological science. But the ambiguous definition of this historical nature of geology at its early stage of development added to the confusion and hindered the serious consideration of the best arguments of the scriptural geologists by their geological opponents. As the 19th century progressed, the question of origins (astronomical, geological, and biological) was moving rapidly away from assumptions rooted in Christianity to a semi-deistic, agnostic or atheistic framework. The rear-guard action of the scriptural geologists was too little and too late to stop this cultural shift in world view.

It is intriguing to see history repeat itself. By the time of the publication of Darwin's book in 1859, the scriptural geologists had almost become an "extinct species" of the human race. Lyell's uniformitarianism had conquered geology. No one would have predicted that by the 1970s Lyell's dogma would be significantly challenge by "neocatastrophism."[202] Still more shocking (and distressing to evolutionists) has been the development of "young-earth creationism" in the last half of the 20th century. It will be obvious to anyone who is familiar with the literature of this contemporary movement that their interpretations of the geological and biblical records regarding creation, the Flood, and the age of the earth are essentially identical on the main points (though much expanded in detail) with those

202 A number of books have appeared on this matter, such as Derek Ager's *The New Catastrophism* (1993), which lists others.

of the scriptural geologists.[203] This might seem surprising, since there is no historical, literary link between the modern creationists and the scriptural geologists. In fact, based on the writings of young-earth creationists that I have read, the scriptural geologists were generally unknown before my research started to be published. But given their identical commitments to the inspiration, inerrancy and authority of Scripture, and their common view of Genesis as literal history, it is understandable that their interpretations of the fossils and rocks would be in such close agreement.

Unlike the scriptural geologists, the young-earth creationist movement is growing stronger with the passage of time. It is now worldwide in extent with literally thousands of Ph.D. scientists involved.[204] The movement has published technical research journals and a popular magazine (with global distribution) for several decades,[205] as well as hundreds of books, tapes, and videos in many languages. With the growth of this movement, the "intelligent design" movement,[206] and the debate about evolution in many countries, it seems likely that the controversy that began at the time of scriptural geologists will intensify in the years ahead. Those interested in learning more should visit the various creationist websites and their online bookstores, e.g., <www.icr.org>, <www.answersingenesis.org>, and <www.creationresearch.org>.

203 The book by John Whitcomb and Henry Morris that launched the modern movement, *The Genesis Flood* (Philadelphia, PA: Presbyterian and Reformed Pub. Co., 1961), and John Morris's *The Young Earth* (Green Forest, AR: Master Books, 1994) are just two examples that will make this clear.

204 Debora MacKenzie, "Unnatural Selection," *New Scientist*, no. 2235 (April 22, 2000), p. 35–39, writes about the creationist movement from the perspective of a concerned evolutionist. Henry Morris, *History of Modern Creationism* (Santee, CA: ICR, 1993), provides names and addresses of many creationist organizations worldwide.

205 For example, *Creation Research Society Quarterly*, which can be ordered on the web from <www.creationresearch.org> and *TJ* (formerly *Creation Ex Nihilo Technical Journal*) and *Creation Magazine* (a family magazine), both of which can be ordered at <www.answersingenesis.org>.

206 For a good introduction to the intelligent design movement, which began in the early 1990s, see Phillip Johnson, *The Wedge of Truth: Splitting the Foundations of Naturalism* (Downers Grove, IL: InterVarsity Press, 2000) and William Dembski, editor, *Mere Creation: Science, Faith, and Intelligent Design* (Downers Grove, IL: InterVarsity Press, 1998).

BIBLIOGRAPHY

REFERENCE WORKS

Addison, W. Innes. *Roll of the Graduates of the University of Glasgow*. Glasgow, 1898.

Allibone, S. Austin. *A Critical Dictionary of English Literature*. 3 Volumes. London, 1877 [1858].

Anderson, Peter John, ed. *Fasti Academiae Mariscallanae Aberdonensis*. Vol. II. Aberdeen, 1898.

British Biographical Index.

Brown, Phillip A.H. *London Publishers and Printers c1800–1870*. London: British Library, 1982.

Burke, John. *History of the Commoners of Great Britain and Ireland*. 4 Volumes. London, 1836.

_______. *Burke's Landed Gentry*. 3 Volumes. London, 1965–72.

Catalogue of the Graduates . . . of the University of Edinburgh. Edinburgh, 1858.

Catalogue of the Royal Society.

Cameron, Nigel M. de S., ed. *Dictionary of Scottish History and Theology*. Edinburgh: T & T Clark, 1993.

Crockford's Clerical Directory. London, 1860.

Foster, Joseph. *Alumni Oxonienses: The members of the University of Oxford 1714–1886*. 4 Volumes. London, 1887.

Gilbert, Richard. *The Clerical Guide*. London, 1836.

Gillispie, Charles C. *Dictionary of Scientific Biography*. 16 Volumes. New York: Scribner, 1970–80.

Hastings, James, ed. *Encyclopaedia of Religion and Ethics*. 13 Volumes. Edinburgh: T & T Clark, 1908–26.

Historical Register of the University of Oxford 1220–1900. Oxford: Clarendon, 1900.

Hume, Abraham. *Learned Societies and Printing Clubs of the United Kingdom*. London, 1847.

Imperial Dictionary of Universal Biography. 3 Volumes. London, 1865.

International Genealogical Index. Microfiche.

Maunder, Samuel. *The Biographical Treasury*. London, 1851.
Page, William, ed. *The Victoria History of the Counties of England.* 5 Volumes. London: St. Catherine Press, 1925.
Report of the British Association for the Advancement of Science. 9 Volumes. London: John Murray, 1831–1840.
Stephen, Leslie and Sidney Lee, eds. *The Dictionary of National Biography*. 22 Volumes. Oxford: Oxford University Press, 1917.
The British Gallery of Contemporary Portraits. 2 Volumes. London, 1822.
The Clergy List. 17 Volumes. London, 1841–57.
Venn, J.A. *Alumni Cantabrigienses: 1752–1900.* 6 Volumes. Cambridge, 1940–1954.
Walsh, S. Padraig. *Anglo-American General Encyclopedias: A Historical Bibliography 1703–1967.* New York: Bowker, 1968.
Ward, Thomas Humphry, ed. *Men of the Reign*. London, 1885.
World Book Encyclopedia. 22 Volumes. Chicago: World Book, 1987.

NINETEENTH CENTURY PERIODICALS

Annals of Philosophy
Asiatic Journal
Athenaeum
Blackwood's Edinburgh Monthly Magazine
British Critic
British Magazine
British Quarterly Review
Chambers' Edinburgh Journal
Christian Observer
Eclectic Review
Edinburgh Journal of Science, Literature and Arts
Edinburgh Journal of Natural History and the Physical Sciences
Edinburgh New Philosophical Journal
Edinburgh Quarterly Review
Evangelical Register
Evangelical Magazine
Gentlemen's Magazine
Hampshire Chronicle
Leamington Spa Courier
Magazine of Natural History
Mining Journal
Philosophical Magazine
Proceedings of the Geological Society of London
Quarterly Review
Quarterly Journal of Science, Literature and Art
Remembrancer/Christian Remembrancer
Report of the BAAS
Transactions of the Geological Society of London
Transactions of the Royal Society of Edinburgh
Transactions of the Royal Society of London
Whitby Gazette

PRIMARY SOURCES

Ainsworth, Henry. *Annotations upon the five Bookes of Moses, the Book of the Psalmes, and Song of Songs, or Canticles*. London, 1639.
Anonymous. *Alphonse de Mirecourt; or, The Young Infidel Reclaimed from the Errors of Deism*. Birmingham, 1835.
Anonymous. "Brief Notice of the Late Rev. George Young, D.D." *Evangelical Magazine*, vol. XXVII (1849): p. 113–117.
Anonymous. *The Curate's Appeal to the Equity and Christian Principles of the British Legislature, the Bishops, the Clergy, and the Public on the Peculiar Hardships of Their Situation; and on the Dangers Resulting to Religion, to Morals, and to the Community from the Arbitrary Nature of the Laws, as They Are Now Frequently Enforced against Them*. London, 1819.
Anonymous. *Dr. Andrew Ure: A Slight Sketch, Reprinted from the Times and Various Other Periodicals of January 1857*. Published Privately (1874).

Anonymous. "Lamarck's Genera of Shells." *Quarterly Journal of Science, Literature and Arts*, vol. XIV (1823): p. 64–86.
Anonymous. "Memoir of the Late Rev. George Young, D.D." *The United Presbyterian Magazine*, vol. III (1849): p. 97–103.
Anonymous. "No 'More Last Words' on Geology." *Christian Observer*, vol. XXXIX (1839): p. 471–474.
Anonymous. *Remarks on Certain Parts of Mr. Granville Penn's Comparative Estimate*. London, 1826.
Anonymous. Review of *Conversations on Geology* [by J. Rennie]. *Magazine of Natural History*, vol. I (1829): p. 463–466.
Anonymous. Review of George Fairholme's *General View of the Geology of Scripture. Magazine of Natural History*, vol. VI, no. 33 (1833): p. 256.
Anonymous. Review of George Young's *A Geological Survey of the Yorkshire Coast. Philosophical Magazine*, vol. LIX, no. 288 (1822): p. 293–299.
Anonymous. Review of *The History of Europe during the French Revolution* by Archibald Allison. *Blackwood's Edinburgh Magazine*, vol. XXXIII (1833): p. 889–890.
Anonymous. Review of "On the formation of the Valley of Kingsclere . . ." by William Buckland et al in *Transactions of the Geological Society. Magazine of Natural History*, vol. I (1829): p. 249–271.
Anonymous. Review of Robert Bakewell's *An Introduction to Geology. Magazine of Natural History*, vol. I (1829): p. 353–360.
Anonymous. Review of William M. Higgins' *The Mosaical and Mineral Geologies, Illustrated and Compared. Christian Observer*, vol. XXXII (1832): p. 742–751.
Anonymous. Review of William Rhind's *Age of the Earth. Atheneum*, no. 549 (May 5, 1838): p. 321–322.
Anonymous. *Scriptural Evidences of Creation; or, the Mosaic History of Creation Illustrated by Geological Discoveries*. London, 1846.
Anonymous. *Voices from the Rocks*. London, 1857.
Anonymous. "Whitby Literary and Philosophical Society: A Retrospect (1823–1948)." *Whitby Gazette* (January 16, 1948).
Augustine. *The City of God, Books VII-XVI*. Translated by G.G. Walsh and G. Monahan. Washington, DC: Catholic University of America Press, 1952.
_______. *The City of God, Books XVII-XXII*. Translated by G.G. Walsh and D.J. Honan. Washington, DC: Catholic University of America Press, 1954.
_______. *The Literal Meaning of Genesis, Vol. 1*. Translated and introduction by J.H. Taylor. New York: Newman Press, 1982.
_______. *The Retractions*. Translated by Sister Mary Inez Bogan. Washington, DC: Catholic University of America Press, 1968.
Babbage, Charles. *The Ninth Bridgewater Treatise, a Fragment*. London, 1837.
Bacon, Francis. *Advancement of Learning*. Oxford, 1906.
_______. *Novum Organum*. Translated by Andrew Johnson. London, 1859.
_______. Ibid. Edited by Thomas Fowler. Oxford, 1878.
_______. *The Works of Francis Bacon*. 10 Volumes. London, 1819.
Bakewell, Robert. *An Introduction to Geology*. London: J. Hardy, 1813.
_______. Ibid. Second edition. London: J. Hardy, 1815.
_______. Ibid. Third edition. London: Longman and Co., 1828.
_______. Ibid. Fourth edition. London: Longman and Co., 1833.
_______. Ibid. Fifth edition. London: Longman and Co., 1838.
Best, M.C. *Six Thousand Years Ago*. Bath, 1844.

Best, Samuel. *After Thoughts on Reading Dr. Buckland's Bridgewater Treatise*. London: J. Hatchard and Son, 1837.

_______. *Sermons on the Beginning of All Things As Revealed to Us in the Word of God*. London: Simpkin, Marshall and Co., 1871.

Beudant, F.S. "Extract from a Memoir Read to the Institute on the 13th of May 1816 on the Possibility of Making the Molluscae of Fresh Water Live in Salt Water, and Vice Versa." *Philosophical Magazine*, vol. XLVIII, no. 22 (1816): p. 223–227.

Blomfield, E. *A New Family Bible . . . with Notes . . . Selected from Matthew Henry*. Vol. 1. Bungay, 1810.

Blyth, Edward. "An Attempt to Classify the 'Varieties' of Animals with Observations on the Marked Seasonal and Other Changes Which Naturally Take Place in Various British Species and Which Do Not Constitute Varieties." *Magazine of Natural History*, vol. VIII (1835): p. 40–53.

_______. "On the Psychological Distinctions between Man and All Other Animals; and the Consequent Diversity of Human Influence Over the Inferior Ranks of Creation, from Any Mutual and Reciprocal Influence Exercised Among the Latter." *Magazine of Natural History*, N.S. vol. I (1837): p. 131–141.

Boys, Thomas. *A Word for the Bible*. London, 1832.

Brande, William. *Outlines of Geology*. London: John Murray, 1817.

_______. Ibid. Second edition, 1829.

Brander, Gustavus. *Fossilia Hantoniensia Collecta*. London, 1766.

Brown, James Mellor. *Reflections on Geology*. London: James Nisbet, 1838.

Brown, John. *The Self-interpreting Bible*. 2 Volumes. London, 1816 [1791].

Buckland, William. "Address Delivered on the Anniversary, 19 Feb. 1841." *Proceedings of the Geological Society*, vol. III, pt. 2, no. 81 (1841): p. 469–540.

_______. *Geological and Mineralogical Considerations with Reference to Natural Theology* ("Bridgewater Treatise"). 2 Volumes. London: John Murray, 1836.

_______. "Geological Society Anniversary Address of the Rev. Prof. Buckland, Pres., Feb. 21, 1840." *Philosophical Magazine*, 3rd ser. vol. XVII, no. 113 (1841): p. 508–541.

_______. *An Inquiry Whether the Sentence of Death Pronounced at the Fall of Man Included the Whole Animal Creation or Was Restricted to the Human Race*. London, 1839.

_______. "On the Vitality of Toads Enclosed in Stone or Wood." *Edinburgh New Philosophical Journal*, vol. XIII (1832): p. 26–32.

_______. "Professor Buckland's Reply to Some Observations in Dr. Fleming's Remarks on the Distribution of British Animals." *Edinburgh Philosophical Journal*, vol. XII, no. 24 (1825): p. 304–319.

_______. *Reliquiae Diluvianae*. London: William Pickering, 1823.

_______. *Vindiciae Geologicae*. Oxford: University Press, 1820.

_______. *The Works of Francis Bacon*. 10 Volumes. London, 1819.

Buckland, William and William D. Conybeare. "Observations on the Southwestern Coal District of England." *Transactions of the Geological Society*, 2nd ser. vol. I, pt. 1 (1822): p. 211–316.

Bugg, George. *Appeal to Truth. A Farewell Sermon Preached at the Parish Church of Lutterworth, Leicestershire, on Wednesday Evening, Dec. 30th, 1818, in Consequence of the Author's Dismissal from His Curacy by the Lord Bishop of Lincoln, Being the Third Time He Has Been Removed under the Influence of Existing Laws: Delivered before a Large Audience, to Whom This Sermon Is Affectionately Inscribed, and Published at Their Request and Expense*. London: L.B. Seeley, 1819.

_______. *The Book of Common Prayer: Its Baptismal Offices, Catechism, and Other Services Explained and Justified, in an Address to the Churchmen of Kettering and Its Neighbourhood*, 1840.

_______. *The Country Pastor: Fifteen Sermons*. London: L.B. Seeley, 1817.

_______. *Friendly Remarks on the Rev. J.W. Cunningham's Conciliatory Suggestions on the Subject of Regeneration*. London: L.B. Seeley, 1816.

_______. *Hard Measure; or, Cruel Laws in Liberal Times Illustrated in an Authentic Narrative of the Sufferings Endured and the Pecuniary Loss Sustained by the Rev. George Bugg, A.B., in Three Dismissals from His Curacies under the Influence of the "Curates' Act," without a Fault Alleged.* London: L.B. Seeley, 1820.
_______. *The Key to Modern Controversy or the Baptismal Regeneration of the Established Church Explained and Justified; in Reference to the Late Charge of the Bishop of London.* London: Seeley, Burnside and Seeley, 1843.
_______. "Letter to the Editor." *Christian Observer*, vol. XXVIII (1828): p. 235–244, 308–311, 367–374, 428–433.
_______. *Scriptural Geology*. 2 Volumes. London: Hatchard and Son. 1826–27.
_______. *Spiritual Regeneration, not necessarily connected with Baptism.* Kettering: T. Whitlark, London: L.B. Seeley, 1816.
Burnet, Thomas. *Sacred Theory of the Earth.* London, 1816 [1691].
Burton, Charles J. *A View of the Creation of the World in Illustration of the Mosaic Record.* London, 1836.
Calvin, John. *Genesis.* Translated & edited by John King. Edinburgh: Banner of Truth, 1992. [Original English translation, 1847; Latin original, 1554].
_______. *Institutes of the Christian Religion.* Translated by Henry Beveridge. Grand Rapids: Eerdmans, 1994. [Original English translation, 1845; Latin original, 1559.]
Catcott, Alexander. *A Treatise on the Deluge,* 1761.
Chalmers, Thomas. *Evidences and Authority of Christian Revelation.* Edinburgh, 1814–15.
Charpentier, Jean de. "On Fossil Organic Remains as a means of distinguishing Rock-formations." *Edinburgh Philosophical Journal*, vol. XII, no. 24 (1825): p. 320–321.
Clarke, Adam. *The Holy Bible . . . with Commentary and Critical Notes.* 6 Vol., London, 1836.
Clarke, J.B.B. *An Account of the Infancy, Religious and Literary Life of Adam Clarke.* 3 Volumes. London, 1833.
Cockburn, William. *The Bible Defended against the British Association.* London: Whittaker and Co. Fourth edition, 1844.
_______. *The Creation of the World, Addressed to R.J. Murchison.* London: J. Hatchard and Son, 1840.
_______. Ibid. Fifth edition, 1845.
_______. *A Letter to Prof. Buckland, Concerning the Origin of the World.* London: J. Hatchard and Son, 1838.
_______. "Letter to the Editor." *The Times.* (June 10, 1845): p. 6.
_______. "Letter to the Editor." *The Times.* (June 20, 1845): p. 4.
_______. *A New System of Geology*. London: Henry Colburn, 1849.
_______. *Remarks on the Geological Lectures of F.J. Francis.* London: J. Hatchard and Son, and Whittaker and Co, 1839.
_______. *A Remonstrance, Addressed to His Grace the Duke of Northumberland, upon the Dangers of Peripatetic Philosophy.* London: J. Hatchard and Son, 1838.
Cole, Henry, *The Bible a Rule and Test of Religion and of Science.* Cambridge: Hall and Son, also London: Seeleys, 1853.
_______, transl. *Luther Still Speaking: The Creation, a Commentary on Genesis 1-5.* Edinburgh, 1858.
_______, transl. Luther's *The Flood.* Norfolk, 1883.
_______. *Popular Geology Subversive of Divine Revelation.* London: J. Hatchard and Son, 1834.
_______. *Two Final and Conclusive Letters to the Editor of the Christian Observer, on the Subject of His Review of "Cole's Answer to Professor Sedgwick on Geology," Published in 'The Times' Journal of July 14, 1834, and Remaining Unanswered in Defense of Divine Revelation.* London: J. Hatchard and Son, 1834.

Conybeare, William D. "Answer to Dr Fleming's View of the Evidence from the Animal Kingdom, as to the Former Temperature of the Northern Regions." *Edinburgh New Philosophical Journal*, vol. VII (1829): p. 142–152.

_______. "An Examination of those Phaenomena of Geology Which Seem to Bear Most Directly on Theoretical Speculations." *Philosophical Magazine*, vol. IX, no. 52 (1831): p. 258–270.

_______. "Letter from the Rev. W.D. Conybeare, on Mr. Lyell's *Principles of Geology*." *Philosophical Magazine*, N.S. vol. VIII, no. 45 (1830): p. 215–219.

_______. "Report on the Progress, Actual State, and Ulterior Prospects of Geological Science." *Report of the First and Second Meetings of the BAAS: 1831-32*, 365-414. London, 1833.

_______. "Rev. W.D. Conybeare in Reply to a Layman, on Geology." *Christian Observer*, Vol. XXXIV (1834): p. 306–309.

Conybeare, William D. and William Phillips. *Outlines of the Geology of England and Wales*. London: William Phillips, 1822.

Crichton, Alexander. "On the Climate of the Antediluvian World." *Annals of Philosophy*, N.S. vol. IX (1825): p. 97–108, 207–217.

Croly, George. *Divine Providence; or, the three Cycles of Revelation*. London, 1834.

Cuninghame, William. *Seasons of the End; Being a View of the Scientific Times of the Year 1840*. London, 1841.

Cuvier, Georges. *Essay on the Theory of the Earth*. Translated by Robert Kerr. Edinburgh: William Blackwood, 1813.

_______. Ibid. Fourth edition, 1822.

_______. Ibid. Fifth edition. Edinburgh: William Blackwood and London: T. Cadell, 1827.

_______. *Researches on Fossil Bones*. 4 Volumes. London, 1834.

De la Beche, Henry T. *A Geological Manual*. London: Treuttel and Würtz, 1831.

_______. *Researches in Theoretical Geology*. London, 1834.

Deluc, Jean André. *An Elementary Treatise on Geology*. London, 1809.

Delvinus, Biblicus. *A Brief Treatise on Geology: or Facts, Suggestions and Inductions in that Science*. London, 1839 (second edition).

Dodd, William. *The Holy Bible with a commentary*. 3 Volumes. London, 1765.

D'Oyly, George and Richard Mant. *The Holy Bible with Notes Explanatory and Practical*. 2 Volumes. Oxford, 1823 [1817].

Duncan, Peter Martin. *Heroes of Science*. London: SPCK, 1882.

Eastmead, William. *Historia Reivallensis: Containing the History of Kirkby Moorside, and an Account of the Most Important Places in its Vicinity; Together with Brief Notices on the More Remote and Less Important Ones, to Which Is Prefixed a Dissertation on the Animal Remains, and Other Curious Phenomena, in the Recently Discovered Cave at Kirkdale*. London, 1824.

Ehrenberg, M. "Observations on the Disseminations of Minute Organic Bodies." *Edinburgh New Philosophical Journal*, vol. XXXVI, no. 71 (1844): p. 201–202.

Esmark Jens. "Remarks Tending to Explain the Geological History of the Earth." *Edinburgh New Philosophical Journal*, vol. II (1826–1827): p. 107–121.

F.F. "Dr. Chalmers on Scriptural Geology." *Christian Observer*, vol. XXXVII (1837): p. 446–448.

Faber, George Stanley. *Horae Mosaicae: A View of the Mosaical Records, with Respect to Their Connection with Profane Antiquity, Their Internal Credibility and their Connection with Christianity*. (Oxford University Bampton Lectures, 1801.) London, 1818 [1811].

_______. *The Treatise on the Genius and Object of the Patriarchal, the Levitical, and the Christian Dispensations*. 2 Volumes. London, 1823.

Fairholme, George. "Description of a Species of Natural Micrometer; with Observations on the Minuteness of Animalcula." *Philosophical Magazine and Journal of Science*, 3rd ser. vol. II, no. 7 (1833): p. 64–67.

_______. *General View of the Geology of Scripture*. London: J. Ridgeway, 1833. Second edition, 1838. Philadelphia, PA: Key and Biddle, 1833, and Philadelphia, PA: H. Hooker, 1843.

_______. "Mr. Fairholme on Geological Phenomena." *Christian Observer*, vol. XXXV (1835): p. 346–350.

_______. "Natural History of the Elephant." *The Asiatic Journal*, N.S. vol. XIV, pt. 1 (1834): p. 182–186. The German translation appeared as "Zur Naturgeschichte der Elephanten." *Notizen aus dem Gebiete der Natur und Heilkunde*, vol. XLI (1834): p. 194–198.

_______. *New and Conclusive Physical Demonstrations Both of the Fact and Period of the Mosaic Deluge, and of Its Having Been the Only Event of the Kind That Has Ever Occurred upon the Earth*. London: James Ridgeway & Sons, 1837. Second edition, 1840.

_______. "Observations on Woodcocks and Fieldfares Breeding in Scotland." *Magazine of Natural History*, N.S. vol. I, no. 7 (1837): p. 337–340.

_______. "On the Niagara Falls." *Philosophical Magazine and Journal of Science*, 3rd ser. vol. V, no. 25 (1834): p. 11–25.

_______. "On the Power Possessed by Spiders to Escape from an Isolated Situation." *Philosophical Magazine and Journal of Science*, 3rd ser. vol. I, no. 6 (1832): p. 424–427. The German translation appeared as "Ueber die Fahigkeit der Spinne, sich von einem isolirten Orte aus zu entfernen." *Notizen aus dem Gebiete der Natur und Heilkunde*, vol. XXXV (1833): p. 278–281.

_______. *Positions géologiques en vérifications directe de la chronologie de la Bible*. Munich: George Franz, 1834.

_______. "Some Observations on the Nature of Coal, and on the Manner in Which Strata of the Coal Measures Must Probably Have Been Deposited." *Philosophical Magazine and Journal of Science*, 3rd ser. vol. III, no. 16 (1833): p. 245–252.

Fairholme, George K.E. _______. "The Blacks of Moreton Bay and the Porpoises." *Proceedings of the Zoological Society of London*, pt. XXIV (1856): p. 353–354.

_______. "Observations on the Pteropus of Australia." *Proceedings of the Zoological Society of London*, pt. XXIV (1856): p. 311–312

_______. "On the Australian Dugong." *Proceedings of the Zoological Society of London*, pt. XXIV (1856): p. 352–353.

Fitton, William H. "Notes on the History of English Geology." *Philosophical Magazine*, N.S. vol. II, no. 7 (1832): p. 37–57.

FitzRoy, Robert. *Voyages of the Adventure and Beagle*. 3 Volumes. London: Henry Colburn, 1839.

Fleming, John. "Additional Remarks on the Climate of the Arctic Regions, in Answer to Mr. Conybeare." *Edinburgh New Philosophical Journal*, vol. VIII (1830): p. 65–74.

_______. "The Geological Deluge as Interpreted by Baron Cuvier and Buckland Inconsistent with Moses and Nature." *Edinburgh Philosophical Journal*, vol. XIV (1826): p. 205–239.

_______. "Mollusca." In *Edinburgh Encyclopaedia*, Vol. XIV, 598–635. David Brewster, ed. Edinburgh, 1830.

_______. "On the Value of the Evidence from the Animal Kingdom, tending to prove that the Arctic Regions formerly enjoyed a milder climate than at present." *Edinburgh New Philosophical Journal*, vol. VI (1829): p. 277–286.

_______. "Review of Knight's *Theory of the Earth*." *Edinburgh Monthly Review*, vol. I (1819): p. 356.

Forman, Walter. *Treatises on Several Very Important Subjects in Natural Philosophy*. London, 1832.

Francis, Frederick J. *A Brief Survey of Physical and Fossil Geology*. London, 1839.

Fuller, Andrew. *Expository Discourses on the Book of Genesis*. 2 Volumes. London, 1806.

Geddes, Alexander. *Critical Remarks on the Hebrew Scriptures*. Volume 1. London, 1800.

_______. *The Holy Bible . . . with Explanatory Notes*. 2 Volumes. London, 1792.

Gilbert, Richard. *The Clerical Guide*. London, 1836.

Gill, John. *Exposition of the Old Testament*. 6 Volumes. London, 1810 [1763].

Gisborne, Thomas. *Considerations on the Modern Theory of Geology*. London: T. Cadell, 1837.

_______. *The Testimony of Natural Theology to Christianity*. London: T. Cadell. Third edition, 1818. American edition, Philadelphia, PA: M. Thomas, 1818.

Gosse, Philip H. *Omphalos*. London, 1857.

Gray, John E. "Remarks on the Difficulty of Distinguishing Certain Genera of Testaceous Mollusca by Their Shells Alone, and on the Anomalies in Regard to Habitation Observed in Certain Species." *Philosophical Transactions*, vol. CXXV, part 2 (1835): p. 301–310. A one-page summary of this appeared under the same title in *Philosophical Magazine*, 3rd ser. vol. VII, no. 39, p. 210.

_______. "Some Observations on the Economy of Molluscous Animals, and on the Structure of Their Shells." *Philosophical Transactions*, vol. CXXIII, part 2 (1833): p. 771–819.

Greenough, George B. "Address Delivered at the Anniversary Meeting of the Geological Society (Feb. 21, 1834)." *Proceedings of the Geological Society*, vol. II, no. 35 (1833–34): p. 42–70.

_______. *A Critical Examination of the First Principles of Geology*. London, 1819.

Harcourt, Leveson Venables. *The Doctrine of the Deluge: Vindicating the Scriptural Account from the Doubts Which Have Recently Been Cast upon it by Geological Speculations*. 2 Volumes. London, 1838.

Harcourt, William Vernon. "Address of the Presidency of the BAAS." *Atheneum*, no. 618, (August, 31, 1839): p. 651–654. Partial reprint from *Report of the Ninth Meeting of British Association for the Advancement of Science, Birmingham 1839*, 1-68. London: John Murray.

Herschel, John. *Preliminary Discourse on the Study of Natural Philosophy*. London, 1840. Third Edition.

Higgins, William M. *Book of Geology*. London, 1842.

_______. *The Mosaical and Mineral Geologies Compared*. London, 1832.

Hindmarsh, Robert. *Christianity against Deism, Materialism, and Atheism, Occasioned by a Letter Addressed to the Author by R. Carlile*. Manchester, 1824.

Hitchcock, Edward. "The Historical and Geological Deluges Compared." *The American Biblical Repository*, vol. IX, no. 25 (1837): p. 78–139.

Hopkins, William. "On the Transport of Erratic Blocks." *Transactions of the Cambridge Philosophical Society*, vol. VIII (1849): p. 220–240.

Horne, Thomas H. *A Compendious Introduction to the Study of the Bible*. London, 1827.

_______. *Deism Refuted*. London, 1819.

_______. *An Introduction to the Critical Study and Knowledge of the Holy Scripture*. 3 Volumes. London, 1818.

Humboldt, Friedrich W.H.A. von. *Geognostical Essay on the Superposition of Rocks in Both Hemispheres*. London, 1823.

Hutton, James. *The Theory of the Earth*. 2 Volumes. Edinburgh, 1795.

Jameson, Robert. *System of Mineralogy*. 3 Volumes. Edinburgh, 1804.

Johnsone, Fowler de. *Vindication of the Book of Genesis Addressed to Rev. William Buckland*. London: R. Groombridge, and Simpkin and Marshall, 1838.

Irons, William Josiah. *On the Whole Doctrine of Final Causes*. London, 1836.

Kennedy, James. *Lectures on the Philosophy of the Mosaic Record of the Creation*. 2 Volumes in one. London, 1827.

Kirby, William. *On the History, Habits and Instincts of Animals*. 2 Volumes. London, 1835.

Kirwan, Richard. *Geological Essays*. London, 1799.

Lindley, John and William Hutton. *The Fossil Flora of Great Britain*. 3 Volumes. London, 1831–1837.

Luther, Martin. *Biblia*. Wittemburg, 1548.

_______. *D. Martin Luthers Werke: Die Deutsche Bibel*, 8. Band. Weimar, 1954. [This is a parallel edition of the 1523 and 1545 editions.]

Lyell, Charles. *The Antiquity of Man*. London, 1863.

_______. *Manual of Elementary Geology*. London, 1855.

_______. *Principles of Geology*. 3 Volumes. London: John Murray, 1830–33. [1990 Reprint, Chicago: University of Chicago Press.

_______. Review of *Memoir on the Geology of Central France* by G. P. Scrope. *Quarterly Review*, vol. XXXVI (1827): p. 436–483.

Macbrair, Robert Maxwell. *Geology and Geologists*. London, 1843.

Macculloch, John. "Hints on the Possibility of Changing the Residence of Certain Fishes from Salt Water to Fresh." *Quarterly Journal of Science*, vol. XVII, no. 34 (1824): p. 209–231.

_______. "Organic Remains." In *Edinburgh Encyclopaedia*, David Brewster, ed. Edinburgh, 1830, Vol. XV, p. 681–756.

_______. *Proofs and Illustrations of the Attributes of God from the Facts and Laws of the Physical Universe Being the Foundation of Natural and Revealed Religion*. 3 Volumes. London, 1837.

_______. *A System of Geology with a Theory of the Earth and an Explanation of Its Connexion with the Sacred Records*. 2 Volumes. London, 1831.

Mantell, Gideon A. *Fossils of the South Downs: Geology of Sussex*. London, 1822.

_______. *The Wonders of Geology*. 2 Volumes. London, 1838. Second edition.

Martin, William. *The Christian Philosopher's Explanation of the General Deluge, and the Proper Cause of all the Different Strata*. Newcastle, 1834.

Mildert, William Van. *An Inquiry into the General Principles of Scriptural Interpretation*. Oxford, 1815.

Miller, Hugh. *The Old Red Sandstone*. Edinburgh, 1873. Eighteenth edition, original in 1841.

_______. *The Testimony of the Rocks; or Geology in Its Bearings on the Two Theologies, Natural and Revealed*. Edinburgh: W.P. Nimmo, Hay, & Mitchell, 1897. Identical to original 1857 edition.

_______. *The Two Records: Mosaic and the Geological*. London, 1854.

Morison, David. *The Religious History of Man*. London, 1838. Second edition, 1842.

Murray, Hugh, ed. *Historical and Descriptive Account of British India*. 3 Volumes. Edinburgh, 1832.

Murray, John. *An Account of the Phormium Tenax, or New Zealand Flax. Printed on Paper Made from Its Leaves, with a Postscript on Paper.* London: Henry Renshaw, 1836.

_______. *Atheism Weighed in the Balance of Induction*, post-1839.

_______. *Communications on Coal Mines . . . investigating the causes of accidents in coal mines.* London: Hamilton, Adams and Co, 1844.

_______. *Considerations on the Vital Principle*. London, 1837.

_______. *Description of a New Lightning Conductor; and Observations on the Phenomena of the Thunderstorm.* London: S. Highley, 1833.

_______. *Descriptive Account of a New Shower Bath, Constructed on a Principle not Hitherto Applied to That Machine; also, an Apparatus for Restoring Suspended Animation.* London: Whittaker and Co., 1831. Second edition.

_______. *A Descriptive Account of the Palo de Vaco or Cow-Tree of the Caracos with a Chemical Analysis of the Milk and Bark.* London: Effingham Wilson, 1837. Second edition, London: Relfe and Fletcher, 1838.

_______. "Dr. Buckland's Geological Sermon." *Christian Observer*, vol. XXXIX, no. 19 (1839): p. 400–401.

_______. *The Economy of Vegetation*. London: Relfe and Fletcher, 1838.

_______. *The Elements of Chemical Science as Applied to the Arts and Manufactures and Natural Phenomena*. Saffron Walden: G. Youngman, 1815. Third edition, 1827.

_______. *Experimental Researches on the Light and Luminous Matter of the Glowworm, the Luminosity of the Sea, the Phenomena of the Chameleon, the Ascent of the Spider into the Atmosphere, and the Torpidity of the Tortoise, Etc.* Glasgow: W.R. McPhan, 1826.

_______. *A Glance at some of the Beauties and Sublimities of Switzerland.* London: Longman, Rees, Orme, Brown and Green, 1829.

_______. *Improvements on the Life Boat,* pre-1839.

_______. *Invention of an Effective and Unfailing Method for Forming an Instantaneous Communication with the Shore in Shipwreck and Illuminating the Scene in the Dark and Tempestuous Night.* London: Whittaker, Treacher and Arnot, 1831.

_______. *A Letter to the Right Honourable Earl Grey on Colonial Slavery.* London: Holdworth and Ball, 1832.

_______. *A Manual of Experiments Illustrative of Chemical Science, Systematically Arranged.* London: Longman, Rees, Orme, Brown and Green, 1828. Fifth edition, 1839.

_______. *A Memoir on the Diamond.* London: Longman, Rees, Orme, Brown and Green, 1831. Second edition, London: Relfe and Fletcher, 1839.

_______. *Minor Poems.* Dumfries, 1816.

_______. *Napoleon Never Existed.* Translation from French, pre-1939.

_______. *The Natural History of Poisons.* London, 1830?

_______. *The Natural History of the Silk Worm.* London: Effingham Wilson, 1838. Second edition.

_______. *Observations and Experiments on the Bad Composition of Modern Paper; with the Description of a Permanent Writing Ink, which Cannot Be Discharged.* London: G. and W.B. Whittaker, 1824.

_______. *Physiology of Plants; or the Phenomena and Laws of Vegetation.* London: John Murray, 1833.

_______. *The Plague and Quarantine. Remarks on Some Epidemic and Endemic Diseases; (Including the Plague of the Levant,) and the Means of Disinfection; with a Description of the Preservative Phial. Also a postscript on Dr. Bowring's pamphlet entitled "Observations on the Oriental Plague," etc.* London: Relfe and Fletcher, 1839 (second edition). First edition, London: Effingham Wilson, 1838.

_______. *A Portrait of Geology.* London: Relfe and Fletcher, 1838.

_______. *Practical Observations and Researches on Ventilation and Disinfection, Inclusive of Other Essential Provisions Connected with Sanitary Regulations and the Health of Towns.* London: Whittaker and Co, 1850.

_______. *Practical Observations on the Phenomena of Flame and Safety Lamps.* London, 1833.

_______. *Practical Observations on the Phenomena of Flame and Safety Lamps.* London: Henry Renshaw, 1836. Second edition.

_______. *Practical Remarks on Modern Paper with an Introductory Account of its Former Substitutes, also Observations on Writing Inks, the Restoration of Illegible Manuscripts, and the Preservation of Important Deeds from the Destructive Effects of Damp.* London (also Edinburgh: W. Blackwood), 1829.

_______. Public testimony. *Report from the Select Committee on Accidents in Mines,* 237-48. London: The House of Commons, September 4, 1835.

_______. *Remarks on the Cultivation of the Silk Worm, with Additional Observations, Made in Italy During the Summer of 1825.* Glasgow: W.R. McPhan, 1825.

_______. *Remarks on the Disease called Hydrophobia: Prophylactic and Curative.* London: Longman, Rees, Orme, Brown and Green, 1830.

_______. "Reply to B.M." *Annals of Philosophy,* N.S. vol. III (1822): p. 121–123.

_______. *Researches in Natural History.* London: Whittaker and Co., 1830. Second edition.

_______. "Researches on Hydrocyanic Acid and Opium, with Reference to Their Counter-poisons." *Edinburgh Philosophical Journal,* vol. VII, no. 13 (1822): p. 124–127.

_______. *Strictures on Modern Geological Speculations,* pre-1839.

_______. *A Treatise on Atmospherical Electricity Including Lightning Rods and Paragrêles.* London: Whittaker and Treacher. Second edition, 1830. French edition: Paris, 1831.

_______. *A Treatise on Pulmonary Consumption; Its Prevention and Remedy.* London: Whittaker, Treacher and Arnot, 1830. Second edition, London: Longman, Rees, Orme, Brown and Green, 1831. Another edition, London: Renshaw, 1834.

_______. *The Truth of Revelation, Demonstrated by an Appeal to Existing Monuments and Sculptures, Gems, Coins and Medals.* London: Longman, Rees, Orme, Brown and Green, 1831.

_______. *The Truth of Revelation, Demonstrated By an Appeal to Existing Monuments and Sculptures, Gems, Coins and Medals.* London: William Smith, 1840. Revised and expanded second edition.

Newton, Isaac. *Four Letters from Sir Isaac Newton to Doctor Bentley Containing Some Arguments in Proof of a Deity.* London, 1756.

_______. *Opticks.* London: Bell, 1931. Original in 1704.

Nolan, Frederick. *Analogy of Revelation and Science Established.* Oxford, 1833.

Parkinson, James. *Organic Remains of a Former World — An Examination of Mineral Remains of the Vegetables and Animals of the Antediluvian World: Generally Termed Extraneous Fossils.* 3 Volumes. London, 1808–1811.

Paterson, James. "Parish of Gordon." *The New Statistical Account of Scotland.* Edinburgh, 1845.

Patrick, Symon. *A Commentary upon the Historical Books of the Old Testament.* Vol. I. London, 1738. [Original in 1694].

Penn, Granville. *A Christian's Survey of all the Primary Events and Periods of the World.* London, 1811. Second edition, 1812. Third edition, 1814. Another edition, London: John Murray, 1824.

_______. *Comparative Estimate of the Mineral and Mosaic Geologies.* London: Ogle, Duncan and Co, 1822.

_______. *Comparative Estimate of the Mineral and Mosaic Geologies.* Revised and expanded second edition: 2 Volumes. London: J. Duncan, 1825. Third edition, 1844.

_______. *Supplement to a Comparative Estimate.* London: Ogle, Duncan and Co, 1823.

Phillips, John. "Geology." *The Penny Cyclopaedia*, Vol. XI, 127-51. London, 1838.

_______. *A Guide to Geology.* London: Longman, Rees, Orme, Browne, Green and Longman, 1834.

_______. *Illustrations of the Geology of Yorkshire.* 2 Volumes. York, 1829–36.

_______. *Memoirs of William Smith.* London, 1844.

_______. *A Treatise on Geology.* 2 Volumes. London: Cabinet Cyclopaedia, 1837–39.

Playfair, John. *Illustrations of the Huttonian Theory of the Earth.* Edinburgh, 1802.

Powell, Baden. *The Connexion of Natural and Divine Truth.* London, 1838.

_______. *Revelation and Science.* Oxford, 1833.

Pratt, John H. *Scripture and Science not at Variance,* 1856.

Priestley, Joseph. *Notes on all the Books of Scripture for the Use of the Pulpit and Private Families.* 4 Volumes. Northumberland, 1803–04.

Prout, William. *Chemistry, Meteorology and the Function of Digestion Considered with Reference to Natural Theology.* London, 1834.

Purver, Anthony. *A New and Literal Translation of . . . the Old and New Testament with Notes.* 2 Volumes. London, 1764.

[Rennie, J.] *Conversations on Geology: Comprising a Familiar Explanation of the Huttonian and Wernerian Systems; The Mosaic Geology as Explained by Mr. Granville Penn; and the Late Discoveries of Prof. Buckland, Humboldt, Dr. Macculloch and others.* London, 1828.

Rhind, William. *The Age of the Earth: Considered Geologically and Historically.* Edinburgh: Fraser and Co., 1838.

_______. *Cases Illustrative of the Division of Tendons.* Edinburgh, 1841.

_______. *A Catechism of Botany.* Edinburgh: Oliver & Boyd, 1833.

_______. *A Catechism of the Natural History of the Earth*. Edinburgh: Oliver & Boyd, 1832.
_______. *Class Book of Elementary Geography*. Edinburgh, 1858.
_______. "Contributions to the Hydrology of the British Islands." *Proceedings of the Royal Physical Society Edinburgh*, vol. I (1855): p. 15–17.
_______. "Description of a Species of Worm Found in the Frontal Sinus of a Sheep." *Edinburgh Journal of Natural and Geographical Science*, vol. I (1830): p. 29–31.
_______. *Elements of Geology and Physical Geography*. Edinburgh: Fraser and Co., 1837. Second edition, London: H. Washbourne, 1839. Third edition, 1844.
_______. *Elements of Meteorology*. Edinburgh, 1840?
_______. *Elements of Zoology*. Edinburgh, 1839. Another edition, 1845.
_______. "Examination of the Opinions of Bremser and Others on the Equivocal Production of Animals." *Edinburgh Journal of Natural and Geographical Science*, vol. II (1830): p. 391–397.
_______. *Excursions Illustrative of the Geology and Natural History of the Environs of Edinburgh*. Edinburgh, 1833.
_______. *The Feline Species*. Edinburgh: Fraser and Co, 1834.
_______. *First Class Book of Physical Geography*. Edinburgh: Sutherland and Knox, 1850. Another edition, London: Simpkin, Marshall and Company.
_______. "The Geological Arrangement of Ancient Strata, Deduced from the Condition of the Present Oceanic Beds." *Edinburgh New Philosophical Journal*, vol. XXXVI (1844): p. 327–334. German: Froriep, Notizen, vol. XXX (1844), col. 273–280.
_______. *The Geology of Scotland and Its Islands*. Edinburgh: Edinburgh Printing and Publishing Company, 1842. Other editions, London: Smith, Elder and Company, also in Glasgow and Aberdeen.
_______. *A History of the Vegetable Kingdom*. Glasgow, Edinburgh, and London: Blackie and Son, 1840?
_______. "Notice of Coal Found in the Argillaceous Slate Quarries of Seil Island, Argyleshire." *Proceedings of the Royal Physical Society Edinburgh*, vol. I (1858): p. 439–441.
_______. *Second Class Book of Physical Geography: Embracing Organic Life, and the Geographical Distribution of Plants, Animals and Man*. Edinburgh: Sutherland and Knox, 1851. Another edition, London: Simpkin, Marshall and Company.
_______. *Sketches of the Past and Present State of Moray*. Elgin: G. Wilson, 1839.
_______. *Studies in Natural History*. Edinburgh: Oliver & Boyd, 1830.
_______. *A Treatise on the Nature and Cure of Intestinal Worms of the Human Body*. London: S. Highley, 1829. Another edition, Edinburgh.
Richardson, John. *Choice Observations on the Old Testament*. London, 1655.
Rodd, Thomas. *A Defense of the Veracity of Moses*. London, 1820.
Rogers, Henry D. "On the Falls of Niagara and the Reasonings of Some Authors Respecting Them." *American Journal of Science and Arts*, vol. XXVII, no. 2 (1835): p. 326–335.
Scopes, George Poulett. *Considerations on Volcanos. . . to the Establishment of a New Theory of Earth*. London, 1825.
Scott, Thomas. *The Holy Bible . . . with explanatory notes by T. Scott*. 4 Volumes. Glasgow, 1841.
Sedgwick, Adam. "Address to the Geological Society." *Philosophical Magazine*, N.S. vol. IX, no. 52 (1831): p. 271–317.
_______. "Annual General Meeting of the Geological Society, Presidential Address." *Philosophical Magazine*, N.S. vol. VII, no. 40 (1830): p. 289–315.
_______. *A Discourse on Studies of the University*. Cambridge, 1834. Second edition.
_______. *A Discourse on Studies of the University*. Cambridge, 1855. Fifth edition.
_______. "On Diluvial Formations." *Annals of Philosophy*, N.S. vol. X (1825): p. 18–37.
_______. "On the Classification of the Strata Which Appear on the Yorkshire Coast." *Annals of Philosophy*, N.S. vol. II (1826): p. 339–362.

_______. "On the Origin of Alluvial and Diluvial Formations." *Annals of Philosophy*, N.S. vol. IX (1825): p. 241–257.

_______. "*Vestiges of the Natural History of Creation.*" *Edinburgh Review*, vol. LXXXII, no. 165 (1845): p. 1–85.

Sedgwick, Adam and Roderick Murchison. "On the Structure and Relation of the Deposits Contained between the Primary Rocks and the Oolitic Series in the North of Scotland." *Transactions of the Geological Society*, 2nd ser. vol. III (1835): p. 125–160.

Smith, James. "On the Last Changes in the Relative Levels of the Land and Sea in the British Islands." *Memoirs of the Wernerian Natural History Society*, vol. VIII (1838): p. 49–88.

Smith, James Alexander. *The Atheisms of Geology*. London, 1857.

Smith, John Pye. *Mosaic Account of Creation and the Deluge Illustrated by Science*. London, 1837.

_______. *On the Relation Between the Holy Scriptures and Some Parts of Geological Science* (often referred to as *Scripture and Geology*). London, 1839.

_______. "Suggestions on the Science of Geology, in Answer to the Question of T.K." *Congregational Magazine*, N.S. Vol. I (1837): p. 765–776.

Smith, William. *Deductions from Established Facts in Geology*. Scarborough, 1835.

_______. *Strata Identified by Organized Fossils*. London, 1816.

_______. *Stratigraphical System of Organized Fossils*. London, 1817.

Smithson, James. "Some Observations on Mr. Penn's Theory Concerning the Formation of the Kirkdale Cave." *Annals of Philosophy*, vol. VIII (1824): p. 50–60.

Sowerby, James. *The Genera of Recent and Fossil Shells*. London, 1820–25.

_______. *Mineral Conchology of Great Britain*. 7 volumes. London, 1812–29.

Spinoza, Benedict De. *The Chief Works of Benedict De Spinoza*. 2 Volumes. Translated by R.H.M. Elwes. New York: Dover Publications, 1951.

Stackhouse, Thomas. *A History of the Holy Bible; Corrected and Approved by Scottish Bishop George Gleig*. 3 Volumes. London, 1817 [1737].

Sumner, John Bird. *Treatise on the Records of Creation*. 2 Volumes. London, 1816.

Sutcliffe, Joseph. *Geology of Avon*. Bristol, 1822.

_______. *Short Introduction to the Study of Geology*. London, 1817.

T. "Reviews." *Magazine of Natural History*, vol. I (1829): p. 249–271.

_______. Review of George Young's *A Geological Survey of the Yorkshire Coast* (2nd ed., 1828). *Magazine of Natural History*, vol. III, no. 15 (1830): p. 423–426.

_______. Review of Robert Bakewell's *An Introduction to Geology*, Third edition. *Magazine of Natural History*, vol. I, no. 4 (1829): p. 353–360.

Townsend, Joseph. *The Character of Moses Established for Veracity as an Historian*. 2 Volumes. Bath, 1813–15.

Turnbull, H.W., ed. *The Correspondence of Isaac Newton*. 7 Volumes. Cambridge: Cambridge University Press, 1959–1977.

Turner, Sharon. *The Sacred History of the World*. 3 Volumes. London: Longmans and Company, 1832–1837.

Ure, Andrew. *The Cotton Manufacture of Great Britain*. 2 Volumes. London: Charles Knight, 1836.

_______. *Dictionary of Arts, Manufactures and Mines*. London: Longman, Orme, Brown, Green and Longman, 1839.

_______. *A Dictionary of Chemistry*. London: T. and G. Underwood, 1821.

_______. *Elements of the Art of Dyeing*. London: T. Tegg, 1824.

_______. *A New Systematic Table of the Materia Medica*. Glasgow: Duncan, 1813.

_______. *A New System of Geology*. London: Longman, Rees, Orme, Brown and Green, 1829.

_______. *Outlines of Natural or Experimental Philosophy*. Glasgow, 1809.

_______. *The Philosophy of Manufactures*. London: Charles Knight, 1835.
_______. *The Revenue in Jeopardy from Spurious Chemistry*. London: J. Ridgeway, 1843.
Weaver, Thomas. "Geological Observations on Part of Gloucestershire and Somersetshire." *Transactions of the Geological Society*. 2nd ser. vol. I, pt. 1 (1822): p. 317–368.
_______. "On Fossil Human Bones, and Other Animal Remains Recently Found in Germany." *Annals of Philosophy*, N.S. vol. V (1823): p. 17–34.
Whewell, William. "Address to the Geological Society, delivered at the Anniversary, on the 15th of Feb. 1839." *Proceedings of the Geological Society*, vol. III (1838-43): p. 61–98.
_______. *The History of the Inductive Sciences*. 3 Volumes. London: J.W. Parker, 1837.
_______. *The Philosophy of the Inductive Sciences*. 2 Volumes. London, 1840.
_______. Review of Lyell's *Principles of Geology*. *Quarterly Review*, vol. XLVII, no. 93 (1832): p. 103–132.
Whiston, William. *New Theory of the Earth*. London, 1698 [1696].
Whitehurst, John. *Inquiry into the Original State and Formation of the Earth*. London, 1792. Third edition.
Wiseman, Nicholas Patrick, S. *Twelve Lectures on the Connection between Science and Revealed Religion*. 2 Volumes. London, 1859 [original 1836].
Wood, Nicholas. "Account of Some Fossil Stems of Trees." *Transactions of the Natural History Society of Northumberland*, Vol. I (1831): p. 205–214.
Wood, William. *Index Testaceologicus; or a Catalogue of Shells, British and Foreign*. London, 1825.
Woodward, John. *An Essay Toward a Natural Theory of the Earth*. London, 1695.
Wrangham, Francis, ed. *The Pleiad; or, A Series of Abridgements of Seven Distinguished Writers, in Opposition to the Pernicious Doctrines of Deism*. Hunmanby, 1820.
Young, George. "Account of a Fossil Crocodile Recently Discovered in the Alum Shale Near Whitby." *Edinburgh Philosophical Journal*, vol. XIII (1825): p. 76–81.
_______. "Account of a Singular Fossil Skeleton, Discovered at Whitby in February 1819." *Memoirs of the Wernerian Society of Edinburgh*, vol. III (1817–20 [article dated 1819]): p. 450–457.
_______. *A Catalogue of Hardy Ornamental Flowering Shrubs, Forest and Fruit Trees, Etc.* Whitby: R. Rodgers, 1834.
_______. *The Character of Anne Exemplified. A Sermon Preached in Cliff-lane Chapel, April 27, 1827; Occasioned by the Death of Elizabeth Petrie.* Whitby: R. Rodgers, 1827.
_______. *Christ's Departed Friends Asleep in the Grave. A Sermon Preached in Cliff-lane Chapel, October 10, 1819, Occasioned by the Early Death of Mr. William Hyslop, Etc. with Letters, Etc.* Whitby: R. Rodgers, 1820.
_______. *Christ's Prayer for the Unity of His Church. A Sermon Preached at Edinburgh, September 7, 1819, at the Opening of the Associate Synod.* Edinburgh: J. & C. Muirhead, 1819.
_______. *Compassion for Prisoners Recommended. A Sermon Preached in Cliff-lane Chapel, on Sabbath, January 22, 1809*. Whitby: R. Rodgers, 1809. Third edition, 1809.
_______. *The Death of a Young Seaman Bewailed. A Sermon Preached in Cliff-lane Chapel, December 27, 1818.* Whitby: R. Rodgers, 1819.
_______. *The Downfall of Napoleon, and the Deliverance of Europe Improved. A Sermon Preached in Cliff-lane Chapel, July 7, 1814.* Whitby: R. Rodgers, 1814.
_______. *Evangelical Principles of Religion Vindicated, and the Inconsistency and Dangerous Tendency of the Unitarian Scheme Exposed.* Whitby: R. Rodgers, 1812.
_______. "Geological and Mineralogical Survey of Part of the Yorkshire Coast." *Philosophical Magazine*, vol. LI (1818): p. 206–214.

_______. *The Great Solar Eclipse; or, the Stability of the Covenant of Grace Illustrated by the Unchanging Ordinances of Heaven. A Sermon Preached at Cliff-lane Chapel, May 15, 1836.* Whitby: R Kirby, 1836.

_______. *A History of Whitby and Streoneshalh Abbey*. 2 Volumes. Whitby: Clark and Medd, 1817. Another edition, Whitby: Caedmon Press, 1976.

_______. *Lectures on the Book of Jonah.* Whitby: Clark and Medd, 1819. Second edition, Whitby: R. Rodgers, 1832. Another edition, London: F. Westley, 1833.

_______. *A Letter to the Rev. T. Watson; Occasioned by His Pamphlet Entitled "Evangelical Principles Exemplified."* Whitby: R. Rodgers, 1813.

_______. *The Life and Voyages of Captain James Cook.* Whitby: Horne and Richardson. London: Whittaker and Treacher, 1836. Dutch edition: Utrecht, 1854.

_______. *The Mariner's Refuge. A Discourse to Seamen, Delivered in Cliff-lane Chapel, August 5, 1810, on the Fate of a Part of the Crew of the Aimwell, Who Were Lost in the Greenland Seas, May 27, 1810.* Whitby: R. Rodgers, 1811.

_______. "On the Formation of Valleys, Bays, and Creeks." *Edinburgh Philosophical Journal*, vol. VII (1822): p. 151–155.

_______. "On the Fossil Remains of Quadrupeds, Etc. Discovered in the Cavern at Kirkdale, in Yorkshire, and in Other Cavities or Seams in Limestone Rocks." *Memoirs of the Wernerian Society of Edinburgh*, vol. IV (1821–23 [article dated 1822]): p. 262–270.

_______. "On the Fossil Remains of Quadrupeds, Etc. Discovered in the Cavern at Kirkdale, in Yorkshire, and in Other Cavities or Seams in Limestone Rocks." *Memoirs of the Wernerian Society of Edinburgh*, vol. VI (1826–31 [article dated 1822]): p. 171–183.

_______. *Parallels Between King David and King George. A Sermon Preached in Cliff-lane Chapel, February 16, 1820, Being the Day of the Funeral of His Majesty King George III.* Whitby: G. Clark, 1820.

_______. *A Picture of Whitby and Its Environs.* Whitby: R. Rodgers, 1824. Second edition, 1840.

_______. *Royal Honours Transient. A Sermon Preached in Cliff-lane Chapel, December 6, 1818, Being the Sabbath of the Funeral of Her Majesty Queen Charlotte.* Whitby: Clark and Medd, 1818.

_______. *Scriptural Geology*. London: Simpkin, Marshall and Co. Edinburgh: Oliphant and Son. Glasgow: M'Leod, 1838. Second edition with the *Appendix to Scriptural Geology*, London: Simpkin, Marshall and Co., 1840; *Appendix to Scriptural Geology*. London: Simpkin, Marshall and Co., 1840.

_______. *Speech of the Rev. George Young, A.M., on the Nomination Day, at the Whitby Election, December 11, 1832.* Whitby: R. Kirby, 1832.

_______. *Two Discourses to Seamen — 1st, Praising God; 2nd, Christ, the Seamen's Friend.* Whitby: Clark and Medd, 1819.

Young, George and John Bird. *Geological Survey of the Yorkshire Coast.* Whitby: George Clark, 1822.

_______. Ibid. Revised and expanded second edition. Whitby: R. Kirby, 1828. Another edition, London: Longman and Co.

SECONDARY SOURCES

Anonymous. *Abbotts Ann School 1831–1981.* Abbotts Ann, Hants: Private publication, 1981.

Addinall, Peter. *Philosophy and Biblical Interpretation: A Study in Nineteenth-century Conflict.* Cambridge: Cambridge University Press, 1991.

Ager, Derek. *The Nature of the Stratigraphical Record.* London: Macmillan Press, 1981.

_______. *The New Catastrophism.* Cambridge: Cambridge University Press, 1993.

Agerter, Sharlene R. and Waldo S. Glock. *An Annotated Bibliography of Tree Growth and Growth Rings 1950–1962.* Tucson, AZ: University of Arizona Press, 1965.

Allen, Diogenes. *Philosophy for Understanding Theology*. Atlanta, GA: John Knox Press, 1985.

Ashton, T.S. *The Industrial Revolution 1760–1830*. Oxford: Oxford University Press, 1970.

Aylmer, G.E. and Reginald Cant, eds. *A History of York Minister*. Oxford: Clarendon Press, 1977.

Austin, Steven A. *Mount St. Helens: Explosive Evidence for Catastrophe in Earth's History* (video). El Cajon, CA: Institute for Creation Research, 1994.

Bartholomew, Michael. "The Singularity of Lyell." *History of Science*, vol. XVII, no. 38 (1979): p. 276–293.

Brock, W. H. "Chemical geology or geological chemistry?" In L.J. Jordanova and Roy S. Porter, eds. *Images of the Earth*. British Society for the History of Science, 1978, Monograph 1, p. 147–166.

_______. "The Selection of the Authors of the Bridgewater Treatises." *Notes and Records of the Royal Society of London*, vol. XXI, no. 2 (1966): p. 162–179.

Brooke, John Hedley. "Indications of a Creator: Whewell as Apologist and Priest." In Menachem Fisch and Simon Schaffer, eds. *William Whewell: A Composite Portrait*. Oxford: Clarendon Press, 1991, p. 149–173.

_______. "Natural Theology in Britain from Boyle to Paley." In *New Interactions Between Theology and Natural Science*. Milton Keynes: The Open University Press, 1974, p. 5–54.

_______. "The Natural Theology of the Geologists: Some Theological Strata." In L.J. Jordanova and Roy S. Porter, eds. *Images of the Earth*. British Society for the History of Science, 1978, Monograph 1, p. 39–64.

_______. *Science and Religion: Some Historical Perspectives*. Cambridge: Cambridge University Press, 1991.

Brown, Colin. *Christianity and Western Thought*. Leicester: Apollos, 1990.

Cameron, Nigel M. de S. *Biblical Higher Criticism and the Defense of Infallibilism in 19th Century Britain*. Lewiston, NY: Edwin Meller Press, 1984.

Cannon, Susan Faye. *Science in Culture: The Early Victorian Period*. Folkstone: Dawson, 1978.

Cannon, Walter F. "The Impact of Uniformitarianism." *Proceedings of the American Philosophical Society*, vol. CV, no. 3 (1961): p. 301–314.

_______. "The Problem of Miracles in the 1830s." *Victorian Studies* vol. IV (1961): p. 5–32.

_______. "The Role of the Cambridge movement in Early 19th Century Science." In *Proceedings of the Tenth International Congress on the History of Science*. Paris: Hermann, 1964, p. 317–320.

_______. "Scientists and Broad Churchmen: An Early Victorian Intellectual Network." *Journal for British Studies*, vol. IV (1964): p. 65–88.

_______. "The Uniformitarian-Catastrophist Debate." *ISIS* vol. LI (1960): p. 38–55.

Chadwick, Owen. *The Victorian Church*. 2 Volumes. London, 1971.

Chorley, R.J., A.J. Dunn, and R.P. Bechinsale. *The History of the Study of Landforms*, Vol. 1. London: John Wiley and Sons, 1964.

Clark, John W. and Thomas M. Hughes. *The Life and Letters of the Rev. Adam Sedgwick*. 2 Vol. Cambridge, 1890.

Cleevely, R.J. *World Palaeontological Collections*. London: British Museum, 1983.

Coleman, William. "Cuvier and Evolution." In Colin Russell, ed. *Science and Religious Belief: A Selection of Recent Historical Studies*. Milton Keynes: The Open University Press, 1973, p. 224–237. Reprinted from William Coleman. *Georges Curvier, Zoologist*. Boston: Harvard University Press, 1964, p. 170–186.

Colie, Rosalie L. "Spinoza and the Early English Deists." *Journal of the History of Ideas*, XX (1959): p. 23–46.

Copeman, W.S.C. "Andrew Ure, M.D., F.R.S. (1778–1857)." *Proceedings of the Royal Society of Medicine*, vol. 44 (1951): p. 655–662.

Corsi, Pietro. *Science and Religion*. Cambridge: Cambridge University Press, 1988.

Davies, Gordon L. Herries. "Bangs Replace Whimpers." *Nature*, vol. 365 (Sept. 9, 1993): p. 115.

Dean, Dennis R. "James Hutton on Religion and Geology: The Unpublished Preface to His *Theory of the Earth* (1788)." *Annals of Science*, vol. XXXII (1975): p. 187–193.

Dembski, William A., ed. *Mere Creation: Science, Faith and Intelligent Design.* Downers Grove: InterVarsity Press, 1998.

Dillenberger, John. *Protestant Thought and Natural Science*. New York: Doubleday, 1960.

Douglas, Robert. *Sons of Moray*. Elgin: private publication, 1930.

Draper, John W. *A History of the Conflict Between Religion and Science*. London, 1875.

Dunhill, Rosemary. "The Rev. George Bugg: The Fortunes of a 19th Century Curate." *Northamptonshire Past and Present*, vol. VIII, no. 1 (1983–84): p. 41–50.

Dutton, H.A. "The Age of a 1000 Year Old Fig Tree." *Trees Magazine*, vol. XIV, no. 4 (1954): p. 10.

Edmonds, J. M. "The First Geological Lecture Course at the University of London, 1831." *Annals of Science* vol. XXXII (1975): p. 257–275.

English, Thomas H. *Whitby Prints*. 2 Volumes. Whitby: Horne and Sons, 1931.

Evans, Susanna. *Historic Brisbane and its Early Artists*. Brisbane: Boolarong, 1982.

Farrar, W.V. "Andrew Ure FRS, and the Philosophy of Manufacturers." *Notes and Records of the Royal Society*, vol. 227, no. 2 (1973): p. 299–324.

Fullom, Stephen Watson. *The Life of General Sir Howard Douglas*. London, 1863.

Geisler, Norman L. and J. Kerby Anderson. *Origin Science: A Proposal for the Creation-Evolution Controversy*. Grand Rapids, MI: Baker, 1987.

Geddes, Alastair. *Samuel Best and the Hampshire Labourer*. Andover: Andover Local History Society, 1981.

Gillispie, Charles Coulston. *Genesis and Geology: A Study in the Relations of Scientific Thought, Natural Theology and Social Opinion in Great Britain, 1790–1850.* New York: Harper & Brothers, 1959 [1951].

Glock, W.S. and S. Agerter. "Anomalous Patterns in Tree Rings." *Endeavour*, vol. XXII, no. 85 (1963): p. 9–13.

Goodman, D.C., ed. *Science and Religious Belief 1600–1900: A Selection of Primary Sources*. Milton Keynes: Open University, 1973.

Gordon, Elizabeth Oke. *The Life and Correspondence of William Buckland*. London: John Murray, 1894.

Gould, Stephen J. "Catastrophes and Steady State Earth." *Natural History*, vol. LXXXIV, no. 2 (1975): p. 14–18.

_______. "The Great Scablands Debate." *Natural History*, vol. LXXXVII, no. 7 (1978): p. 12–18.

_______. *Time's Arrow, Time's Cycle*. Cambridge: Harvard University Press, 1987.

Grant, R. "Hutton's Theory of the Earth." In L. J. Jordanova and Roy S. Porter, eds. *Images of the Earth*. British Society for the History of Science, 1978. Monograph 1, p. 23–38.

Grinnell, George. "The Origins of Modern Geological Theory." *Kronos*, vol. 1, no. 4 (1976): p. 68–76.

Gundry D.W. "The Bridgewater Treatises and their Authors." *History*, N.S. vol. XXXI, (1946): p. 140–152.

Haber, Francis C. *The Age of the World: Moses to Darwin*. Baltimore: John Hopkins, 1959.

Hahn, Roger. "Laplace and the Mechanistic Universe." In David C. Lindberg and Ronald L. Numbers, eds. *God and Nature*. Berkeley, CA: University of California Press, p. 256–276.

Hanna, William. *Memoir of the Life and Writings of Dr. Chalmers*. 4 Volumes. Edinburgh, 1849–52.

Harrison, R.K. *Introduction to the Old Testament*. Grand Rapids, MI: Eerdmans, 1969.

Hazard, Paul. *The European Mind: 1680–1715*. Translated by J. Lewis May. London: Hollis and Carter, 1953.

Heidel, Alexander. *The Gilgamesh Epic and Old Testament Parallels*. Chicago, IL: University of Chicago Press, 1946.

Hellemans, Alexander and Bryan Bunch. *Timetables of Science*. New York: Simon and Schuster, 1988.

Hennell, Michael. "The Oxford Movement." Tim Dowley, ed. *Eerdmans' Handbook to the History of Christianity*. Grand Rapids, MI: Eerdmans, 1977, p. 524–526.

Heylmun, Edgar B. "Should We Teach Uniformitarianism?" *Journal of Geological Education*, vol. XIX (1971): p. 35–37.

Hilton, Boyd. *The Age of Atonement*. Oxford: Clarendon, 1991.

Hinton, D.A. "Popular Science in England, 1830–1870." Ph.D. thesis, University of Bath, 1979.

Hodge, M.J.S. "The History of the Earth, Life, and Man: Whewell and Palaetiological Science." In Menachem Fisch and Simon Schaffer, eds. *William Whewell: A Composite Portrait*. Oxford: Clarendon Press, 1991, p. 255–288.

Hooykaas, R. "Catastrophism in Geology, Its Scientific Character in Relation to Actualism and Uniformitarianism." *Meded. Kon. Nederl. Akad. Wetenschappen*, Afd. Let., Nieuwe Reeks, deel 33, no. 7 (1970): p. 271–316.

_______. "Genesis and Geology." In *New Interactions Between Theology and Natural Science*. Milton Keynes: The Open University Press, 1974, p. 55–87.

_______. *G.J. Rheticus' Treatise on Holy Scripture and the Motion of the Earth*. Oxford: North-Holland Publishing Co, 1984.

_______. *Religion and the Rise of Modern Science*. Grand Rapids, MI: Eerdmans, 1972.

Howarth, O.J.R. *The British Association for the Advancement of Science: A Retrospect 1831–1931*. Second edition. London, 1931.

Howse, Ernest M. *Saints in Politics: The "Clapham Sect" and the Growth of Freedom*. London: George Allen and Unwin, 1976 [1953].

Hummel, Charles E. *The Galileo Connection*. Downers Grove, IL: InterVarsity Press, 1986.

Jackson, Benjamin D. *Guide to the Literature of Botany*. London, 1881.

Johnson, Phillip. *The Wedge of Truth: Splitting the Foundations of Naturalism*. Downers Grove, IL: InterVarsity Press, 2000.

Kauffman, Erle. "The Uniformitarian Albatross." *Palaios*, vol. II, no. 6 (1987): p. 531.

King, G.E. and P.J. King. *Abbotts Ann School 1831–1981*. Published privately by the school, 1981.

Klaaren, Eugene M. *Religious Origins of Modern Science*. Grand Rapids, MI: Eerdmans, 1977.

Kuhn, Thomas S. *The Copernican Revolution*. Cambridge, MA: Harvard University Press, 1971 [1957].

_______. *The Structure of Scientific Revolutions*. Chicago, IL: University of Chicago Press, 1970. Second edition.

Laudan, Rachel. *From Mineralogy to Geology*. Chicago, IL: Chicago University Press, 1987.

_______. "The Recent Revolution in Geology and Kuhn's Theory of Scientific Change." P. Asquith and I. Hacking, eds. *Philosophy of Science Association 1978*, Vol. II. East Lansing, MI: Philosophy of Science Association, 1981, p. 227–239.

Lawton, Richard and Colin G. Pooley. *Britain 1740–1950: An Historical Geography*. London: Edward Arnold, 1992.

Lindberg, David C. and Ronald L. Numbers, eds. *God and Nature: Historical Essays on the Encounter between Christianity and Science*. Berkeley, CA: University of California, 1986.

Longden, Henry I. *Northamptonshire and Rutland Clergy (from 1500)*. 2 Volumes. Northampton: Archer and Goodman, 1938.

Lyell, Katharine M. *Life, Letters and Journals of Sir Charles Lyell, Bart.* 2 Volumes. London: John Murray, 1881.

MacLaurin, Colin. *Account of Sir Isaac Newton's Philosophical Discoveries*. London, 1748.

Marston, V. Paul. "Science and Meta-science in the Work of Adam Sedgwick." Ph.D. Thesis. The Open University, 1984.

McIver, Tom. *Anti-Evolution: An Annotated Bibliography*. Jefferson, NC: McFarland, 1988.

McKee, E.D., E.J. Crosby, and H.L. Berryhill, Jr. "Flood Deposits, Bijou Creek, Colorado, June 1965." *Journal of Sedimentary Petrology*, vol. XXXVII, no. 3 (1967): p. 829–851.
Melmore, S. "Letters in the Possession of the Yorkshire Philosophical Society." *North Western Naturalist*, vol. XVII (1942): p. 317–332.
Meyer, Stephen C. "The Methodological Equivalence of Design and Descent: Can There Be a Scientific 'Theory of Creation'?" In J.P. Moreland, ed. *The Creation Hypothesis.* Downers Grove, IL: IV Press, 1994, p. 67–112.
_______. "Of Clues and Causes: A Methodological Interpretation of Origin of Life Studies." Ph.D. Thesis. Cambridge University, 1990.
Millhauser, Milton. *Just before Darwin: Robert Chambers and the Vestiges.* Middletown, CT: Wesleyan University Press, 1959.
_______. "The Scriptural Geologists: An Episode in the History of Opinion." *OSIRIS*, vol. XI (1954): p. 65–86.
Moore, James R. "Geologists and Interpreters of Genesis in the Nineteenth Century." In David C. Lindberg and Ronald L. Numbers, eds. *God and Nature.* Berkeley, CA: University of California Press, 1986, p. 322–350.
Moreland, J.P. *Christianity and the Nature of Science: A Philosophical Investigation.* Grand Rapids, MI: Baker, 1989.
Morgan, Robert and John Barton. *Biblical Interpretation.* Oxford: Oxford University Press, 1989.
Morrell, Jack B. "London Institutions and Lyell's Career: 1820–41." *British Journal for the History of Science*, vol. IX (1976): p. 132–146.
Morrell, Jack and Arnold Thackray. *Gentlemen of Science: Early Years of the British Association for the Advancement of Science.* Oxford, Clarendon Press, 1981.
Morris, Henry. *History of Modern Creationism.* El Cajon, CA: Institute for Creation Research, 1993.
Morris, John D. *The Young Earth.* Green Forest, AR: Master Books, 1994.
Nelson, Byron C. *The Deluge Story in Stone.* Minneapolis, MN: Augsburg, 1968 [1931].
Neve, M. and R. Porter. "Alexander Catcott: Glory and Geology." *The British Journal of the History of Science*, vol. X (1977): p. 37–60.
Numbers, Ronald L. *The Creationists: The Evolution of Scientific Creationism.* New York: Alfred A. Knopf, 1992.
Oldroyd, D.R. "Historicism and the Rise of Historical Geology, Part 1." *Historical Science*, vol. XVII, no. 37 (1979): p. 191–213.
_______. "Historicism and the Rise of Historical Geology, Part 2." *Historical Science*, vol. XVII, no. 38 (1979): p. 227–257.
Orange, A. D. "The Beginnings of the British Association, 1831–1851." In Roy Macleod and Peter Collins, eds. *The Parliament of Science.* Northwood: Science Reviews, 1981, p. 43–64.
_______. "The Idols of the Theatre: The British Association and Its Early Critics." *Annals of Science*, vol. XXXII (1975): p. 277–294.
_______. *Philosophers and Provincials: The Yorkshire Philosophical Society from 1822 to 1844.* York: Yorkshire Philosophical Society, 1973.
O'Rourke, J.E. "A Comparison of James Hutton's *Principles of Knowledge* and *Theory of the Earth.*" *ISIS*, vol. 69, no. 246 (1978): p. 5–20.
Ospovat, Alexander M. "The Distortion of Werner in Lyell's *Principles of Geology.*" *The British Journal for the History of Science*, vol. IX, no. 32, pt. 2 (1976): p. 190–198.
Overton, John H. *The English Church in the Nineteenth Century: 1800–1833.* London, 1894.
Page, Leroy E. "Diluvialism and Its Critics in Great Britain in the Early Nineteenth Century." In Cecil J. Schneer, ed. *Toward a History of Geology.* Cambridge, MA: MIT, 1969, p. 257–271.

_______. "The Rivalry between Charles Lyell and Roderick Murchison." *The British Journal for the History of Science*, vol. IX, no. 32, part 2 (1976): p. 156–165.

Partington, J.R. *A History of Chemistry*. 4 Volumes. London: MacMillan, 1961–70.

Pelikan, Jaroslav, ed. *Luther Works, Vol. I: Commentary on Genesis 1–5*. St. Louis, MO: Concordia, 1958.

Pelikan, Jaroslav, ed. *Luther Works, Vol. II: Commentary on Genesis 6–14*. St. Louis, MO: Concordia, 1960.

Plumb, J.H. *England in the Eighteenth Century*. London: Penquin Books, 1987.

Porter, Roy. "Charles Lyell and the Principles of the History of Geology." *British Journal for the History of Science*, vol. IX, no. 32, part 2 (1976): p. 91–103.

_______. "Gentlemen and Geology: The Emergence of a Scientific Career, 1660–1920." *The Historical Journal*, vol. XXI, no. 4 (1978): p. 809–836.

_______. "The Industrial Revolution and the Rise of the Science of Geology." In M. Teich and R.M. Young, eds. *Changing Perspectives in the History of Science*. London: Heinemann, 1973, p. 320–343.

_______. *The Making of Geology: Earth Science in Britain 1660–1815*. Cambridge: Cambridge University Press, 1977.

Prestwich, Joseph. *Collected Papers on some Controverted Questions of Geology*. London: MacMillan, 1895.

Puryear, Vernon J. "Napoleon I." In *The World Book Encyclopedia*, Vol. XIV:12–17. Chicago: World Book, 1987.

Pyrah, Barbara J. *The History of the Yorkshire Museum*. York: William Sessions, 1988.

Rappaport, Rhoda. "Geology and Orthodoxy: The Case of Noah's Flood in 18th Century Thought." *The British Journal for the History of Science*, vol. XI (1978): p. 1–18.

_______. "Problems and Sources in the History of Geology 1749–1810." *History of Science*, vol. III (1964): p. 60–78.

Rashid, Salim. "Political Economy and Geology in the Nineteenth Century: Similarities and Contrasts." *History of Political Economy*, vol. XIII, no. 4 (1981): p. 726–744.

Raup, David M. "Geology and Creationism." *Bulletin of the Field Museum of Natural History*, vol. LIV (1983): p. 16–25.

Rausch, D.A. "Oxford Movement." In Walter A. Elwell, ed. *Evangelical Dictionary of Theology*. Grand Rapids, MI: Baker, 1984, p. 811–812.

Read, H.H. *The Granite Controversy*. London: Thomas Murby, 1957.

Reardon, B.M.G. *Religious Thought in the 19th Century*. Cambridge: Cambridge University Press, 1966.

Redondi, Pietro. *Galileo Heretic*. Translated by Raymond Rosenthal. London: Penguin Books, 1989.

Reeve, Robin M. *The Industrial Revolution 1750–1850*. London: University of London Press, 1971.

Reventlow, Henning G. *The Authority of the Bible and the Rise of the Modern World*. Translated by John Bowden. London: SCM Press, 1984.

Richardson, Alan. *The Bible in the Age of Science*. London: SCM Press, 1964.

Robinson, Francis K. *Whitby*. Whitby, 1860.

Roberts, Michael B. "The Roots of Creationism." *Faith and Thought (The Journal of the Victoria Institute)*, vol. CXII, no. 1 (1986): p. 21–35.

Robson, John M. "The Fiat and Finger of God: The Bridgewater Treatises." In Richard J. Helmstadter and Bernard Lightman, eds. *Victorian Faith in Crisis*. Basingstoke: MacMillan, 1990, p. 71–125.

Rogerson, John. *Old Testament Criticism in the 19th Century: England and Germany*. London: SPCK, 1984.

_______. Christopher Rowland and Barnabas Lindars SSF. *The Study and Use of the Bible*. Basingstoke: Marshall Pickering, 1988.

Rudwick, Martin J.S. "Charles Lyell, F.R.S. (1797–1875) and His London Lectures on Geology, 1832–33." *Notes and Records of the Royal Society of London*, vol. XXIX, no. 2 (1975): p. 231–263.

_______. "Charles Lyell Speaks in the Lecture Theatre." *The British Journal of the History of Science,* vol. IX, no. 32 (1976): p. 147–155.
_______. "The Foundation of the Geological Society of London: Its Scheme for Co-operative Research and Its Struggle for Independence." *The British Journal of the History of Science*, vol. I, no. 4 (1963): p. 325–355.
_______. *The Great Devonian Controversy: The Shaping of Scientific Knowledge among Gentlemanly Specialists*. Chicago, IL: University of Chicago Press, 1985.
_______. "Introduction." In Charles Lyell, *Principles of Geology* (1830–33). 3 Volumes. Chicago, IL: University of Chicago Press, 1990: vol. I, p. vii–lviii.
_______. *The Meaning of Fossils*. Chicago: University of Chicago Press, 1985. Third edition.
_______. "Poulett Scrope on the Volcanoes of Auvergne: Lyellian Time and olitical Economy." *The British Journal of the History of Science.* vol VII, no. 27 (1974): p. 205–242.
_______. "Lyell's Chronological Model." *ISIS*, vol. 243 (1977): p. 440–443.
_______. "The Principle of Uniformity." *History of Science*, vol. I (1962): p. 82–86.
_______. "The Shape and Meaning of Earth History." In David C. Lindberg and Ronald L. Numbers, eds. *God and Nature*. Berkeley, CA: University of California Press, 1986, p. 296–321.
_______. "Transposed Concepts from the Human Sciences in the Early Work of Charles Lyell." In L.J. Jordanova and Roy S. Porter, eds. *Images of the Earth*. British Society for the History of Science, Monograph 1, 1979, p. 67–83.
_______. "Uniformity and Progression: Reflections on the Structure of Geological Theory in the Age of Lyell." In D.H.D. Roller, ed. *Perspectives in the History of Science and Technology*. Norman, OK: University of Oklahoma Press, 1971, p. 209–227.
Rupke, Nicolaas A. *The Great Chain of History: William Buckland and the English School of Geology 1814–1849*. Oxford: Clarendon Press, 1983.
Russell, Colin A. "The Conflict Metaphor and Its Social Origins." *Science and Christian Belief*, vol. I, no. 1 (1989): p. 3–26.
_______. *Cross-currents: Interactions between Science and Faith*. Grand Rapids, MI: Eerdmans, 1985.
_______. "Noah's Flood: 2: Noah and the Neptunists." *Faith and Thought*, vol. C, no. 2 (1972–73): p. 143–158.
_______. *Science and Social Change: 1700–1900*. London: Macmillan, 1983.
Russell, Colin A., ed. *Science and Religious Belief.* Milton Keynes: Open University, 1979.
Russell, Colin A., R. Hooykaas and David C. Goodman. *The 'Conflict Thesis' and Cosmology*. In the series *Science and Belief: from Copernicus to Darwin*. Milton Keynes: Open University, 1974.
Russell, Jeffrey Burton. *Inventing the Flat Earth*. New York: Praeger, 1991.
Sarjeant, William A.S. *Geologists and the History of Geology.* 5 Volumes. London: MacMillan, 1980.
Secord, James A. *Controversy in Victorian Geology: The Cambrian-Silurian Dispute*. Princeton, NJ: Princeton University Press, 1986.
Shea, James H. "Twelve Fallacies of Uniformitarianism." *Geology*, vol. X (1982): p. 455–460.
Shea, William R. "Galileo and the Church." David C. Lindberg and Ronald L. Numbers, editors. *God and Nature*. Berkeley: University Calif. Press, 1986, p. 114–135.
Sheppard, T. "William Smith, His Maps and Memoirs." *Proceedings of the Yorkshire Geological and Polytechnic Society*, N.S. vol. XIX (1914–22): p. 75–254.
Simpson, Martin. *The Fossils of the Yorkshire Lias*. Whitby, 1884. Second edition.
Smales, Gideon. *Whitby Authors and Their Publications*. Whitby, 1867.
Stephen, Sir James. *Essays in Ecclesiastical Biography*. 2 Volumes. London, 1849.
Temple, Philip. *Islington Chapels*. London: Royal Commission on the Historical Monuments of England, 1992.
Thackray, John. *The Age of the Earth*. London, Institute of Geological Sciences, 1980.

Thaxton, Charles B., Walter L. Bradley and Roger L. Olsen. *The Mystery of Life's Origin: Reassessing Current Theories.* Dallas, TX: Lewis and Stanley, 1992.

Thomson, David. *England in the Nineteenth Century*. London: Penguin Books, 1950.

Toon, Peter. *Evangelical Theology 1833–1856: A Response to Tractarianism*. London: Marshall, Morgan and Scott, 1979.

Weindling, Paul Julian. "Geological Controversy and Its Historiography: The Prehistory of the Geological Society of London." In L.J. Jordanova and Roy S. Porter, eds. *Images of the Earth*. British Society for the History of Science, 1978, Monograph 1, p. 248–271.

Whitcomb, John C. and Henry M. Morris. *The Genesis Flood.* Grand Rapids, MI: Baker, 1977 [1961].

Whitten, D.G.A. and J.R.V. Brooks. *The Penguin Dictionary of Geology*. London: Penguin Books, 1972.

White, Andrew Dickson. *A History of the Warfare of Science with Theology in Christendom.* 2 Volumes. New York: Appleton, 1896.

Wilberforce, Samuel. *Life of William Wilberforce*. London, 1868.

Williamson, William C. *Reminiscences of a Yorkshire Naturalist*. London, 1896.

Wilson, Leonard G. "The Development of the Concept of Uniformitarianism in the Mind of Charles Lyell." In *Proceedings of the Tenth International Congress on the History of Science*. Paris: Hermann, 1964, p. 993–996.

_______. "The Intellectual Background to Charles Lyell's *Principles of Geology*, 1830–1833." In Cecil J. Schneer, ed. *Toward a History of Geology*. Cambridge, Mass.: MIT, 1969, p. 426–443.

Woloch, Isser. "French Revolution." In *The World Book Encyclopedia*, Vol. VII. Chicago, IL: World Book, 1987, p. 450–452.

Woodbridge, John D. "The Impact of the 'Enlightenment' on Scripture." In D.A. Carson and John D. Woodbridge, eds. *Hermeneutics, Authority and Canon*. Grand Rapids, MI: Zondervan, 1986, p. 241–270.

Woodward, Horace B. *The History of the Geological Society of London*. London: Geological Society, 1907.

Young, Davis A. *The Biblical Flood*. Grand Rapids, MI: Eerdmans, 1995.

_______. *Christianity and the Age of the Earth*. Thousand Oaks, CA: Artisan Sales, 1988. Reprint of 1982 edition. Grand Rapids, MI: Zondervan.

_______. "Scripture in the Hands of the Geologists (Part One)." *Westminster Theological Journal*, vol. 49 (Spring 1987): p. 1–34.

Yule, J. David. "The Impact of Science on British Religious Thought in the Second Quarter of the Nineteenth Century." Ph.D. Thesis, Cambridge University, 1976.

SCRIPTURE INDEX

NAME INDEX

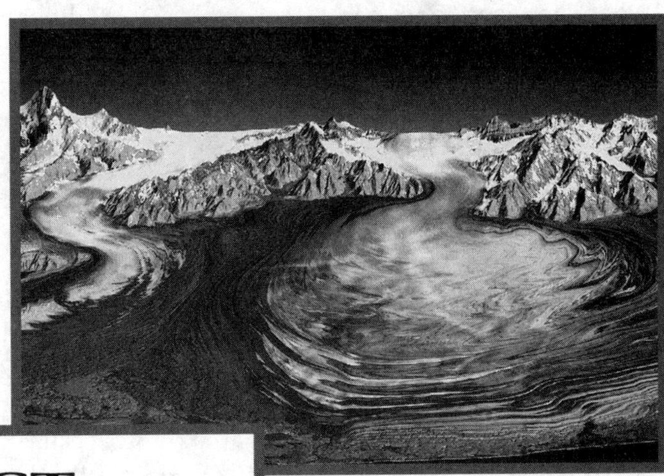

SUBJECT INDEX